A History of European Socialism

A History of European Socialism

Albert S. Lindemann

Yale University Press
New Haven and London

Published with assistance from the foundation established in memory of Philip Hamilton McMillan of the Class of 1894, Yale College.

Designed by James J. Johnson
and set in Aster Roman type.
Printed in the United States of America by
Vail-Ballou Press, Binghamton, N.Y.

Library of Congress Cataloging in Publication Data

A history of European socialism.

Bibliography: p.
Includes index.
1. Socialism—Europe—History. 2. Communism—Europe
—History. 3. Marx, Karl, 1818–1883. I. Title.
HX237.L536   1983   335'.0094   82–40167
ISBN 0–300–02797–4   AACR2

10 9 8 7 6 5 4 3 2 1

For Timothy and Erika

Contents

Introduction:
What Is Socialism?

This book is admittedly and unavoidably personal in focus and organization. It is designed for readers who wish to gain a general understanding of the history of European socialism, and for those who are looking for a solid introduction to socialism elsewhere, since socialism throughout the world has deep roots in Europe. In style and approach I have strived to avoid the format of a "text"—especially insofar as that term implies an encyclopedic survey, weighed down with lifeless detail. My ideal instead has been what might be termed an essay of synthesis, or an interpretive overview, although I make no pretense of having discovered an overarching theory or single theme that makes the whole history of European socialism fit neatly together. I am persuaded, at any rate, that no existing study of European socialism satisfies the needs of the overwhelming majority of potential readers, in English or in any of the major European languages.

I should make immediately clear that in referring to "socialism" I mean more than a study of the linkage of ideas to one another or a description and analysis of socialist doctrines as such. Historians recognize a distinction between histories of socialism alone, of the labor movement, and of the working class—that is, of ideology, institutions (largely trade unions and labor parties), and the workers themselves (regardless of their doctrinal beliefs and organization proclivities). While few historians have kept these categories hermetically separate, for many years the tendency was to concentrate on the history of socialist thought, on socialist parties, and on trade unions, to the neglect of the workers themselves, of history "from the bottom up." In the past fifteen to twenty years a very strong shift of historical focus has occurred. Many of the best minds in the historical profession and in kindred disciplines, particularly younger scholars, have turned to an intensive study of the common workers, not through the prism of socialist party or trade union (which even in their most successful moments never attracted a majority of workers) but from broader, more all-encompassing perspectives. In a related way the so-called "cliometricians," that is, those who have developed methods of gathering quantitative data about the inarticulate lower orders, have opened up many new, fascinating perspectives.

Obviously, these new approaches have made a large contribution, but the enthusiasm that some scholars feel for history from the bottom up and for "reliable" quantitative methods has unfortunately led them to denigrate, or at least to express boredom and impatience with, "traditional" history based on "literary" evidence, since such evidence is often impressionistic and since it calls into play historical imagination leading to generalizations not easily checked by the computer. Moreover, the new history is plagued by a number of serious problems. Much of it is unreadable except by an extremely narrow audience; its sophisticated techniques, often severely limited focus, and recondite conclusions separate it from the large audience that history as a humanistic discipline has long attracted. Its findings, moreover, even when clearly presented and significant in scope, are often less reliable than its champions maintain.

Thus, while the newer historical concerns play a definite role in the following pages, the traditional topics are also well represented. My ideal of an essay of synthesis implies not only avoiding the textbookish but also striving for an integrated and balanced approach, one that examines the relationship between ideology, institutions, and working masses, placing socialist ideas and movements in a "total" historical context. Similarly, although I cannot dwell at length on topics which may be of primary concern to the more traditional academic specialist, I do not ignore those topics. I hope that this work, by the very breadth of its focus, has something to offer even to those familiar with large portions of the history of socialism.

Since I am concerned especially to provide a readable overview, I have avoided cluttering the text with footnotes. The sources of direct, substantial quotations are identified in parentheses. Where my debt to a particular scholar is important or where a significant point of scholarly controversy is touched upon, general references are provided in the text itself. Further particulars may be found in the Guide to Further Reading at the end of each chapter. There is as well an alphabetical bibliography at the end of the book, with more complete bibliographical information.

Any history of socialism must obviously begin with as unambiguous as possible a definition of socialism. But this is not a simple task. Since the term was coined a century and a half ago, it has undergone perplexing transformations. Competing doctrines, such as liberalism and conservatism, not only overlap it but have often been confused with it, and sometimes have been used in an even more bewildering manner. It would be satisfying to be able to conjure up concise and air-tight definitions of these terms, which could then serve as easily available and unfailing guides for the uninitiated. But attempts to provide such definitions have always failed, for the simple reason that language, and particularly the language of political persuasions, evolves in ways that defy easy description. No platonic authority exists that can provide us with a complete or "real" definition of socialism. Instead, our understanding of it must be based on how people have used it in history, even if we find that they have used it with dismaying imprecision. We must thus reconcile ourselves to the uncomfortable truth that often people who call themselves socialists so define their beliefs as to exclude others who also claim to be socialists.

Yet let us not exaggerate the degree of inconsistency with which the word socialism has been used. It is possible to discover certain underlying, abiding themes, a solid core of meaning. We can construct a kind of ideal type of socialism, and of other doctrines with which socialism might be confused, to serve as our guide through the thicket of actual historical usage. In so doing we must of course keep in mind, not only that such ideal types are purely mental constructions, but that abstract definitions rarely correspond exactly with the ideas of real theorists or historical actors, and that no useful definition could possibly encompass all of the individuals who have espoused a given political doctrine.

We can begin by observing that a fundamental concern of all socialists has been for cooperation and *social* justice, with particular emphasis on the needs and rights of the community over the egotistical urges of the individual. In this respect the etymology of the word socialism is a useful key: It was first widely used in the 1830s in opposition to "individualism," to stress man's social nature, his *social*ism, at a time when the individualistic strivings unleashed by the nascent capitalistic system seemed to be destroying much that was humane and beautiful in European civilization.

Thus socialists have tended to stress that human beings are properly gregarious rather than self-sufficient, that they should concern themselves with the welfare of their fellow human beings, especially those weaker or less fortunate. On a more lofty level socialists have stressed that men and women achieve their most highly developed humanity only in society, in cooperative rather than competitive effort with others. This commitment to cooperation rather than competition, to fellowship, solidarity, and sympathy, rather than self-seeking, is the most fundamental and abiding characteristic of the socialistic tradition.

Such attitudes were obviously not completely new in the early nineteenth century. The socialist impulse has deep roots in history. Since antiquity social inequality and heedless individualism have found eloquent critics. Christ himself was a poor workingman whose utterances were full of condemnation of the rich and the proud; he could appropriately be termed a proletarian revolutionary. The Christian tradition has unmistakable socialistic elements, and throughout the history of Christianity various sects have tried to live with "all things common."

But modern socialism differs from such earlier tendencies in several ways. To begin with, modern socialists have normally been secular, basing their theories on human rationality, on specifically human feelings of solidarity, and on natural law, as distinguished from such mystical concepts as divine inspiration, brotherhood in Christ, or divine law. This is not to ignore that many socialists, even those who became militantly anti-Christian, emerged from a Christian background, retained certain Christian habits and sentiments, and even explicitly praised the corporatist habits of premodern Christian society. A number of socialists argued that socialism was a kind of "true" religion, abandoned by the official churches, and indeed many socialists remained Christians. Yet on balance modern socialism has been an enemy of organized religion and of theological approaches to social problems.

A second important difference is socialism's relationship to modernization or the so-called Dual Revolution, the industrial revolution and the wave of political revolutions that swept Europe in the latter part of the eighteenth century, transforming European life. These revolutions stimulated hopes for a fundamentally different world, based on rational human design rather than on tradition or inscrutable forces, and on material plenty rather than want. However, the initial impact of the Dual Revolution appeared remote from these hopes. The growing conservatism of the revolution in France as well as the shocking social conditions of early industrialization outraged those with a vision of a new, ideal order.

A variety of people were repelled by the effects of revolutionary change. Particularly numerous at first were those who considered political upheaval and industrialization to be unmitigated disasters, with no redeeming qualities whatsoever. The socialists by and large held a more positive view. Believing in the feasibility of using new industrial techniques and political institutions for a richer, more harmonious life, they rejected the notion of a return to a traditional, nonindustrial past— although most of them hoped somehow to retain the noncompetitive qualities of that past.

Liberalism was another ideology to emerge with modern times, and in a number of ways its concerns and character were similar to, or overlapped, those of socialism. It could easily be argued that socialism, while sharply opposing itself to liberalism, evolved out of liberal tenets and remained marked throughout its history by that origin. Yet it is important for our concerns to make as clear as possible the underlying concerns of liberals that distinguished them from socialists.

As their name suggests, liberals were characteristically concerned with the concept of liberty or liberation (*liber* is Latin for "free"). They saw liberty as an all-embracing force for good in the world, a force that would ensure progress, happiness, and an almost unlimited perfection of the human personality. In more concrete terms they looked to a free market (as compared to one rigidly controlled or directed by the state); freedom of assembly, speech, and press; freely elected representative institutions—all in the context of a popularly established rule of law. The free competition of individuals was desirable to them. It represented the best way of unleashing human potential, and they accepted that such competition would lead to a degree of social and economic inequality. When they praised "equality" what they meant was equality of opportunity and equality before the law—lack of special legal privilege—not social equality, particularly not if such equality had collectivist implications, or somehow limited individual freedom.

Liberals were committed to the institution of private property, to them a fundamentsl guarantee of freedom and a reward for superior individual achievement. One of the main functions that liberals saw for the state—whose power, they believed, should be carefully limited in most respects because of the dangers it posed to liberty—was the protection of property. Liberals tended to consider the failure to accumulate property as a personal inadequacy, and they viewed poverty in general as due to personal laziness or incompetence, rather than to lowly origin or overpowering impersonal forces.

Socialists too were fascinated by the notion of liberation, believing as they did in a freely developing human perfectibility, and most of

them favored free institutions and freedom of speech and assembly. The
key difference came in the socialists' rejection of individual competitiveness. To them it appeared destructive, and they similarly considered that private property preserved unfair and harmful social distinctions.

In understanding the ways that socialism and liberalism overlapped it is further useful to distinguish two main tendencies in the
latter, that is, between what we can call the "whig" and the "democratic radical." The two terms have had many applications in history.
For our purposes, however, it can be said that the whig-liberal tendency was distinguished by a hostility to popular rule, which the whig
feared would degenerate into rule by the mob. The whig was attracted
to elitist, oligarchic rule and was devoted to the preservation of powerful institutions (law courts, representative bodies, professional organizations) as well as large property holdings, which he believed would
protect liberty by standing in the way of a centralization or usurpation
of power, either by a despot or by the masses. Obviously the whig conception of liberty had much to do with the idea of privilege.

The democratic-radical tendency within liberalism (in France "jacobin," and in England simply "radical"), on the other hand, accepted
popular rule as compatible with liberty—indeed as its most reliable
guarantee—and was concerned to fashion political institutions that
would reflect the direct will of the masses (and not that of privileged
elites, as the whigs would have it). But the democratic radical still retained a belief in competitive individualism, did not oppose moderate
holdings of private property, and rejected collectivism. He was sympathetic to the plight of the working poor and generally opposed great
differences in social status or wealth, but his remedy for poverty remained hard work and individual enterprise. He was willing to see the
state intervene to preserve what he deemed to be fair competition, but
he was reticent to see the state take up the task of enforcing social solidarity and fellowship or of socializing wealth. Still, it was at the democratic-radical pole of liberalism that it began in important ways to
merge into socialism, and many socialists began as democratic radicals.

It is axiomatic for students of European history that ideologies do
not exist as purely abstract statements; they are linked to or express
interests. It is further plausible that class background tends to influence political persuasion, that the poor tend to be attracted to ideologies that in some way favor them, and that the rich look to ideologies
that defend their wealth and justify their position in society. But these

correlations are anything but simple, and much recent scholarship—
particularly that devoted to history from the bottom up—has been
concerned to question easy assumptions about social class and political preference.

Still, by way of introduction we can observe that socialism's following came primarily from the lower orders, where it was gradually
perceived that strength lay in numbers, in solidarity, and that only
through cooperative or collective action could economic and social
oppression be remedied. Perhaps more important, most people who became wage-earning workers came from pre-industrial backgrounds,
where individualism was not a virtue. Thus they were inclined to reject
competitive individualism and its associated liberal ideology and to
embrace ideologies that emphasized cooperation and economic control.

This is not to imply that all wage earners, or even a majority of
them, became socialists at any time in any country, since they obviously
did not, nor is it meant to ignore the role of wealthy and leisured individuals in the actual formulation of socialist theory, since theory was
worked out by intellectuals, who were very rarely manual laborers.
However, on the whole the wealthy and leisured individuals of the
bourgeoisie, or middle class, were attracted more to liberalism than to
socialism. They were normally employers rather than employees, exploiters rather than exploited, and they tended to benefit most from
political liberalization and a free-market economy.

Throughout the nineteenth century democratic radicalism, as defined above, attracted a larger number of workers than did socialism.
This statement would seem to contradict what has just been said. But
democratic radicalism can be considered, and has been considered traditionally, to be the ideology of the petty bourgeoisie, lower middle
class, or small property owner (to use terms that are loosely synonymous and that can include the small businessman, shopkeeper, peasant
proprietor, white-collar worker, and independent artisan). The attractions of this ideology for workers in the nineteenth century can then be
attributed to the petty-bourgeois nature of much of the working class
at that time. A majority of workers for most of the nineteenth century
in Europe owned, or aspired to own, small amounts of property—their
shops, machinery, and tools. They were not yet proletarianized, were
not yet completely without ownership of the means of production, and
still believed it possible to prevent the domination of wage-labor and
factory production.

Anarchism also often attracted the petty-bourgeois worker. This
ideology is even more difficult than the others to categorize with any

precision, since it has many branches and since anarchists have taken a certain pleasure in defying attempts to impose on them the tyranny of a definition. Our first resort, as before, must be to look at the etymology of the word: *an-archos* in Greek means "no-leader," or, more loosely, "without authority." The heart of the anarchists' concern has been to oppose authority, again out of a longing for liberation.

In practice, the authority of the state, although only one of the many varieties of authority repugnant to anarchists, has been the object of their most concentrated hatred. This has been the case because they have seen in the state the origin and bulwark of a panorama of social ills, mostly related to the existence of a society of exploitation and social inequality. The state protects large accumulations of private property and the unjustly acquired goods of the exploiting classes. Anarchists therefore maintain that only with the abolition of the state and its means of repression (police, army, bureaucracy, law courts) will come an end to exploitation and to gross inequality in the distribution of wealth and property.

Anarchists have been frequent opponents of socialists, particularly of those authoritarian collectivists who believe in the central and necessary role of the state in building socialism. But their quarrels have been more like family quarrels, whereas their hostility to the ruling orders, in particular to wealthy bourgeois liberals, has been more fundamental and more intense. For this reason in the following pages anarchism is considered a variety of socialism, generically defined. This is consistent with the preference of most anarchists, many of whom called themselves "libertarian socialists" or "communists."

The term "communism" was coined about the same time as "socialism," but in the course of the nineteenth century it was used, first and foremost, to describe a thoroughgoing egalitarianism and collectivism (and thus was ostensibly embraced by the most desperately poor and exploited workers). Secondly—with less consistency and consensus—it implied a taste for violence. Marx chose to call himself a communist in the late 1840s in order to differentiate his hard-headed, "scientific" theories from the pipe dreams of what he termed "utopian socialism." The term fell into relative disuse in the late nineteenth century, when it was used mostly by certain anarchists, but during the First World War Lenin revived it in order to distinguish his brand of revolutionary elitist Marxism from what he considered the sell-out Marxism of the leaders of the main socialist parties of the time. Both Marx and Lenin also used the term communist on a more speculative level to describe the ultimate society, which would come after an initial, imperfect "socialist" society.

Aside from nationalism, which did not concern itself directly with the social question, socialism, liberalism, and conservatism may be considered the three main ideologies of the nineteenth century. They are best understood not in isolation but in relationship to one another. Indeed, one of the easiest and least equivocal ways of defining them is in their vision of the "enemy." Liberals in the early nineteenth century first distinguished themselves by their attacks on conservatives, on the latter's political and social pre-eminence, based on an "unfair" and irrational privilege. Later, liberals would begin to focus more on the challenge to individual freedom that they believed was posed by socialists. Similarly, as we have noted, socialism first appeared as an attack on liberal individualism, especially insofar as it was used to defend the emerging capitalist system. At the same time—and this will be a recurring theme—socialism can be seen as borrowing from both conservatism and liberalism: from the former's sense of society's organic unity, its binding responsibilities, and from the latter's promise of liberation.

Enough of definitions, which, though useful and necessary, can easily become tiresome. The reader should now have enough of an overview of the uses of the term socialism to begin more confidently a study of socialism's historical evolution. He or she should keep in mind that in the subsequent chapters the term socialism will be used in a generic sense, as an "ism" in opposition to individualism, liberalism, and capitalism, and encompassing all the more narrowly defined varieties of socialism, such as anarchism, communism, Marxism, and syndicalism.

GUIDE TO FURTHER READING

It would be pointless to attempt an exhaustive treatment of the vast and rapidly proliferating literature associated with the history of European socialism. What follows here and in each subsequent chapter is a discussion of an admittedly select number of relevant titles, although I think I have not often missed standard works or those of major importance. My main goal has been to provide the interested reader with the means to satisfy—rather than overwhelm—his or her curiosity concerning subjects found to be of special interest in the main text. The more advanced student should also find in these essays a basis for further exploration in the monographic and primary literature in given areas. I have particularly noted those works that have extensive or otherwise useful bibliographies. This first essay deals with works of general scope; those following each subsequent chapter focus on the appropriate specialized studies.

As I have said in the Introduction, no existing study of the history of European socialism satisfies the needs of most potential readers. The books of George Lichtheim, a scholar of catholic interests and penetrating intellect, deserve recognition as prominent and sophisticated efforts. Among them are his *Short History of Socialism* and *Marxism, A Historical and Critical Study*—the latter by far the more ambitious and successful work, and more than a study of Marxism per se. Both of them suffer from distracting idiosyncracies, however. These include a self-indulgence and arbitrariness in matters of focus and organization, and a pithiness of style that all too often takes on tones of haughty, Germanic obscurity, frustrating rather than instructing the reader. A beginning student may well find himself confused and resentful as he stumbles over the pecularities of Mr. Lichtheim's prose and overall approach. Still, his books, others of which will be referred to below, have established a high intellectual standard and cannot be ignored.

Carl Landauer's *European Socialism* is clearer and more readable, but is marred by his prolixity when dealing with subjects of special interest to him or concerning which he had personal experience (for example, Germany in the Weimar years) and his neglect of certain other areas. (He seriously slights French socialism—except for its syndicalist variety, concerning which he has some very interesting remarks—and does not even attempt to deal with English socialism.) Thus, this 2,000-page, two-volume work, in spite of some excellent chapters, is more a personal statement than a balanced study. Its usefulness as an overview is also limited in that it breaks off in the mid-1930s.

Leszek Kolakowski's *Main Currents of Marxism*, a three-volume, 1,600-page work, is breathtaking in its scope, thematic unity, and penetration. It ranges far beyond Marx and the Marxists. It is both scholarly and clearly written, although its encyclopedic aspirations result at times in lifeless summaries of the thought of peripheral figures. It is the best of intellectual history, although its concentration on thought, to the neglect of political actions, creates problems of interpretation for figures like Lenin and even Kautsky. But on the whole it is a monumental achievement that must be placed near the top of the reading list of any serious student of Marxism and of socialist thought generally.

G. D. H. Cole's five-volume study, *The History of Socialist Thought*, has long been a standard work, but its length as well as its encyclopedic style tend to disqualify it for all but the most indefatigable readers. It is, in spite of its title, much more than a work of intellectual history. It is best considered a useful work of reference, stressing narrative rather than analysis.

Harry Laidler's *History of Socialism* is in much the same mold: While judicious and generally reliable, it is ponderous and poorly integrated—a 1,000-page, uninspiring textbook—rather old-fashioned in approach and dated in sources. Like Cole, Laidler has devoted a few sections of his book to socialism outside of Europe.

Suffering from an opposite failing is Norman MacKenzie's *Socialism, A Short History*, which is merely a brief essay, too short and superficial to be of use to most readers. Another short volume, R. N. Berki's *Socialism*, is designed not as a general history of socialism but as an essay on aspects of it, using a general historical framework. Engagingly written and full of stimulating interpretations gathered from a broad learning, it spans a period from the late eighteenth century to contemporary Europe and America.

Alexander Gray's *The Socialist Tradition*, another dated and over-long volume, is for the most part a series of juxtaposed intellectual biographies rather than a full-scale history of socialism. It contains a good bit of basic information but frequently lacks analytical penetration or integration. The value of the work is diminished by a mocking hostility to socialism and by a pompous and verbose style, interlarded with inept efforts at humor.

Julius Braunthal's two-volume *History of the Internationals* comes close to being a general history of the political side of socialism. It too is often textbookish, and is flawed by a polemical tone, especially in the second volume, where the author's passionate anti-communism clouds his judgment.

A handy volume for those beginning students who would like to read primary sources is Albert Fried and Ronald Sanders, *Socialist Thought*, which provides selections from the writings of the major socialists, as well as a few of the more important documents in the history of socialism. See also Irving Howe, *The Essential Works of Socialism*.

Michael Harrington's *Socialism* may be considered a forceful apologia for democratic socialism and, in particular, an effort to demonstrate, not always persuasively, the democratic essence of Marxism. It is highly readable, intelligent, and full of original insights and interpretations.

Élie Halévy's *Histoire du socialisme européen*, a rewarding work by a renowned intellectual, remains unpolished and incomplete, since it was published posthumously from the lecture notes of his students. Some of the material in this book can be found in English in Halévy's *Era of Tyrannies: Essays on Socialism and War*. Maxime Leroy's three-volume *Histoire des idées sociales en France* covers more than socialist ideas but is generally a first-rate study, invaluable for reference. A dated but still useful set of volumes, thirteen in all, some of which have aged far better than others, was put together under the general editorship of the great socialist Jean Jaurès: *Histoire socialiste, 1789–1900*. Focusing on socialism from the standpoint of the working class is Édouard Dolléans's three-volume *Histoire du mouvement ouvrier*. Dolléans is a prolific if facile writer, and these volumes are mostly rapid and at times cluttered narrative rather than analysis. Jacques Droz has organized a number of eminent French scholars to collaborate on the *Histoire générale du socialisme* (vol. 1 deals with socialism from its origins to 1875; vol. 2, 1875 to 1918; further volumes are promised). The result is a sprawling work, some of whose chapters are excellent, others little short of slipshod. Annie Kriegel's *Le Pain et les roses: Jalons pour une histoire des socialismes* is an often fascinating set of essays dealing with select topics of socialism.

Histories of socialist and working-class movements in individual countries rarely encompass the full period from the French Revolution to modern times, and many have been written by journalists, former activists, or popularizers with rather low standards. Recently, however, scholars have begun to move into the field. Paul Louis's *Histoire du socialisme en France* is journalistic in style, packed with facts and figures, but weak on analysis. Daniel Ligou's *Histoire du socialisme en France, 1871–1961* is a not always reliable and often unimaginative work by a moderate socialist, dealing primarily with party politics. Hedwig Wachenheim's *Die Deutsche Arbeiterbewegung, 1844 bis 1914* is scholarly but readable. One of the best national histories, although now dated, is Max Beer's two-volume *History of British Socialism*, which has seen many updated versions since the original German edition of 1912. A most instructive and sophisticated study, dealing with English politics in general, which gives considerable attention to the English labor movement, is Samuel H. Beer's *British Politics in the Collectivist Age*. Franco Venturi's *Roots of Revolution* is an authoritative study of nineteenth-century Russian populism, definitive if also so overwhelming in detail as to daunt most readers.

Two works with the same title, *Socialism since Marx*, do not cover the entire period since the French Revolution but nevertheless are efforts at general, readable overviews. The first, by Leslie Derfler, is badly marred by textual errors, making it unsuitable for the beginning student, although it was composed with that student in mind. It suffers from careless and murky composition in places, although some of its sections are worthwhile. The second, by Robert Kilroy-Silk, gives signs of having been too rapidly composed, but the author has at least written a readable book of manageable dimensions, which also deals with non-European socialism.

A number of works, like the above-mentioned book by Samuel H. Beer, are not exactly histories of socialism or the labor movement but still offer broad, important statements about these subjects. *To the Finland Station* is a jewel of historical writing by the recently deceased doyen of American literary criticism, Edmund Wilson. It describes the revolutionary tradition of the nineteenth century, leading up to the Russian Revolution. Melvin Lasky's *Utopia and Revolution* is stimulating and wide in scope, if somewhat overwhelming (726 pages). Adam Ulam's *The Unfinished Revolution* concentrates on Marxism and Russian communism, combining a felicitous style with sparkling insights. Ulam is a productive scholar whose many works will be referred to in later chapters, but he is at times flippantly unsympathetic to socialists and communists. Wider ranging but also brilliantly unsympathetic to socialism, or at least to certain traditions within it, are Joseph Schumpeter's *Capitalism, Socialism, and Democracy*, J. L. Talmon's *The Origins of Totalitarian Democracy*, and Carl Popper's *The Open Society and Its Enemies*.

To discuss the vast literature on industrialization, modernization, and their social implications would take us far afield, but at least three stimulating but very different general studies can be mentioned: *Studies in the Development of Capitalism*, by the Marxist Maurice Dobb; *The Unbound Prometheus: Technological Change and Industrial Development in Western Europe from 1750 to the Present*, by David Landes; and *The Social Origins of Dictatorship and Democracy* and *Injustice, The Social Bases of Obedience and Revolt*, both by Barrington Moore, Jr.

The most recent re-interpretations of the history of socialism are best followed in the periodical literature of the past ten to fifteen years. The following list, by no means exhaustive, contains most of the more important or more relevant to the history of European socialism.

Annales: Économies, sociétés, civilisations
Comparative Studies in Society and History
Dissent

Geschichte und Gesellschaft
History Workshop
International Labor and Working Class History
International Review of Social History
Internationale Wissenschaftliche Korrespondenz zur Geschichte der deutschen Arbeiterbewegung
Journal of Economic History
Journal of Interdisciplinary History
Journal of Social History
Labor History
Le Mouvement social
Past and Present
Radical History Review
Revue d'histoire économique et sociale
Russian Review
Social History

The Roots of
Socialism

1

INTRODUCTION

Although this study centers on European socialism since the French
Revolution, it is important at the outset to gain some sense, however
impressionistic, of historical continuity, of the deepest roots of socialism. Although the actual word is only about a hundred fifty years old
and significant socialist movements only a hundred, it is possible to
trace an enduring quest for community and cooperation, and, by the
seventeenth and eighteenth centuries, a growing belief in the possibility of constructing a "rational" and "natural" social order.

Civilization, wherever it has arisen, has entailed a differentiation
of social function and prestige. A complex hierarchy of social strata (for
example, rulers, priests, warriors, and laborers, in the earlier stages)
has allowed comfort and leisure for the few, at the price of onerous labor for the many, the exploited "proletariat." Thus social tension and
civilization have gone hand in hand, although most civilizations have
succeeded for long periods in masking or rationalizing social differences and thus permitting a degree of social peace.

It might be going too far to assert that an unequal distribution of
riches in a society naturally leads to social tension, for it is a moot point
whether all human beings possess some inherent sense of justice that
impels them to demand a humane treatment of their fellow beings. But
at least we can observe that most of the civilizations that we term
"western" have at some time in their history seen such protests, at least
by a minority. And, in most of these civilizations, leading intellectuals
have worked out elaborate speculations concerning how society might
be organized along more just or desirable lines, especially when times
of trouble or rapid change have threatened established ways.

PREMODERN SOCIALISM,
FROM ANCIENT TIMES TO THE ENLIGHTENMENT

The Graeco-Roman and Judeo-Christian traditions, the main intellectual heritage of western civilization, are rich in proto-socialist thought. This comes as no surprise, since the best-known periods of Greek, Roman, Jewish, and Christian history are filled with episodes of violent conflict between rich and poor, exploiters and exploited.

Plato's *Republic* may be considered the first great example of far-reaching philosophical speculation or "utopian" thinking on political, economic, and social matters. The program set out in it—the abolition of private property, the family, and other guarantees of privacy (or "selfishness"); the establishment of a rationally ordered hierarchy of political functions; the central and overriding concern with creating an elite of virtuous, selfless citizens—would have an enduring influence on later utopian speculation.

Plato's model was by no means the only one to exercise such influence. The actual Greek states with which he was familiar and from which he developed his theories served as ever-fascinating examples, particularly Sparta and Athens. The special way that the Greek city-state, or *polis*, drew its citizens into total involvement in civic or political (the word comes from polis) affairs has remained a powerful ideal. Greek political philosophers, most notably Aristotle, asserted that only through participation in the political community, in the polis, could the human personality flower into its full potential. In various forms all modern socialists, with the possible exception of some anarchists, looked to the creation of modern institutions that could recapture—and indeed go beyond—the sense of vital community of interests, of mutually stimulating relationships, of the polis.

The Judeo-Christian tradition, although not distinguishable in any clear way from the Graeco-Roman (since Christianity absorbed so much from classical models), has also formed the basis for much of modern socialist thought. In certain ways the message of the prophets of Israel presaged that of later socialists, especially in its protest against the new social inequalities that were being introduced into Hebraic society by an encircling complex of civilizations—the more advanced, imperial cultures that surrounded and indeed often conquered the early tribes of Israel. In this light the prophets appear as proponents of an older, egalitarian-pastoral value system, a code of stern and virtuous simplicity. Their values were threatened, either by direct domination or more subtle corruption, by the cultures of the cosmopolitan, poly-theistic civilizations of the Eastern Mediterranean.

One can suggestively describe the prophets, then, as profound conservatives, even reactionaries, if that term can be freed from its neg-ative connotations. To be etymologically exact, a reactionary is merely someone who "reacts" against deeply troubling developments and who hopes to return to a more satisfactory past. Thus, virtually all proto-socialist or premodern forms of socialism were reactionary. The linking of a belief in progress with social protest is characteristic of modern times; previously, the overwhelming majority of society, humble as well as mighty, feared rapid social change, and protest tended to center around a yearning for the past. Only in the nineteenth century, and then hardly in an unqualified manner, did large segments of the population begin to accept social change as progressive in the sense of promising a brighter future.

With these points in mind it should not seem perverse, having al-ready described Christ as a proletarian revolutionary, to label him also as a reactionary, for he was firmly in the Jewish prophetic tradition. Following his example, Christian protest repeatedly emphasized the need to return from a growing worldliness, sophistication, and individ-ualistic assertiveness (or "pride") to the simplicity and selfless virtue of the first Christians.

On the other hand, Christ's message and its interpretations by early Christians, most notably Paul, radically transformed traditional Jewish religious pre-occupations, particularly by universalizing them, by opening them to the wider Graeco-Roman culture of the time. It both borrowed from and challenged that culture, incorporating Greek philosophy and Roman law while rejecting many of the values of the Greeks and Romans. The early Christian glorification of the poor, of social outcasts of all sorts—even the ugly, sick, and physically de-formed—was radically opposed to the strongly aristocratic values of the Graeco-Romans, with their love of the finely formed and the beau-tiful, their relative lack of concern for the tribulations of the poor. Christ crucified as a symbol was diametrically opposed to the Venus di Milo, and Plato's philosopher-king would have considered the credulous, un-washed mass that flocked into the early Christian communities to be fit only for the role of helot-slave.

Modern socialists have shared the Christian sense of sympathy for the poor rather than the Graeco-Roman disdain for them. The parallels continue on many levels. Early Christians sought to live communistically, without private property, "with all things common," subordinating individual desires to the needs of the community in Christ. (Certain Anabaptist sects, for example, the Hutterites, have conformed to that early ideal since the Reformation, and continue to thrive in the twentieth century.) As socialists excoriated the capitalists, so early Christians asserted that the rich could never be accepted into heaven. The Day of Judgment has obvious similarities to the day of revolution, and the Christian notion of salvation, coming only after a time of great suffering, found a modern form in Marx's description of capitalist development as a necessary if painful prelude to socialism. In a broad sense the Judeo-Christian or prophetic manner of crying out in tones of moral outrage against the sins of the day was taken up by modern socialists, although they incorporated into their message not only the ardent moral tones of Isaiah and Christ but also the coolly analytical and secular logic of Plato and Aristotle.

The egalitarian-communist origins of early Christianity faded from view as it became the official religion of the Roman Empire and as the Church entered forcefully into the world of power and influence. The religion of proletarian martyrs became that of wealthy prelates and the occupants of the corridors of power. Still, the Church's origins and Christ's own at times embarrassingly unequivocal strictures resulted in a continuing tension within the Church, a tension that was only partially relieved through the existence of monasteries and nunneries, where the Church's idealists had a chance to live according to what they believed to be Christ's original message.

From the fourteenth through the seventeenth centuries, a time of profound change in Europe, the Church became less and less capable of managing this inner tension, and the dramatic collapse of Church authority in large parts of Europe in the sixteenth century encouraged the establishment of a number of egalitarian sects which called for a return to the practices of early Christianity. In itself this call was hardly new, but it took on far greater importance than it had before. Violent class conflict and civil war raged in Europe, and while these struggles were always couched in biblical language, unmistakably social issues were at stake. Frequently, nineteenth-century socialist agitators would look back to these times for inspiration and justification.

On a theoretical plane no doubt the most famous and influential expression of proto-socialist ideas in the period of the Renaissance and Reformation was Sir Thomas More's *Utopia*, published in 1516. More's pamphlet, one of a score of similar pieces produced in the period, describes a settlement supposedly discovered by a sailor-explorer. As its ambiguous title implies (*eu topos* in Greek means "good place," while *ou topos* means "no place"), More's *Utopia* did not describe an ideal that he actually believed could ever be put into practice, and thereafter "utopian" came commonly to mean "attractive but unrealistic." Like the perfect state in Plato's *Republic*, More's distant isle was free of private property, distinctions in dress were not permitted, and society was so perfectly organized as to be free of strife. Sir Thomas conceived his pamphlet primarily as a device to underline the evils of the day rather than as a program of immediate or even distant reform. *Utopia* can be considered a fairly traditional religious tract, not a daring flirtation with forbidden ideas. It views evil, for example, in a traditional Christian manner, as an individual rather than social problem. Yet the *Utopia* was a tract that many later socialist thinkers would consult and would attempt to integrate into a more modern context.

The period from the late seventeenth through the eighteenth centuries, termed the Enlightenment by historians, has usually been seem by them as providing the intellectual foundations of modern times. In large part the thought of this time returned to Graeco-Roman roots, attempting to strip away Christian accretions to classical thought. The *philosophes*, the tone-setting and popularizing intellectuals of the Enlightenment, provided socialists (and, more typically, liberals) with a characteristic secular-rationalistic vocabulary and with some of their most fundamental values.

The philosophes thought of themselves as emerging from a period of darkness, a time when people's minds were in the grip of the rankest superstition and Christian bigotry. The philosophes achieved what Peter Gay, a leading interpeter of the Enlightenment, has termed a "recovery of nerve," a growing confidence in the power of critical intelligence to unravel, without divine guidance, the mysteries of the universe and of the social world.

This was a recovery rather than a discovery because the philosophes were quite consciously recovering rather than discovering for the first time the confidence that the ancients had in people's ability to govern the world through reason and nature. Yet there was a new element in the philosophes' confidence: an optimism about the future, a belief in unending progress, a grandeur of aspiration that not only went far beyond Christian belief but also exceeded that of the ancients, whose hopes for mankind were qualified by a profound sense of the unavoidable tragedy of the human condition. It was this aspect of Enlightened mentality that particularly appealed to the socialists. Their own plans for the future bespoke an optimism and grandeur that were unprecedented in history.

To have such faith in the human personality, in what people could create for themselves, was ultimately contrary to Christian dogma, to the notion of Original Sin, which made recourse to ecclesiastical guidance based on Christian Revelation necessary. The Church and the philosophes had few doubts about this fundamental incompatibility of beliefs, and here also the socialists would follow the lead of the philosophes. The most prominent socialists of the nineteenth century viewed organized religion—though not always the religious impulse—as parasitical and without social worth, except to the ruling orders. Marx set the tone for most other socialists in describing religion as an "opiate of the masses," a perpetuator and rationalizer of the unjust social system of the day.

In spite of their fundamental incompatibility, Enlightened paganism and Christianity did share certain central values, in particular a sense of compassion for the suffering of others, what is normally if vaguely referred to as humanitarianism. But for the philosophes humane values were based upon a conception of human life as good in itself, not good because human beings were created by God. While critical of Christianity, however, the philosophes were rarely atheists, and most were strongly attached to the notion of rewards and punishments in an afterlife.

Indeed, as recent scholarship has emphasized, the philosophes, while believing in the powers of unaided human reason, still recognized its limitations, that human passions usually determine action. But in contrast to Christians they tended to view those passions more sympathetically and to reject the prevailing Christian view that passions usually led to sin and destructiveness. In short, they believed that reason and passions could be harmonized, that a more rational and natural existence would lead to greater happiness. This belief they handed down to the socialists.

Given the desirability and feasibility of social transformation in the direction of more rational and natural standards, a question logically ensued: How exactly was this transformation to be accomplished? It is significant that none of the most important philosophes believed in violent revolution, not even Rousseau, although many later revolutionaries, socialists included, would cite him in support of their actions. The philosphes were mostly gentle men, attached to rational and witty discussion in the *salons* and coffeehouses, not to action in the world.

They would have had no place in the upheavals of 1789–99, if they had lived so long, and most did not. One of their most optimistic members, Condorcet, a firm believer in the progress of the human spirit, did have the misfortune of living so long and was driven to suicide in the revolutionary Terror. Even Thomas Paine, a man not only of Enlightened views but a revolutionary activist of sorts, soon found himself out of favor with the revolutionaries in France.

In approaching the problem of how society was to be reformed, the philosophes accepted as axiomatic that any political system should be designed to benefit all of the people, not just a privileged class. A corollary of this view is that the consent of the governed should be the basis of political action and authority, which itself strongly implied that the reforming action should be linked to the initiative of the people— all of which points to the Enlightened origins of nineteenth-century democratic radicalism and, less directly, of democratic socialism.

However, the philosophes were far from unanimous in this line of reasoning, since many of them doubted the ability of the people, at least in their present state, to act in rational ways. The belief that popular rule is compatible with liberty and progress was not at all widely accepted in the eighteenth century. Many eighteenth-century thinkers, like most ancient political philosophers, were inclined to consider the people ignorant, irrational, and fickle. They believed that popular action was often irrationally destructive and, furthermore, often cynically manipulated by reactionary interests.

Such perceptions of the common people would trouble many nineteenth-century thinkers, not the least of whom were socialists. As noted in the Introduction, the "whig" tendency of liberalism was based to a large degree on distrust of the masses. However, another, rather antithetical tendency existed among the philosophes, especially those on the Continent. Voltaire, for example, was attracted to what became known as "enlightened despotism," which meant rule by an enlightened monarch with despotic powers to do for the people the things which they were not yet clearsighted enough to do for themselves. In variously altered forms this tendency persisted, from Babeuf to Lenin: These socialists believed that an elite of some sort would have to act in the interests of the people, even if the people did not always give that elite its full or formal support.

But with all philosophes, as with all socialists, the ultimate goal was a time when all members of society would, through education and generally improved material conditions, be capable of rational reflection and accurate recognition of not only their own interests but those of the community at large. And virtually all philosophes and socialists believed that such a time could not begin until those currently in power had been in some way removed.

REVOLUTIONARY CHANGE IN EUROPE

Europe experienced unprecedented change beginning in the late eighteenth century. France, *la grande nation*, the most important nation in Europe, was swept by wave after wave of political revolution, while Great Britain increased its industrial productivity to the extent that it finally surpassed France in power and influence. These two revolutions, political and economic, have been termed the "Dual Revolution" by E. J. Hobsbawm, a scholar who has made extremely important contributions to the history of socialism. Other scholars have preferred other terms, such as "modernization," a more diffuse notion, rich in connotations, that has the advantage of suggesting that the combination of political and industrial revolutions—as well as a network of change in many other areas—marked the advent of modern times.

Whichever term we prefer—and much debate surrounds them—it is important to recognize that Europe in the late eighteenth century was moving rapidly away from an older, relatively static world based on tradition, legal privilege, and general acceptance of the status quo, to a new one of restless, dynamic change. Central to this newly forming world was the use of more "rational" (that is, more efficient and productive) techniques of manufacture and administration (in government, education, the military, as well as in industry). Increasingly, efficient performance rather than custom, privilege, or divine sanction became standard to which those in the leading positions of Europe's states, societies, and economies were held. Linked to this rationalization of European life, although in some ways contrary to it, were growing demands for democratization, for the participation in power of a wider social spectrum than the traditional ruling aristocracies.

It is of course possible to see in all of this a reflection of the rationalistic ideals of the Enlightenment. Just as those ideals may be said to have established the intellectual foundations of modern times, so the Dual Revolution marked the transformation of Enlightened ideals into practice: Economically the British paved the way; politically the French offered the most influential model. Both provided the context for modern socialist theories.

These two most palpable aspects of revolutionary change were obviously interrelated, although the nature of that relationship is by no means entirely clear. A kind of simplified or textbook explanation has often been presented as follows. Economic growth is impeded by the provincialisms, restrictions, and anachronisms of a traditional order; investment, trade, and invention cannot flourish in the context of provincial tolls, reverence for custom, and religious obscurantism. Conversely, political and institutional reform does not become a pressing matter until economic growth has begun to exert pressure on existing institutions, since the expansion of trade and manufacture means an increase in the numbers and power of the urban bourgeoisie, and this ascending class in turn demands rationalized, liberalized institutions to further its interests in nonagricultural production, in the free movement of manufactured goods and of ideas.

This picture, while widely accepted, presents a number of problems, not the least of which is the implication that the Dual Revolution, or modernization generally, may be in some sense termed "bourgeois" or part of a "bourgeois revolution." Most socialists, especially those influenced by Marx, were convinced that political and industrial revolution was orchestrated by the bourgeoisie for its own benefit, and for Marxists thereafter the concept of bourgeois revolution became a key tool of historical interpretation. But recently scholars have challenged the concept on many levels: The rising bourgeoisie, they maintain, has been used to explain too much—not only the Enlightenment and the sequence of political revolutions from the mid-seventeenth to the twentieth century but also phenomena as diverse as the Renaissance, the Reformation, the rise of the nation-state, and even the revival of learning and economic activity in the eleventh and twelfth centuries. Moreover, it is peculiar that although the bourgeoisie kept rising every century, the older ruling elites remained remarkably much in place in most countries.

Other historians have expressed impatience with the concept of the "bourgeoisie," at least as a social grouping with clearly identifiable interests and consciousness. In France, for example, where of course the term originated, "bourgeois" in the eighteenth century referred to an extremely heterogeneous category, not easily identified with business interests, with enthusiasm for new industrial techniques, or with commitment to overthrow of the Old Regime (indeed, certain bourgeois elements benefited from legal privilege). Many revolutionary leaders in France were of noble origin, and very few of them were directly linked with business interests. Similarly, it is difficult to show that they thought of political revolution primarily in terms of clearing the way for the expansion of industry.

Yet, while recognizing the difficulties of a simplified Marxist framework—and it is of course not only Marxists who have embraced the notion of bourgeois revolution—it would be premature, at least in this author's opinion, to deny that in most countries from the late eighteenth century on government came increasingly under the influence (though not necessarily the direct rule) of what can be loosely termed "business interests," as opposed to those of landed and titled privilege, and that those interests were linked, however elusively, with at least an important part of the bourgeoisie.

Often this influence was accomplished in the context of revolutionary upheavals or the threats of them, as in France and England. But even in an area like Germany, where such upheavals were relatively weak or abortive, and where the bourgeoisie was submissive and "junkerized" (that is, dominated in values and partly absorbed by the old landed aristocracy, or Junkers), business interests repeatedly won legislation favorable to industrial growth. Similarly, even in Germany members of the bourgeoisie made inroads into those important political and military offices that had previously been the exclusive domain of the old aristocracy.

But to retain this carefully hedged notion of bourgeois revolution—and we will return to it—is far from asserting that the French Revolution represented a victory for only the bourgeoisie. The years 1789–99, considered as a whole, have exercised an ineffable, even mystical, effect on subsequent generations, on people of the most varied social origin. For many later socialists the events of those years seemed to have the same kind of appeal as the events of Christ's life have for Christians. Socialists looked to the story of the Revolution as a kind of holy book, wherein they received inspiration and learned vital lessons. In the writings of many nineteenth-century socialists such terms as Thermidor, the Mountain, the *enragés*, and names like Robespierre, Marat, Hébert, and Babeuf appear repeatedly with the assumption that they would be as familiar as biblical references had been in the past. Prince Kropotkin, the late nineteenth-century anarchist, chose a revealing image when he wrote, "the blood shed . . . [in the French Revolution] was shed for the whole human race" (pp. 581–82).

For the less mystically inclined, the Revolution still had appeal simply as a magnificent drama, a promethean effort to transform the human condition. Later socialists read with pounding heart the story of the storming of the Bastille, the Oath of August 4, the rally of the Paris Commune to *la patrie en danger*. For many Europeans the heroic pose of being a revolutionary had a profound appeal, one which persists to this day.

The calling of the Estates General in France in the spring of 1789, arising from the prolonged fiscal insolvency of the French crown, was the prelude to an unforeseen and unprecedented series of developments. The Third Estate—that is, the nonnoble, generally nonprivileged elements of French society (peasants, workers, but also the wealthy merchants and professionals who constituted the greater part of the actual deputies and who were normally included in the category of "bourgeois")—gained a clear majority, after complicated maneuvers, and then declared its intent to launch upon a vast program of Enlightened reform.

This reforming zeal was propelled by constant pressure from the masses, both in the urban centers and in the countryside. Popular violence was soon turned not only against the king, as was at first the case, but also against the privileged orders. A series of *journées* or revolutionary "days" followed one upon the other, the most famous of which was the storming of the Bastille on July 14. The fall of the Bastille was soon followed by the so-called "Great Fear" in the countryside. Peasants, spurred on by rumors of roving brigands and aristocratic plots, attacked and burned *châteaux*, destroyed manorial records, and refused feudal obligations. On August 4, in an emotional session, the National Assembly declared what amounted to the abolition of feudalism, of the legal-institutional framework of the Old Regime.

The detailed program of reform hammered out by the National Assembly, which took final shape in the Constitution of 1791, owed much to Enlightenment thought, classical precedents, and the example of the American Revolution. Although the promulgation of the Constitution depended upon popular pressure and support, in certain ways it may be said to have been opposed to the desires and interests of the lower classes. And here we return to our earlier point: The Constitution of 1791 favored the interests of France's bourgeoisie over those of the landed nobility or of the propertyless common people. The Constitution abolished the legal privileges of the nobility and dissolved the other corporate bodies recognized by the monarchy. The morass of legal and administrative jurisdictions of the Old Regime was replaced with a rationalized, liberalized code for all of France, doing away with the myriad of taxes, obligations, and restrictions previously imposed on France's population.

The Assembly's desire to introduce a liberalized or free enterprise economy in France, by putting an end to the previous impediments to free trade, removed many of the protections which had been enjoyed under the Old Regime by individuals and corporate bodies (such as guilds, religious orders, and municipalities)—and here, no doubt, the interests of certain members of the bourgeoisie were hurt. A liberal economy promised to free much of France's productive capacity, presumably facilitating the enrichment and advancement of her bourgeoisie. But at the same time it made likely an increasing level of insecurity for her less wealthy citizens.

The Constitution of 1791 began with the Declaration of the Rights of Man and the Citizen, followed by a General Preamble, which stated in broad terms the guiding principles of the new constitution. When one evaluates the Constitution as a document favorable to bourgeois interests, it is worth noting that the equality proclaimed in the Declaration was a formal legal equality: "Men are born and live free and equal under the laws. Social distinctions may be established only on the grounds of common utility." Spelled out in later sections of the Constitution this meant that only the more affluent part of the population was given the vote (in other words, now the standard was money rather than birth) and only the very wealthy were allowed to hold high public office. The poor and those who held relatively little property (about three-fifths of the adult male population) were relegated to the status of "passive citizens," still equal under the law to all other citizens but not permitted to take an active part in politics.

Yet, certain of the Constitution's passages, especially in the Declaration and Preamble, were sufficiently ambiguous to lend themselves to more extreme, even proto-socialist interpretations. Interesting in this respect are those passages that describe government as existing solely for the benefit of its citizens; if a government fails to serve this purpose, its citizens have the right and even the duty to destroy it and establish a new government.

This belief concerning the right to revolution, the right to oppose tyranny, had ancient roots and was held widely in the eighteenth century by men as diverse as Jefferson, Paine, and Babeuf. The popular classes in Paris, radicalized by their deteriorating material condition, judged that the Constitution of 1791 was inadequate and that the leaders thrown up by the first wave of revolution had not performed adequately. A new series of journées in 1792 led to the convocation of a new assembly, the Convention, and to the composition of a new, far more democratic constitution, known as the Constitution of 1793. It was, however, never put into practice, since a series of extreme crises obliged the Convention to continue ruling through special committees, the most notorious of which was the Committee of Public Safety.

This leftward swing of the revolution had been predicted by aristocratic observers in the early months of the Revolution. They had warned both the king and the bourgeois members of the National Assembly that to attack the concept of privilege was an action fraught with danger, since the poor would soon assert that the existing unequal distribution of wealth also reflected privilege. And in fact by 1790 a few extremist writers and orators were insisting that "equality of rights" had no meaning to the propertyless, since they had no effective way to take advantage of those rights.

By 1793 revolutionary agitators loosely referred to as the *enragés* ("the enraged ones") were openly preaching a kind of class warfare and urging the masses on to violence to bring about social justice. Thus the issue became couched in terms of the "privileges" of wealth versus the misfortunes of poverty. As Albert Soboul writes, in his book *The Sans-Culottes*, "In addition to the conflict between the Third Estate and the feudal aristocracy, two Frances appeared to be confronting one another: that of the artisan and journeyman, the shopkeeper [that is, the *sans-culottes*], on the one hand, and the large, powerful merchants, the leaders of industry, on the other" (p. xxix).

Yet this conflict was different in nature from the more familiar nineteenth-century conflict, as portrayed by Marx, between the industrial capitalists and the masses of propertyless factory proletarians (in fact, there were very few factory workers in Paris in the 1790s, and other propertyless workers appear to have been politically apathetic). The issue was not the socialization of concentrated industrial wealth but rather the equal or "fair" distribution of property. Put in other terms, this was not a class conflict of a modern sort, based on relations of production; it was founded on moral distinctions, deeply rooted in the Judeo-Christian tradition, between the virtuous poor and the immoral rich. As R. B. Rose, in his *The Enragés: Socialists of the French Revolution?*, comments, ". . . even an outright class-war measure like the purge of aristocrats from the army cadres was defended by the *enragés* primarily because aristocrats were notoriously potential counterrevolutionaries and not because they were exploiting landlords or *rentiers*" (p. 88).

The previously mentioned "reactionary" tendencies of the lower orders came notably into play here also, for the program of the leaders of the sans-culottes generally rejected liberal ideas, especially of an economic nature, and looked instead to a return to the controls and responsibilities of the Old Regime. This primarily backward-looking stance of the sans-culottes, in addition to their persistent attachment to the idea of individual enterprise and small property, disqualifies them from being considered the first modern socialists. At the same time, through their belief in the desirability of cooperative association and the need for state intervention to control the market and aid the needy, they did focus attention on some of the fundamental concepts that would be developed into full-fledged socialism by nineteenth-century theorists.

Proto-socialist demands did find a certain response in the Convention in the years of the Terror (1793 and 1794), but at no time was the enragé element of the sans-culottes able to win a majority in the Convention or in the Committee of Public Safety. Robespierre and other relatively moderate jacobins maintained a position of pre-eminence, and they were not interested in egalitarian social revolution. However, they did get involved in a number of projects favored by the proto-socialist extremists.

The first of these, state-directed industrial production, was imposed upon the Committee by the pressing needs of war production, to fend off invasion and internal uprisings. Private enterprise was either unable or unwilling to provide the revolutionary regime with the war materials it required. The second, the Law of the General Maximum, was enacted by the Convention in late September 1793, stipulating maximum prices for a number of products considered vital to the common people—bread, meat, fuel, clothing—and also establishing maximum wages at a level presumably beneficial to the working population. Both of these measures had precedents in the Old Regime, and France's jacobin leadership made it clear that they intended to return to practices respecting private enterprise and the market economy as soon as the pressures of war were eased. Finally, the Decrees of Ventôse were intended to seize the property of wealthy traitors to the revolution and to redistribute it to the patriotic, revolutionary poor. But significantly they never went into effect. Thus much of what might be incautiously considered "socialist" precedent during the Terror has little substance.

The eclipse of the Committee of Public Safety in 1794 was followed by the "Thermidorean" reaction (so called because it came in the month of Thermidor in the revolutionary calendar, 1794). Most of the revolutionary leaders of the Terror were executed in the swing back to the Right. The ensuing regimes, first the Directory, and then a series of governments under Napoleon's domination, moved away from the egalitarian democracy of 1793 back toward the principles of the Constitution of 1791 (limited franchise, secure property rights, free trade), with particular emphasis on stability and elitist direction.

Yet even under the Empire of Napoleon, and indeed under the monarchical restoration after 1815, the Old Regime was not re-introduced in any fundamental sense. The privileges of the landed nobility and church, feudal land tenure, the old methods of taxation and administration, workers' guilds, the old representative bodies had forever passed from the scene.

This lasting "bourgeois revolution" in France was in basic outline either imposed upon or copied by nearly all of continental Europe. However, even with the carefully qualified notion of that revolution that we have been so far using, we do not avoid some of the problems earlier alluded to. While the political-institutional transformation of France after 1789 apparently did open up channels of career advancement to members of the bourgeoisie, it did not result in any dramatic freeing of productive capacity—did not, in other words, allow the French rapidly to duplicate the industrial revolution that was gathering speed in Great Britain. Since the nature of economic growth became a key concern for socialists, and since they were also concerned with the notion of bourgeois revolution, it is important for us to examine, however briefly, some of the reasons for France's continuing economic backwardness as compared to Great Britain for most of the nineteenth century.

We can begin with a seemingly paradoxical observation: Not only were the political-institutional changes of the French Revolution in themselves insufficient to allow or stimulate rapid industrial growth, those changes and the overall experiences of the revolutionary years in France helped to erect some barriers to industrial expansion. One immediately apparent way that this was true was in the tremendous expenditure of national energies and wealth in revolution and war. Capital that in Great Britain went into industrial investment, and human inventiveness that went into technological improvements, tended to be consumed in France for the needs of revolution and war.

More broadly, by the eighteenth century the English enjoyed a number of particular advantages in regard to industrial development, even when compared to the French, who still were regarded as the favored inhabitants of *la grande nation*. As an island, well provided with harbors and navigable river systems, England possessed natural advantages in trade and commerce. Wide vistas of possible profit, in internal trade, but more spectacularly in trade with the Continent and with far-flung colonial areas, stimulated her commercial classes.

England did not have a numerous nobility of privilege in the French or German sense. She did have a small peerage, which possessed a few relatively unimportant privileges, but the children of English peers had the same civil status (in matters of taxation, legal rights, and so forth) as other Britons. Similarly, the next level below the peerage, that of the squirearchy or gentry, while monopolizing the positions of power and prestige in England (such as the justices of the peace and county sheriffs), still could not lay claim to special legal or fiscal immunities. Thus it could be said that England's legal-institutional revolution antedated that of the French by a century, although her business classes continued to wage a gradually victorious battle in the nineteenth century to obtain clearer title to political power (most notably in the Reform Bill of 1832) and further economic liberalization (for example, in the repeal of the Corn Laws).

These differences between England and France—the commercial setting, the relative lack of privilege for England's upper orders—helped to instill in her population, to quote David Landes, "an exceptional sensitivity and responsiveness to pecuniary opportunity. This was a people fascinated by wealth, collectively and individually" (p. 34). Both the peerage and the squirearchy practiced primogeniture (that is, passing on title or estate exclusively to the eldest son), which meant that most of the children of peers had to discover ways to earn their own living, often in trade or other "nonnoble" activities. Even those who retained title and land were unusually attuned to the opportunity of making money, although normally they worked through intermediaries, such as commercial farmers, stewards, and other agents.

All of this helps to explain another significant difference between French and English development: their contrasting patterns of agriculture. The reforms of the French Revolution tended to satisfy the long-standing desires of French peasants for a clear title to individual plots of land, and throughout the nineteenth century France remained predominantly a country of small peasant enterprise. The French Civil Code provided for the splitting up of the patrimony, thus furthering the parcelization of French landholding and probably encouraging the French peasants to limit the size of their families in order to prevent an endless division of ancestral holdings. An opposite trend had prevailed in England: For most of the eighteenth century, under pressure of England's profit-oriented, upper-class landholders, the English yeomanry, or peasant small-holders, were gradually deprived of their plots. In the place of the small-holdings were assembled larger units, through the Enclosure Movement (so called because the newly organized larger properties were marked off or enclosed by hedges or fences). The larger holdings were put under the direction of managers who introduced economies of scale, technical improvements (in seed, fertilizer, harvesting techniques, and so forth), and market-oriented innovations of all sorts.

In short, while the French countryside remained relatively static, under the aegis of conservative and backward peasant proprietors, the English countryside became ever more dynamic and productive, undergoing what some scholars have termed an "agricultural revolution," preliminary to England's industrial revolution.

The disappearance of small, limited enterprise in the English countryside helped to favor, in the long run, conditions necessary for industrial expansion. However, the expropriation of the yeomanry did not directly, or in any easily perceptible way, provide the plentiful and mobile supply of labor needed by the early factories. It was not, in other words, a simple case of the uprooting of a rural population and its forced movement into the factories. Indeed, the transformation of English agriculture associated with the Enclosure Movement actually increased the demand for farm labor, and from about 1750 to 1830 the population of England's agricultural counties doubled. However, in the long run, in England as in all industrializing countries, the agricultural population declined in relation to the urban-industrial population.

In a way that also confounds facile assumption, the agricultural revolution did not in any directly measurable way provide the excess capital accumulation over consumption thought to be necessary for rapid industrial growth. Debate on this matter has been sharp, but suffice it to note here that empirical findings have questioned whether large, forced savings or harsh exploitation of labor actually characterized the English case. To cite David Landes once again, the cost of industrial machinery and plant at the start of English industrial expansion was not particularly great, and "it was the flow of capital . . . more than the stock [of it] that counted" (p. 78).

It is not the intention of this section to explore the economic and technological history of the industrial revolution, but rather to provide some overall impression of the dynamics or logic of industrialization, and more specifically to make clear to the reader how much more was required than legal-institutional liberalization. We might go on to investigate such matters as the importance of raw materials, demand, communications and transport, technological innovation, and so on. But what for our purposes is most essential to comprehend, to return to the words of the first paragraph of this section, is how in the late

eighteenth century complex forces were unleashed that were ill-under-
stood and that often turned against those who first applauded them.
This apparent perversion of the initial premises of a rationalized and
humanized order—political, economic, and social—was what stimulated the first socialists into theory and action.

PRIVATE PROPERTY AND GREED: ROUSSEAU, THE COMMUNIST PHILOSOPHES, AND BABEUF

To relate society's ills in some way to the institution of private property—without actually calling for its abolition—was a fairly common
practice in the eighteenth century, as it had been among many of the
ancient thinkers most frequently read by the philosophes. Even the
proposition that the law is a device to protect the accumulated property of the rich and to rationalize the exploitation of the poor had ancient roots and was not unfamiliar during the Enlightenment. Similarly, the conviction that simplicity in possessions and overall life-style
was conducive to virtue, or more directly that great wealth and intellectual sophistication were obstacles to it, was held by many Enlightened thinkers. Again, the classical and Christian roots are obvious.

This cluster of notions became particularly identified with one of
the most celebrated of the philosophes, Jean-Jacques Rousseau. Of the
great thinkers of the eighteenth century he was the most quotable, and
he was clearly the most quoted by jacobins, of both moderate and more
extreme persuasion. At the same time he was one of the most difficult
and least understood of Enlightened thinkers—if indeed that term may
be accurately applied to him, for his thought represented the beginning of an emotional rebellion against much that was typical of earlier
Enlightened thought, and he eventually became a pariah among the
philosophes.

His position in the history of socialism is similarly ambiguous:
While frequently cited with approval by leaders of the sans-culottes and
by Babeuf, Rousseau can more persuasively be termed a prophet of
radical individualism than of cooperation. Nevertheless, taken out of
the context of the convoluted and often murkily rhetorical web of ar-
gumentation so typical of his work, many of Rousseau's statements appear to have revolutionary socialist content. One of the best-known examples may be found in his *Discourse on the Origin of Inequality among
Men* (1755), where he wrote:

The first man who, after enclosing a plot of land, saw fit to say: "This is mine,"
and who found people who were simple enough to believe him, was the true

founder of civil society. How many crimes, wars, murders, sufferings, and horrors mankind would have been spared if someone had torn up the stakes and filled up the moat and cried to his fellows: "Don't listen to this imposter; you are lost if you forget that the earth belongs to no one, and that its fruits are for all!" [Pp. 234–35]

The casual reader might be surprised to learn that Rousseau by no means advocated the end of private property—a conclusion that shakily emerges only after a most careful examination of the context of the above passage. Any number of other similarly deceptive passages could be adduced from Rousseau's work. To provide a particularly notorious example, in the *Social Contract* (1762) Rousseau worked out the notion of the "General Will," which, simply stated, referred to the will of the people, reflected through the prism of the rational needs of the polity. It was not a mere expression of a majority opinion (which might well be misinformed, corrupted, or otherwise dangerous to a society's health and future). If people should unwisely oppose themselves to the General Will, it might become necessary to "force them to be free." Rousseau blended this concept into a framework that borrowed much from the model of the Greek polis, of the dynamically bound-together political community previously described.

A number of modern commentators, led by J. L. Talmon, have described Rousseau as one of the intellectual founders of modern totalitarian dictatorships. Other scholars have convincingly defended him from such charges. It is hard to deny, however, that revolutionaries, during the decade 1789–99, frequently cited Rousseau and used some of the intellectual tools he provided to justify theory and action that may be perhaps best termed democratic-authoritarian and that no doubt in some ways resembled later totalitarianism (although totalitarianism is itself a problematic concept).

The communist philosophes, of whom only two of the better known will be briefly examined here, went beyond Rousseau in important ways. (These men did not call themselves "communist," since the term did not gain currency until the 1830s, but they influenced later thinkers and activists who explicitly embraced the term.) They had a more consuming interest than Rousseau in the problem of avarice, and were willing to go to greater lengths to combat it. They began with a criticism of private property that sounded similar to his, but they took the step of actually calling for its abolition and the establishment of a society based on an egalitarian-communal ownership of property.

The writings of Gabriel Bonnot de Mably (1709–85) have passed into almost complete oblivion in the twentieth century. This decline is interesting because he was one of the eighteenth century's most popular writers, the brother of the now far more famous Condillac, and well into the nineteenth century many editions of his work were published. His writings combine a slavish admiration of Plato (and Plato's implicit ideal, Sparta) with—paradoxically—an Enlightened-Stoic belief in natural human equality.

Mably developed the notion of equality beyond the metaphysical assertion of the Stoics that everyone possessed a divine spark, and beyond the liberal belief in equality before the law. He even rejected the popular eighteenth-century notion that important differences in people could arise through such influences as climate and geography. He granted that unhappy experiences in society or nature might alter or brutalize some, but their fundamental equality remained untouched. What he meant is not entirely clear, but most often he seemed to be insisting upon people's equality of needs—the "equality of the human stomach," as Babeuf and his followers would graphically put it.

It is possible that this uncompromising assertion of inalterable human equality was what so widely intrigued Mably's contemporaries. One might futher speculate that his strictures against the unproductive and lazy found a ready hearing among the growing numbers of those who resented the privileges of a parasitical nobility. Yet Mably was not a modernizer in this sense. He was unconcerned with expanding material production as such. He believed that "virtue" (centering around a selfless concern for others and a fair or equal distribution of goods) was far more important than material abundance. And far from praising trade and commerce as a source of new wealth, he expressed deep contempt for merchants—they had few friends among intellectuals—condemning them in quite traditional terms as motivated by an antisocial greed and a readiness to exploit their fellow men.

Mably struggled with the old problem of how it was that people's antisocial or egotistical instincts tended to overcome their co-existing inclinations to sympathy and altruism. His unusual solution was to propose that private property be done away with, thereby dissolving the destructive potentials of greed that arise through the unequal holding of property and other material wealth. At the same time, rather than believing it possible to destroy egotism altogether, or to deny its persistence, he tried to use it in a positive way. He believed that society could be so arranged as to encourage the play of what he termed "*considération*," or public esteem. People's desire to gain considération could both gratify their natural egotism and induce them to perform socially useful tasks. In various guises, this also was a fairly common eighteenth-century notion.

Mably's theories may be said to have spoken more for the past than for the future in that he largely shared the reactionary concerns of Plato, Christ, More, and other premodern spokesmen of social protest. He, like them, had a low opinion of the potentials of human rationality on the average, and looked to a stern regimentation under state control and harsh measures for dealing with social parasites.

The man we will call "Morelly" was an even better known communist philosophe than was Mably, but only because well into the nineteenth century his theories were confused with those of the celebrated Diderot, and thus earned him much respectful attention. Morelly himself remains an obscure figure, whose birthdate and even first name are still unknown to us. Like Mably he pointed an accusing finger at possessions and possessiveness: "The only vice that I perceive in the universe is *Avarice*; all the others, by whatever name they are known, are only variations . . . of this one. . . ." He believed that society should be so organized that natural self-love could flower into general benevolence or love for all. The existence of private property, even when equally divided, prevents this flowering; it corrupts natural self-love into cancerous greed. "I dare to conclude . . . that all division of goods, whether equal or unequal, and that all private *property* . . . is, in all societies, what Horace [the classical philosopher] calls 'material for the highest evil'" (Fried and Sanders, p. 18).

These ideas were set down in a work entitled *The Code of Nature*, designed to establish, as Morelly put it, "a model of legislation conforming to the intentions of nature." This effort to go beyond vague Enlightened statements about the need to hark back to nature was greeted with lively interest, but upon examination it proves disappointing. It borrowed heavily from More's *Utopia* and often is comically arbitrary in detail. A more serious criticism is that Morelly does not, in most instances, offer a basis in nature for his proposals. He simply presents communistic legislation as if its natural foundations were self-evident, and such is hardly the case.

These statements of communist theory, largely forgotten today, take on indirect importance insofar as they were picked up by a more imposing figure in the history of socialism, a man who may be considered the first communist revolutionary, a heroic martyr to the cause who would inspire generations to come: François Noël (or "Gracchus," as he liked to call himself, in reference to a celebrated Roman revolutionary) Babeuf.

Babeuf was even less original in thought than the communist philosophes. His ideas are a rather graceless amalgam of the writings of such philosophes as Rousseau, Mably, Morelly (who he believed was

Diderot), and of the demands of the sans-culottes. Babeuf is a figure of great historical importance, looked back upon in admiration by later revolutionaries, not because of the originality or coherence of his ideas but because he stepped into the world of violent revolutionary action in the name of socialization of wealth for the poor. His pronouncements were not presented as leisurely platonic dialogues but as hardhitting manifestos. He was part jacobin, in other words, attracted to the political devices of the Committee of Public Safety during the Terror, but stepping beyond jacobin ideology.

To understand how Babeuf came to be a communist revolutionary it is revealing to look briefly at his early life. He had spent a number of years as a keeper of manorial archives (*commissaire à terrier*) tracing the legal foundations of various claims to aristocratic privilege, in particular those relating to taxation. Thus he pored over old records for legal evidence to justify a more and more onerous taxation of the peasantry. But he found it distasteful to be, as he put it, a custodian of "the repulsive secrets of the nobility" (Scott, *Babeuf*, p. 1).

The Revolution, by abolishing feudalism, also did away with Babeuf's job. He threw himself into political activity, winning a substantial popular support in his native Picardy—as well as the hostility of the local nobility. In 1793 he was forced to flee Picardy to avoid a jail sentence (he had been caught inserting the name of a poor peasant as the owner of a plot of land that actually belonged to a local noble). He headed for the center of revolutionary activity, Paris, and arrived just in time to witness the onset of the revolutionary Terror. He promptly got himself again arrested and spent the period of the Terror in jail.

Babeuf was released in July 1794, after Robespierre had been guillotined and the Thermidorean reaction had begun. The period following Robespierre's downfall was a deep shock to the revolutionary from Picardy: The common people of Paris shivered and starved while the *nouveaux riches* flagrantly displayed their wealth. The new government that emerged from the Thermidorian reaction, the Directory, forcefully jettisoned the economic controls of the Terror, severely limited the franchise, and stifled every effort at protest.

It was in this context that Babeuf began to organize the famous "Conspiracy of the Equals," which planned to overthrow the Directory and re-establish the Constitution of 1793, at least as a minimum program, although Babeuf himself looked to a new dictatorial committee of public safety and, ultimately, a collectivist society. Others in the Conspiracy retained more distinctly democratic-radical or sans-culottist ideals, but in May 1796 the communists and the radical-jacobins smoothed over their differences against the common enemy. They spread leaflets, established contact men and agitators in the lower-class sections of Paris, and began to send agents into the provinces.

Within a few months the plot was uncovered, and in August 1796 Babeuf and other leaders were arrested under a law which established the death penalty for anyone advocating the return of the Constitution of 1793. Babeuf was carried in an iron cage to Vendôme to stand trial before a specially constituted court. It was at this time that he made his famous defense, which, when later published, became a breviary for communist revolutionaries. The court, to no one's surprise, found Babeuf guilty. After a gory failure at suicide, he was executed in May 1797. Babeuf had insisted upon "real equality or death." He was given the latter, and the cause of communism had acquired its first revolutionary martyr.

Babeuf's rather syllogistically linked beliefs were based on the familiar Enlightened notion that people have a natural right to happiness. But he further asserted that happiness was impossible without "real equality," that is, social equality, which he also termed a natural right, indeed "the first desire of nature." If a society failed to fulfill its obligations in these regards, then it was to be considered tyrannical, and a person had no moral obligation to obey its laws. On the contrary, one had the duty to struggle against it, to overthrow it.

Other revolutionaries of the time, such as Thomas Paine or Thomas Jefferson, also urged a worldwide struggle against the Old Order. What distinguished Babeuf from this company—and indeed from the more radical jacobins—was his conviction that until private property was abolished real equality and thus happiness could not be assured. After the revolution and the abolition of all aspects of private property (including inheritance, idle wealth, the exploitation of the propertyless) there would be a community of goods and property, and the state would see to a continuing equality of distribution.

The state would have other important duties. In order to preserve the "precious principle of equality," those in power would need to take measures that would prevent the naturally superior (unlike Mably, Babeuf appeared to believe that such individuals exist) from translating their superiority into material advantage. If such men laid claim to greater recompense because of their greater productivity, they must be branded as "conspirators against society" who "must be reduced to such a state where they could do the work of only one man." Babeuf believed that "it is both absurd and unjust to pretend that a greater recompense is due to someone whose task demands a higher degree of intelligence, a greater amount of application and mental strain; none of this in any way expands the capacity of his stomach" (Fried and Sanders, pp. 65–66).

Babeuf justified going to these lengths to preserve equality because he believed that people would continue to be miserable without it, that a happy, harmonious society demanded strict equality. Further, his ideal society was both ascetic and fundamentally static. Although he did make a few stray comments about the potential benefits of machinery, he had little sense of the expanding vistas opened up through technology and industrialization. In this sense his views still overlapped with the anti-liberal, backward-looking, sans-culottists, and more generally with the premodern communist tradition, which was concerned with the moral aspects of "fair" distribution rather than with the promises of liberation through endlessly increased productivity. In a related way, his ideal communist state was concerned with equal distribution, and ignored collective production. He envisioned the shopkeeper and artisan as beneficiaries of a state-controlled community of goods; he did not look to state-directed, centralized, and rationalized productive units.

Babeuf seems to have given considerable thought to Rousseau's concept of forcing people to be free. He urged that the common people, or the "proletariat" (a long-dormant classical usage he revived) be active in their own redemption, but he was painfully aware that the oppressed could easily be deceived concerning their own true interest. He thus openly accepted that the communist state might, at least in its initial stages, have to be organized along despotic-military lines, at least until the ignorant masses had been brought up to a proper consciousness.

This direction of Babeuf's thought suggests his connection with a by now hoary cluster of ideas identified with the more extreme revolutionaries of the nineteenth and twentieth centuries. This has often been termed "communistic," and it does have obvious points of connection with the premodern communist tradition we have already much referred to, although it also adds some significant new elements. It asserts that what the majority of the people happens to think at any given moment is not of decisive importance to a revolutionary. More important is the question, What kind of men are in power? Are they intent on oppressing the people, or do they wish to help them? In either case it might be possible for leaders to win majority support, but if benevolent leaders fail to win a formal majority they are still justified in retaining power. Indeed, they are even justified in resorting to terror against the people, for the people's own good, in the name of the General Will. In a related way, revolutionary violence to gain power can be defended as a kind of self-defense. That is, while in normal parlance aggression is thought of in terms of one person or one country attacking another, the revolutionary asserts that social systems are also aggressive, that one class "attacks" another (that is, exploits its labor), and that those under attack have the right to self-defense, the right to social revolution, in order to bring down the "aggressive" social system.

The thoughtful revolutionary recognizes that the moment for revolution must be chosen carefully, since a poorly orchestrated revolt will lead to repression and futile bloodshed. But at the same time the prospect of *some* bloodshed cannot dampen the resolution of the clear-sighted revolutionary, since the system in existence is already violent. In a society of exploitation and repression great numbers of people die daily, if not through policemen's bullets then through overwork, malnutrition, lack of medical care, and a host of other factors related to the existence of an oppressive class system. In other words, violence is always present and cannot be avoided. The revolutionary must try for an "economy of violence"; he must try to use violence as rationally and sparingly as possible to attain the goal of ending violence.

It might easily be concluded that a short but effective bloodbath could be justified, since countless generations in the future could thus be saved from daily violence. Stated in this way the matter takes on anguishing dimensions, especially if the revolutionary takes fully into consideration the great obstacles to success. Yet one should keep in mind that even conservative political philosophers have recognized the right to use violence to end tyranny, *if* the oppositionist is convinced that the overall level of violence will diminish once the tyrant has been deposed. But how can one ever be certain?

These remarks are not offered as a description of the actual form of Babeuf's own thoughts—which only dimly suggest such conclusions—but as an introduction to a persistent and indeed still vigorous revolutionary communist mentality. We must not forget, of course, that Babeuf was presented with a regime, the Directory, that seemed to him monstrously evil, that condemned the majority of Frenchmen to malnutrition and disease while a parasitical and corrupt minority basked in luxury. He reacted from the depths of his being. And so have revolutionary communists ever since.

THE DEMOCRATIC-RADICAL TRADITION

Democratic radicalism was a variety of liberalism and thus not in any rigorous sense socialistic; it was emphatically distinct from revolutionary communism. Yet elements of it may be said to have had socialistic potential. Many democratic radicals developed into socialists, and even in embracing socialism as more "advanced" they often continued to agitate for democratic-radical reforms as a necessary first step on the way to socialism. At the same time, many socialists clarified their own position by exposing what they believed were the inadequacies of democratic radicalism (which nevertheless long remained far-and-away more important than either socialism or communism in terms of the breadth of its appeal and the numbers of its following). Thus the first socialists were doubly marked by democratic radicalism, and socialism throughout the nineteenth and twentieth centuries would carry unmistakable signs of these early associations.

One of the easiest ways of identifying democratic radicalism is in terms of what it represented to its enemies. From the conservative Right, democratic radicals were singled out as men of intellectual pretension but shallow understanding, enamored with simplistic, Enlightened verities, "logic choppers" and "little men"—clerks, artisans, petty tradesmen, school teachers, and unsuccessful lawyers—out to destroy venerable traditions and institutions, insensitive to the social value of the privileged orders. Socialists criticized the democratic radicals for their narrow commitment to private property, individual enterprise, and the free market, and for their failure to appreciate the full implications of industrialization. Even main-line liberals, while often involved in political alliances with the democratic radicals, viewed them with distrust, as fractious types, inclined to exaggeration in their egalitarian, reforming zeal.

The adjective "democratic" has been chosen here—although the figures under discussion here did not consistently use the term themselves—because the democratic radicals characteristically believed in institutions of popular or democratic control, such as universal manhood suffrage, secret ballot, and frequent elections, in order to maintain a strict vigilance by the people over their elected representatives. In a related way they demanded freedom of speech, press, and assembly, although in practice some of them were inclined to be suspicious of the "misuse" of those freedoms by the privileged. Opposition to privilege of birth was a central concern, uniting the most diverse of democratic radicals.

These general remarks find a sharp focus in the thought of Thomas Paine (1737–1809), the most famous and influential of the democratic radicals. In social origin and mental set Paine much resembled the leaders of the popular classes of his time. He worked for a while at his father's trade as a staymaker, followed by a stint as a petty official of the British government, as a shopkeeper, tutor, and, finally, as a journalist in America, where he found his true calling.

Paine's popularity is no doubt explained in large part by these origins. He had little formal schooling, and he was not an intellectual of any real stature; but he knew the language of the new reading public—the self-made, independent, ambitious men of the time, who were not yet sharply divided into employers and employees, and for whom individual enterprise had real meaning. He was able to articulate their inchoate feelings into powerful, vivid prose, and his writings enjoyed an enormous popularity.

Paine eloquently defended both the American and French revolutions, and conservatives came to see him as a very dangerous revolutionary. Undeniably he personified in an unusually distinct fashion the sense of boundless aspirations associated with the Enlightenment: He wrote of "a scene so new and transcendently unequalled by anything in the European world, that the name of revolution is diminutive of its character, and it rises to the regeneration of man." And further: "The present age will hereafter merit to be called the Age of Reason, and the present generation will appear to the future as the Adam of the new world" (Hobsbawm, *Labouring Men*, p. 1). Yet, compared to a revolutionary like Babeuf, his sans-culottist fellow conspirators, or even later nonrevolutionary socialists, Paine appears moderate. He attacked the landed class and its privileges but never questioned the sanctity of private property. He glorified competitive private enterprise and the free market. He shared little of Babeuf's anguished attachment to the lowest and most downtrodden in society. In a manner typical of eighteenth-century thought, Paine recognized a distinction between the people and the mob, that is, between the sober, hardworking part of the population and the propertyless poor, the latter without regular employment or skills, with no real stake in society, and prone to unruly fits of violence. Paine's ideal society was the America of the late eighteenth century, or, less clearly, the social forces favored by the French Constitution of 1791.

Yet there were elements in Paine's thought and in the democratic-radical tradition in general, that, especially in a changing historical context, bordered on a more socialist perspective. Although in general hostile to the notion of a strong state, Paine believed it both possible and desirable to remedy poverty and inequality through the action of the state, for example through a vast program of public education. This was not a state-imposed, Babouvist equality; Paine was advocating equality of opportunity, which implied that some would succeed and others not, and that an inequality of actual fortunes would continue to exist, though one of considerably narrower dimensions than in existing society, and one based on merit rather than birth. This sense of equality of opportunity rather than material or collectivist equality was central to the democratic-radical tradition.

Paine did not limit his suggestions to opening up educational opportunities. While bitterly denouncing the lavish expenditures of the British monarchy in support of the military and privileged orders, he proposed expenditures of comparable dimensions for the disadvantaged, in the form of family allowances and old-age pensions. At the same time, these expenditures were to be financed by a reformed tax system, which would include a progressive income tax.

Paine did not himself consider these measures to have socialist implications. His family allowances were designed to make the poor independent and self-reliant, and his progressive income tax was mild. Its real intent was not a redistribution of wealth on any significant scale but rather a shifting of the burden of taxation from the middle and lower orders to the upper. What he did not foresee in his easy, typically Enlightened optimism was how much the state would in fact have to do in order to provide meaningful aid to the underprivileged. And, in a related way, he had little appreciation of the vast bureaucratic machinery that would be necessary to administer family allowances, old-age pensions, mass education, and a progressive income tax (at least if modern experience with these measures is any accurate guide).

Paine believed that every institution, every law, every political measure should be subjected to a simple standard: Does it make people—all people, not just a select few—happier? But he did not really subject that standard to thorough scrutiny. That task was taken up by the English utilitarians (also called Philosophical Radicals, or simply Radicals, in England). As presented by Jeremy Bentham (1748–1832) and refined by James Mill (1773–1836), utilitarianism showed how far Enlightened thought, building in this case upon classic as well as eighteenth-century hedonistic philosophy, could go in the direction of rejecting tradition, divine sanctions, transcendental inspiration, and similarly imprecise notions.

Stated in simple terms, the utilitarians believed in reducing pain and increasing pleasure: All laws and institutions should prove their usefulness or utility (thus "utilitarianism") to the general purpose of the greatest happiness (that is, pleasure) of the greatest number. As Bentham wrote in his *Introduction to Principles of Morals and Legislation* (1789), "Nature has placed mankind under the governance of two sovereign masters, *pain and pleasure*: it is to them alone to point out what we ought to do, as well as determine what we shall do."

Since all of the existing systems in the world failed to provide for the greatest happiness of the greatest number, the utilitarians concluded that all existing systems of morality and formal law should be abolished—by gradual reform rather than violent revolution, however—to be replaced by systems more useful to the increase and perpetuation of happiness.

What would be the outline of such a system? Before proceeding to the actual proposals of Bentham and Mill, it will be useful for our purposes to examine briefly a contemporary of theirs, the famous philosophical anarcho-communist William Godwin (1756–1836), whose presuppositions resembled theirs but who arrived at some very different conclusions.

Theorizing on the same axiomatic foundation as the utilitarians—that is, that the world is made up of rational individuals who seek pleasure and avoid pain—Godwin concluded that the greatest number of people would be happiest if there were no law, no state, no official morality, no church. He affirmed that whatever conflicts arose between individuals could best be resolved through reasonable discourse. If one person desired something that another possessed, the recourse should not be, on the one hand, to steal, or, on the other, to seek police protection, but rather to discuss the matter rationally.

In effect, then, Godwin so elevated the power of reason that he short-circuited the entire effort to find a more reasonable system; quite simply, human reason was sufficient to conquer socially destructive selfishness and greed. A kind of enlightened self-interest obviated the need for a system. Before we conclude that Godwin was a man of breathtaking naiveté, we should recognize that he, like Mably and Morelly, advocated radical simplicity of life-style, without private property or material luxuries, and indeed without other such institutional stimuli to greed and invidiousness as marriage and family. When false differences between people, based on social class, wealth, or family, no longer existed, selfishness or greed would wither, reason blossom, and widespread happiness ensue. This was different, however, from the communism previously discussed, because Godwin's point of departure, like that of Bentham and Mill, remained that of the self-seeking individual whose instincts were in no way to be brought under the sway of a collectivist-authoritarian state.

What particularly distinguished Bentham and Mill from Godwin was that they believed property and possessions were essential to the attainment of happiness. They thus set for themselves a whole range of problems that Godwin believed he could ignore. The existence of private property implied continued class differences, since a wealthy father would hand down his riches to his progeny. The protection of property was recognized by all philosophes, we have seen, as a complicated, tricky question, entailing a powerful state, police, courts of law, and numerous other devices to keep the propertyless, the have-nots, in line. Property, especially when distributed in unequal amounts, encouraged envy, social conflict, and dissatisfactions of all sorts.

Put in other terms, Bentham's conclusion was that "criminality" (that is, the efforts of some people to seize or steal the property of others, or in other ways to take "unfair" advantage of them) represented a permanent problem. Thus legal devices of some sort were necessary in order for people to live harmoniously and productively together. What concerned Bentham was that these devices be rational or utilitarian, rather than based on privilege.

Rejecting the possibility of a natural or spontaneous harmony of interests, Bentham had to arrange an *artificial* harmony. To use his special language, the state would have to introduce "sanctions" of pain, in the form of legal punishment, to prevent one person's profiting from the pain of another. If a man desires to steal a pair of shoes, the legal punishment for such a crime must exceed any pleasure the man might derive from it. Being rational as well as self-interested, he will make a pain-pleasure calculation and desist, particularly when he sees that the punishment is certain and swift (a rather important proviso in Bentham's system). The role of reason, while nowhere near as vital as with Godwin, was still important here. Bentham believed that even in the context of social inequality and private property some people would choose rationally those things that contributed to the general, rather than their individual, happiness. But most would not, and thus government was necessary to reinforce reason.

The audacity of Bentham's ideas and their totalistic attack on privilege and existing institutions were attractive to democratic radicals. Utilitarianism provided an uncompromising philosophical foundation for the kinds of reforms that men like Paine desired. Nevertheless, many democratic radicals were somewhat uncomfortable with certain aspects of utilitarianism, above all with its simplistic sense of the inner workings of the mind, of the role of passion in human affairs. Utilitarianism seemed to them to an uncomfortable degree modeled on the thought patterns of the merchant and businessman, those people whose minds were dominated by daily calculation of profit and loss.

There is little question that in practice it *was* defenders of business interests, believing that industrial productivity and prosperity would result in the greatest happiness of the greatest number, who often appropriated Bentham's ideas in the nineteenth century. But their use of his ideas does not alter the fact that the same ideas could be used for more egalitarian, less business-oriented purposes.

Another seminal thinker of the eighteenth century, Adam Smith (1723–90), was similarly used—or misused. That is, Smith's ideas, along with those of such other economic theorists as Thomas Malthus and David Ricardo, were appropriated by those seeking to defend the early industrial system in England; yet Smith himself could more accurately be termed a democratic radical than a defender of capitalism as it grew up in the nineteenth century.

Smith was distrustful of any claim that it was possible to rebuild state and society from the ground up. Much influenced by the eighteenth-century philosopher of skepticism David Hume, he was persuaded that it was possible to work out realistic reforms only within the context of a given historical reality, in a commonsensical, piecemeal manner.

But Smith's moral philosophy while differing from the utilitarians' in this respect, approached theirs in that he believed people were moved by instincts of self-gratification and self-preservation. In addition, however, he believed that sympathy, a spontaneous sentiment or emotion that had little to do with a rational assessment of individual advantage or social utility, was a powerful force in society. Similarly, rather than a pleasure-pain calculus, Smith believed that happiness came "from a consciousness of being loved."

What put Smith squarely in the Enlightenment tradition was his belief that humanity's basically passionate nature could be put to rational use. However, he did not see this rational use as did either the utilitarians or the communist philosophes. That is, rational use did not entail a totalistic remaking of the human environment. Rather, as he saw it, certain rights should be assured—and clearly among them was the well-established right to property and all that it entailed—certain limited ground rules established, and then individual passions would be the propellants, the main stimuli to action. From the interplay of these passions would emerge public good.

This perspective should make it clear how Smith could, after first earning a reputation as a moral philosopher, nonetheless advocate a free-market system. His *Wealth of Nations* (1776) argued that each man seeking his own economic advancement contributes best to the overall wealth of society. Competition between buyers and sellers or between employers and employees assures high quality, low prices, fair wages, growing productivity. Thus, the "invisible hand" of the market assures an economy far superior to any possible through state intervention or other kinds of planning.

However, the interventionist state that was the object of Smith's criticism was not that proposed by the communist philosophes. It was rather the mercantilist economic system that the British government had built up, which by 1776 was a convoluted network of trading rights that were granted to privileged companies and supported by tariffs, navigation laws, and bounties. Smith believed that these privileges benefited primarily the merchants concerned and caused great social and economic harm. Thus, far from being a spokesman in any narrow sense for bourgeois or business interests, Smith was a critic of the greed and monopolizing spirit of the large merchants and manufacturing interests. Indeed, Smith waxed eloquent over the conditions of the poor and underprivileged in eighteenth-century England. He believed, in addition, that a free market would lead not only to greater productivity but also to greater social and economic equality and to greater social justice in general.

We are now in a better position to understand how Smith can be seen as providing ammunition for democratic radicals in England. This perspective also helps us to understand some of the foundations for the differences between the English and French democratic-radical traditions: They were worked out in the context of different historical experience and different stages of economic development. Smith's ideas may be seen as liberal or economically liberating in the context of a situation where the state had long committed itself to the protection of special, large-scale commercial interests, to the neglect of the interests of the common people. In France such tendencies, while present, were relatively less important. The sans-culottist tendency in jacobinism still looked to state controls as a way of protecting popular interests, and suspected economic liberalization of favoring the large-scale commercial and manufacturing classes. Both Smith and the leaders of the sans-culottes conceived of themselves as attacking privilege and wanted to redress the balance in the direction of individual enterprise. Both believed that their ideas would help the relatively powerless in relation to the corrupt power brokers, who were little concerned with overall social welfare.

Without any doubt Smith's own sympathies lay with the underdog. It is also a fair guess that had he lived to see some of the nineteenth-century fruits of the free market and individual enterprise (such as growing industrial concentration and a widening gap between capitalist wealth and proletarian poverty), he, like many later democratic radicals who had earlier found inspiration in the *Wealth of Nations*, might have approved of a more forceful role for the state in defending the poor.

The taste for the protecting role of the state, entailing in particular the regulation of property, remained from the beginning stronger among the French democratic radicals. Moreover, the jacobins, especially in their more extremist, sans-culottist wing, mixed into their esteem for the hard-working independent craftsman and peasant a distinctly stronger taste for association and fraternal aid. Both fraternity and equality meant more to French democratic radicals than liberty, and they looked to the state to protect, preserve, and propagate fraternal feeling and equal status. We thus can readily perceive the jacobin strains in Babeuf's thought. In the English case individual liberty seemed more important: In Paine, Bentham, and Smith the vision of the free individual prevailed over that of the rights of society or the delights of egalitarian brotherhood. In a related way, the concept that the highest good consists in "virtue," a concept rooted in classical philosophy and centered around the notions of self-abnegation, responsibility, and social justice, remained a key theme for French democratic radicals, but less important for their English counterparts.

The lasting attachment of the French to classical and premodern themes makes it possible to some degree for us to consider English democratic radicalism as the more forward-looking, the more open to the acceptance of modernization of the two. Without a doubt contemporary democratic radicals in France and England grew to feel rather different from one another. Paine, while first received as a hero in France and elected as a delegate to the Convention, soon fell out of favor, largely over issues of individual rights and the powers of the central state. And, as the English and French drifted toward war, one of the attractions of utilitarianism was that it freed the English democratic radicals of the taint of the enemy's jacobinism. (Bentham detested the jacobins as much as he did the Tories, and argued that both based their political positions on totally false philosophical premises.) The notion of the highest good as defined by a pain-pleasure calculus exercised relatively little appeal in France; it seemed somehow lacking in nobility and appeared to promise a society of squabbling and solely self-interested individuals.

English democratic radicals were by no means unaffected by a yearning for a return to certain aspects of premodern society. It is in this context that one final English democratic radical should be mentioned. William Cobbett (1763–1835) was twenty-five years younger than Paine, but shared with him popular origins, experience with both the American and French revolutions (where he came to harbor an abiding hatred of the jacobins), and a gift for colorful, hard-hitting language that had considerable resonance among the lower orders of society. In one sense his story belongs to the next chapter, for his most important writing was done in the 1820s (especially his *Rural Rides*) and 1830s and was in direct response to industrialization, whose impact was by now far clearer than in Smith's or even Paine's day. But in a more important sense he belongs to the pre-industrial world of the democratic radicals.

Cobbett's roots were rural, while Paine's were urban, and that difference, as well as the difference in their ages, helps to explain the rather different emphases of their thought. Cobbett hated towns and nearly all that was associated with them. He idealized the middle ages and rejected what he believed to be the corrosive rationalism of Paine, the philosophes, and those he derisively termed the "Scottish feeelosophers." He bitterly attacked the new factories, the railroads, the filth and slums that were appearing in England. With one breath he lyrically evoked the delights of English rural life—now being rapidly despoiled by profit-hungry industrialists—and with the next he expressed a seething hatred for Jews, foreigners, Dissenters, Evangelicals, university graduates, and socialists.

Yet Cobbett's romanticized vision of the middle ages did not make of him a consistent defender of the eighteenth century Old Order. He had great contempt for the aristocracy, its privileges and the corruptions of the state it directed. He generally identified himself with measures of democratic-radical reform of parliament and believed in free trade, freedom of expression, and careers open to talent. But he mixed into this standard Enlightened fare a nativist revulsion against modernism, against cosmopolitan civilization, against rapid change and foreign influence. Insofar as democratic radicals closely followed Cobbett's lead, they tended to move away from any connection with socialism. Yet, on the other hand, his thought prepared many to later embrace socialism: His emphasis on the community, on the organic unities and aesthetic delights of pre-industrial life, and his distaste for the acquisitive, competitive qualities of early capitalism were all taken up and elaborated upon by the first socialists.

GUIDE TO FURTHER READING

Readers wishing to familiarize themselves with socialistic tendencies in premodern times could begin with the opening chapters of Laidler, Gray, Popper, or Talmon, discussed in the bibliographical notes to the Introduction. Norman Cohn's *In Pursuit of the Millennium* is an engaging and influential work that attempts to relate medieval and early modern chiliastic movements to modern revolutionary and totalitarian trends. Christopher Hill's many controversial works, among which are *Society and Puritans in Pre-revolutionary England* and *The Century of Revolution*, study particularly the social dimensions of the revolutionary upheavals in England in the seventeenth century.

A stimulating and erudite study of the Enlightenment, which devotes considerable attention to the classical roots of eighteenth-century thought, is Peter Gay's two-volume *The Enlightenment*. Talmon and Gray give special attention to the communist philosophes. Herbert Marcuse has composed a stimulating introductory essay in *The Defense of Gracchus Babeuf*, translated and edited by J. A. Scott. The notion of the revolutionary "economy of violence" is brilliantly explored in Sheldon Wolin's *Politics and Vision*. Further important studies of Babeuf and Babouvism are David Thompson, *The Babeuf Plot*, and Albert Soboul (ed.), *Babeuf et les problèmes du babouvisme*.

For the reader unfamiliar with the main lines of the French Revolution, Georges Lefebvre's *The Coming of the French Revolution* provides an approachable introduction to the opening stages. His two-volume *The French Revolution* carries the story to 1799 and should satisfy even the most advanced student, although Crane Brinton's *Decade of Revolution* is far more readable. R. R. Palmer's two-volume *Age of Democratic Revolution* covers the wave of revolutions in the late eighteenth century from an international perspective. His *Twelve Who Ruled* concentrates on the Terror in the Revolution. The social foundations for extremism in the Revolution are examined by Albert Soboul in *The Sans-Culottes*. Two studies that deal in particular with the relationship of socialism and the Revolution are R. B. Rose, *The Enragés: Socialists of the French Revolution?*, and Peter Kropotkin's *The Great French Revolution*.

A vast literature, of a quarrelsome sort, exists on early industrialization in England and Europe. T. S. Ashton's compact study arguing the conservative point of view, *The Industrial Revolution, 1760–1830*, provides a good introduction. E. J. Hobsbawm's essays in *Labouring Men* and E. P. Thompson's *Making of the English Working Class* offer the reader spirited but scholarly contrasts to Ashton's views. Hobsbawm's *Age of Revolution, 1789–1848* explores the many aspects of the Dual Revolution. Reference should again be made to Landes's *Unbound Prometheus*, discussed in the bibliographical notes to the Introduction, which contains excellent chapters on the beginning stages of industrialization along with ample bibliographical information.

A useful and solid study of the English side of what is here called the democratic-radical tradition is John W. Derry's *The Radical Tradition, Tom Paine to Lloyd George*. From the French side, an excellent short introduction is Leo A. Loubère's "The Intellectual Origins of Jacobin Socialism," in the *International Journal of Social History* 4 (1959): 415–31. Robert Kelley's *The Transatlantic Per-*

suasion, while not concerned with socialism as such, is extremely useful in clarifying the elusive complexity of the radical and liberal impulses. D. H. Munro has written a sophisticated and penetrating philosophical study, *Godwin's Moral Philosophy*.

Finally worth mention is Robert Heilbroner's engaging if frothy popularization of the thought of the classical economists, as well as that of later economic theorists, *The Worldly Philosophers*.

The First Socialists, 1800-1848   2

INTRODUCTION

A profoundly transformed world was emerging in the early nineteenth century in Europe, and many observers believed that socialism would be, or should be, the ultimate form of this new world. But the immediate post-Napoleonic period was one of a temporary conservative and reactionary resurgence. The early part of the century was also a time of romanticism, which, with its idealization of medieval society and its distaste for the rationalism and atomized individualism of most Enlightened thought, easily lent itself to reactionary purposes. But since romanticism also strived to break away from rules and restrictions, implicitly it was also a liberating and even revolutionary notion. As the century progressed, romanticism became more and more associated with the Left. The Revolution of 1848 may be considered a revolution of romantics, and prior to that time many socialists, especially in France, took on romantic airs, substituting for the utopia of the past, cherished by reactionary romantics, the utopia of the future, where a new kind of brotherhood and social harmony would prevail, taking advantage of the new industrial techniques. These socialist ideas slowly percolated from isolated intellectuals to the lower orders, whose own backgrounds and experiences with industrialization and political reform caused them to be ever more receptive to new world views.

THE UTOPIAN SOCIALISTS

The three main Utopian Socialists—Fourier, Owen, and Saint-Simon—differed from one another in a number of fundamental ways, but they had enough in common to justify considering them together. (Étienne

Cabet, often included in their ranks, will be considered in the following section.) They lived at approximately the same time, only twelve years separating the oldest, Saint-Simon, from the youngest, Fourier. All were alive between 1770 and 1825, and they did their most influential writing in the first twenty-five years of the nineteenth century. Although condescendingly labeled with the term "utopian" by Marx and Engels, they were not utopian in the sense that Sir Thomas More was, for they fully believed that their ideal societies could be established in the immediate future. The label utopian has been accepted by subsequent generations, not necessarily out of simple agreement with Marx and Engels that the Utopians failed to recognize the only "scientific" answer to the social question but because their thought patterns resembled those of the religious sectarian, the recent convert, the visionary, the romantic.

It is useful to consider the Utopians not in any strictly chronological order but rather according to how perceptively they dealt with the challenge of industrial society. Arranged in this way, Charles Fourier (1772–1837) appears as the most utopian of the Utopian Socialists. That is, although he was certainly aware of what was happening in England—he was an eloquent critic of laissez-faire liberalism and the factory system—he rejected industrialism. Moreover, his projects, when compared to those of Owen and Saint-Simon, strike us as fantastic, lacking a firm sense of reality.

Indeed, there is much in Fourier's writing that is pure twaddle, to say nothing of being often contradictory, confused, pretentious, repetitive, and long-winded. At times the contents of his pages resemble the fantasies of someone on an LSD trip: He writes of androgynous planets which copulate, oceans of lemonade, anti-bugs and anti-lions (to replace the existing noisome and dangerous ones), and six moons circling the earth.

But it would be wrong simply to pass Fourier off as an absurd eccentric. If one is able to wade through the nonsense, he offers even the modern reader some fresh and audacious views of the human condition.

Fourier was a relatively isolated thinker, the origins of whose ideas cannot be confidently traced. He had no formal academic training, and claimed to be bored with the learned tomes of the philosophes. Working as a traveling salesman during the day, scribbling away in the evenings, he was mocked and ridiculed by critics and established intellectuals. He had no meaningful contacts with any political organizations nor did his thought patterns correspond in any clear sense to the

proto-socialist elements of the democratic-radical or communist traditions.

This is not quite to accept Fourier's own claims to utter originality
and epoch-making genius. His ideas did reflect, consciously or unconsciously, certain typical Enlightened themes, in a rough but at times
imaginative way. "Reason" and "nature" were key terms in his writings:
He described himself as the "Messiah of Reason," and, like Rousseau—
another outsider among established intellectuals—he criticized in emotional terms what he believed to be a crushing and unnatural "civilization" (meaning, vaguely, bourgeois society). Put into modern language, Fourier proposed a completely nonrepressive society, where
basic human drives would not be repressed or sublimated but rather
satisfied and even cultivated.

Like Rousseau and most of the jacobin Left, Fourier detested all
things English, not least of all their rapidly emerging industrial society
and the theorists who reflected and rationalized it. He held in special
contempt the utilitarian vision of rationally calculating atomistic individuals; he believed that genuine fulfillment could come only in a society that was tightly, emotionally bound together. Thus, Bentham's system, designed to force people to quell many of their natural desires,
was both wrong and unrealizable. Human nature, Fourier believed,
was created by God, and organized society should respect that nature,
not combat it. Thus he could also not accept the jacobin concept of
social cohesion, achieved through a repressive General Will. He had
personally suffered persecution during the Terror, narrowly missing the
guillotine, and he harbored a lasting hostility toward the jacobin Republic of Virtue.

Fourier was born into a well-established family of cloth merchants and spent most of his life in commerce, but from an early age he
rebelled against his work, lamenting that it was his fate to be "participating in the deceitful activities of merchants and brutalizing myself in
the performance of degrading tasks" (Riasanovsky, p. 3). He spent his
early years in Lyons, where he had a chance to observe at first hand
the efforts of the Lyonnais silk workers, or *canuts*, to organize in their
own self-defense. Similarly, he made contact with a strong local tradition of utopian speculation. Here too he observed with deepening disgust the rampant commercial speculation, the cycles of inflation, and
the industrial stagnation that prevailed when the free-market economy
was re-established under the Directory.

Fourier shared the general concern of Enlightened thinkers to elevate productive labor, to rescue it from long-standing classical and aris-

tocratic denigration. But while Fourier was interested in rational reorganization and efficiency he by no means accepted the bourgeois work ethic or the older Judeo-Christian sense that work is unavoidably arduous. And while his ideal looked to self-contained agricultural production, he did not even accept the democratic-radical tendency to view agricultural labor as relatively pleasant and ennobling compared to the degraded and monotonous work of the factory hand. For Fourier manual labor, as it currently existed, whether in factory, workshop, or field, was intolerably dehumanizing. But he believed that it was possible to make all work into play, to make it pleasant and desirable, deeply satisfying psychically. This was a vision of lasting fascination for nineteenth- and twentieth-century socialists.

The device that Fourier believed would make possible this nonrepressive social cohesion, this Eden of joyous labor, he termed the *phalanstère*. A typically untranslatable neologism—his works are replete with them—the term was apparently coined by Fourier to suggest the ancient Greek phalanx, where men were tightly linked together, forming a highly interdependent and impenetrable fighting unit. Fourier's phalanstère was to be a self-contained community, housing 1,620 members (a number based on his calculation that there were 810 different psychological types, doubled to give one of each sex), with a myriad of subdivisions designed to encourage a dynamic interplay of various human passions. Here the Law of Passional Attractions would be allowed to operate unimpeded for the first time in history. (Fourier believed that his law explained the attractions of human bodies to one another, just as Newton's gravitational laws explained the attractions of planetary bodies—although Fourier believed that his own discoveries were much more important.)

Fourier distinguished twelve fundamental passions: five of the senses (touch, hearing, taste, sight, and smell), four of the "soul" (friendship, love, ambition, and parenthood), and three, finally, that he termed "distributive." These last three he gave special names, and they require special explanation.

First, *la Papillone* (deriving from the French word for "butterfly"), which refers to the human love of variety: A worker quickly tires of one kind of task, just as lovers, in spite of the power of their initial attraction, soon find themselves casting loving glances elsewhere. Fourier had a deep contempt for Christian morality, which made people feel guilty when in the grips of this God-given and perfectly natural desire for variety, in work or in sex. For the same reasons he abhorred Adam Smith's vision of a society of specialists, performing day after day the same labors. Whatever the productive advantages of such monotonous labor, only stunted and repressed human beings could result. Society should strive to eliminate all tedious or otherwise unpleasant jobs, learning, if at all possible, to do without the products derived from such labor.

The second of the distributive passions, *la Cabaliste*, had to do with rivalry and conspiracy. While in previous and existing societies this passion had been the cause of much grief, in the phalanstère it would be put to good use. (Fourier believed that all passions could be corrupted and thus made socially harmful; only in the phalanstère would they find their properly balanced and harmonious expression.) Productive teams would vie with one another to produce the most delicious peaches or the most durable, attractive shoes. Their competition would satisfy a natural passion, while at the same time contributing to socially necessary production. And the harmful aspects of competitive commerce in "civilization" would not be reproduced because production would keep the overall good of society in mind, rather than encouraging individual profit in the market, based on exploited labor.

Finally, *la Composite*, the distributive passion, which Fourier considered the most beautiful of all. Insofar as it is possible to make sense of Fourier's descriptions, this seems to entail the combination of two or more different varieties of passions—the sharing of a good meal (sensual) in good company (social, of the "soul"), while conspiring (*la Cabaliste*), perhaps, to arrange a sexual orgy with the couples at the next table.

This last remark suggests some of the special and renewed interest of Fourier's writings for modern consciousness. He was an ardent advocate of sexual liberation and an awesomely consistent defender of sexual preferences that were not accepted by organized religion or existing society. He believed that the only sexual activity that could properly be forbidden involved inflicting pain on someone against his or her will. He was willing to accept both sadism and masochism, among consenting partners, as well as sodomy, sapphism, pederasty, bestiality, fetishism, sex between close relatives—any sexual activity, in other words, that satisfies the God-given needs of certain individuals.

Similarly, Fourier was a radical feminist. He considered the position of women in contemporary society to be little better than slavery. He set down the postulate that the level of any civilization could be measured by the extent to which its women had been liberated. It would be imprecise, however, to say that Fourier wished to introduce equality between the sexes. He believed that their manifold and very real differences, physical and psychological, would contribute to passional satisfactions. He firmly rejected patriarchy, or family units led by a paterfamilias, and he posited conditions in the phalanstère that would make family life, at least as it was known in western civilization, nearly impossible. He believed that existing family structure and traditions were responsible for the subjugation of women; they also discouraged sociability, by encouraging people to turn exclusively inward, to spouse and offspring, rather than outward, to society.

Fourier believed that important natural differences existed not only between men and women but also between various human beings. He believed that social and economic equality was neither attainable nor even desirable. However, he envisaged no extreme differences in wealth. In the phalanstère there would be no poor. Its members would range from those of comfortable income to those of relative affluence. The key point was that these differences would not contribute to envy and strife but rather to a natural harmony by satisfying different emotional needs.

Fourier enjoyed little success in his lifetime. The communities that were established by his followers lasted only a short time and in fact did not much resemble his ideal, particularly in such matters as relations between the sexes. Indeed, most of his writings on sex were not even published until the twentieth century. In the 1830s and 1840s groups calling themselves Fourierist won a following, but they propagated only certain elements of his thought—his criticism of commerce and the bourgeois family for example—and were not ready or able to introduce a phalanstère as Fourier conceived of it.

In considering Robert Owen (1771–1858), we move into a significantly different historical context and theoretical framework. Although Fourier and Owen resembled one another in being self-taught intellectuals, without university education, involved in the textile industry yet radically critical of it, Owen was not repelled by his work, nor did he live out his years in isolated theorizing. Rather, he became, paradoxically, a highly successful industrial entrepreneur, quickly moving up, at least for a while, into the charmed circles of the wealthy and politically powerful, enjoying almost univeral admiration. By the 1830s and 1840s Owenism (a term which he disliked and discouraged his followers from using) became nearly synonymous with English socialism.

Owen understood the implications of industrialization more clearly than did Fourier and accepted them in a more positive spirit. He was more open to the new techniques of factory production, to the new machines and new disciplines, seeing in them the promise of growing productivity and general human happiness, whatever the initial aberrations and irrationalities of the system.

But this is to get ahead of our story, for in the beginning Owen appeared as little more than a benevolent factory owner, involved in paternalistic improvements in the lives of his employees, and speaking a language that seemed in large part to hark back to a pre-industrial moral economy, to a rejection of modern commercial and industrial civilization. For this reason, prominent among Owen's earliest admirers were members of the rural gentry and Tory politicians, among whom such antimodern ideas were common.

Broad notice of Owen first came through his operation of a textile factory in New Lanark, Scotland. Taking over just after the turn of the century, he introduced such improvements as shorter hours, healthier and safer working conditions, after-hours recreation, schools for children and adults, renovated housing, an end to child labor, and insurance plans financed by payroll deductions. What was remarkable above all was that he not only improved the welfare and general morale of his workers but continued to make a handsome profit. Before long New Lanark became a world-famous tourist attraction, where visitors of every description, from royalty to common citizens, came to observe Owen's reforms in action.

What endeared Owen to England's Tory squirearchy was that he, a successful industrialist, attacked the theories of Adam Smith, Malthus, and Ricardo, the political economists who had provided a widely accepted defense of the factory system. Similarly, in entering the then-heated debates concerning the Poor Law, Owen reinforced the arguments of the older ruling orders. The factory system, he argued, encouraged social irresponsibility, destructive competition, and heartless individualism. In contrast, pre-industrial society was characterized by a pervasive social conscience, by a belief by the upper orders that they had the duty to look after the poor and unfortunate, and by a strong sense of community among the working population. In his earliest work, *A New View of Society* (1813), far from advocating radical change, Owen recommended "a plain, simple, practicable plan which would not contain the least danger to any individual, or to any part of society," and which had the goal of making the poor independent and self-supporting (Harrison, p. 22).

However, Owen's Tory admirers gradually began to perceive that his ideas differed from theirs in fundamental ways, and he more and more broke out of the mold of the simple philanthropist. From his very first writings, it was obvious that, while he attacked individualistic utilitarianism, most of his own intellectual assumptions were closer to those of the democratic radicals than to those of a typical conservative. He rejected Christianity and custom (even while seeing much practical good in the traditions of the past) and looked to the unique guidance of reason and nature. He espoused a thoroughgoing environmentalism: People are now unhappy, immoral, cruel, and greedy because of a bad environment; they could be made happy, moral, altruistic, and cooperative through a good environment. As he proclaimed in the opening page of *A New View of Society*, "Any general character . . . may be given to any community . . . by the application of the proper means . . . which are to a great extent . . . under the control of those who have influence in the affairs of men" (Gray, p. 204).

Owen rejected the democratic-radical emphasis on competitive individual effort because his personal experience convinced him that it had unfortunate social consequences. He still accepted that happiness was the only proper goal of society and asserted that the greatest happiness of the greatest number should be the test of any system. But unlike the industrialist admirers of Smith and Bentham, he did not believe that the best way to assure general happiness was through the increased productivity of a free-market system. Harmonious cooperation and rational planning would be far superior.

Owen thus moved from vaguely utilitarian premises to socialist conclusions. But to be precise, even his utilitarianism had a different emphasis from that of Bentham and Mill. That is, Owen did not really define happiness hedonistically, in terms of pleasure exceeding pain. He believed it was to be derived from the delights of a rational (socialist) existence. The dynamic of his ideal community was not to be the pain-pleasure calculus; instead he offered a moral injunction: People should live for the rational ideal of the greatest happiness of the greatest number. Ironically, although Owen relentlessly criticized Christianity for its moralism, he was in a sense falling back upon a moralism just as irrational and unnatural. But profound and consistent philosophical reasoning was not one of Owen's strengths.

Owen's first plans for the establishment of utopian settlements (utopian in the sense of being divorced from the rest of society and constructed from the ground up according to reason and nature) resembled Fourier's phalanstères in very broad outline, without the dynamics of the Theory of Passional Attraction. Owen called them "Villages of Cooperation," and they were conceived of as self-contained agricultural communities, where the unemployed, particularly those displaced by machines, could find productive employment. Here, as in Fourier's communities, modern factory production for the market was not the object.

Owen was at first supremely confident that his Villages, once a few had been established, would quickly spread, not only because of the inherent attractiveness of cooperative labor, but also because they would easily outproduce privately held economic units. But the Villages of Cooperation did not take England by storm. As Owen conceived of them, they required a considerable initial capital investment, and he could not interest the government in the project. He similarly found few takers in the private sector. Even working-class leaders tended to be suspicious of the Villages at this stage. They did not trust Owen, with his background as factory owner and his contacts with the conservative ruling elite. Symptomatic was the reaction of William Cobbett, who, sensing something Benthamite in the Villages (as a matter of fact Bentham *was* one of Owen's business partners), derisively dismissed them as "Owen's parallelograms of Paupers" (referring to the geometrical forms in which housing in the Villages was to be arranged, which resembled Bentham's famous "Penopticon") (Derry, p. 65).

Indeed, in spite of the approximately 15,000 visitors to New Lanark between 1805 and 1815, during which time it continued to make a profit, it too failed to provide a sufficiently attractive model to spread to the rest of the country. There were a number of reasons for this. Owen's personal qualities, his genius as a businessman and as an inspirational leader, were nearly unique. Few others dared to copy him, although in fact a number of other vaguely similar factories, run on humanitarian principles, also appeared at this time and were able to make a profit.

More important in limiting the attractiveness of the New Lanark model was the fact that Owen's achievements there were not particularly relevant for most of England in the early nineteenth century. The mills of New Lanark were located in an isolated rural area. They depended upon water power rather than steam, and were filled with workers who had been especially brought to the area and provided with housing, stores, and other facilities by the previous owners. New Lanark was operating under conditions that were typical of the initial stages of textile industrialization but were being superseded elsewhere in England.

Owen had previously worked in Manchester, the dynamic center of industrial England, and the epitome of all that emerged from a ferocious scramble for profit, utterly unconcerned with aesthetic and humanitarian values. There is little question that it was in the bustle and chaos of industrial Manchester that Owen developed his distaste for destructive competitiveness and began to grope for a way out of the confines of the laissez-faire economy. In going to New Lanark he had an opportunity to deal with problems of a manageable scale; he had some hope of establishing the kind of rational supervision and humanitarian concern that had been abandoned in the sprawling factories and slums of Manchester.

We should also keep in mind that New Lanark was not properly speaking a socialistic experiment: Owen and his partners owned it, and he directed it personally, with very little active or democratic participation by the workers, and certainly no efforts to establish common ownership were made. Private ownership and the profit motive remained, in spite of the humanitarian measures introduced by Owen. Thus the failure of the New Lanark model to spread was not really a failure of a socialist model but rather a failure of paternalistic humanitarianism.

Even further detracting from the significance of New Lanark was the special nature of its working population. By and large Scottish workers of Calvinistic background had been brought into Owen's factory. They were relatively homogeneous, and were inclined to disciplined, uncomplaining labor, self-improvement, and paternalistic direction.

Thus Owen's assumption that his success in New Lanark equipped him to establish full-fledged communitarian or socialist settlements in other areas, with socially, ethnically, and religiously heterogeneous populations, was a faulty one, as he soon learned. In the early 1820s, finally frustrated with the blindness of his fellow Englishmen, he resolved to establish a new community in America, far from the prejudices and evil habits of the Old World. In 1824 he sailed for the United States, where he was received in Washington with much fanfare and adulation. Then he proceeded to Harmony, Indiana. Having purchased a large piece of land and a settlement previously inhabited by a religious group, he hoped that here at last, in the isolated community he named New Harmony, would he have a free hand to put his ideas fully into practice.

New Harmony was the first and most famous of some sixteen Owenite communities that sprang up in the United States, with a special fecundity from 1825 to 1829. None, however, lasted more than a few years, at least as full-fledged socialist communities. The same was true for the smaller number of such communities subsequently established in Great Britain, the best known of which was at Orbiston, in Lanarkshire. Actually, none of them were ever able to attain Owen's stated ideal (which he himself at times contradicted) of a complete community of goods and equality of remuneration; indeed, sharing of property and responsibility for work were among the most important areas of contention within the communities. But, unlike New Lanark, in every community diligent if also exhausting efforts were made to establish democratic participation and control.

The diversity of backgrounds at New Harmony made for friction, as did the colonists' differing motivations in joining the colony in the first place. Some of the colonists were selfless and idealistic Owenites, but many others seem to have joined merely in pursuit of a carefree existence, of dancing and dallying. Few of the predominantly middle-class colonists possessed the dispositions, manual skills, or physical vigor to cope with arduous, dirty agricultural work. From New Harmony a woman colonist revealingly wrote a friend, "Oh, if you could see some of the rough, uncouth characters here, I think you would find it hard to look upon them exactly in the light of brothers and sisters" (Harrison, p. 185). Before long most of the communities had broken down into hostile factions.

It became painfully apparent that, in trying to deal with the problems that cropped up at New Harmony, Owen lacked his former magic touch. He was no longer dealing with submissive, uneducated, and grateful Scottish workers. Although many of the colonists revered him, they had their own fixed opinions. Particularly the Americans among them, coming from a democratic and relatively egalitarian society, were not ready to accept authority unquestioningly.

Owen did not spend much time at New Harmony, and the advice he offered once he arrived (the colony was set up some time before his arrival) was often of little use. When confronted with dissension and factionalism, he urged the colonists to pause and reflect upon the eternal principles he had discovered: In so doing they would see the error of their ways and become rational. But reason was not such a powerful force among them, however free they might have been of the vices of the Old World, and his eternal principles proved to be an insufficient guide.

The ever-growing difficulties of New Harmony disillusioned the colonists and ate up Owen's personal fortune. With bankruptcy approaching in 1828, he returned to his native country, attracted by the rapid growth of a labor movement that was adopting some of his ideas. A new and different stage of his long career was beginning, to which we will return later in this chapter.

By any careful definition, Claude Henri de Saint-Simon (1760–1825) cannot be termed a socialist. The term is associated with his name because Saint-Simonism, in one of its many forms, after his death, became socialistic, and because, in a related way, several of the key themes of Saint-Simon's thought became central to modern socialism.

The details of Saint-Simon's life—and even more the lives of leading Saint-Simonians—are colorful and frequently bizarre. He was of ancient noble lineage, belonging to a collateral branch of the family of the famous Duc de Saint-Simon who recorded the court life of Louis XIV. During his checkered career he fought on the side of the American revolutionaries, and, returning to France, narrowly missed the guillotine. During the Directory he rose to wealth and prominence, only to lose his fortune, suffer a breakdown, and pass some time in an insane asylum. After his death Saint-Simonian religious cults grew up, proclaiming the advent of a new age, while others preached orgiastic sexual liberation. By the time of the Second Empire (that is, the 1850s and 1860s), bankers, industrialists, and prominent government officials professed admiration for his ideas.

Compared to Fourier's or Owen's, Saint-Simon's position in society did not put him so directly into contact with the negative ramifications of capitalist growth, nor was he apparently inclined to dwell on them. His experience under the Directory is worth noting in this respect: As a friend and associate of the financiers and speculators who flourished following Thermidor, he was just the kind of person who was detested by Fourier—or, even more, by Babeuf. Where these latter two saw corruption and an immoral lack of concern for the common people, Saint-Simon saw expertise, enterprise, and sagacity. Where they looked upon capitalist growth with suspicion, he welcomed it. Where they detested England and its social system, he was an ardent anglophile. And where they were repelled by the falseness and unnaturalness of Parisian society, he thoroughly enjoyed the company of the brilliant artists, scientists, and men of affairs to be encountered in the salons.

For some time Saint-Simon appeared to be a typical liberal aristocrat, a man who spoke a language favorable to the emerging liberal-progressive bourgeoisie. Yet he was consistently more than a liberal, more than a defender of laissez-faire capitalism. As his thought developed, he became more and more concerned about the dangers of unbridled individualism. He is best described not as a liberal but as a theorist of modernism, in a way that is difficult to identify closely with either liberalism or socialism. More than the Classical Economists, more than Owen and Fourier, he perceived the wide-ranging implications of the new industrial techniques of his time, and he attempted to put his perceptions into a broad theoretical framework. He enthroned productivity, organization, efficiency, innovation, technological discovery; however, he did not conclude that these were best achieved in a free-market system or that such a system had any universal application or relevance.

Saint-Simon condemned kings, nobles, and prelates as useless and parasitical. This was a familiar enough theme, but his condemnation broke away from the moralizing and ahistorical tone characteristic of many Enlightened reformers. He believed that in a previous stage of social development kings, nobles, and prelates served a necessary historical role. It was only now, under new conditions, that they had become socially useless. Insofar as be judged them harshly it was for their failure to recognize their anachronistic status and because of the obstacles they were putting in the way of the new social order, led by *les industriels* (a neologism, coined by Saint-Simon, in which he included not only industrialists, but scientists, artists, technicians, and productive citizens generally). Yet, even these obstacles were to be expected, he recognized, since all of recorded history had witnessed comparable struggles between new groups coming into power and older, outmoded groups that struggled futilely to maintain their position.

While the Saint-Simonist vision, particularly as further elaborated by later socialist followers, incorporated manual laborers within the general category of industriels, it did not place them in a dominant or even an important position. While manual labor would be honored and the parasitical laziness of the old privileged orders banned, what would distinguish the new system was not labor as such but its reorganization and the application of technology to it. Thus the highest places of prestige and authority would be assumed by a meritocratic elite of intelligence and creativity. Saint-Simon was unabashedly an elitist. He saw no reason to conclude that manual laborers could, on their own, organize and run an efficient, rational, and otherwise desirable new order. They had need of the authority and direction of an elite. However, managers and laborers would not stand in opposition to one another; they would recognize the mutually beneficial aspects of a rationally organized hierarchy of production.

Saint-Simon was sincerely concerned about the plight of the poor— "the most numerous class," as he called it—but he rejected social and economic equality as a sterile, "negative" concept. He believed that society required a fundamental reorganization so that the most numerous class could be rescued from its current distress, so that destructive individualism and antisocial competitiveness could be remedied, and so that meaningful equality of opportunity could be established. Liberal institutions could not accomplish these goals. Rational planning and reorganization required order and hierarchical control, not parliaments and representative institutions.

In rejecting both democracy (in the sense of popular control) and liberalism in favor of disciplined productivity, Saint-Simon's vision appears to modern eyes to conjure up an oppressive, mechanized society, where spontaneity would be crushed and little room left for diversity, unorthodox life-styles, or opposing viewpoints. Indeed, it is remarkable how much Saint-Simon's ideal society resembles the "technocratic society" that New Left critics in the 1960s condemned for its narrow esteem of productivity over humanity, for its ruthless pursuit of efficiency, even at the cost of crippling the human personality and ravaging the landscape.

Saint-Simon's ideas lent themselves to various re-interpretations. By 1830, that is, five years after his death, his followers had split into several factions. Those heading in a socialistic direction built upon his rejection of individualistic selfishness and corrosive rationalism, his concern for social solidarity and interdependent responsibility. They popularized his ideas, making special efforts to present them in a form attractive to the working class. They made familiar a number of the socialist phrases and slogans of the 1830s and 1840s, such as "end the exploitation of man by man" (to be replaced by the "exploitation of nature by men in union" through science and technology), and "to each according to his work, from each according to his ability." This latter slogan became commonly identified as the program of socialism, as distinguished from the Babouvist-communist slogan of "to each according to his needs, from each according to his ability," although there was considerable inconsistency in this.

In seeking more popular support, the Saint-Simonian socialists also began to question the institution of private property, at least as property was handed down through inheritance, rewarding the children of rich parents regardless of their personal merit or service to society. Saint-Simon had defended private property as the proper reward for achievement, but he by no means saw it as a sacred or natural right; it was simply an institution which was useful in the organization of industrial productivity. His socialist followers emphasized more explicitly that property could not be considered the foundation stone of society but rather a tool of social organization. They eventually advocated the appropriation by the state of all wealth that was gained through inheritance—of economic privilege, in other words. This wealth would then constitute a common pool with which the state could reward its citizens according to their usefulness to society.

The Saint-Simonians put this attack on the rights of inheritance into the context of a liberation of the most numerous class, and as part of a program to enhance productivity. They did not consider the end of inheritance as a step in the direction of communist egalitarianism; they explicitly contrasted their views with those of the Babouvists by insisting that rational association depended upon differences of wealth and inequality of reward. Similarly, while sensitive to the issue of the exploitation of labor through the concentration of wealth, the Saint-Simonians rejected the Babouvist belief that in order to rescue the poor the rich must be expropriated. Rather they believed in an absolute expansion of total wealth and argued that rich and poor would profit by rational association and attention to the techniques of rational productivity.

In short, then, a key contribution of Saint-Simonians was to link socialism solidly with the notion of progress through industrialization, breaking away from the backward-looking tendencies of Babouvist communism and the tendency to conceive of socialism as best achieved in isolated agricultural communities. This, and the identification of socialism with the working class, another Saint-Simonian concern, would be a central theme of the 1830s and 1840s, moving Utopian Socialism away from its initial escapist tendencies toward an integration into historically rooted movements and concrete social and economic realities.

WORKING-CLASS CONSCIOUSNESS IN THE EARLY NINETEENTH CENTURY

Our first task in understanding the linkage of the kinds of socialist ideas described in the previous section with the working class is to establish a clear perception of what the working class actually was in the nineteenth century and how the experiences and mentalities of important numbers of workers prepared them to embrace socialist ideas. Such terms as working class, workers, proletariat, common people, rabble, mob—all of which referred at times to similar or overlapping groups—were rich in emotional connotations at that time; reactions to them helped to delineate Right and Left, and indeed still do.

The Left generally had a favorable and sympathetic image of the lower orders of society, as solid, virtuous (that is, characterized by egalitarian unselfishness), productive, and exploited. The Right tended to

regard the lower orders as brutish and ignorant, filled with petty jeal-
ousy. Marxists have looked upon factory workers in particular as heroic
and endowed with a redemptive mission. To get beyond these mythic
or value-rich visions to the actual workers themselves, in all their many
forms, is a difficult task.

Like "socialism" and also "middle class" the term "working class"
first became commonly used in the early nineteenth century, and its
various meanings have evolved in sometimes contradictory ways. There
now exists no broad consensus among scholars concerning exactly what
"working class" at that time properly refers to. But let us begin with
some common-sense distinctions.

Most simply stated a member of the working class is one who
earns his or her living through manual labor and whose pay is somehow
directly related to that labor, in the form normally of hourly rates or
piecework. A worker can thus be distinguished from a clerk (who nevertheless is sometimes called a "white-collar worker"), whose work is not
manual, or from a professional, who has acquired a highly valued
knowledge and who is able to charge handsome fees to impart it. These
latter two are normally considered members of the bourgeoisie, lower
and middle respectively.

A worker also lacks any significant amount of property, and lack
of property distinguishes him from those landed peasants or yeoman
farmers who, while engaging in manual labor, possess enough land to
provide for their own needs and thus are not dependent upon wages
paid to them by others. In this sense a small-holding peasant and a
shopkeeper have something in common, since most shopkeepers also
engage in manual labor, but their property, that is, their shops, allows
them a degree of independence and security not enjoyed by wage-earning manual laborers. Both the landed peasant and shopkeeper, the most
important elements of the lower or petty bourgeoisie in early nineteenth-century Europe, often themselves hired workers, to help with
harvesting or during rush hours, when members of the immediate family did not suffice. However, the peasant and shopkeeper were unable to
engage in large-scale hiring, as would a noble with extensive landholdings or a factory owner, nor did the limited property of a typical nineteenth-century petty bourgeois provide him with any significant degree
of opulence or leisure.

Many peasants did not own enough land to provide for their
needs, and they thus found it necessary to labor part of the year for
wealthier neighbors, or to find other kinds of supplementary work (possibly at a nearby mine or factory). Some owned no land at all, and

therefore were obliged to hire out their labor daily. Such day laborers were members of the working class rather than of the petty bourgeoisie.

Skilled artisans, ranging from the cabinetmaker through the cobbler and butcher, may be considered the most highly regarded and comfortable members of the working class in the early nineteenth century. They might just as easily be considered petty bourgeois—especially the master craftsmen among them. The artisan usually owned his tools and sometimes his workshop; he also possessed valued and hard-earned skills, which normally provided him with a relatively high return for his labor (in comparison to the propertyless, unskilled worker, though not to the professional). Still, he was obliged to put in long and hard hours, and could not usually aspire to any important accumulation of wealth. In the less developed areas, where guilds were still in existence, as in Germany, the master craftsman exercised a patriarchal and often heavy-handed authority over the journeymen and apprentices under his direction. He thus in many ways enjoyed the position of a petty bourgeois rather than a worker.

A recent re-interpretation of the origins of the French labor movement has persuasively suggested that a further important distinction should be made within the upper echelons of the working class, between artisan and skilled worker, especially for France, but for other countries as well. The author, Bernard Moss, argues that "by placing independent artisans, master artisans, and skilled wage earners on the same footing, [the vague term 'artisan'] obscures the class distinction based on the ownership of capital." Skilled workers, as Moss defines them, experienced the process of industrialization or modernization as a deterioration of their situation, "as a process . . . that tended to unite them with newer elements of the working class," to make of them a group with a sense of insecurity and grievance with capitalist institutions, a "suffering working class," particularly open to socialist ideas (p. 13).

The numbers of such skilled artisans were by no means insignificant. In France, according to Moss, they outnumbered factory workers and remained the primary productive force, the chief source of capital accumulation for most of the century.

Below the artisans, skilled workers, and other manual laborers who found regular employment, there existed yet another category or subclass. Since the middle ages a propertyless poor had barely survived on the fringes of the recognized ranks or estates of society. The most destitute of them—variously referred to as "paupers," "rabble," "canaille" (in French), or "Pöbel" (in German)—usually lacked skill, opportunity, or inclination for regular employment. They similarly enjoyed few firm connections with established social institutions, and among them family life tended to be weak and unstable. They were often brutalized as children, suffering from neglect, malnutrition, and disease. They survived in dirt and degradation through charity (of the church, the municipalities, or the state), begging, irregular menial labor, and crime of all sorts (robbery, prostitution, bunco). Authorities were always concerned about their presence, both because they were a financial drain and because they were believed to be prone to violence in times of bad harvests and scarce food.

Dividing lines between the various categories of working class, from pauper to master craftsman, were not always sharp; one category tended to blend into the next, although conservative contemporaries and, to an even greater extent, state authorities often insisted that the rabble—which they believed was primarily responsible for urban crime and rioting—was to be clearly distinguished from the sober working population. A variation on this theme has been taken up by a recent French scholar, Louis Chevalier, who has argued that there was an actual genetic difference between the *classes dangereuses* and *classes laborieuses* in Paris. What seems more likely is that there was considerable mingling among the various ranks of the poor, whether regularly laboring or regularly unemployed and "dangerous."

Modernization—with its attendant population growth, rural impoverishment and migration, urbanization, and factory production—contributed to this process of mingling by causing a many-faceted transformation of the conditions and categories of the lower orders. Many were put out of work and many found new kinds of employment. Population growth appears to have been especially pronounced—or at least noticeable—among the poor, and many contemporary observers believed that an unemployed rabble was growing at an alarming rate. For such observers the "social question" of the early nineteenth century centered around the problem of what to do about the expansion of this unproductive and dangerous element of society.

In the 1830s and 1840s a considerable literature appeared describing and theorizing about the "proletariat," as the propertyless poor was more and more often called. A conservative Prussian official, Lorenz von Stein, in a widely read and discussed book entitled *Socialism and Communism in Modern France* (1842), linked communist thought with the new mentality of the expanding proletariat. Von Stein claimed that this was a new kind of propertyless poor, one that no longer accepted as adequate the sporadic and meager charity previously accorded it, and which now sought to generalize its own condition by creating a "community of goods" (*Gütergemeinschaft*). It was, moreover—quite unlike the poor of the past—proud, combative, and filled with indignation against the rich: "a dangerous element . . . in respect to its numbers and its often tested courage . . . its consciousness of unity . . . its feeling that only through revolution can its aims be achieved" (Tucker, *Philosophy*, p. 115). For von Stein, a proletarian victory would have meant the end of European civilization, which he believed could not survive without private property as its foundation.

In 1846 Joseph Maria von Radowitz, another conservative German observer, wrote, "the proletariat is taking on giant form, and with it opens the bleeding wound of the present, pauperism" (Conze, p. 118). For Alexis de Tocqueville, the celebrated observer of democracy in America, all of the working population of Europe seemed to be developing along lines similar to those of von Stein's proletariat. In 1848 de Tocqueville warned his fellow property owners that the passions of the working class "instead of [becoming only] political, have become social." Workers were "forming opinions and ideas which were destined not only to upset this or that law, ministry, or even form of government, but society itself" (pp. 12–13).

"Proletarian" thus came to be a term used to describe subversive, rebellious workers, normally though not always assumed to be those involved in grinding manual labor with little job security—miners, dock workers, rural day laborers, road and canal workers, railroad construction workers—nearly all of whom, it should be noted, worked at jobs where greatly expanding numbers were employed, since such work had much to do with industrialization by opening up communication and transport. Revolutionaries were naturally anxious to make "proletariat" and "people" as synonymous as possible: Auguste Blanqui, facing a tribunal in 1839 for revolutionary activity, gave his profession as that of "proletarian," and when the judge objected that this was no profession, Blanqui replied that on the contrary it was the profession of 20 million Frenchmen!

The linking of the term proletarian with factory labor was natural, since factory workers put in long and exhausing hours, owned no property or tools, came from the poorest ranks of society, and had only their labor to sell. By the latter half of the nineteenth century, Marxists would make the term "industrial proletariat" a commonplace, with the auxiliary term of abuse, "lumpenproletariat," serving as a rough equivalent of the older term, rabble.

Certainly not all contemporary observers described the proletariat or, more generally, the working class in the apprehensive tones of von Stein and de Tocqueville. Of particular interest is the account of Friedrich Engels, who had observed working-class conditions first-hand in England in the early 1840s (before his partnership with Marx had been formed), and who had read a great number of contemporary accounts of the working class before writing his classic, *The Conditions of the Working Class in England* (1845). He sympathized with workers, lamented the injustices to which they were subject, saw in them great virtues, and looked to a time when workers would assume control of society. With obvious approval he cited the writings of a minister-doctor team who had worked among the poor in Manchester and who emphasized the generosity and cooperative qualities of the lower orders: "The poor give more to each other than the rich give to the poor. . . . The aggregate sum given each year by the poor to each other exceeds that contributed by the rich in the same period." From his own observations Engels concluded that the English worker was relatively free of the prevailing prejudices of the English bourgeoisie, such as xenophobia, worship of money, extreme competitiveness, and sexual prudery: "A worker looks upon his fellow beings as men, whereas the middle classes look down upon the workers as being something less than human. . . . Workers are more friendly . . . They are quite free of religious fanaticism. . . . Workers live only for this world and try to make themselves as comfortable as possible here below" (pp. 140–41).

Both Engels and von Stein thus tended to see anti-bourgeois, collectivist or associationist values as emerging spontaneously from the working class. (Von Stein made the explicit distinction between the inchoate "communist" beliefs arising from the harsh experiences of the very lowest orders and the more sophisticated "socialist" theories that derived from the imaginings of isolated theorists—and which were far less threatening.)

Modern researchers have refined and revised these views to an important degree. In particular they have emphasized how it was the threatened skilled workers, especially those with some kind of previous organizational experience, relative financial security, and at least a modicum of literacy, who were the most inclined to forge new institutions of resistance and to embrace communist, socialist, or more vaguely associationist-cooperative world views. The truly miserable, the very lowest ranks of society, apparently remained politically uninvolved and apathetic, with little if any generalized consciousness of themselves as an oppressed group with threatened rights and long-range goals. Such was above all the case with the rabble, but it was even true of the earliest factory workers, who tended to come from backward rural areas, lacked skills (they were often women and children), and had no previous experience in industrial life outside of domestic activities. They tended to be so disoriented, intimidated, or overwhelmed by their new surroundings that organized resistance was far from their minds. This statement is not to imply, however, that they were incapable of sporadic outbursts, which, consistent with their peasant backgrounds, tended to resemble premodern rural rioting when bread was scarce or when other immediate and extreme causes of distress were present.

The artisans and skilled workers, while threatened by the new machines and other modernized techniques of production, were not in most cases overwhelmed. Most of them could look back to a history of organized efforts to protect their interests. The most obvious example of such earlier efforts was the guilds, which since the middle ages had sought to control production, price, quality of product, competition, and entry into the trade, as well as to provide insurance against sickness and old age. They were typical, in other words, of the premodern corporatist institutions that were broken up by the advent of the Dual Revolution. Workers with such organizational experiences were willing and able to work out new institutions and to conceive of long-range modes of resistance, sometimes peaceful, sometimes violent. They were also able to theorize—in however unsophisticated a manner—or to respond positively to the theories of others concerning the meaning of the changes around them.

Three specific and instructive examples of such pre- or proto-socialist efforts, of the many that might be described, were the English corresponding societies, the Luddites, and the *canuts*.

The London Corresponding Society, the largest of many kindred organizations to grow up in the late eighteenth century, had the express goal of linking up reforming societies throughout England (thus "corresponding"), hoping to establish a wide and coherent network for political reform. It was democratic-radical in tone and drew from the as yet largely undifferentiated mass of artisans and skilled workers, shopkeepers, small businessmen, clerks, and schoolmasters. A typical evening would be devoted to fellowship, education, and agitation: reading aloud and discussing Paine's *Rights of Man*, and then launching into a wider-ranging examination of political and social problems. Members of the LCS were pledged to work for a "thorough reform in parliament" by demanding "equal representation, annual parliaments, and universal suffrage" (Wearmouth, pp. 13–14).

At the meetings of such societies much emphasis was given to procedural rules of order, sober and rational exchange, and participation by all present—what today might be called "training for democracy," which clearly reflected new perspectives, when compared to the hierarchical, authoritarian institutions of premodern times.

The temper and composition of the societies varied considerably: Some met in private homes and were usually models of decorum; others met in taverns and were more lively, more prone to disruption. Whatever the prevalent tone of the individual societies, in the background of their deliberations lurked the prospect of violent action to redress grievances and to press political reform on parliament. As a frightened correspondent of William Pitt, the Prime Minister, wrote in 1792, "I look around and this country is covered with thousands of . . . laboring men, hardy men impressed with the new doctrine of equality, and at present composed of such combustible matter that the least spark will set them ablaze" (Thompson, p. 103).

As England became involved in war with France, the democratic-radical societies were overwhelmed by the groundswell of anti-jacobin sentiment in England, and the government found it convenient to denounce the societies as not only socially subversive but unpatriotic. Government action against the societies culminated in the Combination Acts of 1799 and 1800, which added considerably to the government's already wide-ranging authority to repress such "conspiracies" as political clubs and nascent trade unions.

The corresponding societies were concerned primarily with political reform. While many of their members had been in one way or another affected by the growth of the new industries in England, parliamentary reform was desired by both the bourgeoisie and working class. Problems emerging from industrial change were not the main topics of discussion at the meetings of the sections. A different kind of rebellion, more distinctly and exclusively working class, began with the episodes of machine breaking that gained particular notoriety in the early decades of the nineteenth century in England and somewhat later on the Continent.

Now the conflict began to focus on the different interests of those engaged in industrial production. It was no longer an alliance of the nonprivileged against the privileged aristocratic establishment. Rather, workers singled out the owners of the new industrial machinery for intimidation, physical assault, and even murder. This was still not class conflict based on a consciousness of a broad social and economic confrontation, since the tendency was to single out individual "evil" owners or masters rather than the entire class of employers (a few of whom indeed openly sympathized with the machine breakers), but it can be considered an opening stage of a new level of consciousness, a crude grappling with new kinds of problems.

The Luddites of England (named after a fictional "King Ludd" or "Ned Ludd") became the most famous of the machine breakers. Luddite conspirators performed various rituals, were sworn to utter secrecy, pledged unquestioning obedience to Ludd (that is, to the organization and its secret leaders), and were subject to the penalty of death if they broke ranks or in any way revealed the secrets of the organization.

For many years a consensus existed among historians that the Luddites were primitive and irrational bands of men, whose consciousness resembled that of the premodern mob (or at least of the conservative vision of the mob as rabid and planless) or of the peasant fomenters of *jacqueries* (the sporadic and desperate food riots in premodern France). But more recent studies by E. J. Hobsbawm and E. P. Thompson have presented a more complex and convincing picture. They agree that Luddism was a desperate effort by men who had been allowed no other means of protest, but they emphasize that machine wrecking was not always or necessarily anti-industrial in the sense of wishing to halt technological innovation. Many Luddites attacked new and old machinery alike, with no particular hatred of the new machines as such. Often not only machinery was destroyed but also raw materials, finished cloth, and the personal property of unpopular clothiers. The goal, in other words, was not always to do away with labor-saving machinery but to exert pressure on employers—a kind of collective bargaining through intimidation—since workers were not allowed to form unions or strike.

Hobsbawn further emphasizes that even if trade unions had been legal, they would have been weak, due to the difficulties of organizing the early weavers. Unionization was unfamiliar and many weavers did outwork (in their homes) rather than in shops or factories, where they would have been more accessible to organizers. Luddism, with its terroristic aspects and its rigidly imposed solidarity, was probably the most effective collective action possible at this stage of working-class consciousness and general social-economic development.

The Luddites were infiltrated by spies and *agents provocateurs* and were brutally repressed. Yet, their efforts were not entirely futile. Hobsbawm comments, "within their limits, one can hardly deny that the Spitalfields silkweavers benefited from their riots" (Hobsbawm, *Laboring Men*, p. 21). Thompson similarly disputes the facile tag of "reaction-

ary," attached to the Luddites because they wished to control the introduction of machinery and because they looked to pre-industrial
precedents for corporate control over production: "At different times
their demands included a legal minimum wage, the control of 'sweat-
ing' of women or juveniles; [efforts] . . . to find work for skilled men
made redundant by machinery, the prohibition of shoddy work, the
right to trade-union combination. All of these demands looked forward,
as much as backward; and they contained within them the shadowy
image, not so much of a paternalist, but of a democratic community, in
which industrial growth should be regulated according to ethical prior-
ities and the pursuit of profit be subordinated to human needs"
(Thompson, p. 552).

Although on the Continent conditions were generally not so developed as in England, the silk weavers, or *canuts*, had a long history of
organizational efforts and at times violent defense of their interests, the
subject of an admirable recent monograph by Robert J. Bezucha. In
1831 and even more dramatically in 1834 the canuts staged major uprisings, with the battle cry of "live working or die fighting." These uprisings, along with the desperate revolt of the starving Silesian weavers in
1844, were among the most widely noted and commented upon disturbances of the early nineteenth century.

The canuts are of particular interest because they did not face
many of the obstacles to the development of class consciousness and
organization that impeded workers elsewhere. Lyonnais silk weaving,
while pre-industrial in methods, was highly concentrated, and the canuts, unlike the scattered English weavers who did outwork, often lived
in densely populated, exclusively working-class neighborhoods. A contemporary observer marveled that in Lyons "each social class was
lodged separately, like the Jews of the middle ages" (Bezucha, p. 31).
Similarly, the Lyonnais silk workers, unlike those early artisans whose
consciousness was marked by hostility to artisans in rival trades, felt
an unusual degree of common interest, since they were all dependent
upon the silk industry in some way. Even the conflict, normal elsewhere, between the master and journeyman tended in Lyons to be
turned into a general hatred by the canuts of the silk merchants, who
set the rates and who were widely perceived as parasitical exploiters.
By the early 1830s the canuts were convinced, with some justification,
that their conditions had been better in the past. They were in other
words relatively privileged workers—even in their depressed situation
of the 1830s among the best paid in France—who were experiencing
loss of status due to changing economic and political conditions. Unlike

other workers, particularly those in factories, the canuts had enough education (there were two newspapers in Lyons that catered to a working-class audience—highly unusual at this time) and enough previous organizational experience to respond in a relatively coherent manner.

The nature of this response was a "mutualist" (as the canuts themselves termed it) consciousness that apparently arose without any significant outside influence by socialists or other activists. Mutualism, a term used widely by later artisanal activists in France, emphasized working-class mutual cooperation, self-sufficiency, and control over working conditions through the creation of producers' cooperatives— free from the predatory designs of merchants and from the ravages of an individualistic society and market economy.

As Bezucha has shown, the uprising of 1834 was not primarily a political insurrection, inspired by jacobin-republican conspirators against the July Monarchy. This conclusion contradicts the assertions of the officials of the Monarchy (whose hysterical reaction to protests in Lyons in fact helped to provoke the uprising), the widespread conviction of contemporaries, and even the preliminary findings of many later historians. There were indeed republican conspirators in Lyons, but their actions and those of the canuts ran parallel rather than being joined together. The Lyonnais worker community tended to suspect the republicans because of their bourgeois backgrounds and because their jacobin ideology accepted free trade and progress through the introduction of labor-saving machinery. In fact many canuts remained monarchists, because under the Old Regime they had been granted special privileges and protections. The Saint-Simonians and Fourierists, who also tried to recruit in Lyons, met with even less success, for the same general reason that their ideas found too few areas of overlap or agreement with spontaneously generated Lyonnais mutualism.

All of this is not to deny that democratic-radical ideas had an important working-class following elsewhere. The Lyonnais example underlines the diversity and complexity of the early nineteenth-century working class—and the dangers of making too-easy generalizations. Yet to recognize these dangers is not to deny the appropriateness and implications of the concept of a "suffering working class," to recall Moss's term, of a new and widening group with a proletarian sense of insecurity and rebelliousness, with a concomitant inclination to embrace anticapitalist perspectives. But socialist theory as such found acceptance among workers only insofar as it somehow matched concrete experience and values lodged deep in traditional working-class culture, or in the culture of those who became workers.

THE FUSION OF SOCIALIST THEORY
AND WORKING-CLASS CONSCIOUSNESS, 1830–1848

By the 1830s in England and the 1840s in France an explicit and nation-wide linkage of socialist theory with the working class began to be apparent. Although a majority of workers remained untouched or at least unmoved by notions of collective resistance and social reorganization, systematic socialist ideas began to move from the circles of isolated bourgeois intellectuals to become part of a broadly based working-class movement.

In England the stage was set in 1824 with the repeal of the Combination Acts and a general loosening up of legislation dealing with trade-union combinations. Underground unions came into the open, and new unions were established. Soon a vast labor offensive was underway, which gathered force for a decade, especially during the industrial depression of 1829–32. During this time Owenism took on a new allure. As J. F. C. Harrison, the author of one of the best studies of Owen and his followers, comments, "For five years [1829–34] the British working-class movement was saturated with Owenism" (Harrison, p. 196).

In the early 1820s a few working-class leaders had shown interest in Owen's theories, but they concluded that there was no way to put his ideas into effect, largely because of a lack of capital. By the late 1820s they were ready to conclude that cooperative trading stores, and the profits they could accrue, offered a way out of that impasse. Such stores had existed since at least the late eighteenth century, but only in isolated areas for limited periods of time. Now enthusiasm for them was rekindled in the context of the labor offensive. The notoriety of Owen's ideas, the constant propagandistic efforts of his followers, gave cooperative ideas a much wider hearing and linked them to a broader, more systematic indictment of capitalism and the profit motive.

The spread of Owenite ideas and the growth of unionization went hand in hand. Unions were often involved in the establishment of the cooperative enterprises that were to build up capital for the eventual establishment of socialist communities, loosely modeled on Owen's Villages of Cooperation, this time to be run by the workers themselves, democratically. Striking union members and cooperative stores often joined hands to form "union shops," where the products of the strikers were sold. By 1830 there were over three hundred cooperative societies, shops, and stores, many issuing their own newspapers and holding impressive capital reserves, and all full of hope.

Owen became personally involved in a related enterprise, the labor exchange, a good example of the blending of artisanal tradition and socialist theory. An underlying idea of the exchange was the labor theory of value (that is, that the value of all commodities was ultimately based upon the manual labor that went into them), linked to the corollary, popular in working-class circles, that capitalists and middlemen merely exploited the labor of others, adding nothing of value themselves. The remedy which Owen put into practice was to establish a store or exchange where money in the capitalist sense would play no role: Workers would deposit their goods and receive "labor notes" in exchange, equivalent to the number of hours they had devoted to the production of the good or commodity in question. They were then free to use the labor notes to buy other goods in the store, which were marked also according to labor time, not price in shillings according to the market.

This idea generated considerable enthusiasm, and before long the exchange was jammed with goods and was doing an active trade. Labor notes from the exchange even came to be accepted as legal tender outside, and at the end of the first year of its existence the exchange showed a profit.

However, like New Harmony, the labor exchange soon faced some fundamental problems. It appealed primarily to local artisans who produced goods that did not require a large capital investment and that were palpably the result of their own labors. Such artisans—cobblers and tailors, for example—had in fact long before exchanged services without the use of money. But such exchange could not satisfy many of the essential needs of working-class families. Food and textiles were not, for the most part, the result of local handicraft production. A textile worker involved in factory production or a day laborer from the farms could not offer commodities that were clearly the result of their own personal labor.

A major problem was the accumulation of stock on the shelves. Some articles did not move. This situation developed not only because the goods of the less efficient, less diligent, or less honest workers cost more, since more time went into them, but also because some goods were in limited demand, whatever the cost. Thus the labor exchange tended to become a dumping ground for unmarketable goods. As Harrison concludes, "In both the exchanges and the [utopian] communities there was the same mixture of idealistic Owenites and freeloaders who hoped to benefit from Owen's generosity" (p. 207).

Owen found it possible to slip away from the troubled and increasingly insolvent exchanges to a new, even more grandiose adventure: He suddenly became aware of his great authority among the working class, and for a brief spell in 1833 he put himself at the head of the working-class offensive of the time.

The unrest of the early 1830s extended much beyond unionization, strikes, and boycotts. The issue of the reform of parliament, an issue dating back into the eighteenth century but which had been effectively crushed during the revolutionary period, came once again powerfully to the fore, when the reactionary Bourbon monarch Charles X, was chased from the French throne and replaced by the more liberal and business-oriented Louis-Philippe. Reformers in England drew courage from events in France, while English conservatives feared revolutionary violence as they had not for a generation. The Reform Bill that finally passed through parliament in 1832 did so only after an enormously complicated series of parliamentary maneuvers and violent confrontations throughout England. A number of historians have concluded that England had not been so close to actual revolution since the seventeenth century.

But the working class had little reason to rejoice at the final form of the Reform Bill. Radicals like Cobbett had long warned that working people could not gain from any bill that could be conceivably passed through the existing parliament. The Reform Bill satisfied middle-class utilitarian reformers because it put an end to "Old Corruption" (the centuries-old practices surrounding parliamentary elections and office-holding), but it largely excluded the working-class electorate, whether artisanal or proletarian. Most labor leaders were outraged, since they had worked with middle-class reformers in putting pressure on the die-hard reactionaries in the House of Lords.

The working-class role in the agitation for reform had been impressive: In London and Birmingham in late 1831 and then again in May 1832, demonstrations of over 10,000 workers had filled the streets. In Bristol rioters gained control of the city for several days. The rapid spread of agitation and the remarkable unanimity concerning the need for reform in the country at large finally succeeded in alarming those in power.

In this context, middle-class reformers—many of whom had themselves become concerned about the prospect of a violent social revolution—found an important part of the older ruling orders favorably disposed to a compromise settlement, one which would head off revolution but which would leave the masses without the vote. As the *Poor Man's Guardian*, a weekly working-class journal of the time, de-

scribed the middle-class advocates of the final version of the Reform
Bill, "[they] projected it not with a view to . . . remodel our aristocratic
institutions, but to consolidate them by a reinforcement of a sub-aris-
tocracy from the middle classes" (Thompson, p. 812). ·

The passage of the Reform Bill of 1832 led to a sharp intensification of working-class hostility to the middle class and badly split the
ranks of the democratic radicals in England. The theory of class conflict
began to appear as a far more important theme than it had before.
Working people became more conscious of themselves as an exploited
group isolated from parliamentary power and thus became more inclined to fall back on institutions of the working class itself. They also
became more open to socialist theory.

This was the background to Owen's entry into the arena of labor
organization. Paradoxically, he himself consistently rejected any notion
of irresolvable class conflict—and indeed did not even believe that the
lower orders should be given the vote, because of their ignorance. But
his main interest was not in parliamentary issues. Instead, giving vent
once again to his millenarian instincts, he conceived of a "Grand National Consolidated Trades Union" (GNCTU) in 1834.

Efforts to link or consolidate all trade unions had been underway
for at least a decade, but only now did they begin to succeed on a significant scale. Their goal was not simply to improve working conditions
through collective bargaining; rather, they envisaged a fundamental
transformation of British industry. Owen blithely predicted that within
five years the GNCTU would gain control of all industry and transform
England's capitalist system into a socialist one.

Although Owen did not share the political concerns of working-
class democratic radicals, his ideas and theirs fused. The *Poor Man's
Guardian* editorialized, "let the Radical take the Owenite by the hand,
and the Owenite do the same by the Radical, for both parties are the
real and only *friends* of the working-people." Both sought to "establish
for the working-man domination over the fruits of his own industry"
(Harrison, p. 215).

Starting with something like half a million members in late 1833,
the GNCTU awakened great hopes. But employers began to fight back.
Among other measures, they passed around the so-called "Document,"
requiring all employees to forswear the GNCTU or face dismissal. The
government also stepped up its repression, with arrests of union leaders
and recruiters. A cause célèbre grew out of the arrest of six Dorchester
day laborers, who had recruited for the union and who were sentenced
to seven years' transportation (the English equivalent of being sent to

Siberia). A great flood of petitions and giant protest demonstrations were to no avail. The "Tolpuddle Martyrs" became a part of working-class legend.

A further source of working-class indignation was the passing of the New Poor Law in 1834, which was seen as one the first important expressions of the new political power gained in 1832 by the industrial middle class. Middle-class reformers had long disapproved of the old Poor Law, which provided either out-relief (simple welfare payments) to able-bodied males who were out of work, or else a rather lackadaisical employment in a parish workhouse. This practice did not adequately encourage the unemployed to get out and look for work or to accept unpleasant work (for example, that available in the new factories), the reformers argued. The old Poor Law encouraged laziness and perpetuated what in the United States would later be known as the "welfare ethic." Moreover, under the old statutes, a man out of work was discouraged from leaving his native parish. Thus the old law diminished the mobility of labor, another important prerequisite of industrial growth and thus of general social well-being, as utilitarian reformers saw it.

The remedy, codified in the New Poor Law, was to encourage movement from the parish and to establish workhouses where those on relief would be obliged to labor productively and arduously. A man consigned to a workhouse would be separated from his wife and family, in order that he not be allowed to enjoy the "domestic pleasures" possible under the old law, and the work he was given was designed to be in no way more desirable than the worst available on the outside. He would then make great efforts to find work before applying for relief.

All of this had a neat Benthamite ring to it, in its application of "negative sanctions" to provide for social utility. But from the workers' standpoint the workhouses were simply prisons, "Bastilles," as they soon termed them. The *Poor Man's Guardian* voiced the conclusions of many workers when it protested, "Of all the governments, the government of the middle class is the most grinding and remorseless" (Thompson, p. 821).

In this climate Owen's continued insistence that the owners of industry could be convinced to join harmoniously with the efforts of the GNCTU, if only an adequate appeal to their reason was made, caused growing restlessness among his working-class assistants and associates, some of whom were working out positions that could be termed proto-Marxist. Within a short time he fell out with his two chief assistants, who urged a general strike as part of an aggressive and violent response to the onslaught of employers and state. These internal divisions, combined with state repression and the tenacious resistance of the employers, contributed to the downfall of the GNCTU by the end of 1834. By 1835 Owen dropped his aspirations to lead the working class, and most Owenite institutions—the cooperative stores, labor exchanges, nationwide unions, and socialist journals—began to dissolve.

In France the revolution in 1830, like the passage of the Reform Bill of 1832, had been accomplished through an alliance of bourgeoisie and working class. The fraternity of classes on the barricades—although in fact relatively few bourgeois actually fought in the streets—had encouraged some workers to believe that the new regime would introduce measures of broad political and economic emancipation. Again, they were disappointed. In France it was the highest echelons of the bourgeoisie, primarily in finance and banking, that were enfranchised, rather than the businessmen and industrialists as in England (of course, in France there were considerably fewer industrialists), and Louis-Philippe, the new king, repeatedly chose his ministers from the ranks of the *grande bourgeoisie*.

Surprisingly few of the deputies elected to the Chamber of the July Monarchy (so called because the revolution occurred in July 1830) had palpable contacts with the world of business and finance. Most were large landowners. Still, there is little question that the new regime was far more sympathetic to business interests than had been the previous one. Contemporaries as diverse as De Tocqueville, Balzac, and Marx disdainfully described the July Monarchy as little more than a joint stock company of the French bourgeoisie. And certainly leading members of the government evinced little sympathy for the conditions and aspirations of the working class; they considered poverty to be the result of laziness or vice, quite simply. And if the poor dared to organize in order to promote their interests, they could expect heavy-handed repression.

The Le Chapelier Law, passed in 1791, was roughly equivalent to the Combination Acts in England, in that trade unions were made nearly impossible. Further emphasizing the subjugation and limited rights of workers in France, employees were required to carry a kind of passport, in which each change of home address and place of employment had to be recorded by employers. Such measures remained in effect, in various forms, until late in the century, and made it more difficult for workers to organize in France, as compared to England.

The linkage of socialist theory and working-class associationist movements was less important and came later in France than in England, yet even in the 1830s there were some examples of this linkage, particularly in Paris, and by the 1840s the working-class followers of the "communist" Étienne Cabet (1788–1856) numbered between 100,-000 and 200,000 (according to admittedly unsystematic estimates).

Cabet is often included among the Utopians, in large part because he was the author of a popular utopian novel, *Voyage en Icarie* (1839). But he developed his theories several decades after Saint-Simon, Fourier, and Owen, and he freely mixed their ideas with those of the Babouvian communists. Moreover, his reputation derives both from his activities among actual workers and as a theorist-propagandist. Early in his life he had participated in Babouvist conspiracies and had spent the years 1834 to 1839 in exile in England, where he was influenced by Owenism and the English trade-union movement. He returned to France in 1839 and by the early 1840s his novel and his journalistic activities had earned him a significant working-class following, so much so that Engels later (1847) described him—with some exaggeration—as "the recognized representative of the great mass of the French proletariat" (Johnson, "Communism," *AHR*, p. 645).

Although himself a middle-class lawyer, Cabet had a sound insight into working-class mentality and knew how to speak the language of the oppressed masses. His newspaper, *Le Populaire*, presaged later developments in mass journalism. It was printed in large type and restricted itself to uncomplicated arguments, endlessly driven home, often with exclamation points. One theme was repeated in an almost monomaniacal fashion: Private property is the cause of the current woes of the working masses, and communism is the simple and wholly sufficient answer. Some of Cabet's socialist critics called him a utopian because they believed that the simplicity of his slogans lulled workers into a false belief that their problems could be easily remedied.

As recent studies by Christopher H. Johnson have shown, Cabet's following came apparently from certain types of artisanal workers. While the most successful Utopian school of the time, the Fourierists, recruited mainly among the *moyens bourgeois*, members of the middle bourgeoisie, relatively few bourgeois associated themselves with Cabet. Icarian communists, as they were often called, were fairly well distributed throughout France, with particular strength among those trades that were experiencing intense competition from ready-made or factory-produced commodities (tailors and cobblers, for example), although not, significantly, from factory workers in such industrializing areas as Lille and Roubaix.

Although the Icarians were considered by some to be part of a broad movement of working-class communism, by the early 1840s Cabet's thought had moved away from notions of class conflict and revolutionary violence (even though the Babouvist slogan, "to each according to his needs," appeared on the front page of Cabet's novel). His pacifism may well have been another source of attraction to those workers who were disappointed by the failures of the communist conspiracies from 1839 to 1841 (described in the next section), or who simply could not accept revolutionary violence. There were undoubtedly some former Babouvists among the leading Icarians. Cabet's continued attachment to Christianity—"true" Christianity—no doubt helped bridge the gap between the traditional beliefs of many workers and new, less familiar notions.

Although Cabet's theories were to some degree attuned to new industrial realities, equality rather than productivity was still his main concern; the utopia described in his novel was stubbornly egalitarian and authoritarian. Even differences in dress were proscribed. In short, the austere, backward-looking themes of jacobin-communist "virtue" prevailed over the Saint-Simonian vision of a liberated society of abundance.

On a more practical level, Cabetian communists and other socialists were reaching a growing consensus concerning the desirability of a jacobin-republican state form that would commit itself to active intervention in the economy to aid the poor. Two Saint-Simonians, Pierre Leroux and Philippe Buchez, disagreeing with the elitist and authoritarian tendencies of the Saint-Simonians in Paris, began working with jacobin-republican organizations there, striving to make more explicitly socialist ideas acceptable to them. Leroux proclaimed "the true republic is socialist" (he was, by the way, probably the first in France to use the term *socialisme*).

Other republicans, taking up this lead, agitated among the Parisian workers, trying to persuade them that only through the establishment of a jacobin-style republic could their cooperative and associationist aspirations be fulfilled. Buchez worked to establish producers' cooperatives—something he was able to see put into effect among the jewelry workers of Paris in 1834—but it was clear to him that such spontaneous cooperative production was possible only among skilled workers, with certain educational levels, who did not work with large machinery and whose production did not require heavy investments of capital; in order for socialist production to succeed in other areas, particularly large-scale factory production, it would be necessary to have substantial state intervention. Buchez looked to the state to underwrite a bank that would provide worker's cooperative associations with easy credit, for example. Leroux proposed to the typographical workers that they form an organization of all their members in France (some 4,000 to 5,000), which would collect one franc per member per week. Within ten years they would in principle have enough funds to establish a giant cooperative printing press, which would put all others, based on private production and profit, out of business.

Such ideas were obviously similar to those spreading in England in the 1830s. In both countries the lack of capital was seen as a key problem, although in France the notion of a wide role for the state was more popular. The theorist and activist who most effectively combined the jacobin view of the positive role of the state with socialism was Louis Blanc (1811–82). His book, the *Organization of Work* (1840), argued that the state should protect the "right to work" (meaning what the phrase literally says, not the current American anti-trade-union usage) and that "social workshops" should be created, partly under state sponsorship, but run by the workers. Like Leroux's printing press, these workshops would be both more humane and more productive than the existing factories and workshops, and thus would spread throughout France.

The wide popularity that Blanc's ideas gained among workers derived palpably from their similarity to existing convictions, resting on concrete experience and often deeply rooted traditions. Even the term "social workshops" had appeared before—for example, among the canuts—but Blanc provided greater sophistication and wider exposure. By the 1840s his writings and other activities had helped to make such slogans as "the organization of work" (as opposed to the free market), "the right to work," and "the social workshops" commonplace in working-class circles.

Meanwhile, the disappointments of the early 1830s in England combined with the indignation over the application of the New Poor Law led to a new effort to win the vote for the common people. This effort, further fueled by the economic conditions of the so-called "Hungry Forties," became known as the Chartist movement, after the "People's Charter," which presented a six-point program of democratic-radical reform of parliament.

The points themselves called for measures of political, not social equality, and certainly not socialism. Yet in spite of this political emphasis, the social question played an undeniable role in the propaganda of the movement, and very few contemporaries believed that the attainment of these political reforms was the fundamental issue. Most were convinced that political democracy in England would be merely the prelude to social democracy or some variety of socialism. Once the impoverished masses had achieved political power, it was widely believed, they would inevitably tamper with the institutions of private property, social privilege, and the market economy. And without a doubt many leading Chartists had just such a prospect in mind.

Chartist agitations shook England mightily in the late 1830s and 1840s, but in spite of huge crowds meeting in torchlight rallies, giant demonstrations, petitions with over a million signatures, and threats of a general strike to force the acceptance of the Charter on parliament, the governing authorities were able to stem the tide. A final petition was derisively turned down in 1848, while revolutions on the Continent were overturning many governments. Chartist agitations persisted after 1848 but gradually faded from view. The 1840s remained one of the most turbulent periods of English history, and at the time many firmly believed that a revolution of the working class, in its growing and increasingly disciplined numbers, would eventually succeed, first in England, and thereafter in the rest of Europe, as industrialization developed there. This was a conviction that became closely associated with the name of Karl Marx, but many held it who knew little of him or his writings.

SOCIALISTS, COMMUNISTS, AND THE REVOLUTIONS OF 1848

The conviction that society needed to be transformed in a fundamental way easily led to the conclusion that a violent revolution or seizure of power was necessary. This was not the conclusion of the leaders of the Utopian Socialist schools; it was associated with communism and the Babouvist tradition. Nevertheless, even the moderate socialists in France were deeply disappointed with the revolution of 1830 and the ensuing July Monarchy; most of them yearned for *la république sociale*, a jacobin republic devoted to the solution of the social question.

In England, in spite of the great unrest of the 1830s and 1840s, the appeal of a revolutionary upheaval that would abolish the monarchy and parliament was never as broad or as persistent as in France. There memories of the revolution of 1789–99 remained vivid, and the model or the beginnings at least of a social republic in 1793–94 gave focus to the hopes for a "second revolution," which would revive and complete the first. The 1820s, 1830s, and 1840s saw numerous working-class uprisings in France and the rest of the continent. By the 1840s in France a linkage began to develop not only between socialist theory and working-class activism but also between those two and the revolutionary mystique—the almost mystical feeling, alluded to in the first chapter, that a political revolution could bring secular salvation, a total transformation of the human condition. All of this came to a climax with the Revolution of 1848 in France.

The repressive nature of the Bourbon regime in France, and even more Metternich's reactionary rule and influence on the rest of the Continent, forced revolutionaries and reformers underground. One of the most colorful and famous of these clandestine groups was the *carbonari* ("charcoal burners," because of an early association with workers in the charcoal-producing areas of Italy), which agitated for the unification of Italy under a republic. Carbonarist conspirators spread to Spain, France, and the rest of Europe, everywhere battling monarchical reaction. A large proportion of the leading democratic radicals and socialists in the 1830s and 1840s in France had had earlier contacts with carbonist organizations.

Philippe Buonarroti (1761–1837), a survivor of Babeuf's conspirators, also worked with the carbonari, and in 1828 he produced a two-volume work, *La Conspiration pour l'égalité, dite de Babeuf*, describing in detail the organization and goals of the Babouvist conspirators of 1796. His book, avidly read by a whole new generation of young revolutionaries, provided an important symbolic link between the martyrdom of Babeuf and the new conspiratorial activities of the 1830s and 1840s.

The now-aged Buonarroti's own efforts to build up an elite band of trained revolutionaries met with little success. But among his many readers was a young man, Auguste Blanqui (1805–81), who became the archetypical revolutionary-conspirator of the nineteenth century. Blanqui was active in every major revolution in France—1830, 1848, and 1871—as well as in plotting a number of unsuccessful insurrections in the years before and in between. He survived several death sentences and passed more than half his life in prison, often under the most appalling conditions. He became the personification of the revolutionary mystique, the man who devoted his life to the cause of the revolution.

De Tocqueville left a memorable impression of him, as seen in 1848: "He seemed to have passed his life in a sewer and to have just left it. . . . He had sunken, wrinkled cheeks and white lips. . . . His clothes seemed to be covered with mold; no evidence of underclothing. A black cloak covered his thin and meagre members" (Deppe, p. 2). For the solid bourgeois or aristocrat he was a satanic agitator, a monster; but for his admirers among the poor of Paris, he became a legend. He was the saint of the revolution.

Like nearly every other revolutionary and socialist leader of the early nineteenth century, Blanqui came from a middle-class family. Young Auguste was an excellent student, and attended the better schools, as did his brother, Jérôme-Adolphe, who became a noted economist of the classical school and an historian of economic thought. As young men both Auguste and his brother moved in the sophisticated intellectual circles of Paris, and for a time Auguste wrote for the *Globe*, an influential, left-leaning newspaper of the time.

Although Blanqui's thought and action has often been placed in the communist tradition, he was not in any direct or simple sense a disciple of Babeuf or Buonarroti. As he had come of age in the late 1820s and early 1830s his intellectual formation was naturally different from theirs. By his early twenties he was familiar not only with Buonarroti's writings but with modern social theory of all sorts. In the writings of his own brother he had extensive exposure to those theories that sought to defend the free market and private ownership. Thus Blanqui could not easily embrace the unsophisticated, reactionary tendencies of Babeuf. He had great faith in progress and science. One of the reasons that, early in his life, he rejected Fourierism was that he could not accept Fourier's belief in a fixed human nature. Such a belief, Blanqui objected, ruled out the possibility of a steady improvement of the human spirit. Blanqui was also ascetic in personal habits and was repelled by Fourier's glorification of the bodily appetites.

Yet, in spite of his familiarity with various theories that dealt with modern industrial society, Blanqui's most fundamental convictions, which he formed by the early 1830s and scarcely altered thereafter, resembled those of Babeuf to a surprising degree, whether through direct influence (which Blanqui explicitly denied late in life) or because these ideas were part of an enduring legacy of advanced jacobinism. Above all Blanqui was attached to what Babeuf had termed "the precious principle of equality." And, like Babeuf, Blanqui expressed a deep sympathy for the poor, an abiding hatred of the rich, and a commitment to an eventual communistic society.

Although he must have been familiar with Saint-Simon's notion that class conflict was rooted in historical development, Blanqui tended to speak of class differences in terms that were remniscent of Babeuf's simplistic and moralistic juxtaposition of a corrupt rich and virtuous poor, who competed for a limited amount of wealth. He believed that in order to remedy the condition of the poor it was both justifiable and necessary to plunder the rich. The rich would not part with their wealth without a struggle, and thus violence was unavoidable.

Blanqui was apparently not much persuaded by the argument, put forward by liberal economists, that a growing industrial productivity would eventually remedy the condition of the poor. Indeed, he felt a lasting ambiguity about industrialism and the factory system: He appeared to be deeply impressed by Fourier's position that industrial specialization was too heavy a price to pay for increased productivity. At any rate, Blanqui did not directly relate the progress of the human spirit to the economic liberation promised through productivity in the factory system; for him, that progress was an independent factor, a force of its own.

In spite of his devotion to the poor, Blanqui, like Babeuf, was persuaded that in their ignorance the common people were not always able to recognize their interests. Thus he was an unabashed believer in elitist leadership: The seizure of power by conspiratorial revolutionaries would lead to the establishment of a jacobin-style republic, headed by a dictatorial committee of public safety.

What particularly marked Blanqui off from his contemporaries was his unwavering devotion to the revolution and his single-minded concentration on the conspiratorial techniques of seizing power. Expectably, he harbored a deep contempt for utopian theorists and for activists who believed that fundamental change could be accomplished through mere propaganda, without revolutionary violence. One is tempted to speculate that the surprisingly simplistic and even retrograde quality of Blanqui's theoretical pronouncements—in spite of his obvious intelligence and considerable education—can be partly explained by his monomaniacal concentration on revolution, on the means of seizing power.

Although he had already been involved in several clashes with the authorities and had served time in jail, Blanqui's most celebrated activity dates from the period following the Lyons uprising in 1834 and the parallel unrest in Paris in that year. Both of these events impressed him. The brutality of the government's response and the ensuing new regulations further restricting the possibility of legal organization on the part of the working poor further convinced him that a carbonari-like secret society was the only answer. The Society of Families emerged from his efforts, so called because the basic unit was a six-member "family," standing at the base of an elaborate hierarchy that was organized in such a way that one leader did not know the other until the moment for action arrived. The Society set about gathering weapons, making ammunition, infiltrating military garrisons, and recruiting new members. By 1836 it had something like a thousand within its ranks. A setback in that year, when the police discovered one of its powder-making workshops, led to its dissolution. But by 1837 Blanqui had established a similar and even more impressive organization, the Society of Seasons.

The Society of Seasons distinguished itself from earlier conspiratorial societies, and indeed from most socialist and jacobin-republican groups, in the extent of its working-class membership (predominantly Parisian artisans) and in its primary concern with the social question. Blanqui's organizational talents also made the Society far more disciplined and action-ready than earlier carbonarist organizations had been. On the twelfth of May, 1839, Blanqui and his cohorts stunningly proved that their society was more than another group of café revolutionaries: With approximately 500 conspirators, taking the authorities of the July Monarchy—and indeed all of Paris—completely unaware, the society seized the Hôtel de Ville (the city hall, the traditional focal point for revolutionary uprisings) and proclaimed the establishment of a republic. It was a surprisingly smooth operation. Gunshops were raided, barricades erected, and other strategic points occupied.

The uprising of May 12 demonstrated Blanqui's command of the mechanics of a conspiratorial insurrection. However, it also revealed his inadequate grasp of the wider dimensions of political power, for as soon as the regime recovered from its astonishment, it called out the National and Municipal Guards, who easily dislodged the conspirators from the Hôtel de Ville and then demolished the barricades that had been built in some of the working-class districts. Most of the leaders of the Society were captured and thrown into jail, later receiving death sentences, although Blanqui evaded capture for five months, living in cellars, in attics, and in the sewers of Paris.

Moreover, the ardent appeals of the Society to the people of Paris to take arms on May 12 fell on deaf or puzzled ears. Even in the working-class sections, where resentment against the regime ran deep, pitifully few rallied to the call to revolution. Blanqui's uprising showed that more was required than a mechanically expert seizure by a conspiratorial elite of symbolic buildings and strategic points in Paris.

As an act of revolutionary heroism and propaganda the events of May 12 might be termed a kind of success: The dedication and discipline of the conspirators impressed many, and the ensuing trials offered a splendid opportunity to spread revolutionary propaganda. Yet the failure of the uprising to spread tended to discredit the notion of revolutionary conspiracies. Throughout the latter half of the nineteenth century and into the twentieth the term "Blanquism" became synonymous, especially when used by Marxists, with a revolutionary putschism without mass support.

For contemporary socialists of more democratic persuasion the coup of May 12 merely confirmed what they had emphasized all along. Louis Blanc was typical in this respect: In condemning Blanqui he reemphasized his belief in open agitation, in the ability of the common people to use the democratic vote to remedy their condition, and in the futility of a revolution that had not first been carefully prepared in the minds of the people.

Yet Blanc's thought also overlapped that of Blanqui. Blanc saw France as divided basically between bourgeoisie and people, the first possessing wealth and independence, the second suffering from poverty and insecurity. Apparently, like most other democratic radicals or jacobins of the time, neither Blanc nor Blanqui gave much effort to a more refined or penetrating analysis. Similarly, Blanc had great faith that a jacobin-republican state would be capable of bringing socialism to France. But a terroristic dictatorship would not be necessary; a democratically elected republic would willingly sponsor social workshops, would guarantee the right to work, would make cheap credit available—in short, would create socialism without the need for dictatorial institutions, for even a brief time.

Blanc's dislike of the bourgeoisie was less intense and less categorical than was Blanqui's. He was perfectly willing to recognize virtues in the bourgeoisie—hard work, inventiveness, frugality—but he believed that the inspiration or direction of the common people was necessary to pull the bourgeois class away from its selfish, money-oriented preoccupations.

Blanc thus looked to a "fraternal absorption" of the bourgeoisie rather than a violent revolutionary triumph over it by the oppressed people. He insisted, in a manner reminiscent of Robert Owen, that the capitalist, financier, and rentier could be won over nonviolently to a socialist system. In part he believed this because he was convinced that a cooperative economy would be more productive than the destructively competitive existing one. The struggle for limited goods would no longer be necessary; all could be secure and free of poverty.

In a related way Blanc was persuaded that modern technology could be a liberating force rather than something that made work more monotonous, arduous, or alienated. In Blanc's proposed social work-shops, one-third of the profits would be turned over to research and development, in order to ensure rapid progress in productivity, until the day that it would be possible for each to consume according to his needs while producing according to his ability.

Étienne Cabet's communism and Blanc's socialism met and re-inforced one another on the issue of peaceful, legal, and gradual change. Cabet vehemently attacked those in his entourage who showed Babouvist tendencies, denouncing them derisively as "immediates," "materialists," and "violents." But his pacifistic approach unlike Blanc's, was based upon a belief that communism represented true Christian religion.

In these regards Icarian communism meshed with yet a third important variety of early nineteenth-century communism that was important in Paris of the 1840s: the religious communism of the foreign-born, primarily German-speaking, journeymen-artisans who had settled there. Estimates of their numbers run from 85,000 to 100,000, and many of them were active and deeply dedicated. One of their organizations, the conspiratorial League of the Just (to be further discussed in dealing with Marx's activities in the 1840s) had been involved in Blanqui's May 12 uprising.

The best known of the German religious communists of the time was Wilhelm Weitling (1808–71). It would be hard to find a better example of the already discussed artisanal worker, associated with pre-industrial handicraft, lacking any clear understanding of the long-range implications of modernization, yet harboring a sharp sense that new productive techniques threatened his livelihood and values.

Weitling was born in Magdeburg, during the French occupation of Germany, from the illegitimate union of a German maidservant and a French soldier. Earning his living as an itinerant tailor, in the manner of a pre-industrial journeyman, and entirely self-educated, he nevertheless became familiar with the works of the philosophes and the major social theorists of the early nineteenth century. But his deepest inspiration and characteristic vocabulary were religious. His book, *Mankind, As It Is and As It Should Be* (1839), was full of biblical quotations, and its vision of an ideal community was based on a return to what he believed early Christian society had been, when people were not primarily motivated by selfish and materialistic goals.

His remedy for the ills of contemporary society was, nevertheless, not religious conversion but political and social revolution. His religious convictions did not prevent his forming a deep admiration for

Babeuf, about whom he read in Buonarroti's volumes, and he accepted Babeuf's belief in the need for a conspiratorial elite to overwhelm the repressive state of the rich and to introduce the "precious principle of equality."

The communism of Blanqui, Cabet, and Weitling, as well as the socialism of Blanc, thus overlapped or linked in many areas, just as each of them freely borrowed from broader or more ancient traditions, such as the jacobin and primitive Christian. Such was the case not only on the level of abstract, formal theory but even more as these ideas sunk into the consciousness of ordinary workers. Indeed, it is obvious that few workers were capable of distinguishing the many nuances of these theories, to say nothing of the array of other, less important reformist and revolutionary theories that were being propagated. The common people who became interested in socialism tended to bunch together, eclectically, slogans and particular convictions. They especially identified themselves with attacks on social inequality, large concentrations of property, a state that protected the interests of the rich and ignored those of the poor, the laissez-faire economy, and a society of egoistic individuals.

It is noteworthy that the years 1839–40 saw not only Blanqui's insurrection and the presentation of the Charter in England but the publication of Blanc's *Organization of Work*, Cabet's *Voyage in Icaria*, and Weitling's *Mankind: As It Is and As It Should Be*. These were, in fact, only among the better known and more influential of a flood of books and pamphlets in those years that attacked France's state and society. (Proudhon's *What Is Property?*, a perhaps even more influential work, also appeared in 1840 and will be discussed below.)

These works represented a kind of opening flourish to the brilliant and intense intellectual life of Paris in the 1840s, leading up to the Revolution of 1848. Paris, the intellectual center of Europe, attracted to its streets leading socialists and reformers from every country in the 1840s. At the same time in Paris many of the social problems that existed elsewhere in Europe were especially blatant. The marked population increase stemming from the particularly fecund reproductive years of 1820 to 1830 in France tended to feed into the capital, sharply increasing the ranks of the unemployed and the dissatisfied in the city. When the agricultural crises that began in 1845 pushed the price of food continually upward, many of the poor in Paris and elsewhere experienced desperate hardships. At the same time, an especially ostentatious opulence manifested itself in the wealthy sections of Paris, while the moral authority of the July Monarchy was shaken by a number of scandals. During this time literally hundreds of food and fuel riots broke out in France.

Such factors undoubtedly provided some of the preconditions for the outbreak of revolution in France in 1848, and even more they helped, once the revolution had begun, to bring about some of its more violent and socially radical episodes. Other factors, such as the inflexibility and insensitivity of the French king and his ministers to demands for moderate reform—which lost them the support of the National Guard, for example—also played a role.

Yet revolution in 1848 spread with great speed throughout most of the rest of Europe, where often very different conditions held from in Paris. Moreover, the diversity of revolutionary demands from country to country seems to argue against any continent-wide unity to the revolutions. Perhaps the most acceptable generalization is that the word "reform"—a protean concept—was on the lips of many different kinds of people in the late 1840s; a diffuse sense of dissatisfaction with the status quo was widespread, whether because of the complacency of the July Monarchy, the reactionary policies of Metternich, or the incompetence of the many principalities and minor kingdoms of central and southern Europe. Then a unique set of events in Paris in February appears to have acted as a catalyst for revolution in France and in the rest of Europe.

To many in Paris "reform" meant political reform, and demands for a broadening of the suffrage became ever more insistent in the 1840s. In a celebrated encounter with François Guizot, the longtime minister of King Louis-Philippe, those demanding a reduction in the property requirements for voting and holding office were disdainfully told that the proper way to get the vote was simply to "get rich" (*enrichissez-vous!*). This statement enraged reformers and thereafter came to epitomize bourgeois complacency (or at least that of the upper echelons of the whig-liberal bourgeoisie). In late 1847 and early 1848, agitation for political reform took the guise of a series of banquets, where, in order to circumvent the restrictions on political gatherings, political speeches were given at large banquets. When Guizot then forbade these, protest demonstrations resulted. They in turn led to bloody confrontations between the forces of order and the Paris masses, which finally resulted in the erection of barricades and full-scale revolt.

Louis-Philippe lost support with astonishing speed: As was the case with his Bourbon predecessor, Charles X, he was chased from his throne in "three glorious days." With Paris once again in revolution the workers on the barricades were determined not to be sold out once more, as in 1830. But the model of the 1790s—and *la république sociale*—was even more before everyone's eyes.

Revolution in 1848 would in fact parallel that of 1789–99 in some remarkable ways, but nevertheless France by mid-century had changed in important ways. While the country had not industrialized on a scale comparable to that of Great Britain, nevertheless the issue of capitalism versus socialism—that is, two modern ideologies which had scarcely been at issue in 1789—very quickly came to the fore in Paris. Indeed, demands for a resolution of the social question were posed with such speed and urgency that those interested primarily in political reform were both surprised and alarmed. To the initial list of candidates for the Provisional Government were quickly added, under pressure from the Paris masses, the names of Louis Blanc and "Albert," a metal worker connected with various socialist and communist organizations.

The Revolution of 1848 in France may be said to have begun on the twenty-third of February, with the demonstrations in support of the banqueteers. By the twenty-fifth and twenty-sixth unruly crowds gathered in the square in front of the Hôtel de Ville, demanding that a social republic, with the red flag as its symbol, be established. Other demands included "the right to work" and "a new commune." The moderate republicans of the Provisional Government were firmly opposed to these demands, and the romantic poet Lamartine, who assumed de facto leadership of the government, made full use of his eloquence to preserve the traditional republican tricolor (a point of considerable symbolic importance). In other areas subtly deceptive promises were made, defusing passions for a while. To Blanc's own demands, enthusiastically acclaimed by the Paris crowds, that a Ministry of Labor and Progress be created for him, the controlling moderates of the government responded by establishing the Luxembourg Commission, with Blanc at its head, to study the condition of the working class and to make recommendations to the government. The Commission was given little real power; it was hardly more than a debating society, and Blanc was thus isolated from real influence in the revolutionary government. At the same time, the Minister of Public Works, Alexandre Marie, an open anti-socialist, was put in charge of the National Workshops, which were to create work for the unemployed. These were established as an ostensible response to the demand for social workshops, but their organization and purpose had little to do with Blanc's ideas, and the jobs they undertook much resembled those provided by the *chantiers de charité*, a kind of outrelief, make-work program long provided by French governments to see the poor through periods of extreme distress.

However, nothing on the scale of the National Workshops had previously been attempted. By the end of March the Workshops had enrolled 21,000 workers, and by the end of April 94,000. Paying wages to such great numbers became enormously expensive, and in relation to this expense little work was accomplished. Indeed, one of Marie's purposes in operating the National Workshops was to discredit Blanc's socialist ideas.

Nevertheless, other less equivocal gains were made: Restrictions on organizations were lifted, and scores of unions, clubs, and other societies sprang up; a ten-hour workday was declared; slavery was ended in the colonies; the Second Republic was proclaimed, and a constituent assembly was to be elected on the basis of universal manhood suffrage. At first these measures appeared to placate the workers in Paris, and for a while they seemed to join in the general euphoria among virtually all classes and interests in society. In early March Lamartine joyfully declared that the new regime had "eliminated the terrible misunderstanding . . . between the classes" (Lougee, p. 81).

It is again revealing to compare the responses of Blanqui and Blanc to these initial developments, for their differences were much less than might be imagined. Released from prison and immediately making his way to Paris, Blanqui refrained from any immediate calls to social revolution or even secret plans for it. He was impressed by the extent to which the workers of Paris and other regions of France had begun to act in February as active agents, conscious of their interests, capable of spontaneous organization, and willing to fight for a new society. But he was also deeply suspicious of the intentions of the Provisional Government and feared the implications of the immediate application of universal suffrage, because most common people remained under the tutelage of the older ruling orders.

Blanc's statements at this time were remarkably similar. He was perfectly willing to use violence against the monarchy and, once the Provisional Government had been established, to use the threat of popular violence to counter its moderate, anti-socialist intentions. He drew back only on the issue of a conspiratorial coup or the use of terror to gain power.

Blanqui's and Blanc's high regard for the wage-earning workers in Paris was matched by the alarm that these workers awakened in the other classes of society. De Tocqueville summed up the panicked reactions of a great many when he wrote that the socialist workers were the sole victors of the revolutionary events of February and March and the bourgeoisie the main losers.

Similarly, although one can with some justification contrast the class-conscious, forward-looking socialist ideology of the wage-earning workers who were active in Paris in 1848 with the backward-looking convictions of the sans-culottes of the 1790s, the socialist and communist workers of Paris were hardly typical of France as a whole, nor did they represent a clear majority of the Paris population. Moreover, as George Rudé emphasizes in his *The Crowd in History*, in the provinces popular agitation tended to retain a late-eighteenth century and anti-industrial character: The châteaux of the aristocracy were attacked; Jewish homes and synagogues were wrecked; state forests were ravaged; and in some areas Luddite attacks on textile and railroad machinery occurred.

General elections were not long postponed, in spite of the protests of Blanc and Blanqui, and the premonitions these two held concerning them were justified: The number of conservatives and anti-socialist deputies elected under universal manhood suffrage was comparable to the number elected under the restricted suffrage of the July Monarchy—indeed, in terms of social origin a heavier proportion of the new deputies were rich and privileged. The overwhelming conservatism of the French peasantry, the tendency of the newly enfranchised to vote for familiar names (usually members of local elites), and the rural distrust of towns were fully revealed.

Very likely this conservatism was stronger by the spring of 1848 than it might have been, had the elections been held in late 1847. The constant unrest in Paris, the notorious boondoggling in the National Workshops, a new tax imposed upon the peasants—which they believed went to support shiftless troublemakers in the capital—all helped to turn the countryside to the right. Moreover, in contrast to the situation in 1789, the peasants of 1848, with some exceptions, had no particularly pressing grievances that they expected the revolutionary regime to remedy.

A strongly anti-"communist" trend gathered force in Paris itself. The euphoric mood of early March vanished as soon as those who had previously enjoyed even the slightest privilege came to realize what sacrifices the reforms of the Second Republic might entail. Many feared profound economic dislocations or onerous taxation if socialist experiments were continued. Those who had any property at all came to fear the aspirations of those below them. Symptomatic was the protest demonstration by certain units of the National Guard on March 15, against the "proletarianization" of their ranks, which until this time had been proudly monopolized by the petty bourgeoisie. Even more ominous for socialist hopes was the confrontation on April 16. Word had spread through Paris that there was to be a massive demonstration of workers, headed by Blanqui and other leaders of the extremist clubs, that would force the government to accept "communist" demands. When a crowd of workers did appear at the Hôtel de Ville on that day, they were confronted with a rapidly mobilized National Guard. With bayonets mounted, the Guard humiliated the workers by forcing them to pass through a narrowly formed lane, while the troops jeered "down with the communists!"

These developments pushed Blanqui toward plans for a desperate uprising and Blanc to utter despair. A climax was reached in the infamous "June Days." From the twenty-third to the twenty-sixth of June Paris was the scene of a terrible and bloody struggle. The forces of order, under General Cavaignac, ruthlessly shot down great numbers of barricaded workers, and thousands that were not shot down in the streets were imprisoned or sent into exile.

The "terrible misunderstanding between the classes" had not been eliminated. Yet the June Days did not represent a simple confrontation of classes, in spite of what Marx would later argue in his famous pamphlet *Class Struggles in France, 1848–1850* or more conservative observers, such as De Tocqueville, would also tend to see it. Both Marx and De Tocqueville, so different in background and sympathies, believed that the June Days were the opening chapter of a fundamentally new kind of struggle, a portentous clash of capital and labor, of propertied and unpropertied. In fact, class lines were much less clearly drawn than that. A more accurate way of describing the barricade fighting in June is as a conflict between those who supported the idea of the social republic—a vague one, to be sure—and those who feared such a republic as a "communist" device. Thus socially the parties to the conflict appear to have been on the one hand small, relatively insecure producers—not just propertyless wage earners and class-conscious socialists—and on the other citizens with more secure existences (shopkeepers, merchants, landlords). Moreover, the social dimension was often blurred: There were rich and poor on both sides of the barricades, and other factors, such as generational conflict, apparently played a role.

Marx and De Tocqueville were certainly correct in asserting that the confrontation of June 1848 was different in nature from those of the 1790s, but it was not as different as they believed. The most that can be said for Marx's viewpoint is that alongside the predominantly artisanal workers on the barricades were significant numbers of workers from the railroad industries of the Paris suburbs and that they appear to have acted in a particularly class-conscious and organized fashion. How much this new industrial proletariat would fulfill, with the growing modernization of Europe, the promise that Marx saw in it is a central theme of the following chapters.

GUIDE TO FURTHER READING

George Lichtheim's *The Origins of Socialism* is the best overall study of socialism in the first half of the nineteenth century, although it suffers from the same problems as his other books. It is concerned primarily with what Lichtheim terms the "filiation of ideas." This work contains a most impressively detailed set of bibliographical notes.

The thought of Charles Fourier can best be approached through the admirably compact study by Nicholas Riasanovsky, *The Teachings of Charles Fourier*, and the edited collection of Fourier's writings (including some of his long-censored sexual texts) in Jonathan Beecher and Richard Bienvenu, *The Utopian Vision of Charles Fourier*. See also Mark Poster, *Harmonian Man: Selected Writings of Charles Fourier*.

Numberous formal biographies of Robert Owen exist, but the interested reader is well advised to begin with J. F. C. Harrison's *The Quest for the New Moral World: Robert Owen and the Owenites in Britain and America*, which is a penetrating, readable, and thoroughly researched study, a model of scholarship. It contains an ample bibliography.

Frank Manuel has authored or edited a number of works dealing with French Utopian thought, among which are *The Prophets of Paris* and *The New World of Henri Saint-Simon*. A standard work on the Saint-Simonians is Sébastien Charléty, *Histoire du saint-simonisme, 1824–1864*. Martin Buber has composed a sympathetic study of the Utopians in his *Paths in Utopia*, and there are some stimulating pages on the subject in Sheldon Wolin's previously mentioned *Politics and Vision*.

Peter Stearns's *European Society in Upheaval* is an approachable introduction to modern European social history, although it has been criticized for carelessness in certain areas. The general histories of the working class, discussed in the Guide to Further Reading of the Introduction, should be useful, especially Wachenheim and Dolléans, to which should be added the scholarly yet imaginative short volume by Bernard H. Moss, *The Origins of the French Labor Movement: The Socialism of Skilled Workers*. The prolific works of Werner Conze, for example his *Die Arbeiterbewegung in der nationaler Bewegung* (this in collaboration with D. Groh), are rich sources for Germany. The previously discussed works of E. P. Thompson and E. J. Hobsbawn (*The Making of the English Working Class* and *Labouring Men*) offer sophisticated treatment of the working class in the early nineteenth century. They attempt to rehabilitate, though only in a qualified fashion, the classic but now much maligned works of the Hammonds (for example, *The Town Labourer*).

George Rudé's *The Crowd in History, 1730–1848* offers many insights and re-interpretations of the relationship between pre-industrial crowds and modern working-class movements. Robert Bezucha's monograph, *The Lyons Uprising of 1834: Social and Political Conflict in the Early July Monarchy*, is a much broader and more valuable study than its title might indicate, and provides a fascinating microscopic view of an important sector of France's economy.

An excellent introduction to the Revolution of 1848, stressing social and economic history, can be found in Robert W. Lougee, *Midcentury Revolution, 1848: Society and Revolution in France and Germany*. William L. Langer's *Political and Social Upheaval, 1832–1852* offers a broader and more detailed account, very impressive in scholarship. Long a standard account, highly readable and covering the entire continent, is Priscilla Robertson's *The Revolutions of 1848*. Roger Price's *The Second French Republic, A Social History* takes account of the more recent scholarship, as does the collection of articles edited by Price, *Revolution and Reaction: 1848 and the Second French Republic*. Primary documents from the revolutionary period, with a sophisticated commentary, can be found in Maurice Agulhon, *Les Quarante-huitards*. Scholarly accounts of the revolution in Germany can be found in Rudolf Stadelmann, *Social and Political History of the German 1848 Revolution*, and P. Noyes, *Organization and Revolution, Working-Class Associations in the Revolutions of 1848*. A scholarly yet approachable discussion of the social projects of the Provisional Government in France has been written by Donald McKay, *The National Workshops*.

The revolutionary tradition, from the jacobins to the communists, has been studied from a number of differing viewpoints in the following works: John Plamenatz, *The Revolutionary Movement in France, 1815–1871*; Elizabeth L. Eisenstein, *The First Professional Revolutionist: Filippo Michele Buonarroti (1761–1837)*; Frank Deppe, *Verschwörung, Aufstand, und Revolution: Blanqui und das Problem der sozialen Revolution*; A. B. Spitzer, *The Revolutionary Theories of Auguste Blanqui*; Maurice Dommanget, *Les Idées politiques et sociales d'Auguste Blanqui*; and Carl Wittke, *The Utopian Communist, A Biography of Wilhelm Weitling*.

Christopher Johnson's *Utopian Communism in France: Cabet and the Icarians, 1839–1851* provides fascinating information on the social foundations of Cabetian communism. On Louis Blanc see Leo A. Loubère, *Louis Blanc, His Life and His Contribution to the Rise of French Jacobin Socialism*. David Jones, *Chartism and the Chartists*, discusses the more recent literature and attempts a breakdown of the social classes of the Chartists.

The Maturation of Socialism, 1850-1870

3

INTRODUCTION

From the perspective of the history of socialism, the quarter century following the watershed of 1848 presents a double aspect: On the one hand, it was a low point, especially the decade of the 1850s. Anti-socialist and anti-revolutionary forces appeared to have triumphed. On the other hand, a German-Jewish exile named Karl Marx was working out a powerful synthesis of socialist theory, the main lines of which he and his colleague Friedrich Engels had already sketched out by the mid-1840s. Marxism in its mature form came to overshadow all competing socialist theories, especially as it was interpreted by theoreticians, largely German, in the latter years of the nineteenth century. Its position was further enhanced by the victory of Leninist Marxism in Russia in 1917, and it has continued to exercise a special fascination to this day.

For these reasons a considerable proportion of the following chapter is devoted to Marx as a revolutionary activist and to an overview of Marxist theory as such. Such an overview presents serious difficulties, for although Marx was an incomparably learned man, with a brilliant, penetrating mind and catholic intellectual tastes, on a number of important points the clarity of his thought and writing leaves much to be desired. Robert Heilbroner, writing in the March 9, 1972, issue of the *New York Review of Books*, admirably stated the problem:

Marx continues to brood over our intellectual life. In view of the immense impact that he has had on history, the fact would hardly be worth noting were not his writings so often baffling. The famous historical essays and a few parts of *Capital* still have the effects of thunderbolts, but much of his earlier work, not to mention the tedious chapters in the later volumes of *Capital*, are murky in a way that rouses both skepticism and impatience. That we nevertheless go on reading Marx, torturing ourselves by trying to penetrate the obdurate prose, can only be ascribed to a stubborn conviction that there is *something* of inestimable value beneath this opaque surface, if only we could discern exactly what it is.

That much of the scholarship dealing with Marx has been distorted by an unusually ardent political partisanship presents a further difficulty in arriving at a balanced understanding of his life and thought. His enemies have had in some ways an easy job in portraying him, in diabolical tones, as an intellectual forerunner of modern totalitarians, a man personally driven by a lust for power, a cold contempt for humanity. He was undeniably a scurrilous partisan, overbearing and contentious in many of his relationships. Yet a contrasting portrait of Marx as a warm family man with a profound love of humanity can also be plausibly drawn.

With such contrasts, balance that is also discriminating is difficult. What is attempted here is to glean from both hostile and friendly scholarship a relatively impartial picture that will serve the reader whose primary concern is not hagiography or demonology but rather as accurate and dispassionate an understanding of Marx as possible.

THE YOUNG MARX AND THE GENESIS OF MARXIAN COMMUNISM

Accounts of Marx's thought often follow Engels's lead in describing Marxism as a synthesis of German, French, and English intellectual traditions, in particular German philosophy, English political economy (or Classical Economics), and French socialist theory. This simplistic formulation is perhaps acceptable as a kind of shorthand, so long as one does not overlook the extent to which these three traditions overlapped and influenced one another. Certainly what is most impressive about Marx is not so much his strictly original insights—he often said as much himself—as the way that he attempted to pull together early nineteenth-century theory and practice into a coherent whole.

By the conditions of his early life Marx was well situated to effect such a synthesis. Born into a secularized Jewish family in Trier, a quaint and ancient city along the Moselle River, not far from the French and Luxembourgian borders, Marx was early exposed to French thought and culture. His father, Herschel, embraced Enlightened values and was intimately familiar with the major philosophes. During the period of the French Revolution and the Napoleonic Empire—before Marx's birth—Trier became part of France, and as a consequence Jews became full citizens. However, when Trier was taken over by Prussia after the fall of Napoleon, Herschel converted to Christianity, assuming the Christian name Heinrich to spare himself and his family the inconveniences that official status as Jews in Prussia would have entailed.

Thus young Karl, born in 1818, was brought up in an atmosphere of Enlightened humanism. He did not identify himself as a Jew, nor did he embrace in any deep-felt fashion the Christian faith that his father had so opportunistically adopted. In fundamental but not always obvious ways Marx's values remained those of the Enlightenment. From an early age he accepted a belief in the potential development of humanity through critical reason, leading to an eventual secular paradise. Similarly, he identified with the exploited and downtrodden, and his vision of the Good was intimately linked to the idea of liberation, both from material and human-created bonds. In the essays that Marx wrote upon graduating from his local high school (*Gymnasium*) in 1835, he stressed that

we choose the career in which we can do humanity the most good. . . . Experience rates him as the happiest who has made the greatest number happy, and religion itself teaches us the ideal for which we all strive, to sacrifice ourselves for humanity. [Nicolaievsky, p. 14]

Not long after finishing his university work, in the early 1840s, Marx wrote, from a much more developed position,

Communism is the positive abolition of *private property*, of *human self-alienation*, and thus the real appropriation of human nature through and for man. It is, therefore, the return of man himself as a *social*, i.e., really human, being. . . . Communism . . . is . . . a fully developed humanism. . . . It is the *definitive* resolution between man and nature, between man and man. [Tucker, *Reader*, p. 70]

The second passage is couched in the language of German idealist philosophy, which constituted an extremely important element of Marx's intellectual formation. It is at the same time the most esoteric for the ordinary reader. The difficulties are somewhat reduced if one keeps in mind that German idealist philosophers and those who developed from them struggled toward conclusions similar to those of the philosophes and other Enlightened thinkers like the early socialists. Learned obscurity has long remained an esteemed trait of German intellectuals, and German philosophers of the early nineteenth century employed concepts of the most abstruse variety, made all the more unapproachable by a vocabulary that was perplexingly recondite. The triumph of reason and the expunging of irrationality were central concerns for German philosophers, as was the case with the philosophes, and these concerns in both instances led first to a criticism of religion, then to a criticism of the political, social, and economic status quo, although by a very circuitous and philosophically sophisticated path for the Germans.

G. W. F. Hegel (1770–1831) became the seminal thinker of German idealism. One of his central concerns was to rebut the philosophical conclusions of the Enlightened empiricists, such as John Locke and David Hume. While they, like other eighteenth-century thinkers, used the tools of critical reason, their philosophy led toward a position that could be termed suspicious of reason in a larger sense. They asserted that sense experience is our only sure guide, and therefore we must be careful of "unaided reason"; we must proceed cautiously and not propose courses of action for which we can find no guide in experience. The potentially conservative implications of this position were succinctly stated by Hume: "'Tis not reason which is the guide of life but custom." Thus a possible conclusion from the empiricists' standpoint was that the promethean efforts of the revolutionaries in France to remake their world from top to bottom according to reason and in defiance of custom, or the wisdom of the centuries, were foolhardy, even reckless. The reader will recall that Adam Smith, partly under the influence of Hume, believed only in piecemeal reforms guided by historical experience.

As far as Hegel and other German philosophers were concerned, the English empiricists, and above all Hume, seemed to threaten philosophy itself. This was an upsetting prospect for many Germans who considered themselves a highly philosophic people whose fulfillment was achieved in the realm of the spirit rather than in the practical, material world. Hegel countered by arguing that the human mind was far more than a passive register of experience; human reason could master the truth about the outer world, above and beyond the confines of mere experience, since the human mind and outer reality were fundamentally of the same nature and both developed according to an organic-dialectical model. (The implications of these terms, further examined below, are far-ranging and at times obscure. Suffice it to note here that "organic" emphasizes resemblance to a living organism, while "dialectical" asserts the pervasiveness of change through strife, opposition, and contradiction.)

In the hands of the so-called Young Hegelians the organic-dialectical model provided the intellectual tools for an even more corrosive attack on contemporary Christianity than that launched by the philosophes. Whereas the latter strived to expose the inherent unreasonableness of religion, its superstitions and logical absurdities, the emphasis of the Young Hegelians was that traditional religious beliefs and practices reflected the needs of Christian communities at a given stage of historical development but became irrelevant or anachronistic over time, as peoples evolved. Broadly analogous points, it will be remembered, were being made at about the same time in France by Saint-Simon and his followers.

Hegelian philosophy, while hardly as direct or lucid as that of the philosophes, was often more rich and subtle. Hegel himself reflected upon some of the ambiguities of historical change and argued that progress, or what he termed the realization of Reason in history, could not occur as simple linear development, without setbacks and suffering. Strife, confusion, and alienation all served larger rational purposes. For example, the upheavals of the French Revolution, even the Terror and the despotism of Napoleon, must be viewed as ultimately necessary to the final triumph of Reason. Hegel thus argued that a study of the tribulations of human history was the means by which dialectical understanding could comprehend the workings of the spirit or *Geist*, that is, the ultimate guiding force in history. These overall perspectives would emerge, in altered form, in the thought of Marx.

Marx's first contacts among the Young Hegelians in Berlin brought him to a position of radical atheism, but he soon became dissatisfied with their philosophical idealism, with their belief that change in matters of economics, society, and politics could occur only *after* people's minds had been changed—a conclusion broadly similar to that of many early nineteenth-century socialists, who likewise looked to persuading their contemporaries through reason, not force.

For these reasons Marx found much of interest in the writings of another Young Hegelian, Ludwig Feuerbach. Feuerbach's best-known work, entitled *The Essence of Christianity* (1841), can be seen as a culminating attack by the Young Hegelians on Christianity. He asserted that man exists only as matter; the conflict between the subjective and objective worlds, between mind and matter, so central to much of philosophical and theological speculation, was an imaginary, unreal one. God as Spirit has no reality; indeed, no divinity of any sort exists, whether it is called Yahweh, Zeus, or Geist. All of these are creations of men's minds, figments of their imaginations. This was the meaning of the title *The Essence of Christianity*: The essence of Christianity is man's estrangement or alienation from himself through a religious fantasy life. Man projects his own aspirations and ideal qualities—for example, those of creator—onto the figure of God. God did not create man. Man

created God. The thought processes of the Godhead were thus not ultimately responsible for man's being and his history (as Hegel and the
Christians believed); rather, man makes his own history, and indeed
makes or creates what has been presented as the divine thought processes. Man conjures up a heavenly world through imagination or "self-
alienation."

But this fantasizing causes man to feel abased and to suffer in
comparison to his idealized god, that is, his idealized self. The only way
for man to come into himself, to gain real freedom to express his human
creativity, to realize his own godlike nature, is to rid himself of religion,
of his fantasy-god. In so doing men will "wake up," escape from self-
alienation. They will recognize one another as godlike and therefore
worthy of the love they have wasted on a nonexistent deity. This awakening, in other words, will be the basis of a true, radical humanism.
Thus Feuerbach reached conclusions much like those of the philosophes
and of the early socialists.

While impressed with Feuerbach's materialistic emphasis and his
attack on the religious impulse, Marx soon carried his analysis further.
He asserted that beyond religious alienation the material world itself
was a more fundamental factor. It is not only man's intellectual creations, his myths and deities, that oppress him, but his self-created
world of matter. Waking up would not be quite enough, since the world
of matter was more than a bad dream; it was real and had to be
changed.

Marx's thoughts about this real material world were much influenced by his reading of the French socialists, his contacts with other
Young Hegelians, and indeed his study of Hegel's own writings. They all
had impressed upon him the collective or social nature of human productivity. But modern civilization had perverted this social quality. The
egotism and greed prevalent in contemporary industrial society had led
men to prey on each other's creativity or productivity. Modern men did
not produce together for the common good; individuals exploited the
labor of others and accumulated it in the form of capital or money.
Indeed, private property in the form of capital had become an object of
worship in bourgeois society. Man's alienated material productivity
was comparable to his alienated religiosity, and his worship of money
was replacing his worship of God.

We are now in a position to better appreciate the meaning of the
quotation cited above, from Marx's early writings (beginning "communism is the positive abolition . . . of human self-alienation . . ."). We can
also perceive more clearly why Marx felt it important to give serious

study to the contemporary theoreticians of capitalism, such as David Ricardo. Using a play on words typical of the Young Hegelians, Marx observed that he had set out to master the "unholy forms" of alienation (that is, capitalistic production) just as Feuerbach had described the "holy forms" of alienation (that is, religiosity).

It was about this same time and through related lines of reasoning that Marx began to perceive the means by which it would be possible to step beyond the idealistic remedies to the social question proposed by some of the Young Hegelians and the Utopians. Marx was familiar with the numerous studies of the proletariat published in the late 1830s and early 1840s, such as those by von Stein, von Radowitz, De Tocqueville, and Engels. He was particularly impressed with these writers' descriptions of the workers as rebellious and seeking to generalize their condition. Here, Marx concluded, could be found the "material force that would achieve philosophy," which in plain language meant the force that would achieve what mere ideas or appeals to conscience could not—the establishment of a rational (that is, socialist or communist) order and the end of alienation through a social revolution led by the proletariat.

In the context of these Young Hegelian cerebrations, the factory proletarian emerged in Marx's mind as the ideal type of the alienated man, that is, one whose material production oppressed him, stood as "other" to him. And from this perspective Marx embarked on a more thoroughgoing Feuerbachian-style transposition of Hegelian philosophy. He replaced Hegel's notion of Spirit as creator with "proletariat." Thus, rather than the Spirit externalizing itself in thought objects, it was man as proletarian who externalized himself in material objects, from which in turn derived institutional and intellectual creations. And just as Hegel had emphasized that the study of history opened up an appreciation of the development and thus the inner nature of Spirit, so Marx asserted that man cannot be understood abstractly, divorced from his historical evolution. The history of man's productivity—his machines, social institutions, ideological creations—all add up to a definition of him. In the philosophical jargon that Marx used at this time, he wrote that the sum total of man's creations equals "the human psyche, sensually considered." History is the record of man's progressive self-realization, of his realizing his true humanity by establishing a oneness with his creations.

These last sentences point to an issue of much debate among scholars of Marx, that is, to his notion of human nature. It is beyond question that he rejected any notion of an unchanging human nature—

much of his scorn for the utilitarians had to do with what he considered their simplistic belief in human nature as a timeless, given quality, which rationally sought pleasure and avoided pain, regardless of historical context. Yet it is going too far to assert, as does the eminent Marxist scholar Louis Althusser, that Marx (at least the mature Marx, after he had abandoned his earlier humanist perspectives) viewed human nature as completely plastic, under the sway of the forces of historical change. The issue is too complex and technical to follow with any thoroughness here, but in a recent work (*Marx's Interpretation of History*) Melvin Rader argues persuasively and with unusual lucidity that central to Marx's thought, throughout his life, was the conflict between man's essence and existence. Man strives, in history, toward the realization of his human potential, and that potential has to do with identifiable qualities: sociability (the basic socialist viewpoint that man is a social animal), productivity (or creativity, especially in the direction of the rational, harmonious, and beautiful), desire for freedom and universality (from irrational constraints and limited visions), yearning for wholeness (for full development of all faculties, rather than stunted specialization).

Marx by no means limited himself to philosophical speculation. His philosophical studies were paralleled by his work as a radical journalist and political activist. In 1842 he became the editor of the *Rheinische Zeitung* (Rhenish Journal) in Cologne, which for a short time became one of the leading newspapers in the south of Germany. Marx was not yet a communist, although his newspaper took an active interest in the social question, generally from the standpoint of democratic radicalism.

Before long Marx ran into difficulties with the Prussian authorities, and in 1843 the *Rheinische Zeitung* was suppressed. Marx's experience at the hands of the Prussian bureaucrats speeded along his disillusionment with the idealists' belief in the potency of critical reason. He won all the debater's points against the censor, but this victory made no difference; his paper ceased to appear. He wrote at the time, "the weapon of criticism can certainly never be a substitute for criticism by the weapon; physical force must be overthrown by physical force; and theory will be a physical force as soon as the masses understand it" (Nicolaievsky, p. 67).

These experiences contributed to his disillusionment also with his homeland, and he thus decided to take up residence abroad, where one could breathe more freely. Paris was especially attractive to him, since he was at this time reading French socialist and communist authors.

He became convinced that what was now necessary was an alliance of German theory and French practice, and, in accordance with this conviction, he arranged to collaborate in the publication of a journal entitled *Deutsch-Französische Jahrbücher* (*German-French Chronicles*).

His plans to emigrate were complicated by the fact that he was, as he wrote to a friend, "head over heels in love." His prospective bride, Jenny von Westphalen, was an unlikely match for a young man in his position. Jenny was four years older than Karl, was known as the belle of Trier, and was the daughter of a highly respected noble (who had befriended Marx years before). Karl and Jenny were secretly engaged, and she waited for more than seven years while he pursued his studies at the university. Apparently she was the only woman during these years in whom he showed any serious interest, and she equally resisted all other offers, although she could have had her pick of suitors. It seems to have been one of those rare examples of a profound affection that lasts through the many vicissitudes of life. And for Jenny these would be at times crushing: She would pass much of her youth in the most sordid slums of London, suffering the disfigurement of smallpox, and losing child after child to disease and malnutrition.

Jenny never reproached her husband for these disasters, nor did she ever seem to have regretted marrying him, although she often regretted living. And Karl does seem to have been a man of warmth and tenderness within the family circle. Wilhelm Liebknecht, a leading figure of the German socialists in the latter half of the nineteenth century, later rhapsodically described the outings of the Marx family and friends to Hampstead Heath, outside London, where they would sing, declaim passages from Shakespeare, play hide-and-seek, and ride donkeys— Marx himself sometimes serving as a braying mount for the children.

The death of Edgar, Marx's favorite child and only living son, shook him and his wife to the depths of their being. Marx wrote to Engels, "Bacon says that really important people have so many contacts with nature and the world that they easily get over any loss. I am not one of those people. My child's death has affected me so greatly that I feel the loss as keenly as the first day. My wife is also completely broken" (Nicolaievsky, p. 261).

This was merely one of the family's many tragedies during the terrible years in London, in the 1850s and 1860s. But arriving in Paris in the autumn of 1843 Karl and Jenny were full of great expectations. Here he was able to meet the great socialists of the age and to come into contact with socialist workers, both German and French. His friendship with Engels also began to blossom in Paris, the beginning of one of the most remarkable and productive partnerships in history. Although Engels's background was different from Marx's—Engels came from a pietistic Christian family in Barmen, in the industrializing Wuppertal—he traveled much the same ground through Hegelian-Feuerbachian philosophy, French socialism, concern for the working class, to communism.

Marx and Engels agreed that one of the first practical tasks before them involved the propagation of their theories among the German workers with whom they had established contacts in both Paris and London. While many of these workers considered themselves "communists" and were highly suspicious of bourgeois intellectuals, they still felt the need for a more satisfactory theoretical statement of their position. Such was especially the case after the failure of the Blanquist coup in 1839, which had required that a number of them flee to England. There they came into contact with leaders of the Chartist movement and with a relatively advanced, democratically constituted workers' movement. In London they formed a "workers' union"—more like an educational and friendly society than a trade union, which partly served as a legal cover for their conspiratorial organization—the League of the Just.

Within a short time Marx came to exercise a powerful influence on the German communists in London and Paris through a correspondence society that he helped to establish. By early 1847 he and Engels were invited to join a reorganized League of the Just, soon to be renamed the Communist League, which was to be restructured on more open and democratic lines, although it was still somewhat secretive in nature. The two young intellectuals were asked to help draw up a statement of its goals. It was this statement that developed into the *Communist Manifesto*.

The *Communist Manifesto* is a powerful work, full of incisive judgments and effective rhetorical flourishes, although its immediate influence on the revolutions of 1848 was practically nil. With it the term "communist" took on far broader, richer, and more progressive implications than had previously been the case. Indeed, the communism of the *Manifesto* had only tenuous connections with the communist tradition as it had so far developed. The German artisans of the League of the Just had earlier accepted the term "communist" when under the influence of Weitling. Many had also been favorably impressed with Cabet's communistic doctrines or had been attracted to the ideas of Babeuf, Buonarroti, and Blanqui, from whom Weitling had of course also borrowed. Marx and Engels retained a certain respect for this line of communism—it at least had rallied to its banners real revolutionary workers—but they also maintained a critical distance from it, largely because of its conspiratorial nature and its impatient belief in the immediate possibility of a communist society.

Certain aspects of the earlier communist tradition did appear in the *Communist Manifesto*—most notably the vision of a final property-less existence, preceded by a time of violent class struggle and an eventual revolutionary showdown between bourgeoisie and proletariat—but they were worked into a more sophisticated, forward-looking framework, one that emphasized the benefits of the capitalist stage of development. In places the *Manifesto* seemed almost a paean to the creativity of the capitalist bourgeoisie (which had "during its rule of scarcely 100 years . . . created more impressive and more colossal productive forces than had all preceding generations together" [Tucker, *Reader*, p. 339]), although sharper and more passionate were the passages denouncing the capitalists' egotism and inhumanity.

The *Manifesto* was particularly concerned to spell out the ways in which the communism of the Communist League was superior to all earlier varieties of socialism and communism (which it variously dismissed as "reactionary," "conservative," "utopian," or "petty-bourgeois"). This superiority was based upon the League's hard-headed understanding that only through capitalistic development, only after capitalism had proletarianized the mass of the population and had created an economy of abundance, could a socialism (or communism) worthy of the name be achieved.

There is evidence that not all of the League's members enthusiastically embraced Marx's and Engels's interpretation of communism. It is thus plausible that Marx and Engels, having achieved a general victory for their point of view, felt obliged to offer some element of compromise to pacify the more impatient communists. It should be remembered that the *Manifesto* was a publication of the League, not of Marx and Engels personally, and it was subject to revision and overall approval by the League's membership. If such considerations played a role in the composition of the *Manifesto*, as Richard N. Hunt plausibly argues, then one of its more puzzling passages is explained. In its very last section, when speaking of impending revolution in Germany, it asserts that "the bourgeois revolution in Germany will be but the prelude to an immediately following proletarian revolution" (Tucker, *Reader*, p. 362).

This assertion appears to contradict the argument of the *Manifesto*'s previous pages, where the need for capitalist development was emphasized, since Germany in the 1840s was still far behind England and France in that respect. This passage, and a few other statements by Marx and Engels, especially in the following two years, about "permanent revolution" (that is, the rapid passage from the bourgeois-capitalist to the proletarian-socialist stage), about the dictatorship of the proletariat, and about the use of revolutionary terror were decisive in providing a later basis for Leninist communism. But they did not reflect the main emphasis of Marx's and Engels's thought of the time, which aside from insisting upon the importance of capitalistic development also remained attached to the notion of democratic-majoritarian rule. One certainly cannot deny that Marx in particular made a number of statements invoking revolutionary terror and the need for dictatorial methods—and interpretation of these has been and will remain a key problem for students of Marxism—but to this writer at least they are best explained as exceptional rather than typical, reflecting the need for compromise or, on other occasions, reflecting revolutionary excitement or the bitterness of defeat.

Marx's wide-ranging activities after the outbreak of revolution in February 1848 offer some illumination of these ambiguities. He found that among the German exiles in Paris enthusiasm for the revolution was especially high because they expected revolutionary armies to march out of France on a crusade of liberation, as they had done in the 1790s. In this the exiles saw eye-to-eye with the Blanquists, who conceived of foreign war as a way of accelerating the revolution, again with the 1790s in mind. The exiles feverishly set about establishing military formations, which they believed would form vanguard units of the French armies of liberation.

Marx took a rather jaundiced view of these preparations. He urged the German exiles to remain in France at least until revolution broke out in Germany, and he predicted that decisive struggles between the French proletariat and bourgeoisie were soon to be fought. Only after the proletariat had emerged victorious in France, that is, after it had won a decisive majority to its banners, would it be possible to speak of revolutionary wars of liberation. German revolutionaries could thus more profitably serve their cause by remaining in France to aid the French proletariat.

But Marx's words fell mostly on deaf ears. He was even accused—not for the last time—of revolutionary cowardice. The revolutionary passions of the Germans in Paris were further fanned when news arrived in mid-March, first from Vienna, that Metternich had been deposed, and then from Berlin, that the Prussian regime had acceded to revolutionary demands. On April 1 a German legion of would-be revolutionary liberators marched off from Paris, only to be decisively crushed, as Marx had predicted, once it crossed the Rhine. Yet Marx and other more circumspect members of the Communist League also decided that the time had arrived for them to depart for their homeland, to begin the necessary work of building up revolutionary consciousness and organization.

They left Paris on the same day as the German legion, but individually, Marx to Cologne, Engels to the Wuppertal. Although political consciousness among workers in Germany was much behind that of French and English workers, relatively speaking the most advanced area of Germany at the time was the west, where Marx and Engels headed. A small branch of the Communist League had been established in Cologne since late 1847, led mostly by bourgeois intellectuals who had good contacts with the working class.

One of these was Andreas Gottschalk, a physician who had devoted himself to work among the poor and who enjoyed the confidence of the workers in the city. Shortly before Marx's arrival Gottschalk had presided over the creation of the Workers' Union, which recruited perhaps eight thousand members by early summer. The Union was a combination of political organization, educational association, and trade union, and it soon earned a fearsome reputation among the propertied classes in Cologne. Indeed, even the relatively affluent, democratically minded artisans in the city came to fear Gottschalk's organization.

Once in Cologne Marx became embroiled in vehement differences of opinion with Gottschalk concerning the Union. Marx feared that the Union might scare off possible allies in a broad-based democratic-radical movement, which he believed must first achieve success against the authoritarian-feudalistic state forms in Germany before further progress toward socialism or communism was conceivable. Gottschalk and the Union threatened to isolate the poorer and more desperate elements of the working class, making them vulnerable to repression by the Prussian authorities. But Gottschalk rejected all compromises, tactical or otherwise.

Marx concentrated his own energies into work for the Democratic Union in Cologne, whose relatively moderate goals he promoted in his newspaper, the *Neue Rheinische Zeitung* (The New Rhenish Journal). At the same time, Marx allowed the Communist League, a small and weak group anyway, to dissolve. He believed it was no longer necessary, since open public activity was now possible.

In July Gottschalk was arrested, making the Workers' Union more accessible to Marx's influence, and he strove to pull it into cooperative action with the Democratic Union. In August a congress of all democratic organizations in the Rhineland was held, and Marx was able to play a prominent role in it. But these auspicious beginnings were deceptive. In September, Prussian authorities, emboldened by the march of reaction in France, arrested a number of popular leaders and declared martial law. Again, Marx was a voice of relative calm. While vehemently denouncing the Prussian action, he attempted to dissuade those who were planning an insurrection, since he believed it would not receive wide support and would thus be easily crushed, with possibly disastrous long-range consequences. His arguments were persuasive, and Cologne remained calm, although there was much grumbling in the Workers' Union.

But it was only a matter of time before the full triumph of reaction. Moreover, Gottschalk emerged from jail resentful of the progress Marx had made within the Workers' Union. An open, acrimonious rivalry began between them. Marx continued to insist that a democratic revolution was the only kind possible at that time; only in that way would it be possible for the worker to emerge from "medieval barbarism" into modern civilization. Gottschalk retorted that the proletariat could not be asked to spill its blood in making a democratic revolution so that it could be exploited in a new and more efficient way for generations in the future. Communist revolution must come now, even if it meant a minority dictatorship.

As the tide of reaction rose, and particularly as open, democratic agitation became impossible, the Communist League was revived, and Marx was forced to work with the Blanquists and other more extreme communists. It was during this period of bitter defeat and disappointment that Marx made some of his more dictatorial and even terroristic statements; he seemed to have lapsed into a position very close to the one he had so trenchantly criticized before. He was also nourished by a hope that new economic crises would set the revolution once again in progress. But this was a vain hope. For the next quarter century Europe was to be relatively free of economic difficulties and of revolutionary unrest, and Marx was to retire to his study.

SOCIALISM AT ITS NADIR: 1850–1870

The triumph of reaction in 1848–50 not only sent Marx to his study but cast gloom and pessimism into the ranks of socialists and working-class activists throughout Europe. Many turned away in disillusionment from socialist ideals or else embroiled themselves in hopeless squabbles. At the same time, the 1850s and 1860s were a time of relative prosperity and rapid economic growth. Those in control of the economy benefited more from these trends than the working masses, but nevertheless some of the more flagrant abuses of the 1830s and 1840s were alleviated by a general improvement in the material conditions of the poor.

In England, the most advanced and generally the tone-setting economy, prosperity and growth were particularly notable, and the twenty-five years there following 1848 are usually considered the high point of laissez-faire capitalism. The captains of industry were supremely confident of their future, and the free-market economy was widely considered both vigorous and capable of serving all classes of society well. Many of those who before 1848 had believed that capitalism and the factory system should not, or even could not, survive, now resigned themselves to its permanence.

In these years realism, materialism, science, and prosaic sobriety prevailed over the aesthetic and emotional idealism of the early nineteenth century. And since socialism was generally associated with romanticism, especially in France, those imbued with the new spirit of realism tended to scorn the utopian follies of the socialists. Even the socialist ideologies that in some limited sense survived, such as Marxism and Proudhonism, stressed hard-headed realism and practical, sober agitation.

Efforts to establish independent parties of the working class failed for the most part. Politically active workers were to a large degree absorbed into the democratic-radical wing of the liberal movement, although continual efforts were made both by socialists and by conservatives like Bismarck, Disraeli, and Napoleon III (if he may be termed a conservative) to lure them away from bourgeois-liberal tutelage.

The acceleration of social and economic change in these years did not yet result in a clear predominance of factory production, even in England. In many sectors of the economy, particularly in the service sector and in luxury production, the numbers of artisans and skilled workers not involved in factory production actually increased. It was overwhelmingly such workers who were politically active and who organized themselves, rather than factory workers. In short, the Marxist vision of a class-conscious factory proletariat at the head of the working class, ready to fight for socialism, remained a distant reality.

The absorption of politically conscious workers into a kind of liberal consensus or bourgeois hegemony was strongest in England. English workers shunned socialism with particular decisiveness, and indeed would continue to do so even after the socialist movement had made great advances on the Continent in the latter part of the nineteenth century. English workers appeared to accept the belief that capital and labor could work harmoniously, even to the point of having representatives in the same Liberal Party. Whatever resentments they harbored concerning continued social inequities were mitigated by the widespread belief, again of liberal provenance, that the condition of the working class would continue to improve as the overall wealth of society increased.

One should certainly not conclude that English workers fully identified with their employers—class distinctions were still strong, as was the determination of many workers to protect their collective interests—but at the same time they eschewed radical criticism of capitalism. Talk of socialization of the means of production or of irreconcilable class conflict seemed to most of them unrealistic phrase-mongering, smacking of the heated and discredited ideological intoxications of the 1830s and 1840s.

The trade unions formed in these years were of a craft or sectional type, called the "New Model Unions." Their members were mostly "the aristocrats of labor." These unions resorted to strikes most unwillingly and hesitated to push wage demands aggressively. An all-embracing trade union, like the Owenite GNCTU, with industry-wide organization, seeking to mobilize the unskilled and indeed to speak for the working class in general rather than sections of it, was a thing of the past, and would not be revived in England until the last decade of the century.

The story of German working-class movements and their affiliations with socialist ideology from 1848 on is one of small beginnings and steady growth. There were ups and downs, but the difficulties in Germany had little in common with the roller-coaster episodes of France's revolutionary working class, or with the half-century-long oblivion of socialism in England. The success story of German socialists paralleled that of the German Reich, which, unified under Bismarck's leadership, advanced toward European hegemony—industrially, diplomatically, culturally, and in many other senses—from 1870 on.

The power and influence of the liberal bourgeoisie, and of liberal ideology generally, were less in Germany than in England or France. German liberals had failed notoriously in uniting Germany under a liberal-democratic constitution in 1848; unification was finally accomplished in the 1860s under a Junker-led Prussia and an anachronistic authoritarian-liberal constitution. Economic as distinguished from political liberalization was fairly complete, and the rate of industrial

growth in Germany after 1870 was impressive, but fundamental questioning of the principles of the free-market economy, the wage system,
and the liberal-individualist conception of society continued to attract
a much wider audience in Germany than in England, both on the right
and on the left.

It was thus a less difficult task for German socialists to wean German workers away from the left wing of the liberal movement and to
convince them of the need for a separate workers' party. That much of
the German bourgeoisie had been "junkerized"—that is, that they had
taken on some of the stiff and socially exclusive airs of the Prussian
aristocracy—further facilitated the creation of a separate workers'
party. Worker activists in Germany, and especially inside Prussia, found
that German bourgeois liberals were less willing to work with them for
shared goals (mostly having to do with further liberalization of the
Reich constitution) against the conservatives than was the case in England or in France.

In the early 1860s leadership in the task of convincing German
workers of the need for a separate organization fell to one of the most
colorful personalities in the history of socialism, Ferdinand Lassalle
(1825–64). Talented, flamboyant, ambitious, and enormously energetic,
Lassalle exercised an almost mysterious attraction over the masses. He
rose to rapid prominence in German politics, only to perish tragi-quix-
otically in a duel to defend the honor of a young countess. Paradoxically, this advocate of modern egalitarianism, himself of Jewish origin,
died in the manner of a feudal aristocrat.

Like a number of contemporary German Jews, among whom were
the poet Heine, Moses Hess, and Marx himself, Lassalle had moved
away from the religion of his ancestors to accept a secular humanism,
influenced by German idealist philosophy and French socialist thought.
He had been active in the Revolution of 1848 as a democratic radical,
and his activities at that time cost him a term in jail. In the 1850s he
too retired to his study, devoting much of his time to working out more
advanced political and philosophical positions.

The parallels with Marx are obvious, although Lassalle freely recognized Marx as the superior theorist. The two also differed in important ways, both personally and doctrinally. Lassalle was a warmer man,
less arrogant intellectually, and Lassalle's personal dynamism drew
many to him who only dimly understood his theories—a cause for
much envy and spitefulness on Marx's part. In the area of theory the
most important difference between the two lay in their attitude to the
state. Marx's statements in this regard were subject to shifts in empha-

sis, but in the *Communist Manifesto* the state was described as an organ devoted to the oppression of one class by another. Marx later put special emphasis on the need to "smash" the bourgeois state, replacing its bureaucratic rule with entirely new organs of proletarian dictatorship and direct popular participation. It would then "wither away," once the power of the ruling class had been destroyed and socialism securely established. Lassalle, on the other hand, retained a certain admiration for the existing Prussian state—a common attitude among Hegelians. He foresaw a positive role for it, once it had been democratized (rather than "smashed") and won over to the "moral ideals of the working class," that is, socialism.

Thus Lassalle's view of the state had something in common with such earlier socialists as Blanc, Buchez, and Leroux, in that they all also hoped to introduce socialism through state aid, although Lassalle's Hegelian vision saw the state as standing above society (rather than depending upon it), a supraclass institution, with an ethical mission to resolve conflicts in society and to act somehow as the agent of a transcendental purpose in human affairs.

In most other areas touching on socialist theory, Lassalle was content to borrow from Marx and Engels. One of his more influential popular statements, the "Workingman's Program" of 1862, was little more than a restatement, without explicit recognition, of the themes of the *Communist Manifesto*—giving Marx another cause to resent him.

Under Lassalle's leadership a new party of the working class, the General Association of German Workers, or ADAV (*Allgemeiner Deutscher Arbeiter Verein*) was founded in 1863. ADAV neither received Marx's explicit support nor was in any unofficial sense Marxist. The purpose of the new association, as proclaimed in its program, was to "work by peaceful and legal means . . . towards the establishment of universal, equal, and direct suffrage," which, it asserted, was the only way to assure the end of class conflict in society (Fried and Sanders, p. 380). Programmatically, the ADAV was thus democratic-radical rather than socialist. Nevertheless, it was a working-class party, firmly anti-bourgeois, and it was widely assumed that the ADAV would introduce socialism once workers had gained control of a democratized state.

The ADAV differed from other German parties in a number of respects. It sought to operate on funds collected by enrolling masses of workers who paid modest but regular dues. Other parties of the day tended to be loose affiliations of prominent men who organized themselves periodically for electoral purposes and who relied upon large contributions from a few wealthy supporters. The ADAV was also a more centralized and tightly organized party. Its president was endowed with wide-ranging discretionary powers, providing thus firm, even authoritarian leadership to a party that at the same time elicited more rank-and-file participation than did other parties.

Marx's and Engels's reticence to join with Lassalle was matched by that of a number of German leftists, especially outside of the area of Prussia (and of course Germany was not yet unified). Many of them suspected Lassalle's motives, in part because of the way that he appeared to be flirting with Bismarck and the Junkers. They feared that he was looking to some sort of alliance of the aristocracy and the working class against the liberal bourgeoisie. These skeptics usually remained in left-liberal parties or formed other organizations independent of the ADAV.

Two of the most important future leaders of German socialism chose this path, Wilhelm Liebknecht and August Bebel. But they also found their alliance with the left liberals to be untenable. This was not because the latter refused them meaningful political partnership—social relations in the southern German states, where these two were active, were more flexible than in Prussia—but rather over more doctrinal issues. Many southern liberals were committed to full political democracy, and were even sincerely concerned about the social question, but they could not swallow the idea of social democracy. Bebel and Liebknecht insisted upon radical measures of social reorganization, and gradually their intransigence on these issues drove a wedge between them and the liberals. The final separation came in 1869, when the Social Democratic Labor Party was founded at Eisenach.

The "Eisenachers" became known as the Marxist party in Germany, largely because Liebknecht maintained close relations with Marx and Engels—who were indeed coaching him and Bebel along the road from democratic radicalism to Marxian socialism—and because the Social Democratic Labor Party joined the Workingman's International, in which Marx was prominent. But at this time the term Marxist remained imprecise. The most significant differences in emphasis between Eisenachers and Lassalleans were not closely tied to Marx's teachings. The Eisenachers were more Prusso-phobic, more internationalist, more conciliatory to the bourgeois Left; their organization was run on less autocratic lines, and they asserted that the economic condition of the workers could to some degree be improved in the context of capitalism through the actions of the trade unions (the Lassalleans believed in a version of the Iron Law of Wages: Salaries unavoidably remained near the level of subsistence).

Most of these emphases had to do more with the Eisenachers' southern origin than with any direct inspiration from Marx. The Eisenacher idea of socialism differed little from that of the Lassalleans. Even on the issue of the state the Eisenachers avoided mention of smashing or of a revolutionary confrontation leading to the dictatorship of the proletariat. Instead, they spoke of a "free people's state" (*freier Volksstaat*), which would sponsor a "cooperative system with state credit for voluntary productive cooperatives. . . ." (Lidtke, p. 30). This was barely distinguishable from Lassalle's position, and indeed Marx and Engels objected to the Eisenacher formula, but without effect.

The Lassalleans and Eisenachers were united in 1875 after the unification of Germany, which takes us beyond the confines of this section. But the Eisenacher-Lassallean dichotomy was the source of an enduring tension, one that would affect many of the activities of the united party throughout its period of greatest success in the late nineteenth and early twentieth centuries.

Developments in France differed significantly from those in both Germany and England. For a short period in 1848 and 1849, following the June Days, hopes were entertained for a "social-democratic" alliance against the bourgeoisie, joining together elements of the lower middle class, peasantry, and workers, with demands for easier credit, tax reform, land for the landless, and state sponsorship of workers' associations. This vision of the social republic was in principle milder than that of the "communists" who had been the object of the violence in June.

The prospect of the social-democratic alliance attaining a ruling majority in the Chamber of Deputies was scarcely less threatening than a "communist" victory to the possessing classes, who, in their anxiety for order, rallied to the banners of Louis-Napoleon Bonaparte, the nephew of the first emperor. First elected to the presidency of the Republic in December 1848, with a resounding majority (5.5 million votes out of 7.4 million cast) Napoleon III, as he was soon called, crushed the Second Republic through a coup d'état in December 1851 and established the Second Empire.

Napoleon III's heavy majorities in December 1848 and in subsequent plebiscites depended above all on peasant support, but his image was sufficiently ambiguous to appeal to all classes, causing some scholars to see in his rule an interesting precursor to modern fascism. He attracted peasants who were both outraged at the taxes introduced by the new republic and still mesmerized by the Napoleonic legend. Workers who were disgusted by the failed promises of the Republic since

June were likewise attracted to Louis-Napoleon's banners, and the
petty bourgeoisie supported him in large numbers because he seemed
to be an enemy of the wealthy, while the wealthy believed that he would
restore order after a time of revolutionary unrest, as his uncle had done
fifty years before.

The overall effect of Napoleon III's rule was undeniably to restore
order and to strengthen the institutions of centralized authority. But he
was in no simple sense a tool of the bourgeoisie, in spite of his respect
for the existing social structures and his support of measures conducive
to rapid industrialization. In his youth, and even at times as emperor,
Louis-Napoleon referred to himself as a "socialist." His socialism was of
a vaguely Saint-Simonian persuasion, and from the beginning of his
rule he made a number of decrees designed to assuage the harsh conditions of the poor. Indeed, the overall record of the Second Empire in
terms of its attention to the plight of the poor was superior to that of
either the July Monarchy or the subsequent Third Republic.

Nevertheless, once Louis-Napoleon's authoritarian rule had been
established, most working-class leaders were unimpressed with his
kind of socialism, since it favored great bankers and industrialists, emphasized social order, and encouraged efficient, concentrated modern
industry. This did not appeal to the great majority of politically conscious French workers. Throughout the nineteenth century most of
them remained involved in small-scale production and distrusted concentrated industry. If it is possible to select any one figure who spoke
for them it was Pierre-Joseph Proudhon (1809–65). A considerable number of French working-class leaders in the 1860s accepted the label
"Proudhonian," although they by no means accepted all of his ideas;
they were consistent in this sense with the spirit of his writings, which
rejected system-building and dogma. At any rate Proudhon's works
were so sprawling and contradictory that it was not always possible to
make coherent sense of them.

Proudhon is usually identified as the seminal theorist of anarchism. He was known for a number of radical-sounding aphorisms ("What
is property?—It is theft!"), and the title of one of his books was *Confessions of a Revolutionary*. Nevertheless, he could as easily be associated
with the conservative Right as with the socialist Left—true enough of
many early socialists—but in Proudhon the conservative side was particularly strong. He termed property "theft" only when it became so
concentrated that it lent itself to such abuses as the exploitation of labor and the enjoyment of unearned incomes; he firmly believed in the
ownership of small amounts of property. Even his call for working-class

solidarity appeared to be inspired more by an anti-modern, anti-bourgeois corporatism than by modern industrial experience. He did not believe in violent revolutionary action; rather, he looked to a "revolutionary" change of society through gradual reform, and even this "reform" would be directed against modernizing techniques, especially industrial technology, capital concentration, and bureaucratic management. In matters having to do with the role of the family, relations between the sexes, and the raising of children he was extremely traditional.

Proudhon's overriding concern with free or easy credit and his identification with the small, traditional producer calls to mind Cobbett's version of democratic radicalism. In other ways as well Cobbett and Proudhon shared much: the same convictions concerning the need for independence and self-help, the same nativist hatred of things modern and foreign—notably of Jews, so much identified in their minds with finance, and with grasping, acquisitive capitalists in general—the same rustic origins, the same heated, scurrilous language. Proudhon's ideal society was one of decentralized and free cooperation, devoid of the state in the modern sense, and organized around an economic federalism of small productive units, credit cooperatives, insurance societies.

By the end of the first decade of his rule, when his support from other classes began to falter, Napoleon III made overtures to the workers. He gave permission for some two hundred working-class leaders to travel as delegates to the London International Exposition in 1862. The French worker delegates were powerfully impressed with the relatively high standard of living enjoyed by English workers and attributed it largely to the freedom to organize in England. The French delegates thus came back to France further convinced of the need for revived working-class organizations in their own country.

The year 1862 also saw the first major strike under the Empire, by typographical workers. They were arrested under the existing legislation prohibiting strikes but were then pardoned by the emperor. In 1864 he followed this gesture by introducing a law that gave workers the right to strike, although not yet full rights to freedom of assembly and trade-union association. In 1868, without actually providing legislation, the government let it be known that it would tolerate workers' organizations as it tolerated employers' organizations, although in practice this toleration was uncertain and unpredictable.

These efforts did not win any appreciable number of working-class activists to Napoleon III's side. Their support, at least in overt political terms, went to the growing republican opposition. A few working-class leaders ran for election themselves, rather than being content with representation by left republicans of bourgeois origins, but they met with little success.

In 1864 worker activists, prominent among whom was a Parisian bronze worker named Henry-Louis Tolain (who was one of the above-mentioned unsuccessful worker candidates), produced a much-discussed and influential statement entitled the *Manifesto of the Sixty*. This document supported much of the republican opposition's program—which included demands for freedom of the press, of association, and of assembly—but it was also Proudhonian in tone. Tolain and other authors of the *Manifesto* consulted with Proudhon before publishing it, reaching general agreement with him, although he retained certain reservations: He would have liked a clearer statement in it of differences with the republicans (whose jacobin taste for a positive role for a strong state he rejected); he also feared that trade unions would become bureaucratic and authoritarian, thus exacerbating class tensions and encouraging violence. But the Proudhonian flavor of the *Manifesto* came through in its concern to disassociate itself from any notions of class conflict, revolutionary violence, or communism. It asserted "we do not dream . . . of a chimerical equality that would put everyone in a procrustean bed. . . . Freedom of labor and credit, solidarity. These are our dreams. When these become facts, it will be to the glory and prosperity of our country, which is dear to us, and then there will be no bourgeois, no proletarian, no master class and no working class. Then all citizens will have equal rights" (Landauer, p. 213).

Organizational activity among French workers accelerated by the late 1860s. In 1870 there were something like sixty-five thousand members of unions (*syndicats*) in Paris. Most other leading cities in France saw comparable developments. Many of these syndicats, as well as political clubs, cooperatives, and discussion groups, joined the Workingman's International, so that by 1870 there were perhaps two hundred thousand French members of the International, although affiliation was so informal and easy that these figures are of dubious meaning.

As a consequence, the vaguely jacobin-Proudhonian French section of the International became its largest section. Marx made some inroads among the French, aided perhaps by the Second Empire's abrupt decision, after several years of tolerance, to prosecute the Internationalists as members of an unauthorized association, which turned some working-class leaders in a more militant, revolutionary direction. But far more important in turning French activists leftward and in enhancing Marx's reputation in France—and the world—was the Franco-Prussian War and the ensuing Paris Commune. By this time Marx had also established a reputation as a theorist of great importance.

MARX'S REVOLUTIONARY THEORY

By 1850 the main outlines of Marx's and Engels's theories had been worked out, although in rather disparate and often unsatisfactory forms. The early philosophical works, such as the *Economic and Philosophical Manuscripts*, and the *German Ideology* were not designed for a wide reading public, and were not even published in Marx's lifetime. The *Communist Manifesto* was a popular tract, hardly a formal theoretical statement. Marx later wrote that his *Poverty of Philosophy* (published in 1847, a withering critique of Proudhon's *Philosophy of Poverty*) was the work in which "the decisive points of our view were first scientifically, although only polemically, indicated." Thereafter "the editing of the *Neue Rheinische Zeitung* in 1848 and 1849, and the subsequent [revolutionary] events, interrupted my economic studies, which could only be resumed in the year 1850 in London" (Fried and Sanders, p. 299).

The period of revolutionary upheavals had thus passed for a while, and Marx threw himself into a meticulously thorough study of capitalism, expressing satisfaction with the "enormous material for the history of political economy that is accumulated in the British Museum [and] the favorable vantage point afforded by London for the observation of bourgeois society" (Fried and Sanders, p. 299).

Enough has been said about Marx's mental formation to make it obvious that he approached the study of contemporary capitalism from a different perspective than had Smith or Ricardo. While he used a number of their tools, it was this different perspective that helped him to work out theories that were original and revolutionary in implications. Where Smith and Ricardo had praised the free-market system and believed that its laws were natural and of timeless significance, Marx denounced it and set out to prove that it would pass away, as had earlier systems, by developing internal contradictions, one day reaching the dialectical-qualitative "leap" of revolutionary upheaval.

Marx's radically transformed interpretation of Classical Economics and his related theories of social development, while worked out in staggering detail in his mature writings, lend themselves to a general overview, since he used what has been called an "abstract-deductive" approach. He usually tried to plot out his analysis at a high level of abstraction, to enhance the breadth of his vision and his sensitivity to interrelatedness, and thereafter he adduced progressively more concrete "auxiliary theses." Whatever the merits of this approach, it also has created problems of interpretation, for in addition to the inherent abstruseness and subtlety of Marx's thought, this approach often leads one to wonder whether any given proposition is merely an opening approximation, subject to substantial clarification and qualification by auxiliary theses, or whether it represents something close to Marx's final thoughts on the matter. Moreover, his hierarchy of abstraction—that is, the determination of the relative importance of his various theses—is at times unclear, and this represents a central problem in making sense of Marx's use of such notions as dialectical and organic change, and base-superstructure. These difficulties are compounded in that Marx, never a careful or consistent stylist, left much of his work unfinished or unrevised.

The cornerstone of Marxian economics is the labor theory of value. Most western economists, with the exception of a few left-wing mavericks, have long since avoided the whole question of "value" as a scholastic dead end, leading to few fruitful insights into the working of economic systems, but in Marx's time the labor theory of value was widely accepted, by non-socialists and socialists alike. Marx's socialist convictions, linked to the foundations of his philosophical positions (that is, of man as producer or creator), made the theory all the more attractive to him. But it was necessary to move from the philosophical conception of man in the abstract, to demonstrate precisely how his productivity creates value and becomes capital in the context of modern industrial society.

In his major work, *Das Kapital*, Marx began his discussions of the labor theory of value with certain familiar distinctions, in the accepted manner of contemporary treatises on economic theory. An article produced for immediate use by a producer, as was typical of premodern production, possessed only "use-value"; it was not yet a commodity, which must also have "exchange-value." That is, a commodity must be suitable for exchange on the market and be produced primarily for that purpose rather than for immediate use.

This kind of commodity exchange existed before the advent of capitalism. For modern capitalist exchange to appear, it was necessary to have a specific social setting, one in which money and other forms of property are primarily in the hands of one class, while others possess only their labor power and are obliged to sell that labor as a commodity, that is, for its exchange-value. Such a social system had of course evolved in Marx's lifetime. But before proceeding to a consideration of this state of Marx's theory, it is well to scrutinize how he dealt with the apparent problems involved in the labor theory of value, for the briefest reflection will cause one to question the validity of this theory.

It is not difficult to accept the notion that labor time alone—that is, the actual time spent in producing a commodity—can constitute a viable foundation for exchange among small-scale producers, such as artisans or peasants. Indeed, such a standard existed in early modern history; it was for this reason, in part, that the Owenite labor exchange was easily accepted by many artisanal workers. But Owen's exchange ran into serious difficulties, as did New Harmony, in part because of faulty assumptions concerning the exchangeability of labor time. How does the labor theory of value, or Marx's interpretation of it, come to grips with the obvious differences between diligent and lazy, skilled and unskilled labor, or between pleasant and unpleasant, dangerous and secure working conditions?

Marx and other economists of the time were perfectly aware of these problems, and Marx attempted to deal with them through the introduction of a number of auxiliary theses, most of which had been suggested by Ricardo. Key among these was the notion of "socially necessary labor," which was a way of averaging out such complicating factors as the inefficiency or lack of skill and diligence of any individual workers, as well as dealing with the problem of the production of commodities that society does not need or desire as much as others and that therefore bring lower prices on the market. Marx's labor theory of value, then, refers only to socially necessary labor: This labor is *not* that expended by a single individual; rather, it is the quantity of labor that is necessary *on the average* to produce a given commodity in a given national and historical context. In a related way the time expended by a skilled laborer has to be understood in terms of the time previously devoted to acquiring that skill. A person's productive activity, in other words, while still measurable in terms of labor time, must not be compared in a simple-minded fashion to the productive activity of the unskilled.

The concept of socially necessary labor also encompasses the growing productivity of labor under capitalism: As technology advances in a particular enterprise, its workers become more productive than those in another enterprise that produces the same commodities. The competitive pressures of the capitalist system will eventually force under the less productive, for more labor is expended in the less productive enterprises than is *socially necessary*. This process means that the average rate of labor productivity under capitalism rises continuously, and for this reason it is impossible to equate labor value at one stage of history with that of a later, more advanced period; labor value must be considered within a given historical context. It is not an absolute of any sort.

According to Marx, labor under capitalism sells itself as a commodity, at its market value. This statement means simply that labor's value is calculated like any other commodity under capitalism: It is equal to the amount of labor necessary to "make" or produce it. In other words, the value of labor under capitalism is equal to the amount of labor necessary to feed, clothe, and house a worker, to keep him alive and functioning as a productive unit. Marx's theory of surplus value arises from this line of reasoning.

He points out that the laborer in modern industrial conditions produces considerably more than the value of his labor power, considered as a commodity. A worker toils twelve hours a day, but it requires, let us say, only four hours' labor to pay his exchange-value (that is, to keep him alive and functioning). The remaining eight hours are surplus-value (*Mehrwert*), which the capitalist appropriates for his own purposes. This insight and the conclusions that arise from it constitute what Marx thought was his most original contribution to economic thought.

An important if elusive point to note carefully here is that machines *as such* are not a source of surplus-value. They intensify and multiply labor but do not create it. Human labor is always necessary to make them function. Thus surplus-value can be extracted only from human labor, not from the activities of machines. This point is important because Marx's theories of declining profit and "immiseration" (*Verelendung*) depend upon it.

Marx, like many of his contemporaries, especially in the 1840s, believed that he saw around him an ever more impoverished working class. He and his contemporaries also believed that profit margins were, by mid-century in England, undeniably declining. But, again, rather than contenting himself with commonly accepted empirical or common-sense observations, he sought to demonstrate precisely what it was about the inner nature of capitalist production that was responsible for these trends. He believed that he found the key to the whole matter in the increasing proportion, in modern industry, of what he termed "constant capital." That is, as capitalism advanced, a relatively higher proportion of investment necessarily went into the purchase of machinery and plant (constant capital) than in the purchase of labor power ("variable capital," or wages). This growing increase in the "organic composition of capital," meant that relatively—though not absolutely—fewer man-hours went into production as industrialization progressed. The result in turn would be that the rate of profit would be smaller—though again, not the mass of profit—since there was relatively less surplus-value in the form of human labor to exploit. And because of this relatively declining amount of variable capital in the production process, capitalists would be driven, quite aside from their own greediness, to exploit their workers all the more ruthlessly.

In addition, technological innovation meant continual displacement of workers by machines. And this technological unemployment created a "reserve army of the unemployed," whose existence undermined any efforts by employed workers to force wages up. Employers always would have recourse to the reserve army if their own workers became unmanageable.

Because of these various factors, Marx alleged, the living conditions of the working class would hover constantly at subsistence levels. Thus while he rejected Ricardo's Iron Law of Wages (briefly, that higher wages would only cause workers to produce more children, thus providing new workers to the market and driving wages down again), Marx arrived at similar conclusions concerning the extent to which under capitalism the condition of the working class could be improved in the long run. However, he asserted not only that the working class would *remain* impoverished, he also believed that the situation of workers would become *more* miserable in the long run, until the final day when they could bear it no longer and would revolt against their oppressors, converting capitalism to socialism.

Marx introduced a large number of complicating factors or auxiliary theses into his theories of declining profit and working-class immiseration. In his more refined or qualified model, these are very long-range trends, easily and often reversed in the short run by countertrends. Moreover, he recognized that working-class immiseration had to be judged in terms of the general wealth of a given society. Thus wealthy workers in one stage of development might well be termed deprived in another, later stage when other classes had advanced even more in wealth. From a slightly different perspective, workers will be increasingly exploited, although not necessarily poorer in any absolute sense.

Marx's treatment of the business cycle may also be considered an auxiliary thesis to the theories of immiseration and declining profit. He did not ever fully work out his ideas on the nature of these cycles, but once again what is particularly interesting and significant is the way he tried to explain the recurring booms and busts of business activity in terms of the inner logic of the capitalist system. Previous economists had tended to see these ups and downs as "accidents" caused by the oversights or speculative activity of certain individuals rather than by the nature of the system itself. Marx described them as aspects of the declining rate of profit, which forced bankruptcy upon the smaller and less productive units. This was a godsend for the larger units. They could then buy up the plants of their former competitors, and at a considerably lower price than their actual value. Having done this they could avoid for a time the previous pressures on their profit margin, since they could operate on "borrowed" labor or labor value that had been bought at a bargain. Thus the recoveries and booms that followed crises could be explained: Individual capitalist enterprises got a new lease on life, although only a temporary one. To the superficial, empirical observer it might appear that the capitalist system had recovered, but for Marx this "recovery" was only part of a necessary, longer process that was leading to a fundamental breakdown of the capitalist process.

One might conclude from what has been said so far that the capitalist, the benefactor of the exploitation of the worker, was free to live a relaxed and luxurious life. But although the capitalist certainly could live in style, especially in the boom periods of the business cycle, the pressures of the system made it dangerous for him to use very much of his profit for personal expenditures. Indeed, the less he spent in that way, the more he invested, the more likely he was to succeed, in the capitalist system. A capitalist must continually improve the techniques of production in his enterprise. If he fails to do so, others will be able to undersell him and thus force him to the wall. But in order to improve production it is essential to invest as much as possible in capital growth. Thus the surplus value appropriated by the capitalist must in large part be fed back into investment. At the same time the most successful entrepreneurs come to control larger and larger accumulations of capital.

The growth of capital accumulation and industrial concentration lead, then, to a result that was quite different from Adam Smith's ideal of many small competitive firms. As large units come to prevail in a given industry, the trend is toward controlled, monopolistic, and noncompetitive production, away from laissez-faire. Advanced capitalism becomes fundamentally different from early capitalism; in addition to being incomparably more productive, it is based progressively more on concentrated and collective rather than individual production. Thus from yet another perspective, in Marx's eyes, capitalism was undermining itself from within, preparing for a qualitative change into socialsm.

Marx's chain of economic arguments had obvious implications for other not specifically economic, areas. Indeed, it is artificial to separate his economic from his social, political, or cultural concepts. He believed them integral to one another and took considerable pains to show their organic interrelatedness.

As one can begin a consideration of Marxian economics with the labor theory of value, so the concept of "mode of production" (*Produktionsweise*) is central to his analysis of social developments, which of course mesh with economic. This is a rich, many-faceted notion in the writings of Marx and Engels but one that is often elusive, even confusing. It can be described in simple terms as the way that a given society at a given stage of historical evolution organizes the management of its material environment; or, the way that human productive activity is organized. Marx believed that this mode of production constituted the underlying reality about any society and a key to a fuller understanding of the varieties of political institutions, religion, art, philosophical speculation, and so forth that develop at the same time. To use Marx's language, the underlying reality, the mode of production, is the "substructure" (*Grundlage*) of a society, upon which the institutional and ideological "superstructure" (*Überbau*) rest.

Although some later Marxists used the base-superstructure notion in a simplistic fashion—that the mode of production of a given society was the direct and only significant cause of its state form, art, or religion—Marx's commentary on contemporary historical developments reveal him as supremely aware of a rich interplay of causative factors, not reducible to the mode of production. The issue has been much debated, but Melvin Rader, again bringing clarity to vexingly confused matters, has argued persuasively that Marx integrated the base-superstructure model into a larger organic-dialectical one.

The mode of production operates within the context of class society, of propertied and propertyless—of who controls the mode of production. But the mode of production differs fundamentally according to the level of technological development. Whether a society possesses a backward or an advanced technology will determine the mode of production it is capable of, the kind of class society it builds. A society where production is centered around horse-driven plows and carts will be different from one where tractors and trucks are used, and the difference will be obvious on many levels. Since a tractor, with one person operating it, can do, let us say, the work of ten people working behind horses and plows, then nine people are made superfluous and can then devote their labor to other kinds of production. Across the broad spectrum of society, this kind of displacement means thousands of hands freed for new tasks.

Thus technological innovation, by multiplying the productivity of labor, requires new kinds of social organization to deal with the hands that are freed. Former agricultural laborers, replaced by machinery, migrate into town and become factory workers. As their numbers swell, the town becomes a great industrial city. A whole new range of problems are created: The physical environment is changed, new social classes appear, relations of production are different, and new political forms arise to deal with these new realities. And in the city continuing advances in the techniques of production again multiply the productivity of labor and free new hands, creating ever-new problems and opportunities.

Various institutional responses are elicited by a change in the mode of production. For example, movement from the land requires an end to the feudal regulations tying families to a given manor or parish; labor must be "free," that is, at liberty to travel to find work. The premodern division of land into a quiltwork of plots with their nexus of related personal obligations also stands in the way of a more efficient rural production, one which could make use of new technology. Thus it is necessary to consolidate landholdings. Labor devoted to the maintenance of draft animals is no longer necessary, thus fields can be put into different kinds of production. Everywhere the shockwaves of a change in the mode of production are to be felt.

Marx argued, and many contemporaries who were politically distant from him agreed, that the new mode of production being introduced by the industrial revolution was the ultimate cause of the unprecedented social, political, and cultural changes occurring in Europe. The commercial and industrial systems were bringing with them new ruling elites that were demanding new laws and new institutions of state. In France these pressures had resulted in a series of dramatic revolutions, but in England also pressures for reform favorable to industrial growth found expression in such measures as the Reform Bill of 1832 and the New Poor Law of 1834.

In short, Marx believed that the political upheavals of the late eighteenth and early nineteenth century had to be understood in terms of a changing mode of production that resulted in ever more ambitious efforts by the bourgeoisie to gain complete control of the state—and here we return to the notion of "bourgeois revolution," as discussed in

Chapter 1. As he and Engels had written in the *Communist Manifesto*, "the modern state authority is nothing more than a committee for the administration of the consolidated affairs of the bourgeois class as a whole." (As earlier noted when discussing Lassalle and Marx, the latter's subtly shifting conceptions of the state are not easily summarized. Suffice it to note here that the above concept, which emphasizes the strictly class nature of the state, most clearly reflects Engels's thought. At times, Marx's own emphasis is on the state as a kind of bureaucratized and parasitical entity, less clearly under the direct control of the ruling class. Marx had recourse to such notions particularly when trying to explain "abnormal" states—such as that of Napoleon III—that served to prolong, unnaturally, the existence of a historically condemned class society.)

In a related way, Marx argued, apologists emerged to rationalize and disguise the true nature of the new social relationships, of the new state forms, of the new legal measures. Theorists like Smith, Bentham, Malthus, and Ricardo delivered telling criticisms of the old order and justified the new. Religious movements like the Methodists similarly emerged to serve the needs of the new ruling class by preaching to the poor that their sufferings should be borne with humility and resignation.

Of course, these theorists and the evangelical preachers did not think of themselves as defenders of the interests of a new ruling class; they believed that they were revealing truths of universal and timeless relevance, essential to the general welfare. In the same way, the ordinary capitalist believed that his success was due to personal merit and that the poverty of his workers was explained by their laziness, ignorance, lack of ambition, or perhaps the Iron Law of Wages. And indeed many workers themselves accepted such views—were, in other words, subjected to the hegemony of a capitalist world view.

For Marx both the capitalist and the worker who thought in this way were the prisoners of a "false consciousness." But at the same time, he recognized that this consciousness did serve certain necessary historical functions, just as the exploitation of labor served similar purposes. That is, socialism would not be possible until capitalism had built up the material and social foundations for it. Yet, as the capitalist system developed, the increasingly anachronistic nature of the theories defending it would begin to be revealed. From these trends a revolutionary proletarian class consciousness could begin to emerge, resulting in ever more intense class conflict, which would be channeled into strikes, demonstrations, and the growth of unions and socialist parties.

Comparable class conflict had occurred in previous periods of history, since the exploitation of labor in one form or another had been an aspect of all civilized history, whether it was between serf and lord, as in the middle ages, or between slave and slaveholder, as in ancient times. Each of these previous systems had eventually developed internal contradictions leading to the emergence of new systems.

It was earlier remarked that capitalist commodity production required a specific class context, where one class owned the means of production and the other owned only its labor power, which it was forced to sell as a commodity. There were of course many other kinds of classes in Marx's time and many other relations of production besides those of exploiter and exploited, propertied and unpropertied. The small property owner—shopkeeper, artisan, or peasant—was quite prominent throughout the nineteenth century. But Marx believed that this petty bourgeoisie would disappear, indeed was already disappearing rapidly, leaving only bourgeois and proletarian. Artisans and shopkeepers would be crushed in the competitive struggle by the more efficient and profitable factories and large stores. The ruined artisan and shopkeeper would then be forced to join the ranks of the proletariat. In the countryside a similar development had been in process for at least a century; the peasant was being replaced by the capitalist farmer. Small landholders, unable to withstand the competitive pressures exerted by this dynamic new element in the countryside, were everywhere being forced to join the ranks of the proletariat.

All of this means an enormous growth in the ranks of the proletariat as capitalism grows. The successful capitalists concurrently become relatively fewer, although there is some growth in the "auxiliary" ranks of the bourgeoisie, such as lawyers, politicians, journalists, doctors, and other professionals, who share the attitudes and class identity of the capitalist. A small minority of these, recognizing the voice of the future, join ranks with the proletariat, providing it with leadership and a more advanced consciousness.

The entire process was described succinctly—although probably more simplistically than Marx would have done—by Engels in the 1883 introduction to the *Communist Manifesto*:

economic production and the structure of society of every historical epoch necessarily arising from it constitute the foundation for the political and intellectual history of that epoch; . . . consequently . . . all history has been a history of class struggles, of struggles between exploited and exploiting. . . . This struggle however has now reached a stage where the exploited and the oppressed class . . . can no longer emancipate itself from the class that exploits it . . . without at the same time forever freeing the whole of society from exploitation, oppression, and class struggles. [Tucker, *Reader*, p. 334]

This brings us once again to the question of how and when the capitalist system will break down—or be broken down. From an economic standpoint the breakdown should logically occur when the contradictions of capitalist production can no longer be resolved through the application of various palliatives and when the productive potential of capitalist techniques has been fully developed, making a socialism of plenty possible. From the standpoint of the development of social classes, the breakdown should occur when capitalism has done its work of creating a society composed predominantly of proletarians, when the older individualistic petty bourgeoisie has been assimilated into the proletariat, and when the proletariat has become aware of its historic mission.

To repeat a point earlier made, Marx's most consistent position was that revolution could not come before capitalism had fully matured. He wrote, "new, higher relations of production never appear before the material conditions of their existence have matured in the womb of the old society" (Fried and Sanders, p. 298). Socialism could not appear until capitalism had substantially created it; and in the long run capitalism *could not avoid* creating it.

Did this emphasis on the inevitability of capitalist breakdown justify the tendency among late nineteenth-century Marxists, concerning which much more will be said later, to avoid revolutionary activism, to assume a strongly deterministic belief that all one had to do was *wait* for capitalism to destroy itself? There are unquestionably a number of specific statements by Marx and Engels that describe the coming revolution as akin to the movement of planets, but this view was inconsistent with their philosophical starting point, and in their own lives both were unrelenting revolutionaries, for whom revolutionary will and critical activity were crucial. In most of Marx's writings a violent confrontation between proletariat and bourgeoisie is envisaged, and indeed on a few occasions (most notably in his "Critique of the Gotha Program," that is, the program under which the Eisenachers and Lassalleans united in 1875), he particularly emphasized the need for a dictatorship of the proletariat to destroy capitalism and end the rule of the bourgeoisie.

Milder statements, even those that appear to accept the possibility of peaceful transition to socialism, can also be cited (one of the more famous, Marx's "Inaugural Address" to the Workingman's International, is discussed below), but it can be reasonably well concluded that Marx's commitment to revolutionary activity, if not always to revolutionary violence, was firm. As has been previously much emphasized, Marx was no hothead; he had a sober sense of what was realistic at a given movement. Marx also apparently believed that a revolutionary dictatorship should be brief and supported by an overwhelming majority of the population. Engels later described the Paris Commune of 1871 as conforming to his and Marx's conception of the dictatorship of the proletariat; and the Commune, while a brief and confused episode, was libertarian, anti-elitist, and emphasized popular participation—it was quite distant from the dictatorship of the proletariat established later by Lenin.

Similarly, while Marx believed that intellectuals had an important role to play in raising the consciousness of workers—his own life was after all devoted to such a role—he conceived of intellectual activity and the leadership of intellectuals as ancillary to the development of consciousness through concrete experience by workers in capitalist society.

The socialist and eventually communist society that Marx and Engels believed would emerge after the dictatorship of the proletariat had done its work remains veiled in obscurity, partly because they consciously avoided the kind of detailed and often absurd blueprints characteristic of Fourier or Cabet. Perhaps the safest statement is that Marx remained under the spell of classical conceptions, of the polis and its citizenry, where society and state, public and private spheres were dynamically bound together. But his ideal was not the repressive-authoritarian Sparta, so revered by Rousseau and the communist philosophes, but Periclean Athens, with its democratic and libertarian participation. In some of Marx's earliest writings he implies that the end of alienation in communism would entail the end of the division of labor and the specialization of skills, in terms reminiscent of Fourier—one would work at whatever was appealing, whenever one felt like it. Kindred views appear in a few sections of *Das Kapital* and in Engels's *Anti-Dühring*. How such notions can be made consistent with Marx's economic and social thought, with the progress of technological complexity and the mandates of economic and demographic concentration, remains a puzzle.

MARX, THE WORKINGMAN'S INTERNATIONAL, AND THE PARIS COMMUNE

Most of Marx's mature theoretical reflections were worked out in the 1850s and 1860s, although he was much distracted in the 1850s by the desperate financial straits in which he found himself. He had thrown his own savings and those of his wife into financing the *Neue Rheinische Zeitung*. He was thus nearly destitute when he arrived in London. It was only after an interminable delay that he was able to finish the first volume of what he considered his life work. *Das Kapital* did not appear until 1867, although he published *A Contribution to the Critique of Political Economy* in 1859; *Das Kapital* was a "continuation" and expansion of it, much delayed because of ill health and personal misfortune. Marx never completed the three remaining projected volumes. Engels was thus obliged to do what he could with the unfinished manuscripts after Marx's death in 1883. Two subsequent volumes appeared in the 1880s and 1890s.

It was not until the mid-1860s that Marx was both able and willing to throw himself in a major way once again into political activities. In 1864 the International Workingmen's Association, subsequently known as the First International, began to take shape. It will be recalled that the 1860s saw a revival of working-class activity in France and the establishment of the ADAV in Germany. The London International Exposition in 1862 had permitted workers of various nations to meet one another and to compare their conditions, furthering the belief among working-class leaders that the laboring population of each nation shared important interests. Various contacts grew out of the Exposition, and in April 1864, in a meeting held to express sympathy for the Poles in their struggle against Russian despotism, English and French workers' delegates arranged for a further meeting in September where an international organization of the working class would be founded. Marx was invited to this meeting and was subsequently elected to the committee that was to draw up the founding statutes of the new International.

Marx rapidly emerged as a leading figure of the International. He devoted much of his time to it because he believed that at last a solid organization, primarily made up of workers and based on working-class initiative, had been established. It had distanced itself from conspiratorial tactics and held real promise of attracting a mass following. At the same time, he was perfectly aware that the founders of the International were a diverse lot, most of whom were not socialist revolutionaries, and even fewer of whom could be called Marxists. At first, the most important contingent by far was that of the English trade unionists, whose goals for the International centered around protecting labor standards in England against the importation of cheap foreign labor. In addition to this large delegation were some surviving Owenites and

Chartists, Proudhonists and Blanquists from France, Polish democrats, and nationalist revolutionaries from such countries as Ireland and Italy, for whom the social question was secondary in importance.

Because of this heterogeneity it was all the more important for Marx to proceed with circumspection if he were to establish a leadership role. Thus the "Inaugural Address" that Marx composed for the International was different in tone from the *Communist Manifesto*, or from his other writings of 1848–50 (and significantly the Address is one of the documents most often cited by non-Leninist Marxists). In it he expressed praise for the contemporary efforts to establish cooperative factories and retail stores, and he congratulated the English working class for having won the Ten Hours Bill, adding that this was "the first time that in broad daylight the political economy of the middle class has succumbed to the political economy of the working class" (since bourgeois economists had predicted that any diminution of the daily hours of labor in England would have a disastrous impact on the economy—a contention which proved untrue). Yet in spite of these mild and ostensibly reformist words, Marx made clear his conviction that "cooperative labor, if kept within the narrow circle of the casual efforts of private workmen, will never be able to arrest the growth in geometrical progression of monopoly, to free the masses, nor even to perceptibly lighten the burden of their miseries" (Tucker, *Reader*, p. 379–81).

Similarly, Marx took care to stress his own beliefs concerning the proper organization of the masses. Against the old carbonarist conceptions of men like Giuseppe Mazzini, the leader of the Italian delegation, Marx stressed that the "emancipation of the working class must be conquered by the working class itself," and that the "capture of political power through the vote has become the great duty of the working class." Like the *Communist Manifesto*, the Address ended with the words, "Proletarians of all countries, unite!"

Marx was not particularly successful in weaning the membership of the International away from rival doctrines, nor did he enjoy any clear-cut success in his broader designs to spread the influence of the International among the workers of the world. The International did grow steadily, and his influence in it also increased gradually over the years—more or less Marxist, collectivist programs were endorsed in 1868 and 1869—but never was it anything close to a major force in international affairs, and Marx's own energies were much dissipated in acrimonious struggles with the anarchist followers of first Proudhon and then Bakunin. Once again he was obliged to formulate the same kinds of arguments that he had used against the impatient "primitive communists" like Gottschalk, and again he did so with mixed success.

The Franco-Prussian War of 1870 and the ensuing uprising in Paris in 1871 put tremendous strains on the International and on Marx as a leading figure in it. In spite of the official working-class internationalism of the organization, most of its members retained deeply patriotic feelings. Even Marx's attitude was characterized by a certain ambiguity, which was difficult to explain to those in the International who were inclined to be suspicious of Marx as a German. He openly favored a Prussian victory, not really out of German nationalism but because he believed that a war of national unification for Germany, resulting in the defeat of Napoleon III and the end of the reactionary Second Empire, would be an overall progressive development. And he was faithful to this position: Once Napoleon III had fallen, Marx came over to the side of the French republicans. At the same time, Marx's and Engels's correspondence at this time reveals a strong sense of satisfaction that Germans appeared to be replacing Frenchmen as leaders in Europe, a development which in their eyes meant that their "German" theories would more easily gain an ascendancy over the "French" theories of Proudhon.

When the Paris Commune arose out of the ashes of defeat, Marx became its ardent defender. This was the occasion of one of his most powerful essays, *The Civil War in France* (first delivered to the International and then distributed in pamphlet form). It was through his defense of the Commune that Marx earned the kind of notoriety associated with his name ever since—"the best calumniated and most menaced man of London" (McLellan, *Marx, His Life*, p. 402), as he self-satisfiedly described himself in a letter to a friend. It was widely believed in anti-socialist circles that the International had somehow plotted the uprising in Paris, and behind these intrigues stood the "monster," Karl Marx. It was in a way the high point of his life as an activist.

The genesis of the Commune out of France's defeat in the Franco-Prussian War is a bewilderingly complex story. One of the initial sources of confusion is the diverse ways in which the term "commune" is used. The word often refers to the uprising as well as to the Parisian municipal government, which is what "commune" means in French. All major cities in France have communal or municipal governments. But the Commune of Paris had a special history and a revolutionary mystique, for between 1789 and 1795 it was through the organs of municipal government that the Parisian sans-culottes put pressure on the national government. Above all, the Paris Commune was remembered for its heroic efforts in rallying the population of Paris, in organizing the volunteer armies of 1792–93 around *la patrie en danger*, the fatherland threatened by foreign invasion.

Thus to call for new communal elections in 1870–71 had great symbolic—and more than mere patriotic—significance. The invaders represented reactionary forces, and the military mobilization of the masses in France led to a shift in social and political power, by arming the people, by urging them to take initiative, by establishing "direct democracy." Thus the crushing defeat of the armies of the Second Empire by the Prussians was seen by the Left in France as an opportunity and by the Right as a potentially dangerous prelude to social upheaval, since both Left and Right were preoccupied with visions of events some eighty years before.

Immediately after Napoleon III's capture on the battlefield in September 1870, a republic was proclaimed in France and a Provisional Government of National Defense established. It was composed mostly of moderate republicans—certainly not men who were looking for a fundamental social upheaval. But central authority was rapidly disintegrating, and the stage was being set now for the complex struggles inside Paris of the next eight months. Activists of all shades rushed to join the "vigilance committees" set up by members of the International, and the committees grew in a turbulent, uncontrolled fashion, especially in the working-class districts of Montmartre and Belleville. At the same time the common people were being armed through the rapid expansion of the National Guard—which once again, as in 1848, was becoming "proletarianized."

These developments caused tremors of concern in the wealthier districts of Paris: Would all of this result in "popular excesses," in requisitions, in the growing impudence of the poor, in efforts to redistribute wealth, as had been the case in the 1790s? If communal elections were finally granted—and the demand for them was becoming more insistent by the day—would that not mean an even greater power in the hands of the social revolutionaries in Paris? If the war continued, would not the privations that would inevitably emerge from it intensify the resentments of the poor against the rich?

For these reasons the wealthier classes tended to favor a speedy peace, even if its terms were onerous. For the same reasons the leaders of the revolutionary Left were uncompromising and urged war *à outrance* until the enemy was driven from France. Since the Provisional Government of National Defense came to reflect the interests of those who favored peace, the alienation between it and the popular forces in Paris steadily intensified.

In the vast efflorescence of popular organizations—clubs, National Guard units, newspapers, conspiratorial groups—that emerged at this time, indigenous French ideologies and traditions were incomparably more important than Marxism. There were few if any Marxists among leading activists, especially among those who were native Frenchmen. Even the members of the International were overwhelmingly Proudhonist. Among those of a jacobin coloration an important proportion were explicitly non-socialist, although still committed to social justice and reform. Blanquists and social jacobins made up most of the rest.

However, distinctions between political persuasions were not always clear, and many of the activists of the time resisted classification. All were intensely patriotic, and all harbored a suspicion of the rich and idle, who were assumed to be mostly "defeatist" or even "treasonous." The Proudhonists, while explicitly calling themselves "socialists," (or "mutualists," or "federalists"), were scarcely distinguishable on issues of private property and individualism from the explicitly non-socialist jacobins, but the Proudhonists tended to be men who had taken an active part in the labor movement of the 1860s, while the jacobins and Blanquists had not. Most of the activists of all persuasions came from the Parisian petty bourgeoisie and artisanry, although there were important numbers of déclassé intellectuals of bourgeois origin. Factory workers played only a minor role, especially among the more visible leaders.

Thus, to return to a familiar theme, in spite of the generation that had passed since 1848, one that had seen considerable industrial growth in France, the Parisian activists of 1871 largely resembled those of 1848, and in spite of Marx's defense of them the Communards were not the factory proletarians that his theory predicted would crush capitalism and introduce socialism.

This is not to imply that social reform and even socialism were not key concerns of these activists. Their differences lay not so much in whether or not France should be extensively reformed but rather in whether that reform should be undertaken through centralized state direction or through pervasive decentralization. For the Proudhonists the Paris Commune was to be an independent municipality, significant as a model for the self-governing communes that were to be established throughout France, free from parasitic statism. But for the jacobins, the

Paris Commune was seen rather as a means of exercising enlightened—and, if necessary, dictatorial—leadership over the entire country.

As in 1848 France's rural majority considered it presumptuous for the "reds" in Paris to believe that they had the right to rule in name of the nation at large. Thus when elections to the new National Assembly were held in February 1871 (after all efforts to rally France against the Prussians had failed), a strongly conservative majority was returned: Out of 675 seats only 200 were even nominally republican, and many of these were republicans of a socially conservative stripe. The remaining 475 were divided into monarchist and Bonapartist factions. The Assembly was thus much more conservative than the retiring Provisional Government.

Within a short time serious trouble was brewing between the National Assembly and Paris. The acceptance of the extremely punitive peace treaty by the Assembly was a source of particular outrage in Paris. But the Assembly also passed a number of measures that seemed to the Parisians to constitute downright provocation. One of the Assembly's first acts was to curtail severely the number of those in the National Guard who received pay. For many of the working men in Paris their 1.50 franc daily payment as National Guardsmen was an important source of income; it had come to represent a kind of unemployment relief. The Assembly also declared an end to the wartime moratorium on various kinds of debts (such as rents and promissory notes). Payment with interest was now declared to be due. This measure was especially resented by the lower and lower-middle classes in Paris, since immediate payment would most benefit the wealthy, a large majority of whom had left the beleaguered city. Moreover, the economic dislocation caused by the war meant that most of the poorer citizens had little income with which to pay their debts. Thus the long-standing antipathy between Paris and the provinces took on dimensions of a social conflict, between owners and debtors.

Adolphe Thiers, who had assumed leadership of the National Assembly, arrived in Paris in early March. He encountered an ugly mood, and he quickly concluded that immediate military action should be taken by the Assembly. After bungling an effort at disarming the unruly and angry National Guard and arresting leading revolutionaries, he abandoned the capital, leaving orders for the complete evacuation of the army and of his ministers, who were to join him with the National Assembly, which was meeting in Versailles, some twenty-five miles to the southwest of Paris.

The gauntlet was down. With Thiers out of town, the recently formed Central Committee of the National Guard took over the Hôtel de Ville and assumed general governmental authority over the city. A spontaneous revolution thus occurred in response to Thiers's action. The Central Committee then arranged for elections to the Paris Commune, as had been so long demanded. The communal council that was returned in these elections was dominated by a coalition of Blanquists and jacobins, with a minority contingent of Proudhonists, all far to the left of the National Assembly.

Paris was "free." No doubt in a realistic, long-range sense "Paris libre" was a hopeless, quixotic notion, given the city's isolation from the rest of France and Thiers's grim determination to destroy the communal government. Yet, for a time at least, Paris's citizens appeared strangely able, in spite of the almost continuous noise of gunfire on the outskirts of the city, to cast from their minds the ominous signs of a coming clash with the gathering forces of the National Assembly at Versailles. A kind of holiday spirit prevailed—what Lenin later termed a "festival of the oppressed." The residents of the city took advantage of the fine spring weather to turn out in great numbers for such ceremonies as the burning of the guillotine and the toppling of the immense Vendôme Column (which had been erected by Napoleon I to commemorate his military victories; under the Second Empire it became for the Left a hated symbol of imperial despotism). The poorer citizens thronged to the inner city, from which many of them had been removed by the Empire's extensive urban redevelopment. This influx brought to the *boulevards* a boisterous, plebeian gaiety that had not been seen there for many years. For a short time at least many of Paris's formerly humble residents became actively involved in public affairs, suggesting the popular participation of the city-states of ancient Greece. Even when the gaiety began to ebb, such ceremonies as the funerals for the National Guardsmen who had fallen in the defense of the city became great public spectacles, attended by huge crowds. And, during the very last days, as the Versailles troops were advancing into the city, there were large, oddly festive crowds listening to the last of a series of concerts presented to aid the wounded, widowed, and orphaned of the city.

The Commune enthusiastically launched into a program of social reform. Historians have debated the extent to which the Commune's efforts in this direction can be termed socialist: Significantly the measures introduced were not aimed at an immediate socialization of the means of production or the immediate redistribution of wealth—although there were certainly insistent demands in some quarters for such measures. But whether clearly socialist or not, many of the reforms introduced by the Commune were reforms that had been vainly demanded by the labor movement and by socialists since the 1840s.

The Commune established a Commission of Labor and Exchange, something like the ministry that Blanc had hoped for in 1848 before he was shunted off into the Luxembourg Commission. The new Commission was headed by the Hungarian socialist and friend of Marx, Leo Frankel, and was devoted primarily to improving working conditions in Paris. It also prevailed upon the Commune to allow trade unions and workers' cooperatives to take over those factories abandoned by their owners.

Ambitious projects involving cooperative production and the radical reform of education were undertaken, but too little time was allowed the Communards for them to accomplish much of real significance. Thiers put into effect a strategy he had advocated in June 1848, which involved total withdrawal from the city, weakening it through a siege, and then delivering a lightning blow once the population had been brought to its knees through hunger and privation.

The siege lasted nine weeks. As stocks dwindled, the animals of the zoo were slaughtered for food. Restaurants, true to the spirit of the festival of the oppressed, served up exotic dishes from the flesh of giraffes and crocodiles. But this stage soon passed, and Parisians were forced to eat their pets, stray cats, rats, grass, glue from the wallpaper or from furniture—anything of the remotest food value. In the final battles between the Communards and the Versailles troops, much of the center of Paris was aflame. The fires were either set by desperate revolutionaries who wished to witness the destruction of the homes of the wealthy and the monuments symbolic of the tyranny of the state before they themselves met their end, or else they spread in the intensive bombardments by Thiers's troops. On the barricades no quarter was given by either side. Summary executions by Versailles troops proceeded relentlessly throughout Bloody Week at the end of May. Captives, when they were taken, were often subjected to brutal treatment; contemporary accounts at times call strikingly to mind the horrors of twentieth-century warfare and concentration camps.

The most famous battle occurred at the last great stronghold, in the Père Lachaise cemetery. About two hundred Communards fought in desperate hand-to-hand combat among the tombstones with the Versailles troops. At the end of the battle, 147 of the Communards were taken prisoner, lined up against the back wall of the cemetery, and shot. A large mound still marks the spot where they were collectively buried. From the 1880s to the present day, socialist and communist militants have made a yearly pilgrimage to the *mur des fédérés* (wall of the Communards) on May 23, and now the graves in the surrounding area are filled with famous French socialists and communists of the late nineteenth and the twentieth centuries.

When the last smoke of battle settled, perhaps twenty-thousand Communards had been executed. Many more died in prison, especially in the pestiferous tropical exile prisons. Paris lost something like fifty thousand workers and political activists. As many as seventy thousand others left—those who immediately escaped capture as well as relatives, immediate family, friends of activists—in the repressive months and years that followed.

Revolutionaries gained a new pantheon of heroes and martyrs, and students of revolutions were provided with new lessons to be learned. Marx's own reflections on the Commune have been scrutinized with particular interest because here, as in the case of his writings of 1848–50, are to be found above all the supposed Marxist foundations of Leninism. Marx described the Commune as the first example of working-class rule in the nineteenth century. Implicitly—although he did not himself at this time use the exact phrase—it also represented a concrete historical example of his conception of the dictatorship of the proletariat (as noted, it was Engels who later made this explicit). He believed that the experience of the Commune offered several important lessons to revolutionaries, the most important of which, as already alluded to, was that revolutionaries needed to do more than seize bourgeois state power; they needed to *smash* it, as the Communards had done, to destroy its bureaucratic structures and replace them with structures of direct working-class rule.

Some students of Marx have seen in these remarks evidence of "totalitarian" tendencies. But Marx's position in 1871, as in 1848–50, may be distinguished, in its libertarian and anti-elitist aspects, from that of the Leninists as well as from the Blanquists, as already discussed. Even Marx's criticism of the revolutionaries of 1871 for being insufficiently decisive, for hesitating to use violence pre-emptively against Thiers—a criticism that Lenin particularly valued—cannot facilely be described as showing a proclivity for violent solutions. It must be remembered that Thiers was uncompromisingly intent on overwhelming the revolutionaries in Paris by force. Such being the case a pre-emptive strike by the Communards could have been considered an act of simple self-defense.

The issue here is hardly clear-cut, since Thiers had the support of a national majority, while the Communards were supported only by a questionable majority of a much depleted Parisian population. Even more elusive but of very great importance for later Marxists is a related question, often referred to as the "hegemony" or "leading role" of the working class. Marx's own political activities make it reasonably clear that while he considered the proletariat to be the only consistently revolutionary class in capitalist society he did not necessarily expect that the working class would itself compose a majority at the time of the revolution. It would be sufficient if the revolutionary proletariat won the support of the majority of the population (in other words, assumed a leading role or exercised a hegemony over it, replacing the capitalist bourgeoisie as the hegemonial class). In actual practice, of course, the working class remained far from attaining hegemony in 1871, but it was a goal toward which Marx and later Marxists devoted much of their political activity.

We cannot explore these difficult yet fascinating issues here. Suffice it to remark that enough ambiguity remained in Marx's statements concerning such issues as proletarian dictatorship, the use of violence and terror, discipline and centralization, and working-class hegemony that his various epigones, from Kautsky to Lenin, could plausibly claim fidelity to his thought. Lenin was himself a careful student of the Commune, and he studied with particular interest what Marx believed to be its main practical lessons. Lenin would not be a captive of legalism, bourgeois morality, indecisiveness, or fear of violence. He would make special efforts to win over the peasantry and would insist at all times on a unified, disciplined party of revolution. He considered it a great victory when his own revolution, in desperate straits in 1918, had survived one day longer than the Commune.

GUIDE TO FURTHER READING

A mere listing of the titles devoted to Marx and Marxism could easily fill a volume larger than this one, and each year a veritable avalanche of new books and articles appears, especially dealing with the young Marx and the philosophical foundations of his theories. The following represents a limited selection of those titles that I have found useful or that have been favorably reviewed in professional journals. In the most recent of them one can find further bibliographical references to the scholarship of the past generation.

To begin with biographies that have achieved the status of standard works, Isaiah Berlin's *Karl Marx, His Life and Environment* is a concise and approachable introduction to Marx and Marxism by a world-renowned British scholar. Long considered the definitive biography of Marx, Franz Mehring's *Karl Marx: The Story of His Life* cannot be unqualifiedly recommended to the modern reader, who will likely soon tire of its inflated prose and aggressive partisan-ship. A more modern, less tiresome, yet still admiring full-scale biography is that by Boris Nicolaievsky and Otto Maenchen-Helfen, *Karl Marx, Man and Fighter*. The most exhaustive biography of both Marx and Engels is the multi-volumed work of Auguste Cornu, *Karl Marx et Friedrich Engels*. An admirable recent short study is by Werner Blumenberg, *Karl Marx*. All things considered, the most satisfactory full-scale biography of Marx is by David McLellan, *Karl Marx, His Life and Thought*. This work is not an effort at a major re-interpreta-tion, but it is highly readable, well balanced, and makes use of a wide variety of sources, including the most recent. McLellan has also written, edited, and translated a number of other volumes having to do with Marxism, each of which merits the respectful attention of anyone taking up the study of Marxism.

Readers desiring exposure to more critical biographies and general stud-ies of Marxism have much to choose from. A cut above the many polemical anti-Marxist, nonscholarly works, although still dripping with vitriol, is Leopold Schwarzchild's *Karl Marx: The Red Prussian*. Also highly critical of Marx, al-though from the standpoint of his economic theory rather than his personality, is M. M. Bober's *Karl Marx's Interpretation of History*. A masterly volume, al-ready discussed in the bibliographical essay of the Introduction, is George Lichtheim's *Marxism, An Historical and Critical Study*. Roughly comparable in scope and more gracefully written is Bertram Wolfe, *Marxism: One Hundred Years in the Life of a Doctrine*.

Three concise studies, most helpful in understanding Marxist theory, are Alfred G. Meyer, *Marxism, The Unity of Theory and Practice*; Stanley Moore, *Three Tactics: The Background of Marx*; and I. M. Zeitlin, *Marxism: A Re-exami-nation*.

An ambitious effort to digest and reformulate *Das Kapital* within Marxist lines is *The Theory of Capitalist Development* by Paul Sweezy. A comparable Marxist reformulation of Marx, reflecting a most impressive, catholic learning is Ernest Mandel's *Marxist Economic Theory*.

Richard N. Hunt's *The Political Ideas of Marx and Engels* (vol. 1: *Marxism and Totalitarian Democracy, 1815–1850*; a second volume is forthcoming) is a model of erudition and clarity.

A good selection from the writings of some of the major scholars of Marx-ism can be found in Tom Bottomore, ed., *Karl Marx*. Of the plethora of edited selections from Marx's and Engels's own writings, Robert C. Tucker's *The Marx-Engels Reader* is as good as any. The bibliography in McLellan's biography of Marx, listed above, contains reference to most of the other important collec-tions of primary sources.

The reader who would like to attain a deeper grasp of the philosophical background of Marxism must be prepared to plunge into some esoteric and controversial works. A good beginning would be Leszek Kolakowski's *Main Cur-rents of Marxism*. Widely respected but hardly light reading is Jacques-Yves Calvez's substantial tome, *La Pensée de Karl Marx*. Long a standard work, Sid-ney Hook's *From Hegel to Marx* is at times opaque because of its recourse to technical philosophical jargon. Much more approachable, although the object of considerable scholarly controversy, are Erich Fromm's *Marx's Concept of Man* and Robert C. Tucker's *Philosophy and Myth in Karl Marx*. A more recent work by Bertell Ollman, *Alienation: Marx's Concept of Man in Capitalist Society*, has received critical praise for bringing clarity into this murky area. A useful but by now somewhat dated article that further discusses some of the literature on the philosophical aspects of Marxism is by Daniel Bell, "In Search of a Marxist Humanism: The Debate on Alienation," *Soviet Survey* 32 (April-June, 1960). More recent and a model of clarity is Melvin Rader's *Marx's Interpretation of History*. Representing an opposing and more orthodox Marxist point of view is Louis Althusser's *For Marx*, a book of considerable influence and controversy.

The middle chapters of George Lichtheim's *Marxism* attempt to put Marx's thought firmly in historical context. A broader work dealing with the 1850s and 1860s, particularly attuned to the themes of the history of socialism, is E. J. Hobsbawm's *The Age of Capital, 1848–1875*.

The most recent and generally most satisfactory work in English on the Paris Commune is by Steward Edwards, *The Paris Commune, 1871*, which reflects recent French scholarship, often of a very impressive quality. The hundredth anniversary of the Paris Commune prompted a flood of books and articles, some lavishly illustrated, as for example Georges Bourgin's *La Guerre de 1870–1871 et la Commune*. The *International Review of Social History* devoted the first two volumes of its 1972 issue to essays on the Commune, under the general editorship of Jacques Rougerie, one of the most promising of French scholars of the Commune. John Hicks and Robert Tucker have collected essays in English for *Revolution and Reaction: The Paris Commune of 1871*. They vary considerably in quality and general interest; particularly worthy of mention is Monty Johnstone's "The Paris Commune and Marx's Conception of the Dictatorship of the Proletariat." E. Schulkind, in *The Paris Commune of 1871: The View from the Left*, has collected the comments of later anarchists and Marxists on the Commune. Good short introductions to the Commune are Roger Williams's *The French Revolution of 1870–1871*, a graceful synthesis; and Stewart Edwards's collection of documents, with very useful introductory comment, *The Communards of Paris, 1871*. Older but still valuable studies are Edward S. Mason, *The Paris Commune*, which reflects a more conservative viewpoint, and Frank Jellinek's *The Paris Commune of 1871*, which is a detailed Marxist treatment.

Socialism as a Major Force, 1870-1914

4

Between 1870 and 1914 socialism emerged as a major force in European history. Reformist, Marxist, and anarchist varieties of socialism, socialist trade unions, cooperatives, newspapers, and a myriad of related organizations grew with a speed and regularity that soon awakened new anxieties in the ranks of Europe's ruling elites. The high point of capitalism from the 1850s through the 1860s was followed from 1873 to the early 1890s by what was considered at the time to be a "great depression." It mostly affected England and particular sectors of the economy, above all agriculture and heavy industry, and entailed a slowing of the rate of growth rather than an actual decline. While mild by the standards of the 1930s, it nevertheless delivered a rude shock to capitalism and the confident liberal ideology associated with it. In some ways it was more disturbing to bourgeois tranquillity than the violent outburst of the Paris Commune.

Other factors also tended to undermine confidence in the viability and permanence of the free-market system. The rising flood of cheap grains from North America caused farmers and large landowners to clamor for renewed tariff barriers, just as many industrialists, alarmed by the unexpected economic fluctuations of the 1870s and 1880s, also looked to government protection. Thus in many quarters, aside from those of the working class, there were insistent demands for state intervention, and in most of Europe's states, tariffs and other varieties of state involvement in the workings of the market were introduced.

This climate proved favorable to a revival of interest in socialism. Many other factors favored recruitment to socialist causes: the expansion of industry, spurred now by a so-called "second industrial revolution" that favored heavy concentrations of capital and labor; the growth in the numbers of urban workers; the rise of mass literacy; the extension of the franchise; and the generally greater assertiveness and visibility of the lower orders. By 1914 socialists in most western European countries could point with pride to large parliamentary delegations, influential daily newspapers, strong trade unions, and devoted, card-carrying members of socialist parties, in most of these respects unmatched by either their liberal or conservative competitors.

THE SPREAD OF MARXISM IN THE 1880s

The attractions of Marxist theory for the working-class parties that began to emerge in the 1870s and 1880s can to an important degree be attributed to the status of Marxism as the most sophisticated and "scientific" analysis of capitalist development. It was a theory that offered a coherent explanation of the difficulties in which the capitalist system found itself in those years, and that furthermore showed capitalism as inexorably preparing the advent of socialism. Other, older ideologies like Blanquism or Proudhonism, while retaining a following, tended to pale in comparison with the imposing body of Marxist theory. Moreover, industrial workers were becoming an ever more important element of the working class, consonant with Marx's theories, and efforts to recruit them into disciplined class-conscious parties now met with greater success. Still, the vast majority of unskilled factory workers remained outside the ranks of socialist organizations, and the most prominent figures in most socialist parties remained former artisans, skilled workers, or members of the leftist bourgeois intelligentsia.

In the 1880s a particular effort was made to popularize Marx's theories, to make them more accessible to a growing reading public, workers and nonworkers. Extremely important in this effort was Engels's publication of a work usually known as the "Anti-Dühring" because one of his purposes in writing it was to refute the theories of Eugen Dühring, an anti-Semitic economist who had gained some popularity at the time and who advocated a reformed capitalism through a strong labor movement. Three general chapters of the Anti-Dühring were translated for the French- and English-speaking world in the early 1880s as Socialism: Utopian and Scientific. The chapters were not primarily a polemic against Dühring; rather, they provided a clear and simple exposition of the main tenets of Marxism, somewhat fuller and more didactic than the Communist Manifesto (which also began to find a mass readership at this time), but more approachable to the average reader than most of Marx's own works. Even intellectuals like Karl Kautsky and Eduard Bernstein, who became leading theorists of the

German social-democratic movement in the 1880s and 1890s, were first strongly attracted to Marxism by reading the *Anti-Dühring*. Kautsky observed that "no book has done so much for the understanding of Marxism as this one" (Steenson, p. 35).

Interest in Marx's writings was widespread in the 1880s and 1890s. Many intellectuals who would never be associated with a Marxist movement nevertheless recognized a large debt to Marx in their own intellectual development. Among those who did join Marxist organizations, however, the process of digesting Marx's ideas was a long and difficult one. Indeed, even among those politicians and working-class activists who worked to build up Marxist movements in the major countries of western Europe in the late nineteenth century, Marxism remained imperfectly and superficially understood—a cause for repeated lamentation on the part of Marx and Engels. Further, the parties that became known as Marxist retained in their programs elements that were contrary to Marx's teachings. Shortly before his death in 1883, Marx, in following the flailings of the self-proclaimed Marxists in France, despairingly observed to Engels, "one thing is certain: *I* am not a Marxist!" (Nicolaievsky, p. 403).

Even for the party that came to be regarded as a model for Marxists, the party that resulted from the unification of the Eisenachers and Lassalleans and that was known for most of its long history as the SPD (*Sozialdemokratische Partei Deutschlands*, or Social-Democratic Party of Germany), such remarks were applicable, above all in its first years of existence. After unification in 1875 most of the party leaders not only failed to give serious study to Marx's writings but often avoided the advice proffered from London (where Marx and Engels continued to reside). It will be recalled that the Gotha Program of 1875 was the cause of a searing, though nonpublic, critique by Marx, in part because of what he considered its muddleheaded democratic phraseology but above all because of the Lassallean elements retained in it.

Those who were least inclined to take Marx seriously were the so-called moderates in the party, most of whom had been associated with the Lassallean ADAV and who held seats in the Reichstag. Under the influence of such men the SPD entered into the parliamentary life of the new Reich with a surprisingly positive and hopeful spirit. But this spirit was not easy to maintain. Although Bismarck had seen fit to give the vote in Reichstag elections to all adult males, he detested democrats and socialists, above all Marxists. As soon as the social democrats had united and had begun to show promise of rapid growth, Bismarck began a series of attacks on them, culminating in the Anti-Socialist

Laws of 1878. This legislation crippled social-democratic activity in a wide variety of areas, including trade unions, consumers' cooperatives, educational societies, even glee clubs. The main area legally left open to the social democrats was election to the Reichstag, although here too their activity was much inhibited (Bismarck had tried to convince the Reichstag deputies to outlaw social-democratic parliamentary partici- pation but without success). For the next twelve years the SPD became a kind of outlawed party, its followers put under police surveillance, its leaders arrested, intimidated, or driven into exile.

Such attacks of course undermined the moderates' hopes that the SPD could play a positive role in the political life of the new Reich. However, the SPD leadership did not really fight back vigorously. Rather, it did its best to abide by and adjust to the conditions of the Anti-Socialist Laws, hoping they would be repealed. To Bismarck's ir- ritation, the social democrats, after a temporary setback in the early 1880s, went from victory to victory at the polls.

The party leaders' hopes that Germany's liberals would rally to their side, that they would firmly oppose Bismarck's highly illiberal policies and repeal the Anti-Socialist Laws, proved vain. Inevitably this new evidence of the feebleness of German liberalism reduced the hopes even among social-democratic moderates for class cooperation. The SPD became ever more clearly a class party. Similarly favorable to the Marxist perspective, the Bismarckian state appeared inflexibly hostile, unlikely ever to be won over peacefully to social reform and real liberal- democratic procedure. The curtailment of trade-union activity was es- pecially resented by workers; it helped further to convince many of them that on the one hand the government was inalterably opposed to their aspirations and on the other that the social democrats were their only true friends.

Thus, if many of the refinements of Marxist theory remained dimly understood by SPD militants, and if they refused an actual revo- lutionary counteroffensive against Bismarck, his actions and the gen- eral political climate in which the social democrats found themselves forced them to move away from the more positive Lassallean attitude to the state and to abandon hopes for class cooperation. At the same time the 1870s and 1880s in Germany were a period of rapid economic development, punctuated by disorienting ups and downs of the market. German social democrats could thus find in Marx's writings not only a sophisticated explanation of their political situation but also of the rapid expansion of large industry, the disappearance of the older trades, the proletarianization of much of the labor force, and the overall urbanization of German society.

Indeed, the social democrats were not the only ones to draw anti-capitalist conclusions from these economic and social trends. The 1880s witnessed a flurry of anti-capitalist literature and theorizing, much of it by anti-bourgeois conservatives who looked to a strong authoritarian state to remedy the social question in Germany.

Bismarck himself viewed the economic disruptions of these years as an opportunity to win over the lower orders, to place workers on the side of his authoritarian state. But the program of social legislation he offered, while it may well have reduced the level of insecurity and resentment among manual laborers, failed to wean them away from their growing attachment to the SPD and its affiliated trade unions, or— nearly as bad in Bismarck's eyes—to shake the fidelity of Catholic workers to Catholic political and trade-union institutions in those areas, such as the Rhineland, where there was a large Catholic working class. Of course, many German workers remained outside the orbit of either the SPD or the Church, and Bismarck's policies may well have encouraged a subliminal acceptance, from workers of all persuasions, of the state's role in defending the poor. But he clearly failed in his main purpose of destroying the political power of the socialists and the Catholics in Germany.

In 1890 Bismarck was unable to obtain a renewal of the Anti-Socialist Laws (they had been renewed every two or three years since 1878), and the SPD then reconstituted itself, with relative freedom of action, although the possibility of a re-introduction of legislation hostile to the party continued to hang over its head. The new party program adopted at Erfurt in 1891, which was worked out by the leading party theoretician, Karl Kautsky, with the collaboration of Engels (who lived on until 1895), struck a more openly Marxist tone than had been the case with the Gotha program. The preamble above all drove home such themes as the inevitable concentration of heavy industry, the growth of monopoly production, the proletarianization of the labor force, immiseration, class conflict, and the final resolution of capitalist contradictions through socialism and the end of class society.

However, the ensuing list of specific demands, or minimum program, although expunging the Lassallean elements of the Gotha program, such as the references to state-aided producers' cooperatives, was still one favoring democratic-radical reform that could in principle—however unlikely in practice—have been promulgated under the existing Reich government without a political upheaval. These demands contained, in other words, no explicit mention of a revolutionary proletarian dictatorship or of socialization of the means of production. Indeed, even the Marxist preamble skirted explicit advocacy of a violent seizure of power or of a proletarian dictatorship. Such reticence, while understandable given the threat of renewed anti-socialist legislation, in fact reflected more than mere tactical caution, as would become abundantly clear in the following years.

The evolution of Marxist movements in France in these years provides some revealing contrasts. In some ways the most prominent French Marxists were more explicit and dogmatic in their Marxism than were the Germans. Marx's son-in-law, Paul Lafargue, who married Laura Marx in 1864, was in constant contact with Marx and Engels, and Jules Guesde was usually more inclined to seek and to follow Marx's and Engels's advice than were either Liebknecht or Bebel. But the conditions under which the French Marxists had to work—political, economic, social, and cultural—were significantly different from those in Germany.

From the beginning French Marxists were faced with powerful competitors for the allegiance of the French working class, competitors who were often militantly anti-Marxist rather than subtly resistant to it, as was the case with the moderates in the SPD. French Marxists were thus obliged to distinguish with relative precision their position from that of the democratic radicals, since the jacobin tradition exercised a still powerful attraction among French workers. It was with good reason that Guesde considered the "radicals," as they were now called in France, to be key competitors of the Marxists, whereas in Germany a comparable democratic-radical movement in the 1880s and 1890s was weak and no longer a serious competitor to the SPD. In addition there were the Blanquists, Proudhonists, and Bakuninists, among the older pre-Marxian, anarchist, or Utopian persuasions, plus such newer tendencies as the Independents, Possibilists, Allemanists, and anarcho-syndicalists (discussed below). The latter part of the nineteenth century witnessed a dizzying confusion of sectarian socialist conflicts in France. The solid and lasting unity of the German social democrats after 1875 long eluded the French socialists.

The diversity of French socialist tendencies and the stubborn resistance of the French socialists to unification were also encouraged by the country's peculiar economic and social structures in the nineteenth century. Although French industry expanded steadily, its overall rate of economic growth in important ways fell behind the growth rates of Ger-

many, the United States, or even Russia. France did not experience so
sudden a transformation of its economic and social structures. In 1870
just over half of its active population was engaged in agriculture; in
1914 the figure was still over 40 percent. The rate of change in Germany
was much more rapid: For approximately the same period its rural
population dropped from two-thirds to one-third of the total. Similarly,
France's total population in those years grew only slightly, from 36 to
39 million, while Germany's soared from 41 to 65 million, resulting in
the movement of something like 20 million of its citizens into urban life
and modern industrial employment. This great movement from rural
to urban life had no clear parallel in France, which remained more typically a country of small enterprise and luxury production, of independent peasants, of shopkeepers, and of skilled artisans who worked in
small shops rather than factories.

     Thus, at a time when the potential following of the SPD was in-
creasingly proletarianized, concentrated, and deeply threatened by
modern industrial techniques, French Marxists had to contend with a
working class that remained relatively heterogeneous and independent,
and one that constituted as well a significantly smaller proportion of
the total French population. It is plausible to assume that such workers,
by their national environment and their very conditions of work, would
normally be less inclined to accept a theory that emphasized the inevitable triumph of modern, concentrated production and the concomitant need to organize in a centralized, disciplined mass party. The
skilled worker or artisan exercised an important degree of job control,
was less affected by economic booms and busts, and did not experience
the collective, disciplined life of the factory worker. The considerable
social distance between factory hand and owner was less important in
the small workshop; owner and employee usually worked together, and
notions of the inevitability of class conflict seemed less appropriate. For
many French workers solidarity and cooperation were more likely to
find expression in small-scale producers' and consumers' cooperatives
than in mass parties or in trade unions that emphasized disciplined
and concentrated organization in order to advance working-class interests, through collective pressure either on employers or on the institutions of the bourgeois state.

     These various structural factors no doubt help explain why social-
ism, and more particularly Marxism, spread far less rapidly in France
than in Germany. (As a very rough approximation it can be said that
from the 1880s to World War I the French socialist movement remained
about one-tenth the size of the German; the disparity in parliamentary

support was not so great, whereas the German trade unions were even more than ten times as large as the French.) However, the scholarship of the past ten to fifteen years that has painstakingly examined particular trades or geographical areas, "from the bottom up," has revealed how bewilderingly complex were the correlations between political affiliation and occupational identity, and indeed how careful one must be in equating industrial growth and the spread of socialism or Marxism.

In a monumental study of the workers of the Lyonnais region, Ives Lequin has discovered that anarchism flourished among all kinds of workers and that while the industrial workers of Roanne gravitated to Guesde's Marxist organizations so did the artisans in Lyons. The coal miners and metalworkers of the Stephanois basin—usually seen as the epitome of hard-bitten proletarians—were attracted to the Independents, who, with their emphasis on parliamentary reform and class collaboration, were supposedly more attractive to petty-bourgeois democratic radicals.

Further confounding Marxist perspectives, in those areas that saw a rapidly accelerating pace of mechanization and concentration before World War I, with a concomitant lessening of emphasis on skill, increased resentment and working-class militancy did not result, but rather quiescence and apathy. As Barrington Moore notes in *Injustice, The Social Bases of Obedience and Revolt*, the ability of German social-democratic trade unions to win wage contracts "remained concentrated in smaller firms where conditions remained similar to those of a workshop in a handicraft. Before the war [social-democratic] Free Unions had made hardly any inroads into heavy industry, iron, steel, or chemicals. In other words, the Marxists had yet to gain a foothold in the core of the modern industrial proletariat" (p. 183).

Still more surprisingly, some of the areas in France with high proportions of socialist members and voters had almost no industry and a sparse population. Tony Judt and Maurice Agulhon have shown that the peasants of the Var rallied to socialism, even to Marxist variants, for a complex set of reasons that had little to do with the march of modern industry. The residents of the Var had long ago shaken free of the influence of both the Catholic Church and the large landholding *notables*; they had strong local traditions of municipal cooperation; and since at least the time of the French Revolution they had been strongly leftist. In only one limited way does it seem that the forces of industrialization propelled the peasants of the Var toward socialism: Those communes that produced wine for a wide market tended also to vote heavily for socialism, ostensibly because they had come to understand the importance of political considerations in seeking to remedy their sense of grievance with impersonal economic forces, and because, more generally, their livelihood drew them into a wider world than was the case for most peasants.

The contrast between political situations in France and Germany also helps explain why Marxism was more readily embraced by German than by French Socialists. Bismarck's authoritarian Reich favored an elite of Junkers and Rhenish-Westphalian industrial magnates who were contemptuous of the notion of popular rule and were certain to resist violently any efforts to introduce it. (Universal manhood suffrage existed for elections to the lower house, or Reichstag, but the Reichstag could not dismiss the chancellor—a power that lay solely in the hands of the kaiser—and within the powerful Kingdom of Prussia, which encompassed a major portion of the Reich, no attempt was made even to construct a façade of popular rule.) The French Third Republic, established after the fall of the Commune, while initially in the hands of conservative and vehemently anti-socialist politicians, was nevertheless a liberal-democratic parliamentary system. Its political elites, unlike those of Germany, shifted according to changes in popular opinion and changing historical realities.

The temptation, in short, for French socialists and other reformers to believe in the possibility of peaceful reform through the liberal-democratic state, once a majority had been won, was understandably greater than for German socialists, who were more likely to conclude that only through an ultimate destruction of the existing state could the will of the German masses for democratic rule and socialism be expressed.

In this light, Guesde's principled rejection in the 1880s of the parliamentary-reformist path may be seen as another factor in the initially poor showing of Marxists in France. Guesde's critics believed that he was adopting a dogmatic position, one that might be appropriate for Germany but not for France. And there is little denying that Guesde's position parroted that of Kautsky at this time: Electoral campaigns and the parliamentary arena generally were to be considered primarily as opportunities to make propaganda, occasions to denounce capitalism and the ruling class. No meaningful reforms could be passed through parliament so long as real power—that is, power based on the ownership of the means of production—remained in the hands of capitalists and other wealthy elites.

One of the more ironic aspects of the spread of Marxism in France—and the situation is full of ironies—is that some of Guesde's most prominent opponents were more familiar with and sensitive to the nuances of Marx's writings than was Guesde. What they often objected to most were Guesde's stiff and authoritarian manners, his "uncritical admiration" for the German social democrats, and his "taking orders" from his masters in London—all of which they saw as an importation of Germanic theoretical dogmatism and authoritarian practices into France.

Prominent among his opponents was the remarkable Benoît Malon, one of the very few socialist theoreticians who was of working-class origin. Malon had spent time in exile in Germany, where he learned German, made friends with leading German social democrats, and even translated the works of Lassalle into French. Back in France he founded the important *Revue socialiste* in 1885, in which he preached what he termed "integral socialism," an eclectic mix of French intellectual traditions, as diverse as the ideas of Babeuf and Saint-Simon, Proudhon and Comte.

Malon's integral socialism also included borrowings from Marx, but he emphasized the importance of ideal as well as material factors in history—a notion that was, as we have seen, not necessarily opposed to Marx's own views, but was certainly different in emphasis from Guesde's Marxism—and he looked to all the oppressed, not only workers or factory proletarians, to take up the cause of socialism. He thus hoped, unlike Guesde, to recruit members of the bourgeois Left into a new socialist party, and his efforts in that direction were important in converting a number of former radicals, most notably Jean Jaurès, the future leader of the unified socialist party.

Malon believed in the gradual raising of working-class consciousness through struggle for concrete reforms, above all reforms in local governing bodies. Such ideas may be considered Proudhonian-anarchist in tendency, but he mixed into them a more positive attitude to the state—he explicitly accepted Blanc's idea of the state as the financier of industrial cooperatives—and to the republic in particular. The central government would also have to attend to certain unavoidably centralized services, such as the railroads and postal service.

This mix of ideas found support from another important socialist leader of the 1880s, Paul Brousse. He rejected with particular decisiveness Guesde's revolutionary rhetoric and stressed that socialist militants should concentrate on reforms that were immediately possible. Guesde dismissed this "Possibilism" as illusory; the capitalist system, he contended, could not allow real reforms. He further charged that Brousse's reformism and localist approach would tend, by involving socialists in daily cooperation with the bourgeoisie, to dilute working-class identity and to obscure from workers their special role in the creation of a socialist society.

Although Brousse was widely perceived as a reformist opponent of the revolutionary Marxists, he also accepted many of the basic propositions of Marxism. He believed in the long-range tendency toward economic concentration under capitalism, in the evolution of increasingly hostile proletarian and bourgeois classes, in the need for a proletarian party whose eventual goal would be the conquest of political power by any possible means. He even accepted that at some future point a revolutionary class dictatorship might be necessary. The main difference between the Possibilists and Marxists in the 1880s had to do with the immediate questions of party organization and the related issue of the path to socialism. Brousse insisted that because of the uneven economic and social development in France, a decentralized, federalist approach was necessary, one which would give workers in particular areas wide leeway to introduce reforms and even to begin projects of socialization, before any final or nationwide confrontation. Guesde was intent on forging a centralized mass party with a program that was attractive to the unskilled, previously unorganized working class and that looked to the seizure of state power. The introduction of socialism would be necessarily centralized because of the realities of advanced industrial production.

Even the briefest examination of the situation in Great Britain reveals how surprisingly little Marxists from one country had in common with Marxists from another in the 1880s, or, put differently, how much Marxist movements were molded by national conditions. Marxists in Great Britain were very weak, much weaker than in France—a paradox because the English economy was the most advanced in Europe, with the largest concentration of factory workers, and it suffered more than either France or Germany from the ravages of the depression. England was the country, in other words, where one might have expected Marxism to be at its most powerful rather than at its weakest.

To say that Marxism failed to spread in England in the 1880s is not to imply that there was little interest in socialism or in collectivist answers to England's many problems. As in Germany there was widespread questioning of both liberalism and laissez-faire economics, although of course in the English case these had enjoyed a higher reputation and more general popularity in the previous fifty years.

Much of this questioning went under the name of "New Radicalism," whose proponents were increasingly receptive to the notion of a

large role for the state in opening up equality of opportunity and in
remedying the stubborn injustices that characterized industrial society.
Other critics of capitalism went distinctly beyond democratic-radical
conceptions by emphasizing more unequivocally socialist concerns:
above all, cooperation and "fellowship," as opposed to individualistic
competition, and a sense that society was an organic whole rather than
a collection of individuals in the utilitarian sense.

In this regard the evolution of the thought of John Stuart Mill is
instructive. Normally regarded as the classic defender of individualistic
liberalism, Mill, especially toward the end of his life (d. 1873), described
socialism as superior to individualism as a moral and social ideal. He
further expressed a deep faith in gradual human "improvement," that
is, toward a more altruistic-socialistic human nature, although he retained substantial doubts concerning socialism's immediate economic
feasibility, before human nature had been so transformed.

Such remarks were obviously difficult if not impossible to reconcile with utilitarian psychology (that is, that individual human beings
were now and for all times governed by the pleasure-pain calculus).
That many other English democratic radicals were moving in similar
directions to Mill reflected their dissatisfaction with such egocentric
and simplistic conceptions of the human personality and their yearning
for "higher," that is, more altruistic, political and social commitments.

The enormous popularity in this period of Henry George's Single-
Tax nostrum further reflected a widespread receptiveness to the idea of
a fundamental social and economic re-orientation. George's proposals
were not socialist proposals, at least not at the height of their popularity; he did not desire the socialization of the means of production nor
was he particularly concerned with matters of social cooperation and
fellowship. He merely called for an end, through a single tax, to the
"unfair" fortunes gained through rent in land. Still, his Single Tax was
certainly regarded as drastic, and in its questioning of the sanctity of
private property it set many to thinking in socialistic directions.

Further reflecting and adding to the dissatisfactions of these years
was a significant swelling of the ranks of organized labor. In the decade following 1882 trade-union membership grew from 750,000 to
1,500,000. This growth reflected to an important degree the influx of
unskilled factory workers, whose "new unions," unlike the established
craft and skilled unions, sharply questioned free-market principles and
openly embraced socialist solutions.

But these many tendencies did not yet have major political implications: No major party appeared on the left to challenge the Liberal

Party, whether it be socialist, Marxist, radical, or simply labor. The reasons were diverse. Perhaps most important, Englishmen of all classes by the end of the nineteenth century had grown to accept and even revere their country's established political institutions, and to believe further that the existing Liberal and Conservative parties were capable of producing the necessary reforms of capitalism, as with other social and political problems. Continued measures of social reform and political democratization, which had begun with the Reform Bill of 1832, passed through parliament in the 1870s and 1880s, including a bill in 1883 that brought England close to universal manhood suffrage.

Thus working-class support for established political institutions and a related belief in the inevitability of further reform were more important in England than in Germany or in France. And the taste for domestic tranquillity was at least comparable to that in Germany. Marxists were associated in the public mind with the idea of a revolutionary seizure of power, the destruction of the existing state (which of course meant the revered English monarchy and parliament), and the establishment of a new, dictatorial proletarian state—all distinct liabilities in the English context. Similarly, the tendency of most Marxists to view trade unions as important primarily because they facilitated recruitment for socialist parties—and to disparage the long-range potential of unions in reforming capitalism—did not sit well with those English workingmen who were proud of their hard-won trade unions and who firmly believed that the material condition of English workers had improved because of union activity.

Closely related to these working-class attitudes was the greater flexibility of England's ruling orders compared to those of the Continent, especially in Germany and eastern Europe. With this flexibility went a belief, which was widely shared among the various strata of English society and indeed was becoming a part of English patriotic identity, that Englishmen were more prone to practical compromise, were less subject to the Continent's ideological intoxications—of which Marxism seemed a particularly extreme, dogmatic, and thus foreign variety.

Even among those English intellectuals who were capable of reading Marx's works and who were not inclined to reject them because of their unfamiliar dialectics, relatively few were won over, at least not in any thorough or durable fashion. Many who would later be active in the Fabian Society (discussed in Chapter 6) passed through a stage of initial admiration for Marx's theories, only to abandon them, or significant parts of them, upon closer scrutiny. G. B. Shaw, for example, finally concluded that Marxian economics, above all the labor theory of value, could not be defended. He was obliged, even in the 1880s, to read *Das Kapital* in French translation, but it is reasonably clear that he and other figures who would become important leaders of English socialism in the twentieth century rejected Marxism not through prejudice or ignorance but because upon careful examination they found it wanting.

There were nevertheless some Englishmen who found lasting inspiration in Marx's writings and who wanted to establish an independent party of class-conscious workers. Prominent among them were a number of imposing if eccentric figures, most of whom had previously had little to do with working-class politics. Their backgrounds and personalities were of the most diverse sort: They included the poet-artist William Morris, J. S. Mill's stepdaughter Helen Taylor, Marx's daughter Eleanor, and the Countess of Warwick. Not the least remarkable of them was Henry Meyers Hyndman, who assumed leadership over what became the Social-Democratic Federation, and who attempted to give it what he believed was a distinctly Marxist orientation, although in the process Morris and Eleanor Marx broke away to form the rival Socialist League.

Hyndman met Marx in 1880 and shortly thereafter read the French translation of *Das Kapital*. He wrote Marx that he "learned more from its perusal than from any book I have ever read" (Pierson, p. 60). At approximately the same time he began actively organizing among upper- and middle-class social reformers as well as working-class democratic radicals in London. Hyndman was a man of great personal energy and dynamism but hardly a profound or subtle thinker. Marx was even less impressed with this "Marxist" than he was with the Continental variety, and he was outraged that Hyndman's book, *England for All*, borrowed heavily from his theories without acknowledgment. Like Guesde, Hyndman was often dogmatic and authoritarian, further cause for opponents of Marxism to believe that proponents of Marxism somehow necessarily assumed those Germanic qualities. But unlike Guesde, Hyndman was unable to attract much of a personal following—his personality, probably more than his theories, was widely regarded as repellent.

In his emphasis on the importance of class and on the economic exploitation of workers, Hyndman clearly broke with the individualistic utilitarianism that remained even in the late nineteenth century the most important intellectual tradition of the British Left. Yet he could not shake free of utilitarian thought patterns, from the inclination to consider social issues in terms of the calculation of interest. He wrote,

"It is not the individual who forms the judgment as to the utility, but the class, or the social position in which he is placed" (Pierson, p. 62).

Thus Marx's organic-dialectical conceptions were at least as ill digested by Hyndman as they were by Guesde. Moreover, Hyndman tended, though his statements shifted confusingly, to move away from the idea of a final revolutionary confrontation toward a kind of gradualism. He believed in political decentralization and in an important role for local governing bodies. Even under capitalism, he asserted, there was an undeniable tendency, which Marxists should encourage, for the state to take over responsibilities formerly left to individuals, to substitute "collective . . . for individual effort" (Pierson, p. 64). Such words might easily have come from J. S. Mill or from the Fabian, Sidney Webb. One might even guess that had Hyndman been active on the Continent, he would have found more in common with the Lassalleans or with some of Guesde's opponents than with the avowed Marxists. This very great ambiguity concerning what it meant to be a Marxist would persist, indeed in some ways would intensify, into the twentieth century.

THE SECOND INTERNATIONAL

After the First International had died an ignominious death in America in 1876, Marx and Engels were not enthusiastic about proposals to establish a new one. They believed that before another international could profitably be established, it would be first necessary for doctrinally coherent (that is, Marxist) and solidly organized parties to take root in the principal European countries. As noted, they did not hold the ostensibly Marxist organizations that began to appear in the late 1870s and early 1880s in particularly high regard, not even the SPD, to say nothing of the organizations headed by Guesde and Hyndman.

Yet, whatever Marx's and Engels's reservations, there was a growing sentiment among working-class leaders and socialist activists that a new international organization was needed, that their growing ranks required international leadership. By the late 1880s, after Marx's death, various proposals were insistently put forth for an inaugural meeting. Typically, the Guesdists and Broussists differed vehemently on the issue. But widespread differences also existed between other potential members, most notably between the leaders of the SPD and the Trades Union Congress (TUC) in Great Britain, the first emphasizing the preeminence of the political, the second stressing trade-union organization. It appeared that any international workingmen's organization that might be put together would be rendered impotent by the old problem of factionalism.

For the French the idea of an inaugural congress in Paris in 1889, the hundredth anniversary of the outbreak of the French Revolution, had obvious attractions. Guesdists and Broussists organized rival congresses, to meet on July 14, the date of the storming of the Bastille and a national holiday. After much confusion and no little rancor, the Guesdist congress proved the more attractive and durable of the two. It became in effect the founding congress of the new International Workingmen's Association (also often referred to as the Socialist International or Second International).

At the founding congress some four hundred officially recognized delegates participated, representing most of the major countries of the world. Among them could be counted most of the important socialist leaders of Europe. A high point of the congress was the election of Liebknecht and Édouard Vaillant, a former Communard, as joint presidents. Their handshake, to enthusiastic applause, symbolized to the delegates the international unity and sense of brotherhood of the proletariat, in contrast to the ever more hysterical nationalism and militarism of Germany's and France's ruling orders.

The other delegates were generally much less important than the French and German. Many consciously patterned themselves after the SPD, as did of course the Guesdists and especially the Austrian delegation, led by Dr. Victor Adler. The Italians too were much influenced by German social democracy; however, among them were a number of flamboyant anarchists, who troubled the regular proceedings of the congress, and who also went to the Broussist congress for similarly disruptive activities. Russia was represented by George Plekhanov, a thorough and solid Marxist and a friend of Kautsky, and by Peter Lavrov. The latter, an eclectic thinker, derived much of his thought from the Russian populist movement but remained at the same time on good terms with Engels—on better terms, ironically, than many of the proclaimed followers of Marx and Engels.

In spite of the existence of a competing congress and the occasional disruptions of the anarchists, the general tone of the founding congress of the International was not sectarian—as would so often later be the case. Rather, there was a sense of international solidarity and satisfaction that the isolation of socialists and labor organizations in the years since the Commune appeared at last to be ending. In this spirit much of the congress's proceedings were devoted to hearing reports of the conditions in individual countries. Procedural matters were usually treated in a rather loose and flexible fashion (again, hardly the case in future years), and insofar as resolutions bearing on doctrine were put to a vote, they tended to be broad and uncontroversial in nature.

Although this was ostensibly a meeting of Marxists and revolutionaries, or perhaps better put, of those who rejected the name "reformist," the resolutions that were passed in most cases suggested the probability of an extended period of peaceful evolution rather than imminent violent confrontation. The demands made for an eight-hour day and other protective labor legislation, for example, were obviously to be accomplished under existing capitalist states.

This tendency to assume positions that implied avoidance of immediate confrontation was ridiculed by the revolutionary anarchists at the conference, whose popular image was much marked in the 1880s by a rising wave of political assassinations, bomb throwing, and other acts of anarchist terror. Many leading figures in the Second International, especially among the Marxists, believed that they must come to a reckoning with the anarchists before the new organization could continue to make real progress. The anarchists' irresponsible and brutal activities, as these figures saw it, discredited and demoralized the socialist movement, and gave its enemies an excuse to attack it.

Few if any bomb-throwing anarchists were represented at the congresses of the International, but the anarchists who did attend were a constant source of embarrassment and vexation. They repeatedly and flamboyantly denounced the leading figures of the international socialist movement, especially the Germans, as sham revolutionaries who lacked genuine international feeling. At the International's congress of Zurich in 1893, Bebel was able to get a resolution passed that limited membership to those groups and parties that accepted political action. At the congress of London in 1896 further measures were taken to drive the anarchists out.

This rejection of anarchist collaboration in the International further confirmed the German Marxist domination of the International. Two fundamental positions, strongly put forward by the Marxists, came to be broadly, if not universally accepted: first, that independent working-class parties, free of bourgeois domination or affiliation, should be established in each country; and, second, that parliamentary-political action, as opposed to direct, revolutionary action, should assume primary importance for the foreseeable future. In both of these positions lay an underlying belief in the need to build up, in a sober and steady fashion, free of futile and destructive revolutionary adventures, the independent forces of the working class in preparation for the day when the evolution of capitalism would render it impossible for the existing class states to continue to rule. But the question remained: How long would the period of preparation last?

The "germanification" of the International, as hostile observers termed it, was yet further reflected in what came to be called the "Revisionist Controversy." Beginning as an internal debate that took up the question of reform versus revolution in a way that reflected conditions peculiar to Germany, it was spread to the International, where it was given a "German" solution.

In 1899 Eduard Bernstein (1850–1932) published a book known in English translation as *Evolutionary Socialism*, which derived from a series of articles that he had published in Kautsky's theoretical journal, *Die Neue Zeit*, beginning in 1896. Bernstein's purpose in these writings was to revise Marxism, to bring it up to date, and to make clear how and why Marx's predictions had proved inadequate. Bernstein was a respected party intellectual, an old friend of Engels, and a loyal member of the SPD since the 1870s, when he had suffered persecution and exile for his socialist convictions. Even after the publication of *Evolutionary Socialism* Bernstein continued to consider himself a Marxist.

Bernstein based his critique on a position that questioned Marxian dialectics; he denied, in other words, that tensions or contradictions which would lead to violent revolution were inherent in capitalism. He considered socialism desirable but not inevitable. It would come only if people desired it and worked for it. And socialism would not be the product of a cataclysmic confrontation of bourgeoisie and proletariat; it would come gradually, reform by reform.

With statistics and other carefully assembled factual material Bernstein demonstrated that most workers were enjoying markedly improved living standards. He showed that property was not becoming concentrated in all areas of the economy; indeed, middle-sized incomes and moderate holdings of property were increasing absolutely and relatively. The members of the petty bourgeoisie were not disappearing in large numbers to join the ranks of the proletariat; many shopkeepers and peasants were proving themselves capable of resisting destruction at the hands of large-scale capitalist production. And white-collar workers, who had an essentially non-proletarian, petty-bourgeois outlook, were appearing in growing numbers. Thus in neither social nor economic terms was capitalism developing in the direction of polarization and violent confrontation.

To come to such conclusions at the turn of the century hardly required brilliant powers of observation and analysis. Bernstein's writings eventually caused such a furor in the SPD not because of specific, debatable points of fact and interpretation, but rather because he was a former radical (that is, Marxist) who had come to agree with the party's moderates that the SPD was not a revolutionary party and thus should stop assuming the false pose of being one.

Bernstein had long been a close friend and associate of the SPD's leading theoretician, Karl Kautsky, who was sarcastically dubbed the "pope of socialism" by those who considered him a dogmatist. Bernstein's writings gradually destroyed their friendship and provoked Kautsky, after some initial hesitation, to level his heaviest theoretical artillery in Bernstein's direction. (Even heavier attacks came from the party's extreme Left, headed by Rosa Luxemburg, concerning which more will be said later.)

Kautsky had already proved his mettle as defender of orthodox Marxism in a number of earlier party conflicts, most notably in dealing with Georg von Vollmar, the leader of the Bavarian contingent of the party. Vollmar had urged an "expansion" of the Marxist Erfurt program in order to attract small landholding peasants, who were particularly numerous in Bavaria and other southern German states. In countering Vollmar, Kautsky had insisted upon the essentially proletarian nature of the SPD, on the inevitable disappearance of the peasant petty bourgeoisie, and thus on the fundamental contradiction between the interests of propertyless industrial proletarians and landowning peasants. He warned that Vollmar's proposals would render the SPD indistinguishable from bourgeois democratic-radical reformers. At the congress of Breslau in 1895, Kautsky's positions won the overwhelming support of the party.

Given this opposition to their ideas, Vollmar and other moderates in the party naturally welcomed Bernstein with open arms as a much-needed ally against what they perceived as Kautsky's unbending dogmatism. Yet Kautsky found even stronger party support in attacking Revisionism: At the congress of Hanover in 1899 and Dresden in 1903 the votes in favor of Kautsky's orthodox Marxist resolutions were remarkably lopsided, 216 to 21 and 288 to 11. At Dresden the revered party leader, August Bebel, delivered a blistering indictment of Revisionist spokesmen, charging that they were mostly bourgeois intellectuals or former workingmen who were now enjoying a bourgeois existence because of their secure and comfortable positions in the party and trade-union bureaucracies. Such people, he charged, had lost contact with the sufferings and revolutionary striving of the proletariat.

But Bebel's support—and he was a powerful force within the party—was probably not a decisive factor in these issues. He had opposed Kautsky in dealing with Vollmar at Breslau, yet Kautsky still managed to win a decisive victory there. What was apparently decisive in earning Kautsky strong support within the party were several factors that neither Vollmar nor Bernstein seemed adequately to comprehend: Most party activists felt with intense conviction that the proletariat had a special mission, a historical role to play; and just as intensely they believed in the hostility of the bourgeoisie, in class conflict, since it was an inescapable aspect of their daily lives. Revisionism, with its unapologetic embrace of mundane reforms, threatened to drain the social-democratic movement in Germany of its mystique, of that element of millenarianism that attracted idealists and that gave rank-and-file members a sense of special worth in a society whose established leaders harbored contempt for them. Even social-democratic trade-union officials, who were for the most part moderates and who would later be important in pulling the SPD in a reformist direction, at first voted against the Revisionist resolutions.

Bernstein tended to aggravate suspicions of his intentions by flip and ill-considered statements, such as, "frankly . . . , the goal [of socialism] means nothing to me. The movement means everything" (Steenson, p. 117)—which his opponents in the party saw as clear evidence of his lack of genuine commitment to socialism. Even some of those most friendly to Bernstein were distressed at the way he had presented Revisionism to the party. Ignaz Auer, another long-established party leader, wrote Bernstein, "My dear Eddie, the sort of thing you ask is not done by passing a resolution. One does not say it—one does it!" (Nettl, *Luxemburg*, abridged ed., p. 101).

In his articles and resolutions against Revisionism Kautsky made particularly effective use of the related issues of class conflict and proletarian mission. He described Bernstein's talk of reform through class cooperation as utter nonsense in Germany, since the German bourgeoisie was both unsympathetic to the plight of workers and disdainful of the concept of popular rule. The great majority of Germany's middle-class citizens were not interested in a coalition with the working class for liberal-democratic reform. The only social class in Germany firmly committed to liberal democracy, let alone socialism, was the working class, and if workers wanted democracy, and through it eventually socialism, they would have to rely on their own forces.

On some issues, however, Kautsky was not so intransigent. He did not, for example, attempt to defend Marx's theory of immiseration, in a purely economic sense, against Bernstein's attacks, because the evidence was simply too overwhelming that the material condition of most workers in Germany and most of western Europe had improved rather than deteriorated. But Kautsky did not accept Bernstein's assumption that as the material condition of workers improved class conflict would necessarily diminish. Kautsky believed, on the contrary, that as the German working class grew in numbers and continued to organize effectively, political and social tension as well as conflict with the state and the ruling class would heighten rather than diminish. In this regard Kautsky had much evidence on his side, not only in the renewed efforts to re-introduce anti-socialist legislation but also in the recurring proposals to abolish universal manhood suffrage in Reichstag elections. Indeed, many in power in Germany had undoubtedly begun to think in terms of an inevitable showdown with the workers' movement.

Kautsky's orthodoxy found support not only among the party rank and file. Many party intellectuals found *Evolutionary Socialism* to be doctrinally unsophisticated, little more than shallow journalism. For them it obviously reflected Bernstein's long contact with England and with English political thought, which was largely utilitarian in inspiration and not held in high regard by German dialecticians. It was widely recognized that Bernstein's contacts with the Fabian Society in England had exercised a profound influence on his arguments, and his detractors argued that the Fabians' reformist perspective patently reflected the peculiar nature of English liberalism, especially as it began to blend with collectivist notions by the end of the nineteenth century. As noted, even John Stuart Mill, the classic theoretician of liberalism in England, had envisaged a future transition to socialism. The Fabians, who accepted most of Mill's thought, saw their task as one of "permeating" liberal opinion, of pulling it in a collectivist direction, and they found many liberals in England who were open to their arguments.

But Kautsky and others believed the idea of a similar permeation of liberal opinion in Germany was ludicrous. Kautsky similarly insisted that Germany's rulers were too inflexible and unsophisticated to envisage a long-range strategy of "buying off" a part of the workers' movement with promises of political reform and continued economic advancement, while still retaining the essentials of power for themselves. (Kautsky was deeply distressed to observe how successful this strategy seemed to be in England, where he observed that the leaders of the working class showed far greater enthusiasm for football than for social revolution.)

Yet more than differences between Germany and England were involved. Kautsky became convinced that Revisionism in Germany had attracted so much international attention because it was part of a Europe-wide development at the turn of the century, of what he termed a "renaissance of bourgeois radicalism," this renaissance was a contradictory and ephemeral affair, he believed, but one that was unmistakable in most western industrialized countries and at least temporarily challenged Marxism. For this reason he concluded, and other leading figures in the SPD concurred, that it was appropriate to take up the Revisionist Controversy at the congresses of the International.

Kautsky was concerned about developments in France, where the class-collaborationist reformism of the 1880s found in the 1890s a brilliant and appealing champion in the person of Jean Jaurès (1859–1914). He had begun his career as a member of the Radical Party, but, influenced in part by Malon's writings, he came to lead a growing faction in the Chamber of Deputies known as the Independent Socialists, composed of men who believed that a parliamentary, gradualistic road to socialism was possible in France.

Jaurès's role in the famous Dreyfus Affair exercised particular influence on the development of reformist socialism in France. His energetic campaign in seeking justice for Dreyfus, and in the process defending the republican form of government against the racist and militaristic hysteria of the Anti-Dreyfusards, captured the imagination of a whole generation of young people in France's institutions of higher education and similarly impressed important numbers of French bourgeois intellectuals. Jaurès and his reformist socialist followers stood out as courageous and virile defenders of humane values and liberal-republican democracy against nationalist reaction. (Both Guesde and the anarchists, it should be noted, stood aloof from the Affair, describing it as nothing more than a quarrel between rival factions of the bourgeoisie, and likely to divert workers' attention from the real issues of class conflict.) With the Dreyfus Affair the socialist movement in France was even more than before—and far more than in Germany—bolstered by figures, usually of democratic-radical or jacobin persuasion initially, from the bourgeois intellectual and university communities (as was Jaurès himself). Of course, as already noted, Jaurès also exercised considerable appeal among industrial workers and among the rural petty bourgeoisie.

The passions engendered by the Affair took on political focus in June 1898, when a new government under Réné Waldeck-Rousseau was formed, with the avowed intention of seeking broad support from the

Left in the name of defense of the Republic. Alexandre Millerand, a colleague of Jaurès's in the Independent Socialist Party, accepted a cabinet post in the new government.

For many Marxists and other revolutionaries this entry of a socialist into a bourgeois government, for the first time since Blanc's disastrous experience in the Provisional Government of 1848, was troubling, even if it was only a tactical move in the name of republican defense, and not, as was the case with Blanc, a move that bespoke high hopes for fundamental social change. Yet Millerand did encourage a belief that his presence in the cabinet would result in important reform legislation, and he immediately set to work on a number of bills designed to ameliorate the condition of France's workers.

The nature of Kautsky's concern about these developments was subtle and easily misunderstood. He did not object to Jaurès's role in the Affair: The issues it raised, Kautsky believed, were far too important for socialists to ignore, and they certainly should not leave the defense of important issues of human rights and civil liberties to the bourgeoisie. (Here, as so often, one is reminded of how much more flexible Kautsky was than Guesde.) Kautsky was not even opposed in principle to a coalition of the Left in the name of republican defense; in Germany the tendency to regard all non-socialists as "one reactionary mass," with whom any sort of cooperation whatsoever must be ruled out, was Lassallean, and one that Kautsky (and Marx before him) had long combated. What *was* essential, in Kautsky's eyes—and here was the danger posed by Jaurès and all he stood for—was to avoid domination by or absorption into the concerns and political activities of the bourgeois Left. He observed, "so long as we preserve our proletarian character, corruption from other parties is not to be feared. . . . if we give up our proletarian character, we lose the firmest ground under our feet and become a ball of the most contradictory interests, like the anti-Semites" (Steenson, p. 114).

Thus Kautsky opposed Millerand's entry into the Waldeck-Rousseau cabinet for two related reasons: first, because in the same cabinet sat General Gallifet, a leader of the military forces that had massacred the Communards—making it "shameful," Kautsky believed, for any socialist to be present there—and second, because Millerand's participation at the very highest policy-making level of a bourgeois government unnecessarily exposed him and his socialist supporters—who had by no means yet established a firm proletarian identity—to the dangers of a fundamental compromise with the forces of the bourgeoisie, thus spreading confusion among the working class.

The issue of ministerialism was taken up at the Paris congress of the International in 1900. Guesde and the Italian socialist Enrico Ferri forwarded a resolution that forbade socialist participation in a bourgeois government under any conditions. Significantly, Kautsky, in spite of his reservations about Millerand's actions, found this resolution too restrictive; it failed to preserve "the necessary elasticity for the unfathomable future." He offered a competing one that allowed socialist participation only under extraordinary conditions and with prior party approval (something Millerand had failed to obtain). In light of future developments, the examples of extraordinary conditions that Kautsky offered were both revealing and remarkably prescient: in the case of a "people's war" against an invasion of Germany by reactionary Russia; and if "fundamental democratic institutions" in a country were endangered, with a broad yet firm coalition of the Left as the only remedy (Steenson, p. 134).

The Paris congress supported Kautsky's flexibility rather than Guesde's dogmatism. However, this did not represent any fundamental split between Guesde and Kautsky, as the latter, immediately after the vote, hastened to point out: He still firmly supported Guesde and his group over the other socialist factions that gave their support to the ministerialist experiment. And on the larger issue of Revisionism (not yet brought to the International) and the issue of reform versus revolution generally, so obviously related to that of ministerialism, Guesde and Kautsky were to all appearances in perfect agreement.

The support of Kautsky and the German Marxists generally was important to Guesde in his efforts to dominate the still confused and contending factions of the French socialist movement, and he saw in the issue of Revisionism a convenient opportunity to use both the Germans and the International to forward his plans. He was helped by the disappointing results of Millerand's period in office, for the proposed social legislation made slow progress through the legislature, and before long Millerand was put into the position of defending law and order by lending approval to the authorities' firing upon striking workers.

A more perfect confirmation of the apprehensions that Kautsky and others had expressed could hardly have been imagined, and thereafter Millerand drifted to the right, ultimately becoming, after World War I, a notoriously anti-socialist president of the Republic. But even before then he served as the perfect example, for those who wanted to find one, of how class cooperation and bourgeois political alliances in parliament could corrupt a socialist. Millerand was out of office by 1903, the same year that Bernstein's theories were condemned at the

SPD's Dresden congress. This was also the year of the SPD's most impressive electoral victory yet—eighty-one seats and over 3 million votes—causing many to conclude that the day of socialist triumph was not far off, that the German Marxist emphasis on discipline, class solidarity, and trust in the inexorable laws of historical development were further vindicated.

Guesde then made his move: In coordination with Kautsky and the other leaders of the SPD, he took the Revisionist issue to the International's Amsterdam congress in 1904, and delegates adopted with a strong majority the exact wording of the Dresden anti-Revisionist resolution. Revisionism and ministerialism appeared to be trampled into the dust, and in the next year Jaurès bowed to Guesde in the unification of the most important French socialist factions around a largely Marxist party program. The name that the new party assumed, and would be known by for the next half century, was significant: SFIO (*Section française de l'Internationale ouvrière*, or French Section of the Worker's International), which put emphasis on the new party's international origins and its presumed commitments.

All of this no doubt represented a defeat for Jaurès and a victory for Marxism as interpreted by the SPD and Guesde. Yet in the debates at the Amsterdam congress Jaurès was a powerful orator who made some telling and prophetic points, above all against what he saw as the heavy hand of the Germans in the International. In words that recalled those of the anarchists in years past, Jaurès condemned the Dresden resolution for "trying to apply the rules of action—or rather inaction— that are presently imposed on the German party, which has no revolutionary tradition but rather one of receiving benefits—for example universal suffrage—from above." The German social democrats were in reality without power in their own parliament, he emphasized, in spite of their impressive electoral victories. Their theoretical intransigence was a mask for this political impotence. "Behind the inflexibility of the theoretical formulas which your excellent comrade Kautsky will supply you to the end of his days, you have concealed from your own proletariat, from the international proletariat, your inability to act" (Harrington, p. 75).

The resentments so eloquently expressed by Jaurès's Amsterdam speech led a number of prominent Independents to a final break with organized socialism, and quite a few of them went on, like Millerand, to brilliant parliamentary careers. But Jaurès made genuine efforts to live with the Amsterdam decision and the Marxist program of the new SFIO, in the name of international solidarity and in hopes for a signifi-

cant and lasting unity of French socialists. Although his decision cost
him much personal anguish in the years immediately following Amsterdam, it was one that ultimately allowed him to assume a position
of leadership in the SFIO and indeed a commanding position in the
international socialist community.

THE ANARCHIST ALTERNATIVE

The competition between Marxists and anarchists has already been an
abiding theme of the previous pages. While both opposed bourgeois society, the anarchists saw themselves as offering a fundamental alternative, in a way that the Marxists failed to do, since the latter accepted
modern industrialism, political parties, the use of parliament, and
more generally the necessity of an extended stage of bourgeois-capitalist development during which time social revolution would be impossible. Yet anarchist thought was amorphous: Anarchists recognized no
single master theoretician—it was central to their temper to reject
dogma of any sort—and their organizations were unstructured and
ephemeral. Anarchists would tolerate no central body or corps of bureaucrats giving them orders.

The general anarchistic perspective had much in common with
what philosophers term "existential." There was also, to use a related
term, a good bit of the romantic in anarchists. They made much of direct experience, intuition, and action. They were distrustful of rules and
regulations, of the systematic spirit, of the fruits of pure reason, of bureaucratic structures and representative institutions, of modern progress and of "scientific" or deterministic answers to what they considered the ultimately unpredictable situations of life.

Such attitudes were obviously a bit out of place in the period following the revolutions of 1848, when science, industry, material progress, and powerful nation-states were the keynotes. Indeed, anarchists
have often been considered losers in their most famous struggles—
against nineteenth-century Marxism; against the growth of powerful,
centralized states; against the bolsheviks; and against modernism generally. It is significant that many socialists of the 1880s, for example,
Guesde, Malon, and Brousse, were first anarchists and then became
Marxists or reformists, while the reverse was very rarely the case (although a number of prominent anarchists, for example Proudhon and
Bakunin, initially expressed admiration for Marx's writings, then
turned against them—or, more accurately, against him).

Whether or not anarchists may be considered losers in the long run, they remained important—more so than is often recognized—in the latter half of the nineteenth century. Their followers, while scattered, inconstant, and often difficult to identify, probably exceeded in absolute numbers for Europe as a whole the followers of the Marxists. (The comparison is not entirely fair, since to be a member of a Marxist organization was usually much more formal and palpable than to entertain anarchist ideas or even to engage in anarchist activities.) Moreover, interest in and respect for anarchist perspectives revived notably in the twenty years or so preceding World War I, when an anti-positivist mood, involving a rejection of the uncritical glorification of science and material progress typical of the 1850s through the 1870s, broadly affected European culture.

Consistent with their existential-romantic rejection of modern state and society, the anarchists did not closely link material productivity with progress, nor would they recognize any clearly progressive inner logic to historical development (where Marxists and liberals saw more or less eye-to-eye). They insisted rather on the notion of moral growth, largely independent of material factors, leading to the construction of a society based on transcendental moral principles, a society whose members would be committed to the abolition of authoritarianism, inequality, and exploitation—in short, to the application of the principle of Justice.

However, the anarchists believed in action, not mere proclamation of airy ideals. Some particularly notorious anarchists, toward the end of the nineteenth and during the early twentieth centuries, reveled in "direct action," heroic acts of exemplary violence, of "propaganda of the deed"—bomb throwing, dynamiting, assassinations—with the expectation, endlessly illusory, that such action would rouse the masses to overthrow their oppressors.

The bomb throwers undoubtedly gained the most attention, but most anarchists expressed a preference for nonviolent solutions. They were nevertheless tolerant of violent acts against tyrannical authority (which for most anarchists meant most of the usual kinds of authority, above all the authority exercised by the modern state). Anarchists with very few exceptions considered themselves revolutionaries—meaning that they believed in a sudden, dramatic transformation of existing society.

Anarchists differed among themselves concerning the desirability of collective effort and socialized institutions, even concerning the extent to which human beings may be considered social or communal in nature. A number of radical individualsts were attracted to a fiercely consistent espousal of liberty, but since they rejected binding social institutions and the related concept of the natural sociability of human beings, they are properly placed outside the socialist tradition. Under the broad rubric of socialistic anarchism a number of important subcategories may be distinguished: Proudhon's mutualism, Bakunin's anarchist collectivism, Kropotkin's anarchist communism, and the anarchosyndicalism of those who attempted to integrate anarchist principles and trade-union organization. To this list may be added, with some important qualifications, the Russian populists (narodniks).

Proudhon, who qualifies as the most original and seminal of anarchist thinkers, was briefly discussed in the previous chapter. His mutualism, exercising its greatest direct influence in the 1850s and 1860s, was the least socialistic of the above-mentioned subcategories. He looked to a decentralized or stateless federation of communes (in the French sense of municipalities) and workers' cooperatives, where the means of production would be "possessed," not "owned," by individuals or small groups and where individual workers would be assured of the fruits of their own labor, without being exploited by moneylender, middleman, or capitalist.

Michael Bakunin (1814–76), Marx's great antagonist in the First International, borrowed much from Proudhon, but he and his followers believed that by the late 1860s it was imperative to adapt anarchist attitudes to the growing reality of industrial concentrations. They thus replaced Proudhon's acceptance of individual possession with the notion of possession by large-scale voluntary associations. They continued to accept, however, Proudhon's insistence that workers should be paid "justly," according to their productivity.

In the late 1870s, Prince Peter Kropotkin (1842–1921) and his anarchistic communist admirers further departed from Proudhon's and Bakunin's emphasis on "just" rewards by calling for the abolition of the whole notion of a wage and price system, thus reverting to the old communistic ideal of a nonpossessive society with some kind of common warehouse of goods. Here the motto "from each according to his ability, to each according to his needs" would prevail.

The anarchosyndicalists drew eclectically from these already-eclectic sources, although they were not much interested in theory—indeed, some were ostentatiously anti-intellectual. In a burst of activity in the early twentieth century they tended to focus on the role of the revolutionary union, or *syndicat*, in bringing down the bourgeois-capitalist state through a general strike and then in constituting the key institution of the new stateless society.

Beyond these nuances having to do with degrees and means of socialization, anarchists differed among themselves in other, sometimes striking ways. Proudhon and Bakunin, for example, held substantially different views of human nature. Proudhon, while recognizing the fundamentally social nature of humans, remained suspicious of many human instincts, and one of the reasons that he advocated the retention of the traditional patriarchal family was that he believed a father's authority was necessary to control the ineffaceably antisocial tendencies in people. Thus in spite of his distaste for the growing power of the modern state, the disciplines imposed by the factory, or even the demands of trade-union solidarity, he was haunted by an appreciation of the possible harm people could cause one another if liberty went completely unchecked, if all authority were rejected. The rule of the father represented a kind of basic minimum if social cohesion were to be preserved.

Bakunin, on the other hand, was more open to the notion of a society that was completely free of constraint; for him human nature needed only full, unqualified liberty to achieve perfection. The vices of his time were largely due, he believed, to the trammels put on human spontaneity, to the established authorities that crushed and corrupted the human spirit. While Proudhon feared the possible outcome of violent revolution, Bakunin believed that the violent destruction of the bonds of law, police, courts—existing civil institutions of all sorts— would not lead to chaos or the tyranny of the lawless but rather to an emancipated humanity. Pushing this remarkable faith in raw human nature to its ultimate expression, Bakunin idealized the least educated, poorest, and most downtrodden elements of the population; they were, he believed, the least corrupted by state worship and the ethic of competitiveness to achieve personal success. Proudhon's ideal, the independent, prudent, hard-working skilled laborer, resembled what Bakunin denounced as a "bourgeoisified" betrayer of the workers' cause. His contempt for theorists originating in the bourgeoisie—like Marx—was even more profound. "The mass is unconsciously socialist," he wrote, "more earnestly and truly socialist than all the scientific bourgeois socialists put together" (Guérin, pp. 34–35).

Proudhon and Bakunin did share an important common concern: They believed that a dictatorship of the proletariat, exercised through the organs of state power, would lead inexorably to a dictatorship of the skilled and otherwise advantaged workers, or even worse, of the bourgeois intellectuals who tended to rise to the top of workers' organizations. The dangers of bureaucratization and the ensuing tyranny of workers over workers were the main reasons that Proudhon expressed severe reservations about the formation of trade unions.

Proudhon's roots were in the rural artisanry of France. Bakunin was a Russian nobleman. Kropotkin, who after Bakunin's death took his place as the leading exponent of anarchism, was also of Russian noble lineage. The attractiveness of anarchist principles in those countries with a large, backward rural population, primarily in the Latin and Slavic areas, and among those social classes, particularly skilled artisans and the old landed aristocracy, that were being rendered irrelevant by the march of modern industry is worth noting. George Woodcock, a penetrating and unusually sympathetic historian of anarchism, writes that "much of the rank-and-file of the movement was made up of artisans, of poor and primitive peasants, of those shiftless, rebellious sections of the lower classes whom Shaw hailed as 'the undeserving poor' and whom Marx dismissed as the *Lumpen proletariat*. . . . The countries and regions where anarchism was strongest were those in which industry was least developed and in which the poor were the poorest. As progress engulfed the classic fatherlands of anarchism, as the factory workers replaced the handcraftsmen, as the aristocrats became detached from the land and absorbed into the new plutocracy, anarchism began to lose the main sources of its support" (Woodcock, p. 470).

While Kropokin was in his early years a supporter of the Bakuninist faction in the First International, his anarchism, in both theory and practice, differed signally from that of Bakunin. Bakunin engaged in endless plots, conspiracies, and revolutionary uprisings; Kropotkin never once manned the barricades, although he spent a number of years in jail, in Russia and the West, for his propagandistic activities. Bakunin had about him a persistent Mephistophelian aura, Kropotkin that of a saint. Bakunin's emphasis was on the destruction of bourgeois society; Kropotkin emphasized the constructive rather than the destructive. Bakunin made sporadic efforts to adjust his ideas to the prevailing tone of scientific materialism, but he remained indelibly marked by his initial romantic-carbonarist enthusiasms. Kropotkin reached maturity intellectually in the 1850s and 1860s and found it much easier to integrate a scientific approach and anarchistic convictions in a clear and convincing manner.

As a young man, in the early 1860s, before becoming involved with anarchism, Kropotkin made a mark as a distinguished scientist, and as a pioneering and widely traveled geographer. At the same time, his intimate contacts with the natives of the Siberian and Manchurian frontiers developed in him a taste for a simple, uncorrupted life, so different from the life he had observed at first hand in the tsar's court. The long Siberian nights also left him with much time for reflection, and it was at this time that he began to read Proudhon. Kropotkin's disgust with the tsarist regime grew steadily, as did a sense of self-indulgence. In a reflection typical of him he wrote, "What right had I to these higher joys [of scientific inquiry] when all around me was nothing but misery . . . , when what I spend to allow me to live in a world of higher emotions must be taken from the very mouths of those who grew the wheat, who had not enough bread for their own children" (Woodcock, p. 192).

Frustrated in his efforts to aid the poor in his own country, Kropotkin went to western Europe. The theories of communistic anarchism that he hammered out in the 1870s and 1880s were hardly novel formulations; precedents could be found from More to Fourier, and the ideal of a communistic society was much discussed in the anarchist circles that Kropotkin frequented, but he presented his ideas in a particularly effective and appealing manner. His many articles on the subject of communistic anarchism, written mostly in the 1880s, were gathered into book form as *The Conquest of Bread* in 1892.

Kropotkin's linking of communism and anarchism, while primarily inspired by fellow anarchists, was interestingly similar to Marx's ultimate vision of the society that would emerge from the dictatorship of the proletariat: There was the same intellectual-aesthetic emphasis (both Marx and Kropotkin thought of bliss in terms of artistic creation and the "higher emotions" related to intellectual contemplation), the same sense of psychic liberation, as well as release from economic and political constraints (Marx too foresaw the end of the wage system and the "withering away of the state," when class differences were no more to be preserved), the same belief in the possibility of "attractive work" to replace the regimented, dehumanizing drudgery imposed by the market and factory systems.

In *Mutual Aid*, composed in the 1890s and published in 1902, Kropotkin built upon the deep-rooted convictions among anarchists and socialists generally concerning the natural sociability or cooperativeness of human beings. But in addition he offered a more empirical foundation: His observations of animal life in Siberia had long before impressed him with the extent to which cooperation among animals of the same species was a generally much more important factor in their survival than competition between them. And he was convinced that such was above all the case with human beings, because of their "eminently social" intellectual capacities and because of their ability to pass on from generation to generation and from society to society the discoveries of any particular individual or group. Kropotkin thus provided a scientific critique of the widespread social-Darwinist notion of the "survival of the fittest."

The anarchosyndicalists emerged most notably in France, though kindred movements developed elsewhere, especially in Italy and Spain. The anarchosyndicalist movement may be considered an amalgam of those anarchist activists who became disillusioned with the results of conspiracies and terror, and the French labor movement, which was already much influenced by Proudhon's ideas and generally open to anarchist perspectives.

The distaste for political activity among the Proudhonist leaders of the French working class was much enhanced by the bitter experience of the Paris Commune and its ensuing repressions. The conservative republic that emerged from the confused years following 1872 was repellent to many worker activists, all the more so because of the number of republicans, previously known as social reformers, who appeared now to be pre-occupied with intrigues for parliamentary office or the comforts of life in Paris. And the sectarian socialist parties of the 1880s and 1890s further discredited the notion of political activity for many workers. When the anti-union Le Chapelier Law was repealed in 1884, the new legislation included the stipulation that any unions formed should refrain from political activity, a stipulation that was in fact not widely resented.

It is thus not difficult to understand why a strongly antipolitical path was followed by the leaders of most of the syndicats that began to grow up in the late 1880s and early 1890s. Moreover, since France remained relatively slow in its industrial growth, large industrial unions, which in countries like England and Germany were eager for state intervention in their behalf, were relatively unimportant. As former anarchist militants assumed influential positions in the syndicats and the affiliated labor exchanges (*bourses de travail*) around the turn of the century, these antipolitical activities became intensified, and the French labor movement took on a complexion that was remarkably different from the movements in most other industrialized countries. Rather than concentrating on day-to-day reforms and compromises between capital and labor, anarchosyndicalist leaders emphasized class conflict and heralded a revolutionary general strike that would bring down the capitalist order. Rather than working as the auxiliary of a socialist party, on the German model, the anarchosyndicalist CGT (*Confédération générale du travail*, or General Confederation of Labor) expressed contempt for politicians of all stripes, bourgeois or socialist, and for all parliamentary activity.

The anarchosyndicalists were the source of much comment and curious attention in the generation before the war. Perhaps the best known of those who wrote about them was Georges Sorel (1847–1922), a retired engineer and idiosyncratic man of letters. In the 1890s he had contributed much to the propagation and digestion of Marxism in France, but his writings on anarchosyndicalism, above all his *Reflections on Violence* (1908), attracted much more attention—both for their brilliance and their perversity.

Sorel was not himself active in the anarchosyndicalist movement, nor were the anarchosyndicalists directly influenced by him, although his theories have subsequently become ineradicably associated with their activities. He was fascinated by the psychological impact on French workers of what he termed "the myth of the general strike." By "myth" he did not exactly mean "illusion"; rather he defined it as a powerful image or idea capable of moving masses of people, of shaking them from their lethargy, of giving their daily activities transcendent meaning. The myth of the Day of Judgment, powerful in earlier Christian times, was a counterpart to what Sorel considered the general strike to be in his time. The validity of such myths did not particularly concern him; what did was the manner in which myths could inspire people to heroic action, to self-sacrifice, to a break with "bourgeois" routine.

Sorel was a typical representative of the aforementioned anti-positivist trend of the early twentieth century. Much of his reasoning was anything but clear or consistent, but he appeared to be indifferent to the ultimate goals of the anarchosyndicalists. What interested him was the spectacle of violent class conflict itself—the struggle of an intransigent proletariat and a similarly determined bourgeoisie. The inherent nobility and vitality of the spectacle, not the sordid matters relating to the improvement of the conditions of the workers, were what mattered to him.

But these were the heated cerebrations of an eccentric intellectual (one who later became involved in anti-Semitic movements and who was considered by Mussolini to be one of the prophets of fascism), not the proclamations of workers themselves. Indeed, without denying the reality of class hatred for many French workers, or the special fascination that the promise of the general strike held for some of them, it appears that the majority of the ordinary workers associated with the CGT accepted only sporadically or incompletely the revolutionary anarchist rhetoric of those who stood at the head of the organization. (It should be remembered, of course, that only a small minority of French workers, far fewer than in Germany or England, joined any union at all.) The CGT was a particularly undemocratic and unrepresentative organization, where an active and overtly elitist minority was able to impose its views on a relatively inactive reformist majority. For example, the militantly revolutionary barber's union, with only a few thousand members, had the same voting strength as the 50,000-member-strong reformist railroad workers' union. This situation was another interesting reversal of the pattern in most other advanced industrial nations, where reformists assumed leadership of the leading union positions and saw their role as one of channeling the demands of their unruly rank and file into practicable, "reasonable," and nonrevolutionary directions.

It would be a mistake, however, to conclude that the anarchist leaders of the CGT concerned themselves exclusively with matters of ultimate revolutionary takeover. Most of the unions that made up the CGT also carefully attended to bread-and-butter issues. In spite of small treasuries and skeletal staffs, the CGT's record of winning local strikes compared favorably with the records of trade unions in Germany and England, where vast union bureaucracies and impressive strike funds became the norm. This too helps explain how anarchist leaders could maintain their position over a rank and file that in its majority did not always share anarchist ideals.

Similarly, the often fiercely anti-patriotic statements of leading anarchosyndicalists, which had no real equivalent among labor leaders in Germany and England and which so scandalized the ruling orders in France, were not widely shared by the rank-and-file members of the CGT. Even among CGT leaders such statements often reflected a hatred for the military as an arm of the repressive bourgeois state rather than a deep-felt internationalism. When war broke out in August 1914, French workers, whether involved in the anarchosyndicalist movement or not, rallied to the banners of national defense with the same delirious enthusiasm as the rest of the French population.

But by 1914 the anarchosyndicalist movement had lost some of the extraordinary revolutionary *élan* associated with its peak years, 1902–08. This loss may be partly attributed to the arrest of the more revolutionary of the CGT's leaders, after a series of ill-fated strikes, which in turn permitted men of relatively moderate persuasion to assume positions of leadership. It was at this time that Léon Jouhaux, who would lead the CGT through the interwar years, assumed prominence. In a larger and related sense, the drift of the CGT in a more reformist direction can be seen as a reflection of France's growing industrialization, with an ensuing loss of influence among those elements of the French working class involved in small-scale, relatively backward production, where anarchist ideas had always found their friendliest reception.

While two of the leading theorists of anarchism, Bakunin and Kropotkin, were of Russian background, the centers of anarchist activity in the second half of the nineteenth century remained in western Europe, primarily in the Latin countries. A significant anarchist movement, explicitly defining itself as such, did not appear inside Russia until the twentieth century, and then it soon was obliterated by the bolsheviks. Yet there was an important movement inside Russia that shared many concerns with anarchism and borrowed heavily from the writings of Proudhon, Bakunin, and Kropotkin. This was the Russian populist or narodnik movement (*narod* means "people" in Russian).

Russian populism is best described as a form of socialism attuned to Russia's peculiar conditions. It was distinct from such western populist movements as that in the United States, which was democratic-radical and explicitly anti-socialist. Within the broad confines of what came to be called the narodnik movement were nearly as many tendencies as within western European socialism, although the movement as a whole may be considered pre-Marxist. Most Russian Marxists of the 1880s and 1890s went through a preliminary narodnik stage, in a way roughly comparable to the anarchist stage of many western Marxists.

A key concern of the narodniks was vaguely Bakuninist in inspiration; they were fascinated by the Russian common people, above all by the "uncorrupted" *muzhik* or peasant and the indigenous institutions associated with Russian rural life. (It is largely for this reason that the narodniks cannot simply be termed socialists in the western European sense, since the latter were characteristically concerned with urban workers as an international phenomenon; they did not nationalistically elevate *their* workers, or peasants, as superior to others—at least not in any theoretical way. More broadly, the narodniks, unlike western socialists, were stimulated to theory and action not by the advent of the Dual Revolution in Russia—at least not in any direct sense—but rather by their own "social question," which had to do with the peculiarities of rural Russia and the problems created by the tsarist state.)

The term "narodnik" was not widely used until the late 1870s, but it subsequently took on a more all-embracing and generic usage, applied to a series of thinkers and activists from the 1840s to the 1880s.

Alexander Herzen (1812–70) was the seminal narodnik theorist. In a celebrated passage, written in 1861, he urged his many readers to "go to the people."

While still in Russia in his youth Herzen was active in a number of left-leaning or socialist coteries. In 1847 he emigrated to the West, never to return. At first an admirer of all things western and modern, he was horrified by the outcome of the revolutions of 1848—above all by the self-satisfied and self-centered bourgeois society that emerged in the 1850s and 1860s. He began then to look with new interest and favor at Russia's native communal institutions and traditions, and the Russian spirit generally.

Herzen's hope, and the hope of all subsequent narodniks, was that Russia could somehow follow a more humane and socialist path to modernization by retaining the village commune (*mir* or *obshchina* in Russian) and cooperative workshop (*artel*). Much of Russia's land was organized into such communes, where private property in the western sense did not exist. Instead, the village elders oversaw the redistribution of land parcels at regular intervals in order to compensate for the natural changes—deaths, marriages, births—in the composition of the village population. In similar ways, the artel was, after the abolition of serfdom, collectively owned and managed by the workers who labored on it.

Herzen and the narodniks after him hoped that the preservation of these cooperative institutions would prevent the spread of the ruinous individualism of the West. A revolution would of course also be necessary to get rid of the tsarist state, with its oppressive taxation, reactionary officials, and obscurantist principles. Changes in the existing communes would be necessary before they would correspond fully to rational, socialist ideals, but they remained the essential basis upon which a socialist society could be constructed.

Herzen belonged to a generation in Russia that could in a general way be identified with the romantic-idealist early nineteenth century in the West. The subsequent generation of narodniks, that is, those active in the 1860s and 1870s, while retaining most of Herzen's fundamental notions, moved away from what they considered his overly belletristic approach; they represented a change of opinion, in other words, similar to that in the West from the romantic 1830s and 1840s to the realistic 1850s and 1860s. In Russia, which did not experience any significant unrest in 1848, the historical catalysts of this change—quite aside from the obvious intellectual influence of the West—were Russia's humiliating defeat in the Crimean War of 1854 to 1856 and the disappointments concerning the terms in which the government finally moved to abolish serfdom in 1861. (Heavy redemption payments were imposed on the land given to the peasants, and the village communes were subjected to strict supervision by tsarist officials.)

N. G. Chernyshevsky (1828–89) was the most influential writer for this generation of narodniks. His thought parallels that of Marx in remarkable ways, although it appears that Chernyshevsky read few if any of Marx's works. Chernyshevsky gave careful attention to concrete economic data, wrote in a simple, direct style (in this he more resembled Engels than Marx, but the point is that he eschewed a highly "literary" style), and emphasized the need for popular initiative in accomplishing revolution in Russia. He believed that class conflict was a necessary aspect of historical development, that the state naturally reflected the interests of the ruling class, and that the class in power would not relinquish it peacefully.

It is thus not surprising that later Marxists in Russia learned much from Chernyshevsky and retained a certain admiration for him. (Lenin chose the title *What Is to Be Done?* for one of his earliest and most important pamphlets; Chernyshevsky had written an extremely influential novel in 1863 with the same title.) But Chernyshevsky retained the narodnik hope—decisively rejected by the Russian Marxists—that Russia's path to modern industrial society would be fundamentally different from that of the West.

(A further ambiguity concerning the meaning of the term "Marxist" in the late nineteenth century was that Marx himself, who had established friendly contacts with a number of narodnik émigrés, spoke favorably of the notion that Russia might avoid western Europe's capitalist stage. This was an embarrassment to those former narodniks turned Marxists, who argued that Russia's indigenous communal institutions would inevitably be destroyed through the introduction of the institutions of private property and the ethic of competitive individualism.)

Chernyshevsky at different times praised both communal decentralization and the role of a rationally constituted state in organizing industry. He appeared similarly ambivalent about the desirability of large-scale industry. Other narodniks were torn on these issues, but one above all pre-occupied them: that is, the mentality of the peasant masses—how much could they be expected to rise up in revolution? how naturally socialistic were they? how much did they require the leadership of some sort of moral-intellectual elite? was violent action or peaceful propaganda the most effective way to raise them from their torpor?

Many of these questions were later debated, in an altered but kindred form, by the Russian Marxists and are best left to the discussion of the origins of Leninism. But their practical implications were very much on the minds of the narodniks in the early 1870s, their time of greatest activist fervor. In the early part of the decade, culminating in the summer of 1874, thousands of militant students spread into the countryside to preach the narodnik message—however imprecise that message remained—and to attain a first-hand knowledge of Russia's peasant masses. This "Going to the People" (*Khozhdenie v narod*), as it became known, was a bitterly disillusioning experience for most of the young activists involved. Rather than encountering oppressed people ready for action, they frequently met with suspicion, incomprehension, and indifference, accentuated by vast cultural differences. The Russian students were in many cases turned over to the tsarist police by the peasants. In the spring of 1875 the movement was sternly and thoroughly repressed.

Thereafter activists took a more violent and terroristic direction. The notorious People's Will (*Narodnaya Volya*) succeeded in assassinating Tsar Alexander II in 1881. The manifesto issued by the assassins at the same time, demanding the calling of a constituent assembly, encountered once again apathy and incomprehension on the part of the people. Thereafter tsarist authorities moved with particular ferocity and thoroughness to stamp out the narodnik revolutionaries.

The year 1881 marked the start of a hiatus in the narodnik movement lasting for over a generation. In the 1880s and 1890s many young intellectuals who still cherished hopes for revolution in Russia turned to Marxism, at a time when it was beginning to spread widely in the West. This interest in Marxist theory especially characterized the anti-terrorist Black Partition, whose members insisted that propaganda among the people, the lifting of popular consciousness—rather than terror directed at the state—was an absolute prerequisite for revolutionary change. Such beliefs blended fairly easily into Marxism, and among the former leaders of the Black Partition was George Plekhanov, who became known as the "father of Russian Marxism."

The appeals of Marxism in Russia were based not only on the patent failures of the narodniks and the status of Marxist socialism as the leading socialist theory in the West. By the 1890s a vigorous capitalism, spurred by western investments, had begun to appear in a number of areas in Russia. The concurrent departure of peasants from the land, from the rural communes, to seek their fortunes in the new factories was the very development that the narodniks had hoped to prevent. Yet the new factory proletariat showed a rebelliousness, in strikes and other forms of industrial unrest, that revived the hopes of many revolutionaries. Before long Marxists were working within the nascent labor movement. In 1898 the Russian Social Democratic Workers' Party, or RSDRP (from its Russian initials), consciously modeled on the SPD, was established. A new chapter in the revolutionary history of Russia had begun.

THE CLASSIC AGE

The quarter century before the First World War has often been described as the classic age of European socialism. It was certainly a time when the leaders of Europe's various socialist parties were optimistic about the future—and ostensibly had good reason to be so. The SPD emerged from illegality to new triumphs, becoming by 1912 overwhelmingly the largest party in Germany. The French socialists achieved unity at long last and grew impressively from 1905 to 1914. Socialists in Belgium, Italy, and Austria-Hungary similarly registered large gains in party and trade-union memberships as well as in parliamentary strength. The congresses of the Socialist International became ever more grandiose affairs, where the pressing questions of the day were debated in grand style by the patriarchs of the socialist movement—Bebel, Jaurès, Plekhanov, Adler, Turati—to the rapt attention of socialist militants. In short, the generation of 1890–1914 was a time of great expectations and accomplishments, one that would be looked back to with nostalgia by many socialists in the harsher, often tragic years following 1914.

The mid-1890s marked a renewed burst of industrial expansion that continued without major interruption, at least without interruption on the scale of the depression of the 1870s and 1880s, until the war. From the turn of the century until 1914 per capita industrial production in Europe rose on an average of nearly 40 percent, over 57 percent in France. The material conditions of most workers improved unmistakably, although the benefits of the growing productivity of labor accrued proportionately less to the lower orders than to the owners of capital and land. This disproportion—in the context of working masses who were better educated, had more leisure, enjoyed better health, and above all had a more positive self-image and higher aspirations—may well have been one of the most fundamental factors in the steady growth of the socialist movements of most countries.

It has already been repeatedly observed from various contexts that factory workers did not rise, as individuals, to provide leadership of socialist movements, nor did they, as a mass, consistently push socialist and trade-union leaders in the direction of a more intense, proletarian-revolutionary perspective. This observation appears to have been the case in the classic age at least as much as in the years before—a conclusion supported not only by the statistical perspectives of the new historical monographs but also from older, more traditional sources.

The German social-democratic movement, in the period of its greatest success in the decade before World War I, saw a widening gap between leaders and broad masses. In recruiting ever greater numbers, in gaining prestige and in appearing to be the voice of the future, the social-democratic movement gathered into its ranks different types from those that rallied to it in the heroic 1880s. Thus while the party could count on a core of dedicated members and officials, the high turnover of the less committed rank and file was a cause of growing concern. A number of party and trade-union leaders openly expressed exasperation with the broad masses of their followers—as lazy, lacking in foresight, concerned overwhelmingly with immediate pleasures, and prone to alternate from unthinking rebelliousness to apathy. Ironically, the attitudes of the working-class elite toward the masses resembled those of anti-democratic bourgeois observers.

Such attitudes were not exclusive to the social democrats in Germany, although they may have been strongest there. The leaders of the anarchosyndicalist movement in France were unapologetic elitists who frequently expressed contempt for the mundane concerns of the average French worker. And as will be discussed below, Lenin argued that an elite was necessary to lead the uncomprehending masses.

The 1905 revolution in Russia—a key event for the classic age of socialism—worked mightily to exaggerate elite-mass tensions in the socialist parties of western Europe. From the revolution emerged new perspectives concerning revolutionary action, new factional alliances and doctrinal disputes, and generally a clearing—or, from another perspective, a poisoning—of the air among European socialists. Revolutionary violence in Russia inspired those under the sway of the antipositivist mood of the time, which in the socialist context took the form of a rejection of determinist interpretations of Marxism, and a related emphasis on action and revolutionary will.

The popular unrest that began to appear in Russia's industrial centers in the 1890s spread and, after 1901, became intense, in both the cities and the vast countryside. The formation of the Marxist RSDRP was soon paralleled by a revived narodnik organization, the Socialist Revolutionary Party, and by the liberal Constitutional Democrats, or Kadets (from the first two letters of their name, pronounced "kah-deh" in Russian). All three called for major changes in Russia's state and society, and of course they all worked largely outside the bounds of legality.

Under such conditions the government of Nicholas II had both the bad luck and bad judgment to become involved in a war with Japan, beginning in January 1904. This conflict starkly revealed the tsarist regime's inability to wage modern war. It staggered from military disaster to disaster, providing its internal enemies with ample evidence of the need for fundamental reform, indeed for revolution.

In dealing with this internal dissent Nicholas and his advisers proved themselves even more inept—if that was possible—than in fighting off the armed forces of an emerging industrial Japan. In January 1905, while the war was still in progress, a major strike in Saint Petersburg developed into a plan to present a petition directly to the tsar, asking for political as well as economic reform. On January 22, a huge crowd of some 200,000, including women and children (whose presence was normally viewed as a sign of peaceful intent), marched to the Winter Palace, singing patriotic songs and headed by an Orthodox priest, Father Gapon. But the tsar did not meet with the crowd. The security forces around the palace panicked, and fired wildly into the demonstrators, killing or wounding hundreds.

This senseless massacre went down in revolutionary annals as "Bloody Sunday"; it acted as a powerful catalyst, turning broad masses of already disaffected people violently against both the tsarist state and Nicholas himself (who had previously benefited from the deep-rooted popular myth that the Little Father truly cared for his people but was surrounded by evil officials who perverted his will). Wave upon wave of riots and strikes rolled across Russia, while unrest in the countryside also increased considerably. Social democrats, Socialist Revolutionaries, and Kadets rushed to give leadership to this ground swell of popular anger, which found institutional form in soviets or revolutionary councils (the Russian word *Soviet* merely means "council").

There existed for a short time a degree of consensus concerning immediate goals among these various opponents of the regime: All agreed on the need for a constitutional government, similar to governments then existing in western Europe, that would provide basic civil liberties. Nicholas vehemently resisted, but he was rudely prodded forward by the rising level of popular violence. In the summer of 1905 the sailors of the battleship *Potemkin* mutinied. By October a fever pitch of revolutionary enthusiasm was reached with a ten-day general strike, called by the Saint Petersburg Soviet, which finally induced the tsar to make real concessions. He issued the October Manifesto, granting Russia a constitution, replete with guarantees of civil rights and a Duma (parliament) with meaningful legislative powers, based on an extended suffrage.

These heady victories generated their own contradictions. In a familiar revolutionary sequence, the once-united opposition fell to bickering, since only a few were completely satisfied with the October Manifesto. The tsar reassembled his forces and from 1905 until the outbreak of World War I he chipped away at the power of the Duma, while reducing the civil liberties initially granted. For Russian revolutionaries the years immediately following the revolution of 1905 were ones of gloom and even despair.

However, the initially successful use of the general strike was viewed with great enthusiasm inside Russia and had considerable impact in western Europe. As already mentioned, the French anarcho-syndicalists were at the peak of their activity, activity they believed would soon result in their own revolutionary general strike. In Germany the year 1905 saw a sharp rise in labor unrest, brought on by an increase in the cost of living and intensified by the growing anti-union aggressiveness of employers' organizations. The SPD's much vaunted success in the elections of 1903 brought with it no real reforms, no improvement in the conditions of the rank-and-file workers; the party's left wing saw in the device of the general strike, so dramatically successful in Russia, something that might divert the SPD from its passive and sterile parliamentarism.

The recent defeat of Revisionism tended further to embolden the left wing in most parties, to make its leaders believe that they should push forward in the name of revolutionary Marxism. With the outbreak of revolution in Russia, it became common for the SPD's left wing to speak glowingly of the need to act "in the Russian manner"—to contrast the spirited, rebellious Slavs with the phlegmatic, law-abiding Germans (although this sentiment was not shared by most leaders of the SPD, who harbored an often ill-concealed sense of cultural superiority to the Russians).

Kautsky was one of several prominent figures vaguely associated with this "Russian manner," in part because of his long-established friendships with numerous Russian émigré Marxists—he was particularly close to Plekhanov—but even more because of his friendship and intellectual partnership with Rosa Luxemburg. She even more than Kautsky had delivered slashing blows to the threat of Revisionism, and by the late 1890s she was emerging as the most articulate and fiery partisan of revolutionary perspectives in the SPD.

Rosa Luxemburg's identification with Slavic revolutionary virtues was natural; she was of Polish-Jewish background, and even though she had emigrated to Germany to find a broader outlet for her talents, she retained a leading position among Marxist revolutionaries in Poland. A woman of great intellectual ability and astonishing energy, she thrived on conflict and confrontation. Revolution in Russia, paralleled as it was by unrest in Germany, France, and other parts of Europe, was exhilarating for her. Even before 1905 she saw her role as one of prodding the timid leadership of the SPD forward—something that did not contribute to her popularity in party circles—but even among the party's leftists she made many enemies, for she was a difficult and at times impossibly abrasive person, in those respects like Karl Marx himself.

Her relationship with Kautsky was thus always precarious; in retrospect it appears to have been doomed, for aside from their contrasting personal traits (he was inclined to be genial and easy-going, and had a much more supportive attitude to party leaders), they came to differ on important issues of theory and action, brought up by the unrest in Russia and the West in 1905.

Prior to 1905 the leaders of the SPD reluctantly accepted the possibility of resorting to a general strike as a defensive measure—if, for example, a new anti-socialist law or further restrictions on the suffrage were introduced—but they rejected the general strike in the anarcho-syndicalist sense, as the ultimate revolutionary weapon launched aggressively by the working class. Kautsky's attitude was also much tempered by caution; he feared that any widespread use of strikes for political purposes might elude the control of the party, leading then to planless violence and possible repression.

Rosa Luxemburg did not ignore the dangers of planless violence or repression, but her attitude to spontaneous mass action was different. She did not fear it, and she was inclined to believe that whatever errors the masses might make in expressing their resentments should be considered an unavoidable aspect of their education, of their growing class consciousness, of the practical experience necessary to make successful revolution eventually. Her emphasis was above all on the need for action, on aggressive activity by the working class. She could not long abide the tendency of Kautsky or Bebel to emphasize the defensive, the need for control, to endlessly postpone confrontation. To most of the moderate leaders of the SPD, her ideas simply appeared "Russian" and inappropriate to Germany, since they had their origin in Russia's lack of representative institutions and in the related need for clandestine, audacious action against an impossibly corrupt and despicable regime.

In spite of this tendency to identify Luxemburg with Russians and their peculiar emphases on revolutionary action, she did in fact differ from leading Russian Marxists. To appreciate the real if subtle differences between them, it is necessary to review briefly some of the more important controversies that had already emerged in the RSDRP.

By the time of the 1905 revolution Vladimir Ilyich Lenin had distinguished himself as a man of stubborn tenacity, factional ruthlessness, and unswerving dedication to the cause of revolution. In 1902 he published one of his most influential works, the pamphlet entitled *What Is to Be Done?* This was initially accepted by other members of the RSDRP as a powerful polemical statement in the controversy that was raging within the party concerning the interrelated issues of party organization and working-class consciousness. *What Is to Be Done?* came down on the side of the so-called "Political Ones" (*Politiki*), those who emphasized the need to wage a political struggle among the workers, those, that is, who believed that clear class consciousness of a revolutionary sort could only be brought to workers from outside their immediate class experience. Only intellectuals who "knew more" and who were professional revolutionaries could give proper leadership to workers. The opposing group, the "Economists," emphasized that workers' consciousness was firmly rooted in their economic and social experience, and thus intellectual activists should not try to push them beyond what their immediate experience, in the factories and workshops, prepared them to understand. Lenin stressed in hard-hitting language the need for an elite of professional revolutionaries, organized along clandestine and highly centralized lines—a "general staff of the revolution"— that could deal effectively with the dual problem of the backwardness of working-class consciousness in Russia and of tsarist despotism. Without the leadership of such a revolutionary party, Russian workers could arrive at no more than a mere "trade-union consciousness"; they could perceive only the most immediate causes of their discomforts and would tend to content themselves with piecemeal reforms and the indefinite perpetuation of the political, economic, and social status quo.

By the time of the second congress of the RSDRP in 1903, when Lenin sought to have his ideas incorporated into the party program, many Politiki, among them Plekhanov, finally concluded that Lenin had taken their own ideas too far. Nevertheless, through a series of factional maneuvers, Lenin and his followers emerged as the *bolshevik* (that is, majoritarian) faction of the congress, while his opponents in the party, a mixture of Economists and Politiki, assumed the title *menshevik* (minoritarian). Although Lenin was often in the minority in subsequent years, he clung to the title of bolshevik, and, oddly, the mensheviks, while often in the majority, permanently accepted a name that identified them as the minority faction of the RSDRP.

Luxemburg's differences with Lenin, expressed often in characteristically trenchant language, centered around the issue of the role of the party. She was closer to the mensheviks, although for most of the prewar period she retained a gruff and grudging respect for Lenin—he was indeed one of the few prominent figures in the Russian party or in the International whom she did respect. But she generally avoided any close identification with either mensheviks or bolsheviks.

In important ways Lenin's model was the efficient, smooth-running bureaucratic machine of the SPD, but intensified in its elitist and clandestine aspects because of the peculiarities of the Russian situation. This was the very machine that Luxemburg came to resent as an impediment to the revolutionary spontaneity of the masses. But while Lenin hungered for revolutionary action, the leaders of the SPD did not. His notion of party "control" entailed a sharpening of proletarian resentment, an effort to direct it to political action, whereas with figures like Bebel or Kautsky control meant preventing the masses from engaging in premature or intemperate action. And although Lenin's attitude to the masses might be termed condescending, he rarely if ever expressed contempt for them.

These nuances were less clear before the war than they would later become, and it is worth emphasizing the extent to which Lenin, who was at this time the leader of an obscure faction of a young, isolated party and not the towering figure he would later become, was nurtured by the theory and practice of the SPD. Kautsky, whom Lenin painstakingly studied, observed in his influential work, *The Road to Power* (1908) that "however much proletarian organizations grow, they will never, in normal, non-revolutionary times include the whole of the working class . . . but only an élite" (Steenson, p. 167). As earlier noted, Kautsky denied that parliamentary activity could lead to significant change. Indeed, from 1903 to 1907, a period of relative radicalism for him, he seemed almost to abandon the kind of tactical flexibility in regard to other parties in parliament that he had defended at the Paris congress of the International in 1901, and he now often spoke as if he rejected the possibility of any cooperation at all with liberal-bourgeois parties. In analyzing revolutionary events in Russia in 1905, he expressed deep distrust for Russia's indigenous bourgeoisie and argued that Russia's proletariat would have to take the lead in dragging Russia into the modern era and firmly re-establishing a western-style, constitutional regime there.

Such positions—elitism, rejection of parliamentary reformism, a denigration of the liberal bourgeoisie—have been subsequently characterized as Leninist and offered as examples of an odd, "Russian" perversion of Marxism. Even Lenin's attitude to the peasantry, often seem as highly Russian in its origin, had clear parallels in Kautsky's thought, since Kautsky believed that Russia's peasants were potentially an important revolutionary force and not necessarily the reactionary brutes or unreliable allies that many Marxists believed them to be. He stressed that without the added push from the peasantry, under the general revolutionary leadership of the proletariat (and of course its Marxist party) Russia's historically weak bourgeoisie would almost certainly duplicate, possibly in an even more cowardly fashion, the failure of the German bourgeoisie to overwhelm and eradicate the old order, reaching instead for some sort of compromise with tsarism. (It is important to keep clearly in mind here that Kautsky was not talking about a proletarian revolution in Russia but rather a bourgeois revolution driven forward by the proletariat and peasantry. Thus his earlier criticisms of Vollmar in the German context were not inconsistent with his position on the Russian peasantry, for the Russian situation represented an earlier stage of development, with socialist revolution, he believed, far in the future.)

This relatively radical stage in Kautsky's thought began to change, however imperceptibly, as the high tide of revolutionary hopes in 1905 and 1906 ebbed in western Europe and in Russia. In German social-democratic circles those who were most upset by the notion of political strikes launched a counterattack. The trade-union leaders led the way, but many others who did not consider themselves reformists and who had opposed Revisionism were driven rightward into a factional alliance with the moderates and reformists because they feared that wild-eyed, irresponsible "anarcho-Marxists" were gaining undue influence in the party. Kautsky's position was not quite so simplistic, but significantly he began to criticize the party's Left (whereas before he had defended it) even while continuing to utter harsh words about the growing bureaucratization of the SPD. He now formulated a position that he explicitly termed "centrism," between the overly cautious bureaucrats and parliamentarians, on the one hand, and the heated enthusiasts around Rosa Luxemburg, on the other. (Kautsky's and Luxemburg's judgments of one another at this time illustrate the nature of their break, which became irrevocable: He wrote that she was "an extremely talented woman, . . . but tact and a feeling of comradeship were completely foreign to her" (Steenson, p. 134). She began to find him "heavy, dull, unimaginative, and ponderous," his ideas "cold, pedantic, doctrinaire" (Nettl, *Luxemburg* abridged ed., p. 255).

At the SPD congress at Jena in 1905 Bebel lent his support to a resolution that accepted the possibility of resorting to political strikes, both as defensive and offensive weapons. The trade-union leaders protested bitterly, and from subsequent conferences with SPD leaders, usually held behind the scenes, emerged the famous (or infamous) Mannheim Agreement of 1906. The agreement in effect signaled the abandonment of the traditional leadership of Marxist party over trade union (it had at any rate been somewhat fictional); the unions were given a veto not only over political strikes but over other important party undertakings. Thus reformist union officials gave added weight to the already highly cautious party leadership. The SPD's left wing was of course outraged.

The parliamentary elections of 1907 further intensified trends typified by the Mannheim Agreement. The Chancellor, von Bülow, skillfully exploited the related issues of imperialism and nationalism— highly charged after the native uprisings in German's African colonies and her humiliating experience at the Algeciras Conference following the Moroccan Crisis of 1905—to attack both the SPD and the Center Party. Social-democratic representation in the Reichstag plummeted from the eighty-one seats gained in the 1903 elections to thirty-eight.

Most party leaders considered this an unmitigated disaster and feared what von Bülow might do with his victory. However, the SPD's defeat was not entirely clear-cut: Total votes for the party in 1907 actually increased by approximately 200,000 over the 1903 figures. What was different in 1907 was, first, that nearly 10 percent more voters, primarily nationalistic and anti-socialist in temper, went to the polls, and, second, that Bülow was able to attract former parliamentary opponents among the left-liberal bourgeoisie to his electoral bloc.

The combination of the Mannheim Agreement and the 1907 elections tended further to envenom intraparty relations. The parliamentary reformists in the SPD held up the electoral failure as proof that the SPD's flirtation with revolutionary internationalism in 1905–06 had led to a growing isolation and political impotence. For the party's revolutionaries, on the other hand, the elections underlined the futility of reformist hopes to ally with the left-leaning bourgeoisie for piecemeal reform. Rosa Luxemburg, an outsider from the beginning of her career in the SPD, became disruptively bitter, convinced now that most party leaders, including Bebel, would be endlessly content to confine their activities to parliament; revolutionary action by the masses made them uncomfortable, whatever verbal commitments to revolution they might make.

Most accounts of European socialism in these years agree that these trends within the SPD were duplicated in other parties of the International, that the bureaucrats and parliamentarians pulled their parties slowly rightward between 1906 and 1914. Along these lines, the course of the SFIO is usually cited: After unification in 1905, under the aegis of a Marxist program, it was Jean Jaurès who assumed de facto leadership of the party, rather than Guesde or a representative of the revolutionary Left; and Jaurès also tended to focus the SFIO's attention on developments in the Chamber of Deputies.

Yet Jaurès cannot be facilely lumped together with the SPD *Bonzen*. He is widely regarded as the most attractive, certainly the most beloved, of the prewar socialist leaders. He was a warm yet deeply serious man, who strove incessantly and quite explicitly to bridge the gap between reformists and revolutionaries in France, and he succeeded in gaining the respect of both camps to a greater degree than Kautsky and Bebel. The young Russian revolutionary Leon Trotsky, in exile in France before the war and hardly inclined to gush with enthusiasm over western reformists, left a memorable portrait of Jaurès. He wrote that the French "are a race of men potent in their physical and moral muscularity, unequalled in their courage, profound in their passion, powerful in their will. One had only to listen to the ringing voice of Jaurès, to see his enlightened look, his imperious nose, his thick and unyoked neck, to say to himself: There is Man!" (Goldberg, p. 357).

Jaurès had little cause to be made uncomfortable, as were some Germans, by comparisons with the Russians. The French had a rich and living revolutionary tradition, with which he enthusiastically identified himself. He moved into the socialist camp in the early 1890s in part because he believed the Radicals were edging away from their earlier identification with the social republic and with revolutionary change. Yet he remained throughout his life open to the possibility of reform through class cooperation within the context of the existing institutions of the Third Republic. Thus he gave cautious support to the ultimately disappointing Millerand experiment, but he was also able to adjust to Guesde's victory in 1905. He assumed an attitude of greater intransigence to capitalism and to the existing parliamentary coalitions that served its interests. His militancy was above all inspired by a struggle against the growing threat of war (concerning which more will be said in the following chapter).

Jaurès's militancy did not mean that he was ever willing to embrace the rigid formulas that Guesde had picked up from the German Marxists. Although Jaurès expressed frequent and genuine admiration for German culture in general and for the SPD in particular, in his mind there was never any question that the SPD's Marxism, especially its attitude to the state and the bourgeois class, reflected conditions peculiar to Germany, and certainly did not hold true in many respects for France. Thus in the spring of 1914, when the SFIO won its greatest electoral victory (its parliamentary representation jumped to 103, reflecting 1.4 million votes, 300,000 more than in 1910), Jaurès seriously considered joining, as minister of foreign affairs—where his influence might have been decisive in preventing war—a Radical-led cabinet. He remarked at the time that the SFIO must not "founder on the rocks of scholasticism" (Goldberg, p. 454), although ultimately the Radical-socialist coalition failed to reach fruition.

The leaders of the SPD felt similar temptations in the few years immediately preceding the war, and within the ranks of the social democrats there were kindred musings about the confinements of dogmatism. As the Bülow Bloc ran into difficulties and began to dissolve in 1909, the possibility of some sort of political cooperation with the bourgeois Left, in spite of the many disappointments of the past, became once again attractive. Such was the case especially after the formation, from the merger of various middle-class groups, of the Progressive People's Party in 1910, giving the Germans a rough equivalent, though relatively much weaker, of the French Radical Party. Progressives and social democrats agreed on a number of key issues—the need for reform of taxation and of the suffrage, most notably—and, if they could have worked together harmoniously in both electoral campaigns in the Reichstag, they could have conceivably formed a powerful Left bloc. In the elections of 1912 the SPD abandoned its decades-old policy of rejecting formal electoral alliances. It entered its own candidates in the first round of voting but then agreed to withdraw in favor of Progressive candidates where those candidates appeared to have the best chance of winning; Progressives were to do the same, a practice long familiar in France between socialists and Radicals. The result was a resounding victory for the SPD, which gained a million new voters (from 3.25 million to 4.25 million) and 110 seats in the Reichstag. The SPD had since 1890 been the party with the greatest number of voters in Germany; now it became also the largest party in the Reichstag, having won nearly twice as many votes as the second largest, the Center Party.

That the SPD could be so large a party yet remain isolated from political power was obviously awkward and paradoxical. But for the SPD to exercise political influence under a constitution that did not require the chancellor to have a parliamentary majority what was necessary was a long-range strategy of close cooperation with the Progressives. If the two parties could exercise control over the budget, where a Reichstag majority did have some meaning, they might well have eventually forced their will upon the Chancellor and the Prussian power structure. But such an association with the less-than-respectable social democrats was not attractive to the Progressives (indeed, their followers had been most reticent to vote social democratic in the second round of the 1912 elections, while the disciplined social-democratic second-round voters were responsible, when the SPD candidates withdrew, for virtuallly every seat won by the Progressives).

Thus the 1912 elections did not produce any real shift in the Reichstag; indeed, they further exacerbated tensions within the SPD. The party's moderates still held on to the hope that eventually the liberal bourgeoisie would come to accept the social democrats as necessary allies against the reactionaries; for Rosa Luxemburg and her wing the voting patterns of the Progressive electorate merely offered further proof, if any were needed, that the class interests and class identity of the bourgeoisie could never be reconciled with those of the proletariat.

It was perhaps possible that the liberal bourgeoisie in Germany would have in time become more conciliatory. But time was not something given to these prewar parliamentarians. On June 28, 1914, Archduke Franz-Ferdinand, the heir to the Austro-Hungarian throne, was assassinated at Sarajevo. A completely new stage of European history had begun, one that would transform the world of European socialism.

GUIDE TO FURTHER READING

A number of the general histories of socialism mentioned in the bibliographical notes to the Introduction (for example, Landauer, Cole, Dolléans, and Wachenheim) devote considerable attention to the years 1871 to 1914 and could be consulted for further information on the period. A less onerous approach might be to consult a few of the many biographies of the leading figures of the time. Among the best of these is Harvey Goldberg's *Life of Jaurès*, which pays attention to the international scene, although the main focus is on France. Gary Steenson's admirable *Karl Kautsky, 1854–1938* manages to rescue Kautsky from much of the obloquy and historical neglect that he has suffered since the 1920s. More than simply a biography, Peter Gay's *The Dilemma of Democratic Socialism: Eduard Bernstein's Challenge to Marx* is an excellent introduction to the Revisionist Controversy and to the intellectual world of German social democracy. Covering not only Germany but Russia and Poland as well, J. P. Nettl's *Rosa Luxemburg* is a remarkable piece of scholarship, erudite, sympathetic yet critical, penetrating. Also brilliant and highly readable is Isaac Deutscher's three-volume biography of Trotsky, the first volume of which is relevant here (*The Prophet Armed*). Another highly readable if fat (640 pp.) volume is Bertram Wolfe's study of Trotsky, Lenin, and Stalin, *Three Who Made a Revolution*. (Further discussion of the numerous works dealing with Lenin and Leninism, and with Trotsky, Stalin, and other Russian revolutionaries will be found in subsequent chapters.)

A commendable if unorthodox introduction to the generation before the war is by Harvey Mitchell and Peter N. Stearns, *Workers and Protest: The European Labor Movement, The Working Classes, and the Origins of Social Democracy, 1890–1914.*

The best overall account of the Second International remains James Joll's *The Second International, 1889–1914.* Somewhat heavier reading and less balanced is volume 1 of Julius Braunthal's *History of the Internationals.* Also recommended is Patricia van der Esch's *La Deuxième Internationale.*

A competent and scholarly introduction to the early years of the SPD is Vernon Lidtke's *The Outlawed Party: Social Democracy in Germany, 1878–1890.* Covering a broader period, from the standpoint of a sociologist, is Günther Roth's *The Social Democrats in Imperial Germany.* The best general history of the party prior to the war years is Gary Steenson's *Not One Man! Not One Penny! German Social Democracy, 1863–1914.* A lively and detailed older study of the years leading up to the war and the schism in the SPD is Carl Schorske's *German Social Democracy, 1905–1917.* Sophisticated and broadly interpretive is Gerhard Ritter's *Die Arbeiterbewegung im wilhelminischen Reich, 1890–1900.* Examples of the newer monographs dealing with history "from below" are Klaus Tenfelde, *Sozialgeschichte der Bergarbeiterschaft an der Ruhr im neunzehnten Jahrhundert*, and David F. Crew, *Town in the Ruhr: A Social History of Bochum, 1860–1914.*

David Stafford's *From Anarchism to Reformism* ably studies the activities of the Broussists. Details on the formation of the SFIO can be found in Aaron Noland's *Founding of the French Socialist Party, 1893–1905.* Claude Willard has written a monumental monograph, *Les Guesdistes.* Similarly monumental works of the new social history are Ives Lequin's *Les Ouvriers de la région lyonnaise, 1848–1914* and Rolande Trempé's *Les Mineurs de Carmaux, 1848–1914*, both in two volumes. More approachable are Joan Wallach Scott's *The Glassworkers of Carmaux, French Craftsmen and Political Action in a Nineteenth Century City*, and Tony Judt's *Socialism in Provence, 1871–1914: A Study in the Ori-*

gins of the Modern French Left, although the latter has been criticized for conceptual carelessness. Barrington Moore's *Injustice* borrows heavily from a number of the newer monographs of history from below and offers their findings in a more approachable form.

C. Tsuzuki's *H. M. Hyndman and British Socialism* is rich and penetrating. Stanley Pierson's *Marxism and the Origins of British Socialism* is a model of intellectual history. Also excellent is Willard Wolfe, *From Radicalism to Socialism: Men and Ideas in the Formation of Fabian Socialist Doctrines, 1881–1889.*

Anarchism does not by its nature lend itself to neat or definitive treatment, but appealing introductions can be found in James Joll, *The Anarchists,* and Daniel Guérin, *Anarchism.* More comprehensive is George Woodcock's *Anarchism: A History of Libertarian Ideas and Movements,* which contains an ample bibliography. Leonard Krimerman and Lewis Perry have put together a useful collection of diverse essays on anarchism in *Patterns of Anarchy.* The definitive account of Russian populism is the previously discussed *Roots of Revolution,* by Franco Venturi. Martin Miller's recent biography, *Kropotkin,* is a major contribution. The most recent comprehensive picture of anarchosyndicalism, both from a theoretical and practical standpoint, is F. F. Ridley's *Revolutionary Syndicalism in France.* A lively dissent from the traditional view of the anarchosyndicalists is registered by Peter Stearns in *Revolutionary Syndicalism and French Labor.* A respected older standard work on the French anarchist movement as a whole is Jean Maitron's *Histoire du mouvement anarchiste en France, 1880–1914.*

The Birth of Communism, 1914-1924

5

INTRODUCTION

On July 31, 1914, Jean Jaurès was assassinated by a nationalist fanatic. His death was symbolic of the ensuing death of international socialism as it had existed in the generation before World War I. The decade of war and revolution that followed forcefully accelerated the schismatic tendencies of prewar socialism, forcing socialists to make decisions that they had previously avoided—between patriotism and internationalism, reformism and revolution, party unity and doctrinal consistency. The outbreak of revolution in Russia and the ultimate victory of the bolsheviks, developments that were intimately linked to the war, transformed socialist perspectives in Europe and the rest of the world. The bolsheviks, often ignored or ridiculed by western socialists before 1917, became the presumptive leaders of a renovated world socialism, soon to take up the name "communism." But revolutionary expectations outside Russia, which reached a crescendo in the two to three years following the end of the war, were one by one bitterly disappointed, leaving a deeply divided and disillusioned socialist movement in western Europe and a proletarian dictatorship in Russia faced with gigantic dilemmas.

SOCIALISTS AND WAR

The issue of the appropriate response of socialists to the threat of war had long been debated among members of the Second International. The position of the extreme Left, more or less shared by the anarchists, was that workers should respond with a revolutionary general strike to any declaration of war between the major powers. Those in the center, like Kautsky or Guesde, tended to be fatalistic; they did not think that socialists had the power to stop war, although they drew some comfort from the prediction that war between Europe's major powers would result in social revolution. Kautsky emphasized, however, that this revolution would come at the end of the conflict, with the exhaustion of the contending powers, rather than at its beginning as a result of a preventative general strike and working-class uprising. Right-wing socialists made little effort to mask their deep-rooted patriotism and their determination to support their country in the case of war. All socialist factions were forced to recognize that the masses had by no means been solidly won over to socialist internationalism.

Yet nearly all socialists wished to avoid war. Insofar as they argued that war was inevitable under capitalism and that war would bring revolution this antiwar position was contradictory, but in most of them the values of humanitarian pacifism and the dread of massive bloodshed overwhelmed pure, harsh Marxian logic. Socialists were emotionally engaged against war, and even those who confidently predicted that the inexorable contradictions of capitalism would bring war and revolution worked frantically for peace.

Jean Jaurès devoted much of his career to the struggle against war, and in him the humanitarian revulsion against the prospect of mass slaughter in the battlefield was perhaps the strongest of any socialist leader. But he was caught on the horns of a dilemma: On the one hand he believed in the right, the duty even, of socialists to defend their country from aggressive attack; on the other hand he recognized that all of the major powers were responsible, to varying degrees, for the growing international tension, that all were in some sense "aggressive." In this context how could aggressors and defenders be clearly distinguished? A key element in Jaurès's position, and, one is tempted to add, its fatal flaw, was his conviction that it would be possible in any given instance to identify an aggressor-nation, and, having made this identification, to rally all socialists, even those in the aggressor-nation, against that nation in the interests of peace.

Most socialists doubted that an aggressor could be reliably identified, and, even more important, doubted that once identified, adequate sanctions by socialists could be put into effect. Such doubts were especially troubling to the center faction of the German social democrats. They knew that even though their party had little influence over—or even knowledge of—the foreign policy deliberations of the German government, the SPD could not refuse to defend Germany from attack. As they saw it, Germany, with its advanced industrial civilization, risked being overrun by Europe's most backward and barbaric major power, Russia. And since the working class was far more numerous and far better organized in Germany than in Russia, a general strike in Germany was potentially more destructive of Germany's warmaking efforts than would be a comparable general strike in Russia. Thus, in the event of war, the call for a general strike in Germany, if followed, would open up Germany to Russian invasion, since Russia would be weakened relatively little by a comparable call by her own socialists. This reasoning gave many German social democrats a pretext to dismiss the whole idea of a general strike in case of war as a "reactionary" idea, since, even in the unlikely event that workers joined it in large numbers, it would lead to a Russian victory.

Once the German socialists accepted the legitimacy of defending their country against "the Cossack hordes"—as they were inclined to put it—they involved themselves in some wrenching paradoxes. The logic of European balance-of-power politics had obliged progressive and democratic France to ally with reactionary Russia, and thus, if the Germans were to fight Russia, they would also have to take on Russia's ally, France.

This paradox was intensified for German socialists by the military strategy of Germany's leaders, who reasoned that the only way their country could escape the grave dangers of a prolonged war on two fronts was to attack France first—whether or not she actually attacked Germany—in a lightning campaign, and then turn to Russia. This strategy, the Schlieffen Plan, was based upon the calculation that Germany's power, which was highly mobile, should be concentrated first in the west, knocking out France within six weeks (as Germany had already done in 1870), and then could turn to slow-mobilizing Russia, which would take at least six weeks to get its vast and unwieldy army effectively into the field. What this chain of reasoning meant for German socialists, even those who were not explicitly patriotic, was that if they accepted the idea of national defense against Russia they would be drawn into a position in which it would be difficult to condemn a preemptive offensive action against France.

Russia began mobilizing in early August, forcing German socialists to make these considerations with dizzying urgency. Because of the Schlieffen Plan's six-week schedule, Germany's leaders viewed any mobilization by Russia as an offensive action, indeed tantamount to invasion. Thus, Germany's plans to invade France were immediately activated.

In this context, most working-class leaders in Germany did not even consider revolutionary action. But there still remained the question of what to do about voting war credits in the Reichstag. This was a largely symbolic matter since the votes of the SPD delegates were not necessary for a majority, and even if the delegation abstained from voting or voted against war credits, it did not necessarily follow that the party would then engage in a sustained opposition to the war. On August first the right wing of the SPD parliamentary delegation let it be known that its members would support war credits no matter what the official position of the party (an almost unheard-of breach of discipline in this highly disciplined party). On the same day Kautsky and other party leaders began to draft a statement that assumed the SPD parliamentary delegation would vote against war credits, but they soon learned that a majority of SPD deputies would not even accept abstention, let alone a negative vote. Kautsky then tried to work out a resolution that, while accepting the inevitability of a vote for the credits, contained sharp attacks on the ruling class in Germany and demands that the German government renounce beforehand any annexations or violations of neutrality. But this effort was blocked by the German foreign office.

Thus when it came to a vote in the Reichstag, the SPD delegation voted unanimously in favor of war credits. The minority that opposed a favorable vote in the preliminary caucus accepted the will of the majority, as was the practice of the parliamentary delegation, and voted as a united bloc.

Socialists in other countries, especially those of the Entente, were outraged, even dumb with shock, when the news of this "betrayal" of international socialist principles became known. However, when the turn of the French socialists came to vote war credits, they similarly proclaimed their duty to national defense, and voted unanimously for war credits. They claimed that it was necessary to defend democratic France from the deadly advance of German autocratic militarism. They were not ready to recognize that Germany's action, given Russia's mobilization, could also be termed a kind of national defense. All of these actions pointed back to the reservations that Kautsky and others had articulated before the war concerning how much socialists could do to prevent war.

The question of war had been the basis of debates at a number of prewar congresses of the International. The most important resolution dealing with the contradictions between national defense and socialist internationalism was that passed at the congress of Stuttgart in 1907, and re-affirmed at Basel in 1912, at the last meeting of the International. Appended to a series of typically vague paragraphs was a surprisingly radical passage, sponsored by Rosa Luxemburg and Lenin, which stipulated that socialist parties should strive to prevent the outbreak of war, but if war broke out nevertheless, these parties were obliged to make every effort to end it, including taking advantage of "the economic and political crisis created by the war to arouse the population and hasten the overthrow of capitalist rule" (Schorske, p. 83).

This passage obviously did not reflect the deepest convictions of most of the leaders of the International, but many of them went along with it as part of an effort to assuage the resentments of the revolutionary Left, which was still smarting from the defeats of the preceding year. As war clouds gathered in the summer of 1914, the leaders of Europe's socialist parties did indeed follow the recommendations of the Stuttgart resolution, up to a point. For example, antiwar demonstrations were organized by both the SPD and SFIO, and socialist orators menacingly reminded Europe's ruling élites of the possibility of revolutionary action if war should break out. Yet the most experienced politicians perceived these as empty threats. It was perfectly clear to them that neither the socialist leaders nor the working masses were prepared for sustained revolutionary action if war actually did come.

Once war had been declared, socialists who had the week before cheered antiwar speeches joined in with those of all political persuasions in a paroxysm of patriotic frenzy that exceeded all expectations. Under these circumstances a call by the SFIO or SPD for a general strike would have been quixotic, if not suicidal. As one German social-democratic leader later put it—and the situation was identical in France—he and his comrades voted for war credits to avoid being beaten to death by their followers.

At this point almost no one cared to bring up the resolutions of the Stuttgart congress. Indeed, many socialists who had before the war been strong partisans of internationalist Marxism and admirers of the SPD, men like Guesde, Plekhanov, and Marcel Cachin, now delivered speeches and wrote articles of fervently nationalistic, anti-German, and even racist content. Members of the SFIO joined with leaders of bourgeois parties into a cabinet of national defense, under the banner of *Union sacrée*, a sacred union of Frenchmen, in which class conflict was put aside. In Germany, a *Burgfrieden*, or "civil peace," was declared. Although the SPD did not actually become part of a governmental coalition, its leaders joined wholeheartedly in the war effort. (Significantly, Kautsky rejected the notion of Burgfrieden and was much distressed by the chauvinistic statements of certain party leaders, but he still saw no feasible alternative to support for the war.)

Each of the major powers looked to a quick and dramatic victory, and socialists shared these expectations. Even as it became clear that this was to be a war of stalemate and attrition, the leaders of the socialist parties of the main contending powers were slow to come around to the idea of a negotiated peace, to say nothing of the Stuttgart commitment to exploit the difficulties of the war in order to bring about the downfall of capitalism. The executive body of the International, the International Socialist Bureau (ISB), was in the hands of the French and Belgians, who were adamant in their assertions that the war be fought *jusqu'au bout*—to the bitter end—and that peace was inconceivable until the Germans were expelled from French and Belgian territory, and German militarism decisively crushed.

As the war continued and the grisly toll of death and destruction mounted, not all socialists, even in the occupied areas, could maintain such a stubborn attitude, however, and some began to entertain the idea of a negotiated peace. On the international level, leadership in the cause of such a peace was taken by Italian socialists, leaders of the PSI (*Partito socialista italiano*, or Italian Socialist Party), in conjunction with the Swiss socialists and socialists of other neutral countries. The Italians first attempted to arrange an international socialist conference under the auspices of the ISB, in conformity with the Stuttgart resolution, but they encountered vehement hostility on the part of the French and Belgian leaders of the Bureau. They were finally obliged to call a conference on their own, which assembled in the village of Zimmerwald, Switzerland, in September 1915. This was the beginning of an active, organized socialist antiwar (often termed "Zimmerwaldian") movement.

By the time of the September meeting Italy had become involved in the war—she entered in the spring—but the PSI had managed to be more faithful to its prewar internationalist commitments than the SFIO and SPD. The reasons for this fidelity went beyond the undeniable revolutionary courage and strong internationalist convictions of Italian socialist leaders, and it is instructive to consider them in evaluating the role of the PSI in the Zimmerwaldian movement.

To begin with, Italy had not been invaded in August 1914, and thus Italy's population did not experience the intense fears and bellicose passions that so overwhelmed the Germans and French. And when Italy finally did enter ten months after the war began—abandoning her former Axis allies—her entry was so grossly opportunistic and so obviously the work of a small clique of politicians and demagogues that the bulk of the Italian people remained emotionally uninvolved. Moreover, Italy's common people, those who would do the actual fighting, had ample opportunity to observe the shattering of the initial confidence in rapid victories and the ensuing carnage of trench warfare.

To these factors must be added the "dress rehearsal" for 1914 of 1911, when the Italian prime minister, Giolitti, had launched a blatantly imperialistic campaign into Libya. This threw the PSI into turmoil, resulting in the expulsion of the party's right wing, which had approved of the Libyan campaign. Thereafter the party swung to the left, led by the charismatic young revolutionary Benito Mussolini. In the early summer of 1914, the PSI and the Italian state were on the verge of civil war, culminating in the famous *settimana rossa*, or Red Week, in June.

These prewar experiences meant that Italian socialists were less tempted to join in an Italian equivalent of the Union sacrée or the Burgfrieden. Indeed, while opposition to the war in Germany or France still took great courage, even by the summer of 1915 opposition in Italy was highly popular and by no means limited to the socialists. When the PSI called for a massive demonstration on May 1 against Italy's entry in the war, thousands marched, in spite of the government's outlawing of the demonstration. Matters reached a climax in mid-May 1915, when military authorities took over Turin to crush a general strike there.

In spite of this brave start, it ultimately became clear that the PSI too was in no shape to engage in a life-and-death struggle with the forces of order. Thus the party's leaders adopted a neutral position, "nè aderire nè sabotare," that is, officially they would neither join nor sabotage Italy's war effort. This position too could be described as a failure to carry out the Stuttgart resolution, especially since, unofficially, Italian socialist trade-union leaders became actively involved in the war effort. However, the Italian socialists did continue their efforts to convene an international antiwar conference, with the Zimmerwald meeting as the result.

Those who responded to the invitation to come to Zimmerwald belonged primarily to the prewar Left and extreme Left of the parties of the International. Some came because of revolutionary internationalist convictions, but most were motivated by a simple desire to express socialist opposition to continued stalemated warfare. Except for the PSI, none of the major western parties sent official representatives. Indeed, most of those who appeared did so against the adamant opposition of their parties' leadership. However, three more or less official delegations represented the socialist parties of Russia.

Among the often uncertain and deeply divided delegates at Zimmerwald, Lenin cut a striking figure. He was full of uncompromising certainty. His indignation at Europe's leading socialists knew no bounds; even the leaders of the PSI, for whom he had initially some admiring words, he now branded as cowardly pseudo-revolutionaries. Thus most of those who came to Zimmerwald, who saw themselves as members of an audacious minority within their own parties, were dismissed by Lenin as mere "social-pacifists," and he engaged in fiery verbal duels with several of them. G. M. Serrati, the leader of the extreme Left in the PSI, in his anger at Lenin had to be physically restrained by the other delegates.

In reading over Lenin's hard-hitting theses on the war, one is quickly made aware of how little he shared the "soft," pacifistic, humanitarian sentiments of most western socialists. He indeed made much of the distinction between "softs" and "hards" in the socialist movement, and he wanted only "hards"—reliable revolutionaries, unafraid of violence—in his party. Just as he had earlier molded the ideas of the Politiki into such an extreme form, so now he built upon widely accepted Marxist propositions, to be found largely in the writings of Kautsky, but he reformulated them in an unequivocal, some said exaggerated, form, obviously reflecting a Russian perspective, and indeed resembling in certain ways anarchist or narodnik formulations. He rejected out of hand all arguments about the right of socialists to defend their countries against attack. He insisted that there could be no "aggressors" and "defenders," no capitalist country that was in the right while others were in the wrong. There was only one fundamental cause for the war— the imperialistic strivings of all European governments—and thus no one socialist party had any more a right to national defense than any other. The only proper Marxist response to an imperialist war was a call for revolution.

In the same vein Lenin proclaimed that imperialism was also the cause of patriotism among socialists. As he saw it, the extraordinary profits that imperialistic capitalism was able to reap permitted it to "buy off" a section of the proletariat, which he termed the "workers' aristocracy." Higher profits permitted higher salaries for this group, and it gradually came to lose its proletarian identity and to live a life of relative affluence. Composed of skilled workers and bureaucrats in the unions and socialist parties, it lost all desire for revolution. Even more, it did its best to dampen and pervert the rebellious spirits of the more exploited strata below it, and to cooperate with bourgeois authorities by whipping up nationalist passions in the working class.

Lenin perceived even wider implications in imperialism. The high profits made possible by exploiting colonial labor allowed capitalists of the West to feel so secure in their rulership that they could fashion more sophisticated tools of manipulation; they could afford to extend the blessings of formal political democracy and liberal constitutionalism. Universal manhood suffrage, freedom of the press (including the socialist press), freedom of assembly, the right to strike, social welfare legislation—all were found useful by the more prescient elements of the ruling class as ways of pacifying the masses.

In this cluster of ideas one senses borrowings from Kautsky, and indeed the term "workers' aristocracy" had been used by Bebel in his polemic against the Revisionists. But Lenin's use of prewar Marxist orthodoxy was more far-reaching, less flexible. Prewar Marxists and other socialists, such as Hobson, Hilferding, and Luxemburg, had also blamed imperialism for the unexpected longevity of capitalism and for national tensions, but very few of them after 1914 were willing to follow Lenin in his tenacious and narrow consistency. Nor were most of them willing to accept his demands that revolutionaries break away immediately from their old parties, denounce their leaders as traitors to the working class—"social-patriots," to use another abusive epithet from Lenin's impressive armory—and agitate among the poorest proletarians in the factories and at the front in favor of work stoppages, strikes, antiwar demonstrations, mutiny, and finally general revolutionary insurrection. Lenin's most striking slogan of the period—and he was a master at composing them—"turn the imperialist war into civil war!" did not exercise wide appeal in the West.

Thus even more than before the war Lenin's ideas appeared peculiarly Russian to western socialists. And the influence of Lenin's Russian background does seem undeniable: It made sense to view the masses as easily manipulable and prone to self-destructive passions in a country of widespread illiteracy, of weak or nonexistent working-class traditions and institutions, one in which violent, desperate revolts had been common for centuries. Ardent internationalism and revolutionary defeatism had at least relatively greater appeal in a country where the masses had little sense of identification with existing political institutions, and where they were not afraid of losing a relatively high standard of living through military defeat. Marx's old battle cry, "You have only your chains to lose!" had more meaning for the working masses of Russia than for workers in western Europe. Belief in an international socialist revolution, in the same way, exercised an understandably strong appeal for Russian Marxists, who could see that only through massive aid from the industrialized West could Russia enter a stage of socialist development in the near future. Of course such aid would not be forthcoming from a capitalist West; only when socialism had triumphed there could it be undertaken.

Not surprisingly, Lenin remained isolated at Zimmerwald. Most of the other delegates retained hopes of preserving the old International, did not want to split their parties, and hoped for a negotiated peace. Revolution seemed to them a very distant prospect. And they remained deeply divided among themselves. However, the conference did re-establish a degree of socialist internationalism. The French and German delegations agreed to a declaration that began "this war is not our war . . . ," and the conference as a whole composed a resolution that placed the blame for the conflict on the shoulders of Europe's bourgeois governments, denounced those socialists who were cooperating with the war effort, and called for a peace without annexations or indemnities.

The war continued, and in 1916 an end to it through either victory or negotiations seemed no closer. Indeed, some of the most horrifying and pointless battles of the war, at Verdun and on the Somme, occurred in 1916. Inevitably this carnage pushed many socialists toward a more serious consideration of revolutionary alternatives; for them the violence that would accompany a revolution came to appear as possibly the lesser of two evils.

In a structural sense also the never-ending war tended to exacerbate social tensions and to reserve some of the trends that ostensibly reduced class conflict and aided social integration in the years before the war. The unprecedented destruction of the war reduced the amount of wealth to be distributed in the warring countries, and the growth and concentration of heavy industry was tremendously accelerated. This acceleration meant a relative increase in the number of factory proletarians, as workers were pulled from small shops, luxury production, farming, and the retail trade. Moreover, in all warring countries the funneling of workers into the war industries was accomplished in the context of national peril and crisis. The urgent demands of mass production for the materials of war tended to equalize working conditions in the war industries, with harsh factory discipline, arduous work, and long hours. Although pay in the war industries was relatively high and rationing more favorably allocated—in order to attract workers from less vital economic sectors—a marked decline in living standards was evident among nearly all classes.

The evidence is ambiguous concerning the extent to which rapid growth of heavy industry and a decline in living standards favored a parallel growth in proletarian-revolutionary consciousness. Much of the antiwar protest and the violent unrest that appeared toward the end of the war did occur predominantly in the war-expanded industries, above all in the metal industry. The increase of organized workers in those areas was at times remarkable: In France the membership of the Federation of Metal Workers rose from 7,500 members in 1912 to over 200,000 in 1919. In the same year the membership of the German metal workers' union reached 1,250,000, making it one of the largest unions in the history of organized labor. However, this growth and a concurrent restiveness did not necessarily mean a desire for social revolution. As will be more fully discussed below, most of the demands made by the metal workers, even when political, grew out of concerns for concrete and limited reforms rather than the desire for a total overhaul of the system.

The continued stalemate war and the mounting social tensions within each country encouraged the convocation of a new antiwar conference, which met in the small town of Kienthal, again in Switzerland, in April 1916. The pronouncements that emerged from this conference went beyond the vaguely pacifistic tone of those at Zimmerwald; they asserted that no lasting peace could be made without social revolution, and they meted out harsh words to the "socialist warmongers" at the head of the main socialist parties. The delegates at Kienthal might thus be said to have moved closer to Lenin's position, although still few of them were willing to accept his prescriptions as a whole. It would not be until 1917 that the antiwar movement began to attract a mass following in the West, and it would not be until the end of that year that western revolutionaries began to look to Lenin for leadership.

The year 1917 was a turning point in more ways than the obvious one, that revolution broke out in Russia. In western Europe too events of great importance to socialists occurred: The SPD split into opposing parties, the beginning of a series of such splits in its ranks and in the ranks of the other major parties; there were mutinies on the French front; a major working-class insurrection broke out in Italy; the United States entered the war; and serious efforts were made to arrive at a negotiated peace, ultimately without success.

The schism of the SPD, while it was ostensibly something that Lenin had long called for, did not occur along the lines of his program. That is, it did not involve a break by revolutionaries from the party in order to give revolutionary direction to the masses. Rather, the high-handed tactics of the patriotic leaders of the SPD against the growing numbers of antiwar dissidents virtually forced the latter out of the old party and left them with little choice but to establish a new one. The new Independent Social Democratic Party, or USPD (*Unabhängige Sozialdemokratische Partei Deutschlands*), was anything but a centralized and homogeneous Leninist party. Although the overwhelming majority of its membership came from the left and left-center of the prewar party, Eduard Bernstein joined it, because he too, in his desire for a negotiated peace, had incurred the wrath of the party leadership.

In revulsion from the authoritarian excesses of the old party bosses, the USPD's constitution gave great leeway to local and provincial branches. In this sense also it did not resemble the bolshevik model. It was more like the British Labour Party; various groups that maintained a separate identity, such as the Spartacists and the *revolutionäre Obleute* (Revolutionary Shop Stewards), were accepted into its ranks.

The Spartacists, led by Rosa Luxemburg, formed the kernel of the later German Communist Party, but at first they constituted only a tiny fraction of the total USPD membership. As earlier noted, Luxemburg had always retained a grudging respect for Lenin, and now the war brought them closer together. She by no means embraced bolshevism, but she shared with Lenin a deep outrage at patriotic socialism and a belief that revolution was needed to bring an end to the war.

Luxemburg remained an outsider in the USPD as in the SPD, and at any rate she spent much of the war in jail. Those who assumed leadership of the new party were not in her eyes real revolutionaries. Most of them desired peace above all, even if it meant a return to the prewar capitalist status quo. Yet the USPD unquestionably attracted growing numbers of restive, violence-prone workers to its ranks, primarily from the war-expanded industries. Luxemburg hoped, by remaining in the party, to find fruitful grounds for recruiting to the revolutionary program of the Spartacists.

Formal splits did not yet occur in the other major socialist parties, although by 1917 deep divisions had appeared in most of them. Within the SFIO a patriotic majority tried unsuccessfully to stem the growth of a growing pacifistic minority. But here too the party's divisions had little to do with a Leninist program. The leader of that minority, Jean Longuet, a grandson of Karl Marx, was dismissed by Lenin as a cowardly "social-pacifist." The only socialists in France who gained a degree of favorable recognition from Lenin were members of a very small group led by Fernand Loriot, composed of the extreme Left of the SFIO and a number of anarchosyndicalists.

Loriot's group, like the Spartacists, would form the nucleus of a future communist party, but at this time few if any of the more revolutionary leaders in the West gave much thought to gaining Lenin's approval, to agitating in conformity with the bolshevik program. With the Bolshevik Revolution, attitudes in the West began to shift, and in the following years, as it became clear that the bolshevik regime was destined to remain in power, western socialists began in growing numbers to give serious attention to Leninist theory. However, understanding it—and understanding what had happened in Russia in 1917—posed major difficulties for all socialists in the West.

REVOLUTION IN RUSSIA

Much has already been said in Chapter 4 concerning the Marxist conception of revolution in Russia. What needs especially to be kept in mind is that for Marxists the collapse of the tsarist state in February-March 1917 meant the advent of bourgeois revolution in Russia. Something broadly comparable to what had happened in France a century and a half before was now occurring in Russia: An old and no longer historically relevant "feudalism" was being cast aside, to be replaced by the legal and political forms most conducive to the expansion of capitalism—free labor, individual rights, representative institutions, the wage system. Now a new stage of industrial growth would expand productivity and create a sizable proletariat, thus laying down the foundations for the future advent of socialism. Of course capitalism had already begun to establish itself in Russia, but it could not expand as freely and rapidly as possible until a bourgeois framework had been created.

As also described in Chapter 4, Lenin shared with most Russian Marxists and with Kautsky the conviction that because of Russia's historically weak urban development and her dependency on foreign capital investment, her native bourgeoisie could not be expected to duplicate the revolutionary accomplishments of the assertive, self-confident, and historically rooted bourgeoisie of such countries as France and England. The Russian bourgeoisie could not be expected to push hard for a "full" bourgeois revolution and indeed would likely sell out to tsarist reaction, leaving the tasks of building a new state incomplete. Thus Lenin reasoned that the Russian proletariat had to take on its shoulders the task of assuring that the bourgeois revolution was not prematurely halted.

But the working class in Russia constituted far less than a majority of the population. Lenin thus proposed that Russia's proletariat ally itself with her massive, restless peasantry in what he termed a "revolutionary democratic dictatorship of the proletariat and peasantry." This would be a special form of dictatorship, adapted to Russian conditions, to oversee the arduous task of effecting an uncompromised, full bourgeois revolution. Having destroyed the old regime beyond repair and having solidly established a democratic-radical constitution, this dictatorial alliance could then presumably retire from the scene to permit a normal bourgeois stage of development.

However, there were a number of subtle and enticing ramifications to Lenin's line of reasoning, ramifications that promised possible escape from the passive determinism implicit in the framework of Marxian stages. For example, if *socialist* revolution in the West rose up to meet *bourgeois* revolution in Russia—especially this peculiar kind of proletarian–peasant supported bourgeois revolution—then a whole new range of perspectives might open up. With aid from the proletarian regimes of the advanced West, Russia's revolutionary democratic dictatorship of the proletariat and peasantry could move rapidly toward socialism, in effect telescoping the bourgeois stage.

This outline of Lenin's conception of revolution can only serve to suggest the highly nuanced, open-ended, and elusive quality of his thought on the subject before the war. By the eve of the 1917 revolution Lenin had further distinguished important aspects of development peculiar to Russia that suggested the possibility of a rapid move from bourgeois to proletarian stages. First, the Russian masses had already been through a dress rehearsal in the revolution of 1905, permitting them to proceed with fewer hesitations, uncertainties, or errors—and with a greater hunger for socialism. Second, the war had caused an enormous acceleration and intensification of historical trends, creating a highly volatile situation and turning ever greater numbers of Russians into revolutionaries.

Still, the actual eruption of revolution in March 1917 took Lenin, who was in Switzerland, by surprise. He had even lapsed, a few months before, into an uncharacteristic pessimism, observing that the revolution might not come in his lifetime. He had been similarly surprised by Russia's entry into the war in 1914—he quipped that "Nickie" would not do him such a favor as to get into an even bigger mess than in 1904– 05. Certainly Russia's government was no better prepared in 1914 than it had been a decade before to face modern warfare, and World War I was incomparably more of a test, one that Nicholas's government failed miserably. By late 1916 disaffection and disgust with the tsar, the tsarina, and their mad-monk adviser, Rasputin, had spread well into the upper echelons of the government.

Rasputin was assassinated by court nobles in December, in hopes of saving tsarism, but again as in 1905 it was the working class of Petrograd (as Saint Petersburg was now called) that played the decisive role, bringing down forever the tottering tsarist regime. On March 8 food riots led to general insurrection, complemented by mutinies in the armed forces. Within a few days—and Lenin was certainly prescient in predicting this rapid pace—a Soviet of Workers' and Soldiers' Deputies had been organized in Petrograd.

Yet the soviet organizations that appeared so quickly also disappointed Lenin. He was dismayed at how they freely relinquished the accouterments of official power to the Provisional Government, a cabinet-sized group representing a coalition of parties from the old Duma. The Provisional Government was largely bourgeois in composition and was hardly representative of the revolutionary masses, certainly not in comparison to the soviets and their executive organs, where immediate recall established direct and constantly refreshed representation. Lenin had expected the soviets to push unyieldingly for a democratic-radical state; instead they tolerated and even supported what were to Lenin the procrastinations and empty promises of the bourgeois ministers of the Provisional Government.

Accordingly, Lenin's first pronouncements, most notably the "April Theses," published when he arrived in Russia, urged the soviets to assert their power over the Provisional Government—a power that all observers recognized was ultimately in their hands, had they chosen to exercise it. In these pronouncements the ambiguities of Lenin's position—and his surging will to social revolution—began to emerge. Rather than clearly defining soviet power in terms of a thorough bourgeois revolution, he concentrated on measures palpably designed to intensify the hostility of the poor to the rich, and the proletariat to the bourgeoisie, measures that seemed designed to pave the way to socialist revolution in the near future, on the heels of a bourgeois revolution. In short, while Lenin's pronouncements when he first arrived in Russia did not unequivocally call for an immediate proletarian-socialist revolution, he seemed, in a way that troubled many other Russian Marxists—even Lenin's own bolshevik followers—to be narrowing down in an extreme fashion the duration of the bourgeois-democratic stage of development. He seemed to be suggesting that the soviets should not only destroy all remnants of tsarism but also begin preparation for a proletarian dictatorship, pure and simple.

As alluded to when discussing Marx's own revolutionary activities, similar notions could be found in the fourth section of the *Communist Manifesto*, where Marx and Engels stated "the bourgeois revolution in Germany will be but the prelude to an immediately following proletarian revolution." Among Russian Marxists, Leon Trotsky's name had been associated with the analogous theory of "permanent revolution." In the debates within the RSDRP in the early years of the century, he had argued that the Russian proletariat, after making the bourgeois revolution for the Russian bourgeoisie, could not be expected to relinquish power. Rather, the proletarian-led bourgeois revolution would inexorably blend into a second, and proletarian, socialist revolution.

Before the war Lenin had criticized Trotsky's ideas, terming them un-Marxist and likely to lead to "absurd and reactionary results" (Wolfe, *Three*, p. 293), since a proletarian dictatorship and socialism would be impossible until capitalism had created both a working class that was the majority of the population and a productivity of labor that would assure material abundance. Still, even in these earlier debates, Lenin granted that if socialist revolution arrived in the West at the same time that tsarism fell in Russia, then a whole new range of possibilities might open up for Russia. And for that matter, all Marxists, in the West as in Russia, conceived of proletarian socialist revolution as an ultimately international affair; no single country, not even one like England or Germany, would be capable of introducing a full and secure socialism in isolation.

It is significant that Trotsky, who had been a strong critic and persistent factional opponent of Lenin before March 1917, gradually moved closer to the bolsheviks after March 1917. In August of that year he joined the party, with Lenin's blessings. This rapprochement was in part due to Lenin's views on the revolution, which moved in Trotsky's direction, but it was due even more to Trotsky's own acceptance of Lenin's centralized, elitist party. In the early part of the century Trotsky had joined with Plekhanov and other Russian Marxists in warning that a party along the lines envisaged by Lenin could be expected to lose contact with the masses, indeed to begin to assume power over them; then the central committee would come to act dictatorially over the party; and ultimately a leader of the central committee would emerge as a dictator, a nemesis totally in opposition to the goals of Marxism. But in the turmoil of revolution Trotsky came to agree that a Leninist party was essential, and thus by the late summer of 1917 these two brilliant leaders of Russian social democracy, previously hostile, moved together to form a powerful alliance.

While disappointed with the wide confidence initially enjoyed by the Provisional Government and with the support given it by the soviets, Lenin hoped and expected that it would quickly lose its credibility before the masses, and that those masses, under the concrete experience of revolution, would look more and more to the bolsheviks for leadership.

These were realistic expectations. In deciding to continue the war and to launch a new offensive in June, the Provisional Government alienated many of its supporters and drove others who were previously neutral into revolutionary opposition. The mass uprising against the government in July after the collapse of the offensive was an indication of how extensive this loss of prior support had become. Although the bolsheviks were accused of having instigated the uprising, in fact the party's leadership was unwillingly pulled along by rank-and-file pressure, and at the crucial moment Lenin decided that it would be better for the party to associate itself with this ill-planned undertaking than to stand aside—that it was better, in other words, to be wrong with the masses than to be right against them.

Alexander Kerensky, a man earlier associated with the Socialist Revolutionaries but now closer to the Kadets, had by this time become head of the Provisional Government. He denounced the July Uprising as a bolshevik plot and moved forcefully to repress the Bolshevik Party and to arrest its leaders, for which actions he obtained the approval of the soviets. Lenin went into hiding, accused by Kerensky of being in the pay of the Germans, an accusation that seems to have been widely believed, at least for a time.

Now Lenin denounced not only the Provisional Government but the soviets as well; he called for an immediate seizure of power by his party, since reaction was gaining the upper hand, with soviet approval; Russia was no longer the "freest country in the world," as he had shortly before described it. In other words, the bolsheviks could no longer benefit from the political liberties permitted in the flush of optimism immediately following upon the revolution in March, and now there was open warfare between the bolsheviks and the soviet-supported Provisional Government.

Kerensky's anti-bolshevik repressions revived hopes on the right that order could once again be established in Russia, above all in the armed forces, which were by the late summer of 1917 in rapid disintegration. Hopes for a military strongman centered around General Kornilov, who mistakenly came to believe that he could assume such a role with Kerensky's cooperation, or at least by using Kerensky as a front.

But the machinations of Kornilov and those around him aroused not only Kerensky's antipathy but that of the entire Left. When Kornilov made his move, he found overwhelming mass opposition. Railroad workers refused to move his troops, and left-wing soldiers infiltrated the ranks of those under his command, so that most of the forces initially following him melted away.

Thus Kerensky's anti-bolshevik repressions and the threatened rightward swing of the political pendulum ultimately resulted in a much strengthened and more aggressive Left. The slogan "All power to the soviets!" was embraced by an ever wider spectrum of revolutionary activists, who had lost all confidence in Kerensky, the Provisional Government, and the notion of any sort of continuing coalition with the Kadets. This disaffection did not mean, however, that there was a widespread support on the left for a bolshevik takeover, and certainly not for a takeover that circumvented the soviets.

Indeed, Lenin's almost frantic appeals to the leaders of the party to launch an immediate, violent seizure of power at first met with near-universal resistance. The moderate wing of the party, led by Lev Kamenev and Gregory Zinoviev, balked at the very notion of a bolshevik seizure of power. Kamenev had long entertained hopes of a coalition of socialists—menshevik, Socialist Revolutionary, and bolshevik—working through the soviets. He and a number of other leaders were willing to grant that the Bolshevik Party alone might succeed in holding power for a short period. But without the aid of proletarian revolution in the West—which they believed should *precede* socialist revolution in Russia and which was unlikely to break out in the foreseeable future—and without the support of the other still-powerful Russian socialist factions, a bolshevik regime would be hopelessly weak and isolated, certain to fall before the attacks of its external and internal enemies.

Others in the Bolshevik Party accepted the notion of a bolshevik revolution but not Lenin's sense of urgency or his proposal for the role of the party in coming to power; they believed that the masses would not understand or accept a simple coup d'état by the Bolshevik Party. Trotsky was prominent among those who urged gaining the backing of the soviets at the approaching Second Congress of the soviets, which was to meet in the first week of November. And it was Trotsky's views that prevailed in this instance. Thus his prominence in the Petrograd Soviet and its recently created Military-Revolutionary Committee assumed great importance, and it was finally the Military-Revolutionary Committee that was instrumental in the actual seizure of power on November 7 and 8—securing bridges, distributing weapons, winning over garrisons—which culminated in a largely symbolic attack on the Winter Palace, where the Provisional Government was stationed.

It is thus hardly surprising that the bolshevik victory in November was widely perceived, both inside and outside Russia, as a triumph not of the Bolshevik Party but of the soviets. The coup was immediately approved by the Second Congress of the soviets, and various soviet institutions ostensibly played a leading role in defeating the Provisional Government. The new Council of People's Commissars, the cabinet-sized executive body set up to replace the Provisional Government, was formally responsible to the soviets. What was not clearly perceived, however, was the deeper significance of the party's position as the guiding force behind the revolution, behind the approving vote of the Second Congress, and behind the decisions of the Council (which was made up entirely of bolsheviks and headed by Lenin).

In a more rigorous sense this deeper significance easily eludes even those attempting to make sense of these developments with the benefit of a half century of historical hindsight. That is, while it is now clear that the November Revolution was more a bolshevik revolution than a soviet revolution, what the term "bolshevik revolution" really meant, both theoretically and practically, is anything but easy to grasp. Quite aside from the glaring paradoxes that the revolution offered in terms of Marxist theory, even in practical terms the "seizure" of power by the bolsheviks is something of a misnomer. It would be closer to the truth to say that the bolsheviks were "lifted" to power by a wave of popular indignation and resentment in the autumn of 1917. Rather than "ruling" Russia, as the Provisional Government had tried to do, the Council of People's Commissars merely lent its approval to a vast disintegration of previously established authorities, social relations, and legal forms. A kind of gold-rush atmosphere prevailed. The peasants were seizing the lands of the large landowners, the soldiers were deserting their units or refusing to take orders from their commanders, the workers were assuming control over production in the factories, national minorities were setting up autonomous nations—everywhere a gigantic scramble was underway that central authority, weakened as it was, could not realistically aspire to control.

The new regime thus began not by establishing a centralized order but by recognizing a decentralized disorder. The Bolshevik Revolution began as something very close to an anarchist revolution (the land program drafted by Lenin and promulgated by the Council of People's Commissars, significantly, was lifted almost verbatim from the land program of the Socialist Revolutionaries), and had only the remotest relationship to what had previously been accepted as a Marxist program of proletarian dictatorship, which stressed an aggressive use of centralized state power.

In the one area that the Council had a relatively free hand, that is, in foreign affairs, it moved quickly to negotiate Russia's departure from the war. This departure was desperately opposed not only by Russia's former allies in the West but also by those in Russia, including the left wing of the Bolshevik Party, who urged a "revolutionary war" against the Germans, a war that would so inflame the revolutionary passions of the German working masses that revolution in the West would come to the aid of the new Russian regime. But after bitter disputes within the party, Lenin's own policy of a simple treaty with the Axis prevailed, in spite of the onerous terms exacted at Brest-Litovsk, where the Central Powers took over a major part of European Russia.

The Treaty of Brest-Litovsk relieved the bolsheviks of the most immediate danger of a German invasion. But soon after the treaty was signed in early 1918, new threats, hydra-like, appeared. An assassination attempt that wounded Lenin and killed several of his lieutenants provided the bolsheviks with a rationale for organizing the Red Terror, which was directed by the secret police, or Cheka, against internal opponents of the regime. By early 1919 anti-bolshevik White armies threatened Moscow and Petrograd. To stop their advance an impressive Red Army, under the leadership of Trotsky, was put together almost from scratch. By late 1920 the Red Terror and the Red Army had silenced or destroyed the major threats to bolshevik rule. In the process the Council of People's Commissars began to establish a more dictatorial and effective rule over Russia than had been the case in the autumn of 1917.

Yet these heroic victories did not free the bolsheviks from the central paradoxes of their rule, in particular those that had to do with the inadequacy of Russia's industrial advancement to support socialism. From the beginning the Council of People's Commissars did not attempt far-reaching projects of socialist reorganization. In the main urban centers the new regime did oversee an initial period of "War Communism." But that was simply an egalitarianism of destitution—and it was probably the only realistic policy, given the fundamental disruption of Russia's economy, the blockade imposed upon her by the Allies, and the life-and-death struggle the bolsheviks were waging with the White armies. This "communistic" life in the cities was only a small part of the total picture in Russia: The economy was now even more overwhelmingly rural, since in the period of civil war city dwellers in vast numbers had fled into the country in search of the food and fuel so desperately lacking in the cities. Socialization of landholdings was scarcely even attempted, except for a few isolated experiments. In the countryside the bolsheviks, by recognizing the right of the peasantry to seize land and to establish what in effect was private tenure over it, were not establishing socialism but small-scale private enterprise, although the demands of war often meant forced requisitioning of crops. Private exploitation of agriculture constituted by far the prevailing economic form in Russia after the Bolshevik Revolution. Thus, one of the major accomplishments of the bolsheviks was to ratify a kind of spontaneous bourgeois revolution in Russia, that is, one that recognized, however ambiguously, the right of private property for the great majority of Russia's population.

As will be more fully explored in subsequent chapters, the bolsheviks were forced by early 1921 to come to grips with this paradox by allowing "bourgeois" forms of economic activity (that is, small-property free enterprise), even in the cities. This New Economic Policy, as it was termed, ironically called to mind Lenin's earlier conception of a "revolutionary democratic dictatorship of the proletariat and peasantry," which was to be a form of bourgeois revolution, introduced under the leadership of the proletariat and peasantry. The striking difference between Lenin's theories before 1917 and his practice in 1921, of course, was that in the second instance he no longer spoke of a democratic-radical stage that would prepare Russia for eventual socialism. Rather, the bolsheviks, still posing as the party of the proletariat, held on to exclusive power, in apparent defiance of traditional Marxist assumptions.

Whatever the dictates of Marxism, the survival of the bolshevik regime was from any number of other perspectives unexpected, miraculous even. Many in the West—Marxists, democratic socialists, and non-socialists—were dumbfounded at its initial victory and regularly made confident predictions of its imminent demise. They failed, however, adequately to understand certain peculiar apsects of Russian history. For centuries despotic forms of government, where rulers and ruled were profoundly different in education and life-style, had prevailed as ostensibly the only way that Russia's sprawling territories, diverse populations, and relatively backward society could be ruled. The war had intensified the difficulties of governing the country and had so weakened the central government and atomized society that the Bolshevik Party, working through the soviets, offered what seemed to many an important integrating force in Russia, although the discipline

and centralization of the party in the early stages of the revolution has
certainly been exaggerated. Russia's small middle class was destroyed,
and most of its leaders exiled. The urban working class formed a more
cohesive and disciplined, if far less numerous, social base for political
rule than did the peasantry. The peasants were scattered throughout
Russia. They were ignorant, divided into hostile subgroups, often passive, and generally difficult to motivate and organize around national
issues. Moreover, the bolsheviks, even if not the peasants' first choice
for political leadership, had at least put an end to the war and had
seemingly recognized the peasants' right to land, something that most
of the right-wing competitors to the bolsheviks, organized in the White
armies, were unwilling to do. Hence the peasants tended to give at least
grudging support to the new regime during the civil war between White
and Red armies.

But an irreducible fact remained: The Bolshevik Revolution had
not been a proletarian-socialist revolution in the sense understood by
prewar Marxists, whether Russian or non-Russian. The most coherent
rationale, in Marxist terms, for the bolshevik regime was that its existence would help to initiate a revolutionary epoch, that the revolutionary spark in Russia would ignite the combustible material in the West,
where the foundations for proletarian rule and socialism existed far
more than was the case in Russia. Thus a decisive question for the bolsheviks from their first year of rule remained: What would happen in
the West?

REVOLUTION IN THE WEST AND THE ORIGINS OF
WESTERN COMMUNIST PARTIES

A point that Lenin stressed with particular energy, in urging bolshevik
party leaders to seize power, was that revolution was imminent in western Europe, especially in Germany, and that a bolshevik takeover in
Russia would speed things up in the West, advancing the cause of international revolution. In April 1917 German workers had struck in impressive numbers when the government sought to reduce their bread
rations by one-quarter, and in January 1918 a strike initiated over similar issues became political. Centered in Berlin, where close to a quarter
of a million workers stopped working, the strike spread to a number of
other cities, and among its demands were peace without annexations
or indemnities—the very terms that the bolsheviks were offering, unsuccessfully, to the German negotiators at Brest-Litovsk. Thus in one

sense the Bolshevik Revolution was undeniably adding to working-class restiveness in western Europe.

Too much, however, can easily be read into these strikes—as Lenin and other bolsheviks tended to do. As earlier noted when discussing the impact of industrial expansion during the war, working-class protest in the West, while at times violent and intransigent, was not often revolutionary in the Marxist sense. The *revolutionäre Obleute*, the Revolutionary Shop Stewards in the metal industries, who led the January 1918 strikes, were self-consciously anti-ideological and openly suspicious of Marxist intellectuals like Rosa Luxemburg. Few activists in Germany believed that the time for a proletarian-socialist revolution had arrived, and fewer still were inclined at this point to follow any Russian model—although of course what had actually happened in Russia was only dimly perceived and would be the source of much confusion for the next several years. The brutality and effectiveness of the German military authorities in breaking up the strikes tended to reinforce revolutionary pessimism in Germany, although at the same time unquestionably many workers were driven to an ever more profound alienation from Germany's rulers.

However much the November Revolution and the ensuing Brest-Litovsk Treaty may have increased restiveness inside Germany, in the Allied countries and above all in France the treaty resulted in vehement anti-bolshevik feeling. It released Germany's armies from a two-front war to concentrate on the western front, and Germany's ensuing offensive only narrowly failed to capture Paris. This was a time when the bolsheviks were reviled in French working-class circles. Working-class xenophobia, much in evidence before the war even among organized workers, now reached a level comparable to that of August 1914. Prominent figures in the SFIO, a number of whom would later become communists, denounced the bolsheviks as German agents and bloodthirsty barbarians.

Even Lenin's confidence in the proletariat of the West began to waver once he was in power. He had at first maintained that revolutionary Russia could not accept a punitive peace and that if Germany tried to impose such a peace, then Russia would be forced to wage a "revolutionary war," drawing the proletariat of the West into action against its own bourgeoisie. Such ideas were consistent with the entire tenor of Lenin's thought in the autumn of 1917, when he had rejected all caviling about the dangers of immediate revolutionary action. However, once it became apparent to him that the Germans might indeed crush his regime, Lenin reverted to a position similar to that of Kamenev and

Zinoviev on the eve of the bolsheviks' assumption of power. He cautioned that immediate revolution in the West could not be relied upon; at least the revolutionary timetable had become, in his words, "completely incalculable" (Lindemann, p. 34).

In the months that followed the signing of the treaty, Lenin's newfound caution seemed justified, for the war continued and, in spite of unprecedented strains in each country, workers showed little inclination to seize power. The bolsheviks were thrown increasingly on their own resources. Thus, after the heady and relatively easy victories of 1917, the year 1918 was a time of harsh and grueling measures. Not only Brest-Litovsk, but the Red Terror, the activities of the Cheka, and the horrors of the civil war provoked dismay and hostility in the West. Anti-socialist governments and the right-wing press often printed wildly exaggerated and one-sided accounts of atrocities committed by bolshevik forces (that these accounts were biased is by no means to suggest that they were without foundation), but even among those revolutionaries who were most inclined to discount anything that appeared in the non-socialist press, even granting the parallel horrors of the White forces, the terroristic aspect of bolshevik rule was perplexing and embarrassing. At this time western revolutionaries nearly without exception were quick to assert that *their* revolution would be more humane, more democratic, less violent.

For Germans that revolution appeared to be beginning in the autumn of 1918, when, under the weight of impending military defeat, the central institutions of the Reich began to collapse, in ways that were broadly similar to the collapse of tsarist authority in the late winter of 1917. Mutiny spread in parts of the army and navy, and throughout the country revolutionary councils or soviets (*Räte* in German) of workers, soldiers, and peasants sprung up and assumed a de facto authority.

However, these initial broad parallels were deceptive, and quickly the two revolutions began to develop according to a different logic, as one might well expect from two countries so different in social structure and historical experience. In Russia the Provisional Government established in March was composed of former deputies to the Duma, mostly bourgeois democrats and moderate socialists. It did not recognize the authority of the soviets in any formal way, although of course in practice it was obliged to. In Germany Friedrich Ebert, as leader of the SPD, the largest party in the Reichstag and the one least tainted by association with the previous regime, was asked by the previous chancellor to assume political authority until elections could be arranged. Ebert then gathered around him a "Council of People's Commissars"

(*Rat der Volksbeauftragten*) that, like Lenin's council, was responsible to the soviets. However, given the nature of Ebert's appointment, actual responsibility was somewhat equivocal.

In spite of its name and the fact that it was composed entirely of socialist Commissars, three from the SPD and three from the USPD, the German Council did not introduce a program of social revolution. Ebert was the polar opposite of Lenin; in a famous outburst, he admitted that he "hated social revolution like sin" (Scheidemann, vol. 2, p. 261). He saw his task and that of the council as simply to manage affairs until regular elections, on western parliamentary models, could be held. Thus Ebert's Council of People's Commissars had more in common with the Russian Provisional Government than with the bolshevik Council of People's Commissars. Indeed, Ebert was haunted by the fear that he would become a German Kerensky, overwhelmed by ruthless revolutionaries.

Ebert's intent was merely to do away with the "feudal" remnants of the old Prussian-Junker Reich, creating a democratic-radical republic (although personally he was open to retaining the monarchy, suitably tamed by a constitution). But the prospect of pushing on to social democracy, to socialization of the means of production, was on the minds of many German Marxists. Germany was the continental power that Marxists believed was most ready for socialism, because of its high levels of productivity and its degree of industrial concentration, both intensified by the war. Nevertheless, a solid majority of German workers and nonworkers was not yet ready for social revolution. Even many left-leaning Marxist theoreticians argued that the time was not yet auspicious for socialization. Four years of Allied blockade had exhausted Germany's economy and sharply reduced her standard of living, rendering a socialism of plenty inconceivable for many years. These same leaders argued that the capitalists and generals should be made to bear full responsibility for the disasters of the war; socialists should not take upon their shoulders the thankless task of rebuilding a war-torn Germany. In the same way, the technical problems, in terms of organization, planning, the general regearing for socialist production, seemed staggering to many socialist economists. They were driven toward the paradoxical and certainly un-Marxist conclusion that revolution in a highly industrialized, technologically sophisticated, and organizationally complicated economy presented more formidable difficulties than revolution in a backward, relatively uncomplicated economy.

This was equally a most un-Leninist conclusion, at least if we consider Lenin's pronouncements during the war, since he and other bolsheviks had repeatedly asserted that capitalist forms had exhausted themselves and that *only* through socialism could Europe be rebuilt. But German socialists were faced with the inescapable reality that without the cooperation of Germany's bourgeois experts—engineers, managers, scientists, corporate functionaries in both private and public concerns—Germany's economy would collapse. Those experts, while often rendered passive and directionless by the events of late 1918, would certainly not, in their overwhelming majority, cooperate with a proletarian dictatorship, and very likely not cooperate even with a democratically elected socialist regime. The bolsheviks had faced a similar resistance on the part of Russia's bourgeois experts, but because of Russia's backward economy these experts were relatively insignificant in numbers; their emigration was not a decisive factor in challenging the bolsheviks's retention of power—and of course the bolsheviks had not really attempted a program of Marxist socialization.

German socialits had to face not only the potential hostility of urban middle-class experts; in the countryside deep aversion to socialism prevailed. And where the bolsheviks were able to neutralize the Russian peasantry for a decisive interval through promises of land and peace, German socialists could not effectively resort to similar promises. Peasants in Germany were relatively far fewer in numbers and they were not as land-hungry as those in Russia. Also, since the German revolution broke out at the end of the war, the radicalizing effect of a futile war effort was not duplicated in Germany; promises of peace in Germany could not be a factor in gaining support for a socialist program.

The anti-socialist sentiment of the German peasant was in another sense a vital factor in the German revolution, since the German peasants' withholding of foodstuffs constituted a much greater threat in a country that had a dense urban population. The mass exodus to the countryside, which saved many from starvation in Russia, was not a real option for most of Germany's proportionately more numerous city dwellers, who had long lost contact with their rural origins, and who could not escape to the countryside.

The prospect of starvation at the end of the war further inclined nearly all Germans to look to the West, particularly to the United States, whose granaries were full. The United States would obviously not share its surplus with any regime in Germany that contemplated the socialization of the means of production or a proletarian dictatorship. Socialism and dictatorship implied looking to the East, to Russia, but it was all too apparent that a German-Russian alliance at this point would not solve but only intensify Germany's problems, since Russia did not have the necessary foodstuffs to nourish her own population, let alone that of Germany.

The sway that the Allies exercised over Germans because of America's bulging granaries was enhanced by overwhelming Allied economic and military power. Germany had of course lost the war and remained blockaded; at the same time her industrial centers were vulnerable to intervention. There was little doubt in anyone's mind that, had Germany moved in the direction of social revolution, the Allied blockade would have remained and the Allied armies would have further extended their control over Germany's southwestern industrial centers. Here again Russia enjoyed an advantage over Germany, since Russia was not as vulnerable to blockade and intervention—although the Allies tried both—because of her great size and predominantly agricultural economy.

What was probably more decisive, though less tangible, than any of these factors was that most social democrats, and German democrats generally, had traditionally looked to the advanced, democratic West, and instinctively rejected close associations with Russia, the land of despotism and barbarism. They hoped that Germany could finally enter the ranks of the Western democracies as a full and respected partner. And whatever the importance of such factors as bourgeois experts, foodstuffs, and intervention, the minds of men like Ebert and many to the left of him were long conditioned by identification with the democracies of the West and a strong desire to be accepted by them.

As we have seen, there was an element of myth in the notion that the discipline and clear-sightedness of the bolsheviks were responsible for their accession to power, but nevertheless revolutionary leadership in Germany was more faction-ridden and directionless than in Russia. The murders of Rosa Luxemburg, Karl Liebknecht, and many other revolutionary leaders in the so-called Spartacist Uprising of January 1919 represent only one aspect of a general lack of preparedness for revolutionary action in Germany. That Lenin, Trotsky, and nearly every other leading bolshevik escaped harm in the similarly ill-planned and premature July Uprising must be seen as something more than pure accident. No doubt reaction in Germany was more powerful and efficient, and revolutionary forces less widespread and more timid. But the evidence also strongly suggests that Lenin and Trotsky were more impressive strategists and tacticians of revolution and that the Bolshevik

Party, regardless of how much it failed in practice to measure up to Lenin's ideal of an *apparat* of disciplined revolutionaries, was more effective than the KPD or USPD.

Many German social democrats by the end of the war harbored a profound, almost anarchistic distrust of party centralization, due to their bitter experiences at the hands of SPD bureaucrats, who attempted to crush all antiwar dissidence. The splintering of the proudly unified prewar movement into SPD, USPD, and KPD (each of which was further rent by schismatic tendencies) caused many also to despair of the very principle of revolutionary leadership by a political party. Thus they looked to the Räte organizations, and their hopes were fed by the widespread impression that revolution in Russia had been a soviet revolution. But the Räte proved a disappointment also. They consistently and overwhelmingly refused to claim more than provisional sovereignty or to push for social revolution, voting instead in their general congresses in favor of a democratically elected constituent assembly on the model of western parliamentary democracies. The Council of People's Commissars similarly worked for the establishment of a western-style democracy, dissolving itself willingly once a constituent assembly had been elected.

The parallels and contrasts with the situation in Russia are instructive. The soviets in Russia were also at first reticent to assume power, and they too looked to the convocation of a constituent assembly. It was only after an involved process of radicalizing disappointments that they were willing to accept the slogan "all power to the soviets!" But under the guise of that slogan the bolsheviks assumed power, and although they then permitted the promised elections to the constituent assembly to be held, they dissolved the body once it met in early 1918.

The new German constituent assembly that met in February 1919 was decisively opposed to socialization of the means of production and indeed even resisted proposals for institutional reform when they touched upon the old power centers in the army and the state bureaucracy. Thus the new German state that emerged from the deliberations of the constituent assembly, while in formal constitution a model democratic-radical republic (usually called the Weimar Republic), remained anti-republican in most of its military leadership and officialdom.

This pessimistic picture of revolutionary prospects in Germany, no doubt more impressive in historical retrospect, is not meant to obscure the extensive, and, to many at the time, promising social unrest at the end of the war. Millions of German workers and soldiers were filled with indignation against employers, against the military authorities, against the old regime generally, and even against the new regime that was assuming shape under Ebert's direction. Above all, but certainly not exclusively, the workers in the metallurgical industries, who under the direction of the *revolutionäre Obleute* had already staged impressive strikes in 1917 and 1918, now violently confronted the authorities. A Red Army of the Ruhr, formed by workers' battalions, came to control a number of cities.

Metal workers were also among the most radical in Russia in 1917. An early center of bolshevik strength was in the factory committees (*fabrichno-zavodskiye komitety*) and their loosely associated workers' militias or "Red Guards." However, in both cases the term "radical" must be used with caution: While militant and ready for violent action, most of these workers showed little desire for a Marxist-style transformation of state and society. Before the war the bolsheviks had few followers in the metal industries—and the same was true in the other large concentrated factories of advanced production. In Pre-war Germany as well, metal workers were not known for their aggressiveness or revolutionary social-democratic fervor. The rapid growth of bolshevik strength among metal workers appears to have had more to do with the intransigence with which bolshevik agitators within the factories pushed for *immediate* demands having to do with wages and working conditions than with the bolsheviks' overall revolutionary Marxist program. Similarly, in Germany the radicalism of the metal workers centered on immediate issues. Even when these issues were political, they were usually defensive, stemming from fears that reaction would once again gain the upper hand in Germany, with obvious implications for the material situation of workers. These fears turned out to be well founded, since Ebert, in his concern to avoid becoming a German Kerensky, ended up allying himself with the reactionary *Freikorps*, who brutally repressed any signs of German "bolshevism."

Lenin and many leading bolsheviks, especially after Brest-Litovsk, tended to treat every piece of news dealing with unrest in Germany as a sign of imminent social revolution there. Moreover, although the bolsheviks were certainly aware of the many objective obstacles to revolution in the West, they came increasingly, though inconsistently, to stress that the fundamental inadequacy in the West was revolutionary leadership. The success of the bolsheviks in November, so it was argued, had not depended upon mature Marxist consciousness among workers and soldiers but rather upon a mass revolutionary spontaneity, "guided" by the Bolshevik Party. What was needed in the West was a party of genuine revolutionaries who could give leadership to the inchoate revolutionary strivings of the masses. This was the demand that Lenin had been putting forth since the time of the Zimmerwald conference. Nevertheless, the ambiguities and apparent inconsistencies in Lenin's program were as pervasive here as they were in the spring and summer of 1917.

The news of revolutionary disturbances in Germany in late 1918 and Lenin's conviction that new parties of revolutionaries under bolshevik leadership must be established as soon as possible led him to call an extremely hurried meeting of what would become the First Congress of the Communist International (also called the Comintern, or the Third International). But Russia remained blockaded and in the throes of civil war. Many of the groups in the West that Lenin wished to see represented did not even receive the invitations sent to them. Thus the meeting that was held in March 1919 was disappointingly small and unrepresentative.

However, a delegate from the new German Communist Party, or KPD, just formed in December 1918, did make it to Moscow. To Lenin's chagrin, this delegate had received instructions from Rosa Luxemburg, shortly before her death, to oppose immediate creation of a new international. Luxemburg feared a hurried and premature meeting; she was worried that any international created at this time might suffer from an overweening predominance of bolsheviks, a situation that she was convinced would be unhealthy for international socialism and the progress of world revolution.

Her immediate apprehensions proved themselves justified: The bolsheviks completely dominated the proceedings of the congress; all of the major speeches were delivered by bolsheviks; and all of the formal resolutions voted by the congress were composed by them. The delegate from the KPD was overwhelmed by the bolsheviks' enthusiasm for a new international and finally agreed to abstain from voting on whether it should be created immediately. Thus from its very first meeting the Comintern was patently a creation of the bolsheviks, with other parties and groups, even those representing large western countries like Germany and France, playing a distinctly subservient role.

However, confusion piled upon confusion: The image of bolshevism broadcast by the congress and taken home by western revolutionaries was one that clearly corresponded neither to Lenin's prewar thought nor to bolshevist thought as it later became known. To a puzzling extent an explicit and coherent discussion of the role of a Leninist party in making revolution was not offered. Although of course mention was made of the need for a party of revolutionaries who would give leadership, the emphasis was repeatedly on the vital importance of the revolutionary masses and their organs, the soviets. Similarly inconsonant with Leninism as normally understood were the friendly overtures made to the anarchists—old enemies of Marxists—also proponents of revolutionary spontaneity. They were described as courageous if immature revolutionaries, who would be far preferable in a revolutionary situation to the cowardly and treacherous "social democrats" (now a term of abuse, in opposition to revolutionary "communists," as members of the Comintern were to be henceforth called).

This lack of emphasis on the need either for strict party discipline or for a centralized party of professional revolutionaries reflected, in a sense, what had actually happened in the autumn of 1917, as opposed to what should have happened according to Lenin's prerevolutionary theories (or what Bolshevik Party historians would retrospectively argue did happen). In fact, rank-and-file anarchists of various sorts, as well as left Socialist Revolutionaries, did play an important role as allies of the bolsheviks in the November Revolution.

Thus many in the West were attracted to the Comintern because of a sense of solidarity with the vague notion of socialist revolution, even when they had little sympathy for the central tenets of Leninism, if indeed they were aware of them. Anarchosyndicalists, "sovietists" (that is, those who believed in the central role of workers' councils), as well as revolutionary Marxists responded favorably to the calls of the First Congress.

Typically, the demands of the First Congress for schisms and forced exclusions—and here there was little equivocation—were not seriously entertained by most western revolutionaries. They certainly shared Lenin's outrage concerning the actions of patriotic and anti-revolutionary social-democratic leaders, but they were still reticent to split their parties, and no consensus existed concerning which individuals should be forcibly cast out. No important splits occurred in any major western socialist parties in direct response to the urgings from Moscow in 1919, although of course a number had occurred in Germany prior to that time, for reasons indigenous to Germany.

For their part, the bolsheviks were apparently unable or unconcerned for the rest of the year to press their initially dogmatic demands for schisms and exclusions. Even in those few instances when, in spite of blockade and civil war, the bolsheviks were able to obtain enough information to make reasonably informed judgments about develop-

ments in western parties, they did so in ways that were puzzlingly inconsonant with the pronouncements of the First Congress. For example,
when the Italian Socialist Party, the only important western party in a
warring nation to oppose the war initially and to avoid outright social-
patriotism, applied for membership in the Comintern shortly after the
First Congress, its application was quickly accepted by the leaders of
the new International. Yet the Italian party was no by means a disciplined, homogeneous party of revolutionaries. It had a moderate wing,
led by the veteran prewar socialist Filippo Turati (a man who stood to
the right of Kautsky, now considered a renegade by the bolsheviks), and
while many of the party's leaders were admirers of the bolsheviks, they
were at the same time determined to oppose forced exclusions of men
like Turati, largely because such exclusions would mean a split in their
party.

But this apparent disagreement with Comintern pronouncements
did not lead to immediate friction with the bolsheviks. Lenin and his
lieutenants ostensibly abandoned their earlier strident denunciations
of Turati and even went so far as to praise the Italian socialists for maintaining a unified party at a time when schismatic tendencies in the KPD
appeared to be on the verge of destroying it.

Lenin in other ways seemed willing to disregard what had at first
appeared as intransigent pronouncements at the First Congress. When,
in March 1919, a soviet communist regime was able to assume power
in Hungary, primarily because of the collapse of the central government
and the unwillingness of any other groups to assume governmental responsibilities, Lenin spoke words of caution and flexibility rather than
dogmatism. When he saw that Bela Kun, the Hungarian communist
leader, had established an apparently successful coalition with the
Hungarian social democrats—the kind of partnership that Lenin had
vehemently rejected in the case of the mensheviks and had explicitly
warned against at the First Congress—he praised Kun for "going beyond" the Russian model. He further speculated that to do so might be
possible in Hungary because it was more "western" than Russia, and
thus wider options were open to it. Implied here, though not spelled
out, was that the further west one looked, the more democratic a revolution could be, and the less necessary would be a single-party revolution and the harsh measures that had been necessary to retain power in
Russia.

Was this a true shift in Lenin's attitudes, or was it merely another
example of his typical pragmatic response to a given opportunity as
contrasted to the dogmatic theoretical conviction equally typical of him?

It is tempting to speculate that Lenin's theory of the "leading role" of the party was in a state of flux at this time and that if revolution had spread to the West, and if western socialist revolutionaries had been able to assume a leading role in the Comintern, then the very nature of world communism might have been different. Speculating even further, if revolution in the West had come to the aid of revolution in Russia, then the harsh measures taken by the bolsheviks in order to survive would not have been necessary, and a more democratic, humane, "sovietist" revolution would have also been possible in Russia.

But these are only speculations. Revolution in the West failed repeatedly from late 1918 to early 1921, with far-reaching implications. An important turning point was reached at the Second Congress of the Communist International in the summer of 1920. This was the first genuinely international Comintern congress, since now duly elected representatives from all major revolutionary socialist parties and movements were able to travel to Russia. Similarly, at the Second Congress exhaustive theses, resolutions, and the famous Twenty-One Conditions of Admission were composed, to make far clearer the nature of bolshevism and the meaning of membership in the new International. In the spring of 1920 Lenin wrote one of his most famous and influential works, *Left-wing Communism, An Infantile Disorder*, in which he moved away from his equivocations of 1919, reverted back to his earlier suspicion of anarchistic spontaneity, and rejected what he considered the bogus claims to revolutionary "purity" of "left-wing communists" (those who rejected a disciplined party, parliamentary agitation, trade-union infiltration, and other Leninist devices). Moreover, in this work, which was put into the hands of all of the delegates to the Second Congress, Lenin gave free expression to his growing conviction that his theories had universal application and that the bolshevik model of making revolution—or, we might interject, an idealized form of it—should be studied by western revolutionaries in order that they be able to remedy their continued failure. Indeed, in Lenin's words and in the words of other leading bolsheviks at this time lurked a more all-embracing assumption: Not only were bolshevik principles to be strictly followed by westerners, but the Bolshevik Party was the only reliable interpreter of those principles, which were at times exceedingly elusive.

Thus the bolsheviks set out in the latter half of 1920 to create communist parties in their own party's image in all countries of the world. This effort would entail splits in all of the major western socialist parties and imposition of a rigid discipline upon the new communist parties, not only by their own executive committees but by the executive committee of the Comintern, which was completely dominated by bolsheviks. Their unyielding demand for centralized discipline came as a bitter disappointment for many western socialist leaders, who had hoped for a more tolerant, more heterogeneous world communism, but most of them had become so dispirited by their own failures that they were unable to resist the confident, dogmatic pronouncements from Moscow.

At the same time, many young revolutionaries in western Europe had by late 1920 become thoroughly disillusioned with the older generation of socialist leaders, and they looked favorably upon the bolshevik calls for exclusions, schisms, and iron discipline. For these younger revolutionaries the older generation had amply proved that it lacked real revolutionary will. Of course in getting rid of this older generation, younger men, men new to political activism, found that positions of leadership were opened up to them in the new communist parties. In some countries, such as Italy, bolshevik influence was actually in the direction of wider unity and fewer purges than these younger revolutionaries desired. The Moscow leadership had plausible cause to fear that the new communist leaders, in their quest for revolutionary purity, would isolate themselves from the masses and from any real possibilities for action.

The communist parties that were established in the West in late 1920 and early 1921 with the intention of remedying the lack of revolutionary will and know-how in the West faced a distinctly less revolutionary situation than had been the case from late 1918 to late 1920. In most countries by the late autumn of 1920 the working class was exhausted and wary of new revolutionary adventures; workers were dropping out of political parties and unions in great numbers. In every country the communist and democratic socialist parties that emerged from the schisms attracted fewer members combined than they had as single parties before the schisms. (The most important of the new parties were the PCF [*Parti communiste français*], from a split of the SFIO, the majority going to the communists; the KPD, whose ranks were enormously expanded by the split of the USPD; and the PCI [*Partito communista italiano*] from a split of the PSI, a minority in this case going over to the communists.)

For many of those western revolutionaries who joined the new communist parties, the time seemed right for retrenchment, for reorganization, and for rethinking. They were intent on preparing for the next revolutionary wave, which could not be far away. This emphasis on retrenchment became all the stronger after March 1921, when the so-called *Märzaktion*, or March Uprising, was humiliatingly suppressed by the German government. The Märzaktion was an almost comic-opera effort to provoke a revolution, and Comintern agents were deeply implicated. The whole affair tended to discredit the KPD and the Comintern and led to the resignation of a number of important German communist leaders, many of whom had earlier been associated with Rosa Luxemburg.

In the same month in Russia the Kronstadt garrison rose in revolt against the bolsheviks, demanding a return to soviet democracy and an end to the Bolshevik Party's increasingly oppressive control of the state and economy. Detachments of the Red Army, under Trotsky's direction, brutally crushed the uprising. This was a cruel turn of fate for Trotsky personally as well as for the bolshevik régime in general, for the men at Kronstadt had been at one time among Trotsky's most ardent admirers and were the most reliable shock troops of the revolution.

Thus the *Märzaktion* and the Kronstadt uprising, both coming in March 1921, can be seen as a watershed in both Russian history and the history of socialism outside Russia. The greatest period of revolutionary upheaval since 1848 had passed, and revolutionaries in Russia and western Europe found themselves faced with a most unexpected and uncomfortable situation. Inside Russia, proletarian revolutionaries held power in apparent contradiction to Marxist laws of development, while in western Europe, where a proletarian revolution would have been more consistent with Marxist theory, the proletariat had failed to take power, or even to show much interest in exercising it. Thus the new world communist movement, with its capital in Moscow, was based upon gaping paradoxes, which would in turn lead communists of the next generation in directions that few Marxists of the previous generation would have believed possible.

GUIDE TO FURTHER READING

An unusually tendentious literature, even for the history of socialism, exists on the origins of communism in Russia and the West. Much of it has been written by western socialists, embittered over the communist destruction of their hard-won prewar organizations and often deeply influenced by menshevik interpreters of bolshevism. Former communists who became disillusioned with Stalinism have also written prolifically, as have Cold Warriors of a deeply conservative background. But, even when lacking balance, many of their works are still of high intellectual caliber and gracefully written. Two good examples are the works of Isaac Deutscher and Bertram Wolfe, discussed in the previous chapter. Deutscher, who was formerly a leading member of the Polish Communist Party, then a Trotskyite, and who finally assumed a position that is hard to categorize, writes with a fundamental sympathy for the Soviet experience, in spite of its Stalinist perversions, in his biographical trilogy of Trotsky (*The Prophet Armed, The Prophet Unarmed,* and *The Prophet Outcast*), as well as in his one-volume study, *Stalin: A Political Biography.* Wolfe, a former leader of the American Communist Party and later a vehement anti-communist linked with right-wing groups, has written (in his *Three Who Made a Revolution,* and in numerous other books and articles dealing with Marx and communism) far less sympathetically, but still with verve and intelligence. Nettl's biography of Rosa Luxemburg, also previously cited, while extremely sympathetic to its subject—perhaps to a fault—is not quite so obviously moved by political animus. It is an excellent study. Perhaps the most detailed, unrelenting, yet also scholarly condemnation of bolshevism, with a scarcely concealed sympathy for the menshevik point of view, is Leonard Schapiro's *The Communist Party of the Soviet Union.* More readable, if at times irritatingly flip, and equally hostile to the bolsheviks is Adam Ulam's *The Bolsheviks.* Leopold H. Haimson's *The Russian Marxists and the Origins of Bolshevism* is a path-breaking, brilliant study. A recent re-interpretation which successfully distances itself from both right-wing and left-wing interpretations and which argues persuasively that Lenin was a coherent and consistent Marxist rather than a political opportunist, is Neil Harding's two-volume *Lenin's Political Thought* (vol. 1: *Theory and Practice in the Democratic Revolution;* vol. 2: *Theory and Practice in the Socialist Revolution*).

The most complete and useful accounts of the response of the various parties of the International to the outbreak of war can be found in the following: Carl Schorske, *German Social Democracy, 1905–1917;* Gerald Feldman, *Army, Industry, and Labor in Germany, 1914–1918;* Robert Wohl, *French Communism in the Making, 1914–1924;* Annie Kriegel, *Aux origines du communisme français;* and Helmut König, *Lenin und der italienische Sozialismus, 1915–1921.* Each of these can be described as first-rate scholarly works, balanced and well researched, even though Kriegel was herself at one time a notorious Stalinist. Fernando Claudin, also a former communist party functionary, has written a two-volume study of the Comintern, *The Communist Movement, From the Comintern to the Cominform,* which primarily concentrates on the mid-1920s through the mid-1940s, but contains useful information on the earlier period. (More is said about Claudin's work in the Guide to Chapter 7.)

Most of the above works deal also with Lenin's reaction to the war, as well as with various aspects of Leninism. A good general introduction to Leninism is Alfred G. Meyer, *Leninism.* A definitive biography of Lenin, of the dimensions and quality of Deutscher's biography of Trotsky, has yet to be written. The most satisfactory, if still inadequate, of the existing biographies is Louis Fischer's *Life of Lenin.* A more critical, theoretically sophisticated work, though not a biography, is Stanley Page's *Lenin and World Revolution.*

William Chamberlin's balanced two-volume study, first published in 1935, still remains, all things considered, the best overview and general narrative of the Russian Revolution (*The Russian Revolution, 1917–1921*). Shorter, more popular, but still reliable is Robert V. Daniels, *Red October.* E. H. Carr's three-volume *The Bolshevik Revolution, 1917–1923,* although not highly regarded by all scholars in the West, can still be recommended. It is considered by Soviet scholars to be the best of western efforts to deal with the revolution. Trotsky's *The History of the Russian Revolution*, while hardly in all respects a scholarly history, is nevertheless brilliant, both in terms of literary skill and historical insight. Alexander Rabinowitch's two volumes, *Prelude to Revolution: The Petrograd Bolsheviks and the July 1917 Uprising* and *The Bolsheviks Come to Power*, relate, with incomparable detail, balance, and clarity, how the bolsheviks came to power in Petrograd—the precise mechanics, with all the confusion and ambiguity. John L. H. Keep's *The Russian Revolution, A Study in Mass Mobilization* examines in depth the classes, social relations, and structural changes in Russia at the time of the revolution.

Accounts of revolution in the West and the formation of communist parties can be found in many of the above-mentioned studies, particularly in Carr (vol. 3), Kriegel, Wohl, Feldman, and König. The interested reader should also consult Albert S. Lindemann, *The "Red Years": European Socialism versus Bolshevism, 1919–1921*; John M. Cammett, *Antonio Gramsci and the Origins of Italian Communism*; Werner Angress, *Stillborn Revolution*; A. J. Ryder, *The German Revolution of 1918*; Eberhard Kolb, *Die Arbeiterräte in der deutschen Innenpolitik, 1918–1919*; and James W. Hulse, *The Forming of the Communist International*. These are all recent studies by academic scholars rather than former participants, and thus are relatively balanced and thoroughly researched. Volume 1 of Paolo Spriano's *Storia del partito communista italiano: Da Bordiga a Gramsci*, is in a category of its own: The author remains a member in good standing of the Italian Communist Party, yet his works (and this is only one of many) attain a level of objectivity and penetration that is respected by many non-communist scholars. At the other end of the political spectrum, Branko Lazitch and Milorad Drachkovitch's *Lenin and the Comintern* is a monotonously polemical work, but its more than six hundred pages contain some useful and new information.

Helmut Gruber's *International Communism in the Era of Lenin* provides both a judicious selection of contemporary documents and an intelligent commentary on them. Key Comintern documents can be found in Jane Degras, ed., *The Communist International, 1919–1921*. For Germany, see Hermann Weber, *Der deutsche Kommunismus, Dokumente*. For Italy, see Giuseppe Maione, *Il biennio rosso*.

The Democratic Socialists, 1914-1939

6

The creation of a communist movement under Russian leadership immediately following the war weakened but did not destroy the older party organizations. In most countries less than half of the prewar membership converted to the communist cause in the "red years" of 1919–21. A large number of the rank-and-file members of the new communist parties were people who had not participated in the prewar socialist movement and who were awakened to activism by the shocks of war and revolution, although many of the leaders of the new communist parties had been active in the Left of the prewar socialist parties.

This departure of the prewar Left meant that the established leaders of the old parties had to deal with fewer noisy revolutionaries in their ranks, a circumstance which in turn meant that reformist currents could flow through the party ranks with far less obstruction. Since communism became associated with minority dictatorship and revolutionary terror, the old parties were free to emphasize with renewed fervor their commitment to majority rule and liberal-democratic procedures. In most countries this new emphasis brought with it an abandonment of their prewar political isolation and the assumption of an active, positive role in the representative institutions of their various homelands.

The particular forms this participation took were kaleidoscopically diverse, but in most cases the outcome in terms of the goals of socialism was disappointing, even tragic. These were, of course, years of severe economic disruption, of fascist victories, and of Stalinist atrocities. Only in Scandinavia could anything like a victory for democratic socialism be counted. Elsewhere, above all in the German-speaking countries, democratic socialist parties were torn asunder by the contradiction implicit in their decision to cooperate with bourgeois-democratic regimes.

THE GERMAN SOCIAL DEMOCRATS IN WAR, REVOLUTION, AND REPUBLIC

Because tensions with Germany—social, economic, political, intellectual—were so severe, the German social democrats faced the harshest dilemmas of any of the democratic socialists. The SPD, as the largest party in Germany and the party most responsible for the certain of a German republic out of the ashes of the Empire, no longer had a real option to remain uninvolved. And leading German social democrats wanted no more of the isolation of the prewar years; they leaped into the political fray with enthusiasm.

August 1914 had been the turning point in this respect. A large proportion of the German working class and its leaders abandoned any pretense of internationalism and enthusiastically embraced the cause of German victory. This new era of Burgfrieden spelled a fundamental transformation in the position of social democracy in the Reich and of the relationship of the German working class to German society. World War I put tremendous pressures on Germany's political and economic institutions. A totalitarian war, a war that required mobilization of a country's total resources, could no longer permit the luxury of an inflexible elitist-class society, or Obrigkeitsstaat, run by haughty Junkers too proud to work closely with representatives of the lower orders. In order to wage war most effectively, social cohesion founded upon enthusiastic mass participation was an urgent necessity, and the leaders of the SPD and the trade unions provided a most welcome aid to Germany's rulers in mobilizing the masses. Social democrats enjoyed the confidence of the German working masses, and they put it to good use in leading rallies to whip up the passions of war, in visiting the front to keep up morale, in facilitating the movement of labor from one industry to another, and in justifying the government's war aims to the readers of the social-democratic press. And, as the pressures of war intensified, social-democratic leaders also helped by controlling strikes and stamping out left-wing dissidence.

Social democrats did these things out of genuine patriotism, but at the same time they expected compensation. They were particularly interested in obtaining promises of constitutional reform once the war was over, so that their popular support would be finally reflected in proportionate political power. These were not demands for socialization; they merely asked for the political rights and liberal-democratic institutions already enjoyed by the English, the Americans, and the French. The German social democrats were committed to fulfilling the "historic task" that German liberals had not pursued to its conclusion. Indeed, many leading social democrats seemed emotionally more committed to bringing about liberal constitutionalism than to socialization of the means of production, although of course in their minds the one could not occur without the other.

This is not to imply that the leaders of the SPD and Free Trade Unions neglected economic matters. The wartime authorities consulted with them on matters of wages, working conditions, and allocation of resources. And German industrial workers did in fact enjoy an improvement in material condition relative to the middle classes, although the living standard of nearly all classes declined in an absolute sense, especially in the last year of the war.

The upheaval in Germany following upon defeat in late 1918 and early 1919 merely formalized the ad hoc relationships worked out during the war between the older authorities and the social democrats. A new social and political balance established itself in Germany, reflecting new power relationships. Whereas under the Empire the ruling caste had come almost exclusively from the ranks of the Junkers and upper bourgeoisie, under the Weimar Republic these older elites joined hands in an uneasy alliance with the SPD and organized labor. When it became clear in late 1918 that Germany's authoritarian state was near collapse, the large industrialists recognized that the strongest ally they could find against social revolution was organized labor, with its limited and "reasonable" demands. And in order to avoid social revolution the industrialists were willing to pay a price, as long as they retained the substance of their power. On November 12, 1918, an agreement was reached between the representatives of the industrialists and organized labor. Known as the Stinnes-Legien Agreement, it established a new framework of industrial relations under capitalism. It recognized that the social-democratic unions were proper representatives of labor (and thus the industrialists agreed to stop support of company, or "yellow," unions), established collective bargaining, recognized the legitimacy of factory councils, and set up an eight-hour working day in factories (although a secret clause made this last promise invalid if other countries did not also introduce the eight-hour day).

Germany's officer corps was able to strike an even more advantageous bargain, considering the enormous discredit of the military in the autumn of 1918. Friedrich Ebert, as leader of the SPD and nominal head of the provisional government, made a secret pact with the generals, known as the Ebert-Groener Agreement. They pledged themselves to support the new republic with the military forces at their disposal, while he agreed not to tamper with the personnel and privileges of the military aristocracy and more generally not to disrupt the old social order.

These new relationships meant that social democrats had broken out of their prewar isolation and had become to a certain extent part of the new republican establishment. They had accomplished this feat not by a victory over the old order but by a compromise with it. This compromise was more than a reversion to ministerialism, which looked to a coalition of Left against Right; it was a kind of coalition *with* the Right, although it was not of course a parliamentary coalition. Once elections were held in early 1919, the SPD did ally itself with the parliamentary party of progressive liberals (the Democratic Party) and with the Center Party, and thus it dealt with the parties of the Right as parliamentary opponents. But still the underlying power relationships, which transcended parliamentary coalitions and established a new set of ground rules, were determined by the nonparliamentary Stinnes-Legien and Ebert-Groener agreements.

For revolutionaries these departures from Marxist class politics were a "betrayal." But if one attempts to see matters as they appeared to leading social democrats, then the decisions they made take on a more ambiguous complexion. Obviously much depends upon fundamental assumptions and questions of value, however, since if one considers class collaboration in itself evil or inexorably destined to failure, then there is no way that the record of the social democrats can be justified.

The dilemmas the SPD faced in 1918 and 1919 were even more wrenching than those of August 1914. Its leaders and its followers firmly believed in liberal democracy; they did not accept the notion of minority rule or violations of democratic procedure to achieve socialism. But, as the elections of January 1919 made clear, the SPD did not have a majority of Germans behind it. Only a little more than 40 percent of voters, now including the more conservative women voters, cast their ballots for social-democratic candidates. Even in coalition with the Independent Social Democratic Party, or USPD, which in 1919 received about 6 percent of the vote, a majority was still lacking. In any case, the USPD was thoroughly disillusioned by its alliance with the SPD in the Council of People's Commissars in November and December; now it would hear nothing of another effort at cooperation. Similarly, the new-formed Communist Party (KPD) rejected any sort of cooperation with the SPD, although communist electoral strength at this point was insignificant. Thus if the SPD were to attempt to form a government, it had to seek out allies in the non-socialist parties.

Similar dilemmas faced the leaders of the SPD on the issue of compromise with the military. The SPD turned to the Junker generals for protection, on the one hand, because no help was available from other quarters. Both on the Right and on the Left agitators were calling for a violent seizure of power. The experience in Russia had much impressed the leaders of the SPD, who were determined not to be like Kerensky, unable to choose sides and then overwhelmed by a ruthless revolutionary minority. Of course the generals were more than happy to help wipe out the bacillus of bolshevism in Germany before it had a chance to spread.

On the other hand, it must also be recognized that many of the leaders of the SPD, and above all Ebert, unabashedly enjoyed the company of generals, in whose presence they felt awe, and they were flattered by the attentions shown them by previously disdainful aristocrats. It is highly questionable whether the bargain struck with the generals was as beneficial for the SPD as it was for the military. The repressions directed at revolutionaries of the Left got murderously out of hand; many of those who "protected" the republic in 1919 in the so-called Freikorps military detachments were virulently anti-republican and would later join forces with the nazis. Similarly, the failure of the social democrats to push for a thorough renovation of Germany's bureaucratic cadres meant that the republic's police force, courts, embassies, and other government bureaus remained in the hands of men who had formerly pledged allegiance to the Kaiser. These bureaucrats became at best what was termed *Vernunftrepublikaner* ("republicans without emotional conviction"), but they often did their best surreptitiously to undermine the republic.

The social democrats' caution about tampering with the established order in Germany also reflected their keen awareness of the obstacles to social revolution discussed in the previous chapter: the likelihood of Allied blockade and intervention, the hostility of the countryside and the urban petty bourgeoisie, the refusal of bourgeois experts to cooperate in projects of social transformation, the disunity of the working class. The leaders of the SPD wished to prove themselves good democrats in order to win the favor (and the food) of democrats in the United States, England, and France. Those same leaders were perfectly aware that the 40 percent of the vote they had won in Germany's first postwar elections did not represent a vote for immediate socialization, and perhaps not even for socialism as a distinct ideal; many voters cast their ballots for the SPD because of its moderate image, and probably more importantly because of its firm stand against "bolshevism," both in Germany and in Russia.

Since the SPD was the largest party in the first parliamentary coalition of the Weimar Republic, it took over the chancellorship in early 1919. Its coalition partners, the Democratic Party and the Center Party, were in full agreement with the policy of repressing the revolutionary Left in the name of constitutional democracy. But beyond certain limited areas of agreement, the partners of the first Weimar coalition fell out on a number of issues. The left wing of the Center Party, representing Catholic workers, generally supported the SPD's goals of social reform in the direction of protecting the working class, but the right wing of the party and the solidly middle-class Democratic Party were far less enthusiastic about those goals. In the same way, the antireligious ideology of the SPD found some support among the Democrats but adamant opposition from the Center Party.

All three parties were dismayed over the role forced upon them as the signatories of the punitive Versailles Treaty in early 1919, and the social democrats, as the leading party of the coalition, took the most blame. Right-wing demagogues excoriated the social democrats and their parliamentary allies as the "November Criminals," who had brought dishonor upon Germany and its army, "undefeated in the field." Popular outrage over the terms of the treaty and the many other difficulties in which the new state found itself convinced reactionary plotters that the time was at hand to bring down the hated republic. In March 1920 troops under the political leadership of a little-known right-wing activist named Wolfgang Kapp mutinied and marched into Berlin. The government was unable to find troops willing to support it against a move from the Right, and it was obliged to flee the capital. The generals who had until then so efficiently devoted themselves to crushing the revolutionary Left suddenly became reticent to come to the aid of the republic, and many sided openly with Kapp.

The SPD then fell back to its ultimate source of strength, the organized working class, and called for a general strike. The other parties of the coalition joined in support of the strike, and for once the German working class responded with startling unanimity: Work stopped throughout Germany in one of the most successful general strikes ever proclaimed. Within four days the Kapp conspirators were brought to their knees, and the German working class had won a great victory. (It should be noted, however, that this victory corresponded to the more cautious prewar conception of the general strike—as a defensive, rather than aggressive, revolutionary measure—and, perhaps more important, that the strike extended outside the organized working class; even many civil servants participated in it.)

The victory celebrations did not last long. Once an effort was made to move beyond the negative measure of destroying the Kapp Putsch to the positive step of securely re-establishing the Republic, the unity of the working class again dissolved. A promising beginning was made when Karl Legien, the leader of the social-democratic trade unions, proposed that a labor government to be formed, composed of SPD, USPD, and representatives of the Catholic and social-democratic trade unions. The new government's program would be designed to correct some of the mistakes made since November 1918 and in particular to deal forcefully with those in military and government agencies who had failed to support the republic in its hour of need. But the left wing of the USPD, which would in the autumn of 1920 split off to join with the communists, refused to consider such a coalition, and the USPD right wing, while attracted to Legien's proposals, was unwilling to split the party over the issue.

Without the USPD, Legien's labor government could not succeed, and thus another Weimar coalition of SPD, Democratic Party, and Center Party was formed. But it failed to take advantage of the initiative of the general strike to introduce reforms. Moreover, it soon turned to some of the very military men who in March had refused support for the government against the Kapp conspirators. It now called on them to repress revolutionary unrest in the Ruhr valley, where workers were attempting to continue the general strike and to dislodge the older authorities and Kapp sympathizers.

The elections held in June 1920 reflected the deep disappointment felt by Germany's workers and by supporters of the other Weimar coalition partners. Nearly a half of the SPD's former voters deserted the party in favor of the USPD, and the Democratic Party lost approximately the same proportion to the parties on its right. In other words, voters polarized sharply on the right and on the left, with the result that the first Weimar coalition no longer enjoyed a majority in the Reichstag.

The social democrats thus found themselves in a particularly uncomfortable position. Only by adding the People's Party (the party immediately to the right of the Democratic Party) to the former three-party coalition could a new majority be formed. But the leaders of the

SPD believed that an important reason for their stunning decline in June was their party's many compromises with the non-socialists. To form an alliance with the People's Party was likely to be further resented since it was not even a party of the left-leaning bourgeoisie, as was the Democratic, but instead represented big business. Yet if the SPD withdrew entirely from the government, the only possible majority would encompass one or more of the parties of the anti-republican extreme Right, and to the social democrats it seemed highly unlikely that the republic could long survive such leadership.

The final result was that the SPD agreed to "tolerate" a minority center-right coalition (of Center, Democratic, and People's parties). "Toleration" meant not voting against this coalition—and social-democratic votes would have been necessary to bring it down—while at the same time refusing to join it formally. Once formed, the new cabinet quickly declared an amnesty for all but the top leaders of the Kapp Putsch. The social democrats could only watch in impatience and frustration.

The policy of toleration, which seemed so cowardly and passive to many socialist activists and which would be revived in the crisis period of the early 1930s, was symptomatic of the irreducible dilemmas facing the SPD, once it had determined to participate in bourgeois parliamentary politics. Within a short time the leaders of the SPD swallowed their initial aversion to participation in a cabinet with the representatives of big business, and a four-party coalition, known as the "broad" Weimar coalition (the "narrow" included three parties), was formed in 1921 (another was formed later under the leadership of Gustav Stresemann, the leader of the People's Party). The SPD had traveled a long way from its prewar position as the most forceful opponent of ministerialism in the International.

After the shocks of 1918–20 and with the formation of the broad coalition of 1921, the SPD and the Weimar Republic seemed for a time to be regaining the confidence of a majority of Germans. The SPD received a boost, especially in its parliamentary representation, when the remainder of the USPD (after the split at Halle in October 1920) decided to rejoin the parent party in 1922. Since the USPD parliamentary delegation had overwhelmingly opted to reject the Comintern and to stay in the USPD, the new united SPD parliamentary delegation increased to approximately 170 (out of 466), only slightly smaller than it had been before the June elections.

A further hopeful sign was that the SPD was gaining a strong and lasting foothold in Prussia; once the bulwark of reaction under the Empire, Germany's largest state now became a powerful progressive force under its social-democratic prime minister, Otto Braun. He was successful in bringing to the Prussian state government the very reforms that Ebert had failed to achieve for the Reich government. Braun replaced many reactionary administrators with social-democratic activists, gained firm control over the police force, and introduced a number of social welfare measures.

Finally, Ebert was elevated to the presidency of the republic, and although he conscientiously sought to strike a pose above party politics, his position as chief executive of the new republic inevitably reinforced the general sense of social-democratic power and responsibility.

But the hopes of 1921 were soon dashed by France's invasion of the Ruhr in 1923 (discussed in the next chapter) and the subsequent disruptions of Germany's economy, society, and state. The breathtaking inflation of that year—postage stamps came to cost 10 billion marks apiece—wiped out the savings of much of the petty bourgeoisie and further embittered broad sections of German society. The grave situation benefited parties of the extreme Left and extreme Right, especially the latter, and in the elections of late 1923 the parties of the Right were the great victors. Finally, an unequivocally right-wing coalition was put together (the so-called *Bürgerblock*), and the SPD, for the first time in the history of the Weimar Republic, entered into full opposition, without any of the ambiguities of "toleration."

The following years were ones of internal recovery and international reconciliation for the republic, under the general leadership of Stresemann. It was not until 1928, after its success in the elections of that year, that an SPD-led Weimar coalition once again acceded to power. But the social democrats never regained the prestige that was theirs in the immediate postwar period. Moreover, the three-party "narrow" Weimar coalition still could not muster a majority, since the right-wing parties remained strong. Thus a rather shaky four-party "broad" coalition was set up. It included Stresemann's People's Party, but was not led by Stresemann, as had earlier been the case. Indeed, a significant proportion of the leadership of the People's Party disagreed with the notion of working with the social democrats; it was largely Stresemann's personal influence that enabled the coalition to survive, and even so Stresemann's party colleagues made repeated efforts to undermine his conciliatory efforts. His premature death in 1929 resulted in a steady rightward swing of the People's Party, which in turn contributed to the disintegration of the last Weimar coalition in March 1930.

By this time the Great Depression had hit Germany, and the nazi movement had begun the enormous expansion that would end in its triumph three years later. Once again the social democrats found it unappealing to turn to outright opposition, for fear of opening the government to nazi infiltration. Thus they tolerated a minority coalition under Heinrich Wilhelm Brüning, a conservative leader of the Center Party, whose government introduced measures openly detrimental to the condition of the working class.

Perhaps the crowning irony came in 1932 in the runoff election for President of the Republic, when the social democrats felt obliged to support Paul von Hindenburg as the only realistic alternative to Hitler. Hindenburg, a Junker general and World War I hero, was a living symbol of the old regime and all that the social-democratic masses had been taught to detest. Needless to say, the SPD's many compromises in the name of the lesser evil caused further disillusionment in working-class circles and provided material for communist recruitment.

In terms of economic policy the social-democratic record in these years was no more illustrious, and that record certainly appeared paradoxical for a party that had once stood for a class-based rejection of a free-market economy. Social democrats became, in effect, defenders of laissez-faire economics, often—at least so it seems in retrospect—in a most unimaginative fashion. The SPD defended balanced budgets and the gold standard; it hesitated to advocate social services or public works if they entailed deficit spending; and the response of most party leaders to economic depression was to argue that the natural workings of the market would soon reverse the downward trend and that government interference would merely make matters worse. Above all, the SPD opposed any kind of currency manipulation by the government.

To be sure, there were plausible arguments, from the standpoint of German labor at this time, for a number of laissez-faire tenets. The terrible experience of inflation in 1923, when party and trade-union funds disappeared overnight, convinced social democrats that once the currency had been again stabilized, no tampering with it of any sort could ever be allowed again. In the same way, it was argued that deflationary policies, insofar as they meant price reductions, would increase real wages, and that deficit spending policies would increase the government's dependence on borrowing from banks, concerning whose influence on government the socialists were justifiably suspicious.

But whatever the pros and cons of deficit spending and currency manipulation as remedies for economic depression, the solutions proposed by social-democratic leaders were no more imaginative than those of the non-socialists in these years—perhaps less so. At the same time, for social democrats to believe in the need to work within the free-market system made sense only as long as they were convinced that free-market capitalism was still a viable and progressive economic system—in other words, so long as they believed that the system still had a way to go before it had fully prepared for the advent of socialism. Whether by 1931 or 1932 capitalism was still such a viable and progressive system was easily doubted. But German social democrats, and reformist socialists in most other countries (with a few notable exceptions, to be discussed below), had little to offer by way of a program to transform capitalism peacefully and democratically into a socialist or system, or into some mixture of the two systems, in order to put the machines of industry effectively back into production.

THE BRITISH LABOUR PARTY

The history of the socialist and labor movements in Great Britain in the late nineteenth and early twentieth centuries was qualitatively different from that in Germany or in other continental countries. It is because of these fundamental differences that relatively little has been said about Great Britain in the preceding two chapters. A number of interesting and instructive similarities developed in the 1920s and 1930s, however, that brought the British movement more into the ideological arena of continental socialism.

Mention has been made in Chapter 4 of some of the peculiarities of the British situation: that Marxism failed to attract a large following and that the dissatisfaction with laissez-faire principles, while widespread, did not result in the creation of a socialist or labor party with a mass base. Thus, when the socialist parties of the Continent were enjoying their classic age of growth and influence, most workers in Great Britain remained loyal to the Conservative and Liberal parties, especially to the democratic-radical or "Lib-Lab" left wing of the latter. In the revolutionary decade of 1914–24, which so transformed continental parties and saw violent clashes between the old order and the forces of socialist revolution, Great Britain remained relatively calm; revolution was not a realistic proposition there even in the distant future. The English working class was not split into contending communist and democratic-socialist factions. The post-war British Communist Party attracted only a tiny minority of the country's workers, far fewer than the communist parties' followers in Germany, France, or Italy.

The turn of the century, when many continental Marxists had nearly despaired of the English worker (Kautsky's derogatory remarks will be remembered), was just the time, in fact, that a significant change was beginning to occur. The notion of a separate party of labor, not necessarily a socialist party but distinct from the Liberal Party, began to attract a following, first because of a growing disillusionment with the Liberals' commitment to deliver social legislation and then more particularly because of the reluctance of Liberal caucuses to accept trade-union candidates for parliamentary offices.

A decisive step toward amalgamating the various groups of predominantly upper- and middle-class socialist intellectuals with the massive numbers of organized workers came in 1900, when a conference met to consider a new party of labor. It was composed of 129 delegates, including seven from the Independent Labour Party, or ILP (a non-Marxist party, formed in 1893), four from the Marxist SDF, and one from the Fabian Society. The rest came from the Trades Union Congress, or TUC (the central body of organized labor in Great Britain), an indication the relative numerical balance of the various organizations in the proposed new political party.

However, numbers were not the only consideration, especially in the case of the Fabian Society; its leaders would exercise a kind of intellectual hegemony in the future Labour Party, directing it toward a socialism peculiarly adapted to English conditions—a gradualistic approach, that is, making use of English constitutional freedoms. At the same time, the Fabians were not simply advanced democratic radicals—indeed, they were in certain ways unapologetic elitists, who believed in a full-bodied socialist society, which they, as much as the most dogmatic socialists, were confident was approaching inexorably.

The debates of the conference centered around two key questions: the kinds of members the new party would attempt to recruit, and the program or official ideology it would adopt. Significantly, a resolution that proposed that no bourgeois members be allowed in the party was voted down. Equally significiant, a resolution of the SDF's advocating class warfare and revolutionary socialism was decisively rejected. Thus the conference made clear its distrust of "foreign" ideologies; indeed it was reticent to embrace any form of explicit socialism.

The organization that emerged from this conference was at first called the Labour Representation Committee, but a few years later it was formally renamed the Labour Party. In these early years of the twentieth century it was still not nearly as well organized, staffed, or financed as the continental socialist parties. In fact, many of its leading figures doubted that this new party would last long; they tended to see it as a tactical device to pull the Liberal Party toward the left, to a greater sympathy for the workers' cause. But from the beginning the new organization gathered behind it several hundred thousand members (in contrast, the SFIO, at its prewar peak, stood at 100,000). In 1906 the Labour Party was able to elect twenty-nine members to parliament. In the eyes of some labor or socialist activists a promising beginning, but only a beginning, had been made.

The war years, while the cause of serious strain within the Labour Party, did not damage or shatter it. In balance the war may indeed have helped the new party because, in cooperating with the state in its hour of need, Labour won a measure of respectability that it had previously not enjoyed. Labour's gain was roughly comparable to what the SPD gained through the Burgfrieden, although of course English workers in the prewar period had never experienced a comparable degree of exclusion from the nation's political institutions. In addition, whereas the SPD's move constituted a dramatic shift in gears and an implicit betrayal of its Marxist heritage, the Labour Party was not encumbered with such ideological baggage. Some of the groups within the Labour Party did struggle with their socialist consciences over support of the war, but since they were allowed considerable leeway within the party to express their dissatisfactions—far more than was the case within the SPD—their struggles, while often bitter, did not seriously threaten the unity of the Labour Party as a whole.

These tragic years of massacre and destruction pushed the party's center of gravity sharply to the left. The membership of the party grew dizzyingly in the immediate postwar period—from 2.5 million in 1917, to 3.5 million in 1919, to 4.4 million in 1920. The growth of the trade unions was even greater—6.5 million by 1920. These trends inclined union leaders in the Labour Party to view more favorably a policy of complete independence from the liberals, an attitude which was all the more attractive because of Lloyd George's flirtation with the Conservative Party. In 1918 the Labour Party adopted an explicitly socialist platform, composed by the Fabian Socialist Sidney Webb. Entitled "Labour and the New Social Order," it predicted the disintegration of European capitalism and the gradual introduction of a democratic-socialist control of Great Britain's productive forces. The break with liberalism, in other words, was now unequivocal. Webb's program warned that "we need to beware of patchwork. . . . What is to be reconstructed . . . is . . . society itself" (Jarman, p. 122).

The experience of the war helped persuade many practical, non-ideological trade-union leaders that government control of the economy was not only feasible but, more important, beneficial to the interests of working people. As was the case for Germany, the totalitarian mobilization of the economy for war had meant a stringent limitation of the free market and a direct government management of such critical industries as the railroads and coal mines. Through these experiences workers on all levels were led to the conclusion that government control and intervention, rather than leading to ruin, could lead to better wages, less unemployment, and broader measures of social welfare.

The economic difficulties following upon the war, exacerbated from the workers' standpoint by the Conservative government's attack on wages (in an attempt to restore Britain's depreciated currency to its prewar levels), further contributed to the electoral appeal of the Labour Party. By 1922 Labour had become the second largest party. Thus, according to tradition, it was the official party of opposition. Few within the party, however, expected a Labour government in the foreseeable future. But in November 1923, when the Conservative leader Stanley Baldwin suddenly decided to appeal to the country to support a controversial protective tariff, Labour increased its representation to 191, and the Conservatives thus lost their majority.

Since the Conservative Party could now rule only with the support of the liberals, and since they refused to give this support, Labour was called upon to form a government. This unexpected turn of events put the leaders of the young party in a quandary. They could assume power only with the backing or toleration of the liberals; thus, any program of far-reaching social reform out of the question. For Labour to refuse power would have meant passing up the opportunity to further break down prejudices against it, to counter the prejudice that socialists and representatives of the working class could not act as capable and responsible national leaders. (A few years earlier Winston Churchill had contemptuously dismissed the Labour Party as "unfit to govern.") Moreover, a Labour cabinet, even if its accomplishments were minimal, would provide the party with valuable governmental experience, looking forward to the day when it would assume power with a majority backing.

Labour finally decided to try the experiment, although a minority of the party protested loudly. Ramsay MacDonald was elected to head the new cabinet. He came to the Labour Party from the ILP, had headed the pacifist wing of the party during the war, and was generally well received by the protesting left wing, in spite of his upper-class appearance and tastes. He had the look and bearing of a leader—an important factor, given the party's interest in gaining public confidence—was a good speaker, and proved himself adroit in manipulating the party's factions to his advantage.

MacDonald was convinced that his government should try to survive for as long as possible rather than lead a bold but short government that would make propaganda for the necessity of socialism but then go down to glorious defeat. MacDonald assured the country that he foresaw the introduction of socialism only as a very distant project, since the country's economic conditions and the mentality of the population did not yet permit it. Thus his government acted much as a left-liberal or democratic-radical party would have.

MacDonald's main accomplishments while in office (January to October 1924) were in the area of foreign affairs, in reducing international tensions through such initiatives as supporting the Dawes Plan (a more workable plan for the payment of reparations by Germany, which contributed to German recovery in 1924) and opening negotiations for the diplomatic recognition of Soviet Russia. In the area of social policy the Labour government's accomplishments were expectably meager: efforts were made to improve lower-class housing, to open up and reform education, and to reduce unemployment. These were measures that encountered little opposition from the other parties.

In the autumn of 1924 the liberals withdrew their support for the government over an issue having to do with the ongoing negotiations with Soviet Russia, and the country went once again to the polls. This time the issues centered around alleged communists in the government as well as the more general bugbear of the "communist conspiracy" in Great Britain. The campaign was emotional and hard-hitting, envenomed by the publication, shortly before the day of election, of the "Zinoviev letter," which, it was alleged, instructed the British Communist Party on the formation of cells in the army and navy for the purpose of spreading revolutionary, anti-military propaganda.

The letter was later shown to be a forgery, although there was little in it that could not plausibly have come from Zinoviev's pen. Genuine or not, it was put to opportune use by the Conservatives. Thousands of indignant and frightened people, many of whom did not usually bother to vote, went to the polls to vote Conservative, or, more accurately, to vote against Labour, tainted by its overtures to Soviet Russia and its more generally "soft" attitudes to communism.

Even so, Labour increased its own vote by a million (while losing 42 seats). The liberals were nearly wiped out, leaving the once-again overwhelmingly victorious Conservative Party and the only temporarily defeated Labour Party as the future protagonists of the British two-party system.

These political disappointments led the trade-union leaders to reassert themselves. The country's prolonged economic malaise weighed heavy upon the backs of working people, and class tensions were not lessened by the unscrupulous tactics of the Conservatives in the autumn 1924 electoral campaign. Conditions remained worst of all in the coal mines, and worsened further in June 1925 when the owners tried to introduce wage reductions and an increase in working hours. Resistance to these efforts led, by a complex process, to the declaration of a general strike in May 1926.

In spite of the anarchosyndicalist overtones implicit in idea of a general strike and the growing interest among organized laborers in "direct action" because of the disappointments in the parliamentary arena, most of the strikers apparently viewed their actions as a demonstration of working-class solidarity and, relatedly, as a test of strength in industrial relations, not as a move to overturn constituted authority. Still, Conservative leaders like Churchill regarded the strike as a declaration of class war, as a life-and-death struggle between the forces of parliamentary democracy and anarchic revolution. Within the labor movement only the miniscule Communist Party and a few others on the extreme Left interpreted the strike along such lines.

As the strike progressed through its many convoluted stages, English workers learned a lesson so forcefully taught French workers in the spring of 1920: Unless a significant majority of a democratic nation warmly supports the goals of such a strike (as for example had been the case with the strike against the Kapp Putsch), it has little chance of success. In the English case, as in the French, middle-class opinion turned sharply against the workers as the strike progressed. The working class, and the Labour Party, showed a remarkable degree of solidarity, but labor leaders were stunned to discover that what they perceived as a just cause against blind and selfish owners found almost no support outside of their own ranks and those of a small contingent of left-wing intellectuals. The Conservative government was ready with emergency forces to carry on needed services, thousands of constables were armed, and middle-class volunteers often filled in where necessary.

Faced with this kind of opposition the strike fizzled, and eventually the miners went back to work with longer hours and lower pay. The Conservative government in the following year passed a law outlawing sympathy strikes and curtailing other labor activities. Yet, contrary to expectations, class tensions seemed to subside and a generally different sense of perspective prevailed. The general population seemed less concerned by the steady growth of the labor movement, and most labor leaders resolved to avoid similar adventures in the future. The growth of the Labour Party was not noticeably impeded: In the elections of early 1929 Labour again enjoyed a significant increase in support, with 8.3 million votes and 287 seats in parliament, making it the largest party in England, though still short of an absolute majority. Thus when the King again called upon MacDonald to form a cabinet, Labour was once again dependent upon the support of the liberals.

The year 1929 was not an auspicious time for any government to come into power, especially not a working-class government which was dependent upon the toleration of another party and led by men who saw their party's present role as necessarily limited to the confines of non-socialist economic policies. It is an irony of history that both the SPD and Labour Party came back into power on the eve of Europe's greatest depression, and thus both were obliged to shoulder the responsibilities of capitalism in crisis.

The first months of the new Labour government saw an upsurge in business conditions, making possible the passage of a few measures of social welfare, since these did not press unduly on business profits. But in the autumn of 1929, when the world crisis began to spread in earnest, this relatively promising and harmonious period of the second Labour government came to an abrupt end, and the Labour Party, like the SPD, was pushed into impossible dilemmas.

From the beginning of the crisis Labour was faced with the problem that the policies promised in its 1929 electoral platform (that is, efforts to stimulate business and to aid the poor) were inflationary in tendency and would thus tend to undermine the stability of British currency now that world prices were in decline, since Britain's economy was so sensitive to export-import trade. In order to protect British holdings of gold, deflationary policies were called for, which would in turn practically rule out any general scheme of public works, at least as long as the gold standard remained.

The international decline of prices meant new pressures on British wages, and thus the Labour government was put in a position similar to that of the Conservatives in the early 1920s. Labour, like the Conservatives, refused to consider currency manipulation (that is, abandonment of the gold standard or devaluation of the pound)—held in nearly the same horror among Labourites as among social democrats in Germany. Without currency manipulation employers were forced to seek a cut in wages and a reduction of taxes (which would further cut government revenues to support social legislation) in order to remain competitive on the world market. A short-term answer might have been found in some sort of protective tariff (it will be recalled that Baldwin had tried to resort to this in 1923, leading to the elections that brought down his government), but Labour also refused to abandon free trade. Deficit spending was also out, since the party believed in balanced budgets.

The Labour Party was thus trapped between the demands of its supporters for social legislation and the protection of wages, on the one hand, and the objective needs of the British capitalist economy as part of a world economy in crisis on the other. Labour's commitment to such liberal policies as free trade, balanced budgets, and the gold standard further restricted any possibility of adequate reponse. Even the government's considerable effort to extend unemployment benefits (which had left the insurance fund from which these were financed nearly 100 million pounds in debt by 1930) was more of a liberal-welfarist palliative than a socialist policy, in that it involved basically a handout to the poor in order to win or retain popularity rather than a far-sighted program of industrial reorganization.

The agony of the second Labour government lasted until the autumn of 1931, when the cabinet disintegrated into squabbling factions and MacDonald secretly presented the king with plans for a "National" government, made up of dissident Labourites, Liberals, and Conservatives. MacDonald was convinced that Britain's problems could no longer be solved by a single-party government, and thus a cabinet enjoying broad support was essential.

In the elections of 1931 the Labour Party went down to disastrous defeat, its parliamentary strength falling from 289 to 46, although its vote dropped only about 6 percent. Conservatives remained in power for the rest of the 1930s, until the Second World War, while Labour was left to nurse its wounds and rethink its positions.

THE SFIO IN THE INTERWAR YEARS

The socialist movement in France between the two wars was notably different from that in Germany or England. While communism attracted a minority, though a substantial one, of German workers and a miniscule fraction of British workers, the French Communist Party (*Parti communiste français*, or PCF) was created from a decisive majority of the SFIO at the congress of Tours in 1920s. It thus began as the largest working-class party in France. And while the SPD and Labour

Party entered fully into the compromises of governmental participation, the post-schism SFIO remained faithful to prewar patterns, refusing to participate in cabinet alliances with non-socialist parties and asserting its continued belief in class conflict, proletarian revolution, and socialization of the means of production.

Thus, while firmly rejecting Leninism, the SFIO did not embrace reformism. Its efforts to find a *via media* between the communists' fundamental rejection of bourgeois institutions and the SPD's full involvement in them required at times the spinning of some fine ideological distinctions. In order properly to understand these it is useful to review the experiences of the SFIO in the immediate postwar years.

In early 1921 the SFIO, having lost about three-quarters of its membership to the communists, faced a bleak prospect, especially since the converts to communism included a large proportion of the SFIO's youngest, most ardent, most active members. Moreover, nearly all of the SFIO's press, including Jaurès's venerable *L'Humanité*, was lost to the communists, as well as treasury monies, offices, and archives. The main advantage of the rump SFIO after the schism was that it retained most of the party's more experienced leaders. But these men were often set in their ways and vulnerable to charges of bureaucratic decrepitude and *embourgeoisement* (if such a term is appropriate to people who were already overwhelmingly bourgeois in social origin).

Among the older leaders the prewar division of parliamentary deputies, or *parlementaires*, and party officials assumed even greater importance. The parlementaires were usually members of the reformist right wing of the party. In most districts they depended upon voters who were not party members to elect them and thus they tended to be conciliatory and undogmatic. The party officials on the other hand were elected by card-carrying activists, the *militants*, for most of whom ideological purity was important, and thus these officials were generally more left wing and dogmatic than the parlementaires. Since the party officials took it upon themselves to oversee the actions of the party's parliamentary delegation, it is easy to see how tensions built up. Disagreements within the SFIO about such issues as participating in bourgeois coalitions had definite institutional foundations.

The party officials strove throughout the 1920s to rebuild the SFIO, to recover from the disaster at Tours, a task which in part involved re-attracting the members lost in the schism as well as attracting new ones. Because of these goals, SFIO leaders were sensitive to the accusation by the communists that they had "sold out"; they made every effort to prove that *they* were the ones who were faithful to prewar traditions, while the communists had in reality abandoned them. SFIO party officials were thus all the more stubbornly opposed to the efforts of many parliamentary deputies to convert the SFIO into an openly reformist party on the model of the SPD or Labour Party.

Usually the party officials had their way. The first party congress after Tours endorsed a strongly anti-reformist resolution. It not only condemned participation in non-socialist electoral coalitions and cabinets but even prohibited voting for the budgets of bourgeois governments (a temptation, when the budgets included benefits for the working class, as they commonly did before the war). At this time, however, competition with the communists was not the only reason for this dogmatic position: The reactionary *Bloc national*, which had so routed the SFIO in the October 1919 elections, held power until 1924, and thus the SFIO's intransigent hostility to the government was natural.

The early 1920s did see a steady recovery of the SFIO. However, in spite of its efforts to appear more ideologically steadfast than the communists it did not succeed in attracting the unskilled industrial working class to its ranks in any significant numbers. Instead, the SFIO gradually earned support from skilled workers and certain categories of white-collar employees, especially in state government, and there above all among educators. The industrial working class tended to gravitate to the communists, and by the late 1920s and early 1930s the SFIO and PCF came to have distinctive social foundations, as was broadly the case in Germany and other countries with democratic socialist and communist parties.

By 1932 the SFIO had regained its pre-Tours membership of 120,000, and in the elections of 1932 the socialists won 2 million votes, with 132 deputies in the Chamber. They had done considerably better than in 1919, before the schism. In comparison, the communists in 1932 polled only 800,000 votes (down from 1.1 million in 1928), with 11 deputies and a party membership that had dwindled to around 30,000.

These figures reveal an interesting aspect of both the communist and the socialist parties in France at this time, as compared to the situation in England and Germany: Relatively few Frenchmen were willing to join the SFIO or PCF compared to the number who were willing simply to vote socialist or communist. Only one out of fifteen socialist voters felt sufficient commitment to join the party, and the figure was approximately one out of the thirty for the communists (exact calculations are difficult, since the communists kept their membership totals secret at this time, and the turnover in communist party membership from year to year was extremely high). For the SPD or Labour

Party the figure was normally in the range of one out of three. This peculiarity of the French scene contributed powerfully to the previously discussed tensions between SFIO parlementaires and party officials, since the parlementaires by 1932 could claim to represent millions of voters, while the party officials represented only the party's 120,000 members. Yet the parlementaires were required to receive their marching orders from the party officials.

It was vital after Tours to find a leader capable of presiding over the contending factions of the SFIO, but the hallowed memory of Jaurès called forth inevitably unfavorable comparisons. The man who finally did take up Jaurès's mantle was in some ways a surprising one. Léon Blum was an intellectual's intellectual, a man of highly refined literary and artistic sensibilities, from a wealthy bourgeois Jewish family. "A revolutionary—in pearl grey gloves," quipped one opponent. He definitely was not cut in the mold of the prewar patriarchs of socialism, like Bebel or Jaurès, and he did not even possess Ramsay MacDonald's saving grace, his look of authority. With his thick glasses, his limp-wristed gestures, and his weak, high-pitched voice, he hardly seemed up to the role of popular tribune.

Yet in other ways Blum was admirably suited for leadership of the SFIO. He was not closely associated with any wartime faction, as were most of the other potential party leaders. He had the further advantage of having been a personal friend of Jaurès's, and his interpretation of socialism had much in common with that of Jaurès. Nearly everyone, even Blum's enemies, conceded that he had taken an active role in the party out of socialist commitment and a sense of duty rather than personal ambition. His wealthy bourgeois background was thus in a way turned to his advantage, since it was recognized that he was sacrificing secure status in respectable bourgeois society for the cause of socialism. In short, Blum had about him an aura of personal integrity that was valuable in soothing party factionalism.

Blum also possessed a remarkable intellect—subtle, penetrating, thorough. He was capable of making clear the most complicated and elusive issues, of finding his way to the essence of a question, and he had a talent for reconciling the seemingly irreconcilable, of working out doctrinal consensus where none seemed to exist—in this, above all, he resembled Jaurès. Blum put these many abilities to good use in the endless squabbles at the SFIO's party congresses, and he was able to reach a wide audience through his regular column in the party newspaper, Le Populaire.

Blum was a prominent parliamentary deputy, whose speeches

earned respectful attention across the political spectrum. Unlike the communist deputies, Blum viewed the parliamentary podium not merely as a propaganda platform to denounce the capitalist world—although he certainly did make use of that aspect of it—but also as a testing ground for socialists, the rulers of tomorrow. Although he looked to an ultimate revolutionary upheaval, he believed that for the foreseeable future the SFIO should work out a constructive criticism of the present government. By so doing, he reasoned, the party was "serving and preparing the revolution by demonstrating that socialist theory and action could inspire the most useful and just solutions for the present day."

Blum's subtle mind was put to work when the party faced an important challenge in the second postwar elections, in May 1924. It will be recalled that the SFIO had refused in November 1919 to form electoral alliances of any sort, in spite of a new electoral law that gave great advantage to those parties that did so. Consequently, the Bloc national, by succeeding in many many districts in uniting all of the other parties against the socialists, trounced them at the polls. The SFIO leadership was not anxious to repeat this experience in 1924; yet at the same time the idea of forming electoral alliances made the party vulnerable to communist propaganda. But faced with the real possibility of a victory of the so-called *Cartel des gauches* (an alliance of the center and left parties), if the socialists cooperated, the SFIO softened its earlier intransigence and agreed to enter into electoral alliances with the Cartel parties. At the same time, Blum and other dominant party leaders insisted that they would not accept cabinet posts, in spite of a vocal minority in the party that urged them to do so.

The Cartel des gauches was victorious in the elections of 1924, and the SFIO registered a healthy gain, from 55 to 104 delegates in the Chamber. Thereafter, the Cartel, under the premiership of the Radical, Édouard Herriot, and with the general support of the socialists, was at least able to reverse some of the Bloc national's efforts in international relations (the occupation of the Ruhr and Germany's ensuing inflation had occurred the year before), linking up their efforts with MacDonald's Labour government in a policy of international reconciliation.

In the course of the discussions that went on within the party about the SFIO's relationship to the new coalition of the Left, Blum articulated some typically subtle distinctions concerning what he believed the party properly could and could not do in the future. It could not "participate" in power by entering a cabinet, when bourgeois parties dominated that cabinet and when their representatives held the most important offices (in the sense that the SPD had "participated" in power in 1921 in the broad Weimar coalition). But a refusal to participate did not rule out electoral alliances and general parliamentary support. A "conquest" of power, in which socialists would wield exclusive power and would no longer honor bourgeois legality, must wait until economic and social conditions were fully ripe. There was still, according to Blum, a third alternative: the "exercise" of power. In this eventuality socialists, as the dominant party of a coalition, would take over the most important cabinet posts and would give general direction to the government. However, bourgeois legality would be respected and no attempt would be made to introduce socialism, since a majority of the population would not yet support it (the SPD in 1919 had in this sense "exercised" power).

Blum recognized—and the German example abundantly illustrated—that the exercise of power might be a dangerous and painful path for his party to follow. Yet his strong sense of responsibility as a socialist could not justify his party's remaining out of the government if, after it had become France's largest party, the only alternative to the SFIO's exercising power would be for a right-wing government to assume power and introduce legislation harmful to the working class, to the future of socialism, and even to constitutional democracy.

Blum's tripartite distinction of "participation," "exercise," and "conquest" was a synthesis worthy of Jaurès; it offered satisfactions to each of the party's factions, and thus preserved unity while avoiding the sterile protest of the party's 1921 position. It also provided the SFIO with ready-made doctrinal underpinnings for its great moment in 1936, the Popular Front, so that the party's decision at that time to assume governmental responsibilities was less susceptible to charges of opportunism.

Blum was not able to placate all of the members of the SFIO. The right wing became especially restive under his leadership in the late 1920s and early 1930s. One of the more forceful and articulate leaders of this faction of the party was Marcel Déat, often described at the time as the "crown prince" of the SFIO. Déat struggled bitterly against Blum's refusal to lead his party into cabinet coalitions, and he finally broke with the SPIO to form the so-called "Neo-Socialists."

Déat was a brilliant yet unstable young professor at one of France's schools for its governing elite, the *École normale supérieure*, and once he had broken loose from the moorings of the old party, he began to flirt with fascist notions. In attacking what he considered the doctrinaire sterility of Blum and the party officials who surrounded him, Déat spoke of the need for a new socialist dynamism, one that would break out of superannuated patterns, emphasize acts of will and aggression, and recognize the need for authority and the proper role of the nation-state as a rallying point for the working class. Such notions found an echo among the older members of the party's Right, led by the old war-horse Pierre Renaudel (an ardent defender of the Union sacrée), and were heard especially after 1932, when a new parliamentary majority of the Left repeatedly broke down because of negative socialist votes. Finally, Renaudel and some thirty other parlementaires broke party discipline to support Radical-led cabinets, and thereafter joined forces with Déat.

Kindred ideas to those of Déat were being put forward in Belgium by Hendrik De Man, another brilliant intellectual who was also a socialist activist and University professor. As a young man, prior to World War I, De Man had been much attracted to revolutionary Marxism. But with the Bolshevik Revolution, he like so many others became disillusioned with dictatorial methods and discovered a renewed commitment to the personal freedoms guaranteed in western liberal democracies. Still, he retained a profound dissatisfaction with parliamentary democracy. In his eyes the parliamentary regimes of the 1920s and 1930s were intolerably inefficient and all too often venal. Even the workers' parties represented in them were dominated by ambitious and self-seeking politicians, more concerned with party intrigues and advancement of their careers than with the workers' cause. De Man at the same time never masked his patrician distaste for the prevalent low moral and cultural condition of the working masses. His theories and proposals, while firmly committed to the betterment of the masses, were animated by a deep and persistent elitist tone.

With the rise of fascism and the advent of the Great Depression, De Man turned his considerable intellectual powers to the problem of broadening the appeal of socialism beyond the confines of the working class, and above all to the petty bourgeoisie, among whom the fascists were making such inroads. He similarly sought to break out of the confines of stopgap, deflationist remedies for the economic difficulties of the Depression. The range of De Man's reflection and theorizing had already earned him an international reputation by the mid-1920s. He had written with insight and originality on such topics as workers' councils, mass democracy, nationalism, and the inadequacies of Marxist theory in the twentieth century. His answer now to the dual problems of fascism and economic depression was the "Labor Plan" (*Plan du travail*).

De Man believed that the Great Depression was the beginning of the end for capitalism, that the existing social order was doomed. Yet he argued persuasively that any effort at a violent overthrow of existing political institutions would result in a disaster, given conditions in the West. His Plan looked to a democratic government based on "a common front of all productive strata against the power of parasitic money." This meant an alliance of working class and petty bourgeoisie around a program of the socialization of banks and the key industries that exercised a monopolistic control of the economy, as well as a takeover of the largest holdings of landed property. With the power thus gained, the state could, De Man believed, tackle effectively the country's immediate economic problems, even though a substantial private sector with a market economy would remain.

De Man was not only a thinker and writer; he was an effective, trenchant orator. Frenzied enthusiasm for his ideas developed in Belgium, and at its Christmas congress in 1933 the Belgian Labor Party adopted the Plan. The party's formerly hostile left and right wings joined hands, with the slogan "the Plan, the whole Plan, and nothing but the Plan."

De Man's ideas have been dismissed as fascist in tendency and have therefore not been granted the attention and respect due them. (De Man later favored appeasement of Hitler. He did not join the resistance when German troops overran his country, and he did attempt for a while to work with the German occupation, but he did not himself become a fascist in any formal or rigorous sense.) De Man was a major thinker, and in many ways his Labor Plan was prophetic, anticipating the democratic socialist management of economies that were still predominantly capitalist following World War II. But his Plan was never put into effect as he conceived of it—despite the intransigent tone of the slogan adopted under his direction by the Belgian Labor Party. Rather, the party, and De Man himself, found themselves irresistibly drawn into a coalition government in which "the whole Plan" was not feasible, even though a public works program to fight unemployment and anti-deflationary policies were introduced. De Man had previously insisted that this kind of coalition government, with all its compromises, would be totally unacceptable. But when the concrete political situation presented itself, he found himself unable to resist. His personal tragedy was then compounded by his mistaken attitudes to the growing threat of Nazi Germany.

In this Déat and De Man also had something in common, for Déat developed into an ardent defender of appeasement and eventually—

and here the comparison is no longer fair—into a notorious nazi sympathizer. How Déat might have developed had he retained his connections with Blum and the SFIO is impossible to say. Ironically, not long after his break an unexpected chain of events, to be described in Chapter 8, resulted in the formation of the SFIO-led Popular Front. If Déat had only waited a while longer, he would very likely have been granted a post in Blum's new government. But, shunted into the cold, he drifted further to the right, his talents lost to the socialist cause.

DEMOCRATIC SOCIALISM IN AUSTRIA AND SWEDEN

In earlier chapters considerations of focus and space rendered it impractical to deal with smaller socialist movements in Europe, in spite of their often fascinating and instructive special histories. But developments in the interwar period in a number of small countries—the just-mentioned Belgium, as well as Austria and Sweden—illustrate the challenges facing socialists and the labor movement so well that they cannot be ignored.

The country whose absence in the preceding chapters has no doubt been particularly noticeable in Austria, or the Dual Monarchy of Austria-Hungary, as it was called before its breakup at the end of World War I. The Austrian social democrats were important members of the Second International, and Austro-Marxism came to be recognized as a significant variant of orthodox Marxism. Due to the multiplicity of nationalities under the Dual Monarchy, its social democrats had to deal from the beginning in a most direct fashion with the conflict between Marxist internationalism and the nationalist strivings of its citizens. Moreover, since the Dual Monarchy, stretching over the Danubian basin, constituted in the eyes of many socialist observers a natural economic unit, there were compelling reasons to retain the prewar boundaries of the Dual Monarchy and to try to combat nationalist separatism, working for a kind of proletarian internationalism within the confines of a multinational state.

At least such was the way it appeared to many socialists in Austria-Hungary, especially those representing the German-speaking areas. Others, especially in the Slavic regions, from the beginning resisted the notion of a multinational state, whether capitalist or socialist. Even before the war had so accentuated nationalist tendencies within the Dual Monarchy, the sizable Czech component of the Austrian Social-Democratic Party had taken decisive steps toward establishing a fully independent party, not satisfied with the offers of autonomy made to it.

With the breakup of the Dual Monarchy and the collapse of the vision of a special role for its German-speaking inhabitants, most Austrians (that is, those residing in the small southwestern territories of the former monarchy) felt little patriotism for the diminutive state created by the victors at the Paris Peace Conference. They hoped that Austria would be allowed to unite with Germany, and Austrian social democrats fully shared in these hopes. But the Allies would not condone any strengthening of their recently defeated Teutonic enemy. Thus although the Wilsonian principle of national self-determination was to a large degree upheld for the South Slavs, the Czechs and Slovaks, the Poles, the Hungarians, and the Rumanians, the Germans were denied unity and split into the German Weimar Republic, Austria (even the name "German-Austria" was not permitted by the Allies), and the western territories of Czechoslovakia. Nevertheless, the populations of these areas tended to consider themselves part of a German nation in a larger cultural and "racial" (*völkisch*) sense. Developments in Austria and Germany exercised a special influence on one another; socialists in each country looked to and learned from developments across the border.

As a key example, the Austrian socialists consciously sought to avoid what they considered the pitfalls along the path taken by the German social democrats in 1918–20. From the standpoint of men like Otto Bauer (the dominant figure in the Austrian party in these years), Ebert and the SPD had drifted much too far to the right and had collaborated too freely with the older powers of the Reich. Bauer was convinced that such collaboration had led to the disenchantment of many of the former activists of the SPD, the repeated schisms of the party, and the significant following of the communists in Germany. Bauer thus sought to lend a more revolutionary tenor to his party, to the left even of the SFIO. He rejected membership in the Communist International but also strove to maintain a fidelity to prewar Marxist orthodoxy.

Bauer's path seems to have helped preserve the unity of Austria's working-class movement. In Austria the communists remained a tiny sect, hardly more important than in countries like England or the United States, while the Austrian social democrats became proportionately stronger than the SPD, especially as the Twenties progressed.

The Austrian social democrats entered into a political coalition with non-socialists at the end of the war but avoided the "errors" of Ebert and the SPD, for the new Austrian Republic was founded not only upon a fully liberal-democratic constitution but also upon democratized institutions. There was a meaningful reform of the military, police, and law courts; and in general the former ruling elites were deprived of the institutional foundations of their power under the Monarchy.

Although the social democrats quit the coalition in mid-1920, by the mid-1920s they had built up a formidable organization. The social-democratic world within the capitalist world was even more impressive in Austria than in Germany. In the capital, Vienna, out of a population of around 2 million, the social democrats boasted around 500,000 card-carrying members and could count on something like two-thirds of the popular vote in municipal elections. A Viennese social-democratic worker could substantially avoid contact with a world dominated by the bourgeoisie, except in the work place. Many workers lived in attractive apartments, built and operated by socialist-controlled municipalities. Workers could also shop in socialist cooperative stores, listen to operatic performances at the socialist-subsidized opera house, and play chess in socialist chess clubs. Austrian social democracy's intricate network, the marvel of other European socialists, seemed to immunize Austrian workers against the appeals of either communism or fascism.

Yet this idyllic picture, and the Austrian socialists' apparent success in the midst of the widespread frustration and failure of socialists elsewhere, had its unfortunate and even ominous reverse side. The power and prestige of the socialists in Vienna and a few other urban areas were not matched elsewhere. In the rural districts of Austria the party's accomplishments were much resented, and opposition to the social democrats grew steadily more virulent. Even though the party leaders usually avoided the language of violent revolution and class conflict associated with the communists—and even though their actual practice was more conciliatory than some of their policy statements—they were viewed by many non-socialist Austrians as little better than bolsheviks.

The leaders of the Christian Social Party, the other principal party of the Austrian Republic (somewhat larger in popular vote in most elections than the social democrats and the party in control of the federal government), drifted from their brief cooperation with the social democrats at the end of the war to intransigent opposition. Concern on the part of the Christian socials was intensified as the Social-Democratic Party grew in strength with nearly every national election, from around 35 percent in 1920, to 39 percent in 1923, to 42 percent in 1930. Social-democratic spokesmen were not hesitant to predict the inevitable takeover by the proletariat of the federal government within the near future.

Here was posed once again the classic paradox so much discussed by socialists before the war: Would not anti-socialists resort to some kind of extralegal device to crush socialists if socialists seemed to be growing inexorably? Wasn't this kind of steady but slow growth potentially a dangerous thing for socialists who adhered faithfully to constitutional procedure—when their opponents very likely would not?

In Austria the situation was exacerbated by what was basically a two-party system. Contrary to the assumptions of many Americans and British, two opposing parties do not necessarily make for the healthiest kind of relationships within a parliamentary democracy. In Austria the existence of two roughly equal parties seems to have contributed to the growing polarization of Austrian society and to a most unfortunate inflexibility in parliament.

The moderate wing of the social democrats, led by Karl Renner (the father of the Austrian Republic's constitution and the future president of the post–World War II republic) urged conciliation with the Christian socials. But the wing of the party that followed Bauer firmly rejected such efforts, and this wing prevailed. Bauer's attitudes were matched, indeed exceeded, by the leader of the Christian socials, Father Ignaz Seipel. For him, the social democrats, godless and unredeemable enemies, deserved only destruction. His hopes for that goal grew measurably as anti-socialists in neighboring countries—Germany, Italy, Hungary—grew in strength.

Tensions in Austria between social democrats and Christian socials, between countryside and city, between federal government and the municipalities of Vienna reached a snapping point in the summer of 1927, in an incident that came to be known as Bloody Friday. A working-class demonstration got out of control and was fired upon wildly by police. In the ensuing battles demonstrators retreated to the social-democratic party headquarters, begging for the weapons that the party kept hidden. But those in charge at the headquarters did not want to make a revolutionary confrontation of this incident, partly because they believed Austria's neighbors would intervene against them. Weapons were refused the crowd, and, to compensate, the party called a series of protest strikes.

The events of Bloody Friday and the ensuing strikes catalyzed Austrian reactionaries and fascists. Right-wing paramilitary organizations, particularly the *Heimwehren*, gained the support of big business, the Catholic Church, and the federal government itself. Bloody confrontations between Heimwehren and workers' military organizations be-

came regular occurrences, and even in areas where the social democrats enjoyed mass support and held political power, their ability to
rule was severely restricted because their military strength did not
match that of the reactionaries. In the elections of 1930, the Heimwehren, running on a more or less fascist program, received only 8 out
of 165 seats, while the Social-Democratic Party won 72, making it the
strongest single party. But still the social democrats could hope to ally
with no other important party, and thus a coalition of Christian socials,
Heimwehren, and other small right-wing parties formed the new government.

In these elections the Austrian nazis were so weak that they failed
to elect even a single member to parliament. But in early 1933, after
the nazi takeover in Germany, a wave of enthusiasm for nazism rolled
across Austria. Insofar as this was translated into votes and party memberships it was mostly at the expense of the Christian Social Party,
whose leader Engelbert Dollfuss (who had taken over after the death of
Seipel) grew desperate in his determination to fend off both the nazis
and the social democrats. In March 1933 Dollfuss exploited a confused
episode in parliament to prevent its further meeting, and thereafter he
ruled through emergency decrees.

Dollfuss's assumption of a virtual dictatorship was the beginning
of the end for Austrian social democrats. Their destruction was not so
rapid as the destruction of the social democrats in Germany, but Dollfuss was nonetheless determined to nullify their influence inside Austria and to refashion the country into what could be termed a clerico-
fascist state. This was not nazism, which Dollfuss also later outlawed;
he claimed that he wanted to rule Austria according to papal encycli-
cals. His sense of Christian mission did not prevent him, however, from
dealing with social-democratic workers in a most brutal fashion.

Dollfuss's government presented the social democrats with an
even more heightened dilemma than that which had faced the German
social democrats when they decided to tolerate Brüning and to support
Hindenburg for the presidency. Dollfuss still seemed to be the lesser evil
when compared to the nazis, and social-democratic leaders saw no
hope of preventing Hitlerian domination of Austria unless some sort of
broad anti-nazi coalition could be forged. Thus they temporized, hoping that with time Dollfuss would come around to their viewpoint on
these matters.

It was a vain hope. Dollfuss hated Hitler and the nazis, but he
hated Bauer and the social democrats even more. He carried on secret

negotiations with Hitler, which remained inconclusive because Hitler would not recognize what Dollfuss considered to be the highest good, the sacred authority of the Catholic Church.

By late 1933 the social democrats finally decided that further dickering with Dollfuss was futile, and they called upon their followers to be ready to resist violently if basic social-democratic institutions were attacked by the government, or if an openly anti-democratic constitution were introduced. Dollfuss did not rise immediately to the bait but rather continued cleverly to nibble away at the social democrats' positions. As will be described in Chapter 8, he administered the coup de grâce to Austrian social democracy in the following year.

Was the story of democratic socialism in the interwar years one of unrelenting disappointment and tragedy? Not quite, for the socialist labor movement in Sweden was able to mark up some solid successes, although it is questionable whether the Swedish model offers many insights into how other labor movements might have avoided their own catastrophes.

Sweden's social-democratic movement grew up in the late nineteenth century in response to the spread of capitalist industrialism there. Swedish social democrats, like so many others on the Continent, were much impressed by the model of the SPD. The founding party of the Swedish Social-Democratic Party, in 1889, was closely modeled on the SPD's Gotha Program, and thereafter Swedish party leaders followed the lead of the SPD in the condemnation of Revisionism and ministerialism.

Yet there were important differences between developments in Sweden and in Germany. Sweden's ruling classes did not introduce anti-socialist legislation, and the social-democratic representatives in Sweden's parliament did not suffer the pariah status of the German social democrats in the Reichstag. Generally social divisions appeared less sharp in Sweden: Of particular significance for later developments, Swedish urban workers were never so isolated from the rural petty bourgeoisie, or from the peasantry, as were urban workers in Germany and Austria.

A number of other broad factors seem to have played a critical role in determining the special development of Swedish social democracy. Sweden was a long-established, self-confident nation. It had an illustrious history and an unusually homogeneous population, who enjoyed an uncrowded countryside and plentiful natural resources. Her lower classes were unusually well educated; literacy was widespread in the working class before the advent of industrialization. The extreme nationalism and ethnic insecurities that afflicted newer nations caused her less trouble. She had been long removed from the intense pressures of European power politics; she had avoided involvement in the imperialistic scramble of the the late nineteenth century, to say nothing of the limitless destruction of World War I. Thus Sweden's national energies could be focused to an unusually high degree on the solution of her domestic problems.

Sweden was by no means free of social strife, especially in the first decade of the twentieth century, when working-class unrest reached its peak elsewhere, but already by 1911 the Swedish social democrats were faced with the temptation of joining a cabinet coalition of the Left. They finally rejected it, both in 1911 and again in 1914, although they did so with much equivocation, making it obvious that they were leaving open the possibility of future coalitions under more favorable conditions.

More favorable conditions came in 1917, when the social-democratic leader Hjalmar Branting, with the approval of his party, entered into a cabinet headed by a member of the Liberal Party. This was mere "participation" in power, to use Blum's terms, for the social democrats did not hold the controlling positions in the cabinet. But on the other hand, the cabinet, formed to deal with the knotty problems imposed on Sweden by the war raging around her, intervened in the economy to a significant degree, thus helping to undermine dogmatic attachment to the principles of the free market in Sweden. Further, the social democrats were promised a significant measure of democratic reform of the Swedish constitution. Thus Branting's experience could not fairly be compared to that of Millerand, who entered a bourgeois coalition without the explicit support of his party and who accomplished little thereafter for the improvement of the conditions of the French working class.

In 1920, the Swedish Social Democratic Party approved a new party program, which stressed the need for economic planning, and proposed taxation (rather than outright expropriation, either legal or revolutionary) as the means by which collective production would be financed in the future. The party thus prepared itself programmatically for reformist action, and throughout the 1920s Branting went on to participate in a series of minority and coalition governments. These were only moderately successful, but at the same time the social democrats gained political experience and public acceptance.

In 1928 the party did poorly at the polls, and thereafter a series of right-center coalitions ruled Sweden. Thus the Swedish social democrats had the good fortune, unlike the SPD and the British Labour

Party, to be out of power when the Great Depression struck. And public dissatisfaction with the way that the liberals and conservatives handled the crisis permitted the social democrats a comeback in the elections of 1932. This in turn set the stage for their successful leadership of Sweden throughout the 1930s.

The social democrats were still a minority party. Indeed, they won the same number of seats in 1932 that they had won in 1924 (104 out of 230), but they worked out an agreement with the Farmers' Party (which had 36 seats), assuring them of a working majority. The previous government had resorted to the standard deflationary policy of "thrift and reduction of expenditures" to meet the economic crisis and to maintain a balanced budget. Where the Swedish social democrats took bold new steps forward was in proposing public expenditures on many levels, in order to compensate for the lack of investment in the private sector, without worrying about immediate or yearly balancing of the budget.

Social-democratic theoreticians, such as Gunnar Myrdal (later well known in the United States for his study of American race relations and as the winner of the Nobel Prize in economics in 1974), argued that the former attachment to yearly balanced budgets in government merely accentuated the prevailing deflationary trends; if the government reduced its expenditures when the business cycle was down, the overall trend to deflation and depression was thereby increased. Similarly, if government expenditures in social services and public works were put off until a time of economic boom, the economy would then be in danger of overheating, leading to inflation—to say nothing of the consideration that at such times government expenditures were the least needed by society at large. This reasoning was, of course, similar to that of Lord Keynes in Great Britain, and indeed overlapped with De Man's Plan du travail.

One of the difficulties in applying Myrdal's ideas was that the social-democratic government would have to rely upon private lending institutions to finance its deficit spending, and Sweden's financial community tended to be suspicious of these untested and controversial notions. For a while, as an aspect of these suspicions, interest rates began to climb, threatening to make the government's programs more expensive and also to defeat its hope of stimulating the private sector of the economy, since private business enterprise was also discouraged by higher interest rates. But the banks relented, at least in part because they were impressed by the reasoning and credentials of the social-democratic ministers. Here again the relatively flexible nature of relations between classes and their institutions in Sweden played a key role.

In spite of some dire predictions, the new economic policies seemed to work. Under the leadership of Per Albin Hansson, a man widely respected and liked even outside of social-democratic circles (he was affectionately referred to simply as "Per Albin" by the population at large), unemployment was brought down from over 150,000 in 1932 to less than 10,000 by the summer of 1937. And the government was easily able to pay off the debt incurred in the initial stages of recovery.

Ironically, part of the reason for Sweden's recovery was that the growing tensions in the rest of the world were resulting in an armaments boom, which pumped funds into Sweden's armaments industries. The gathering clouds of war also made Swedes in general, even those still attached to orthodox economics, more receptive to the idea of government control and planning, since Sweden's economy could so easily be disrupted by a new war—a lesson they had already learned during World War I.

Swedish social democracy, then, rode out the turbulent 1930s, avoided defeat at the hands of conservatives or fascists, and put the country's economy into order. Even though Sweden could not be held up as an exact model for the rest of the world to follow, it was some comfort for democratic socialists elsewhere to see that their general approach was not somehow inalterably flawed, purely illusory, or jinxed. The experience of Sweden between the wars helped to keep democratic socialist ideals alive, and after World War II, would be occasions for further successes, however modest.

GUIDE TO FURTHER READING

Possessing inherently less glamor and excitement than the communists, the democratic socialists in the interwar years have, with the exception of the Labour Party, attracted far less attention by scholars and others. Thus the best overall introduction to the period remains the study by Adolf Sturmthal, *The Tragedy of European Labor*, which is by now dated but still stimulating and highly readable.

Carl Landauer's *European Socialism*, while a general history, devotes several hundred pages to the Weimar years and performs the valuable service of defending the SPD from its numerous and often overly harsh critics. Much of what has been written in this chapter about the democratic socialists in Germany, England, and Sweden depends heavily upon Sturmthal, Landauer, and other general histories discussed in the bibliographical notes to the Introduction. S. William Halperin's *Germany Tried Democracy* is a general history of the

Weimar Republic but contains much information about the SPD and its travails between 1918 and 1933. Richard Hunt's capable *German Social Democracy, 1918–1933* is less a political narrative than an attempt to analyse trends within the SPD.

Joel Colton's *Léon Blum: Humanist in Politics* carefully traces the evolution of the SFIO as well as Blum's leadership of it. Gilbert Ziebura's superb two-volume biography of Blum, *Léon Blum, Theorie und Praxis einer sozialistischen Politik*, is also much more than a biography. It has been translated into French but not into English. Peter Dodge's *Beyond Marxism: The Faith and Works of Hendrik De Man* is a balanced and perceptive study. Among the work's many merits are that it establishes De Man's position as a major twentieth-century theorist of socialism and defends him against facile condemnation as a fascist.

From the vast literature on the Labour Party, the appropriate chapters from the following can be recommended: Samual H. Beer, *British Politics in the Collectivist Age*; Carl F. Brand, *The British Labour Party: A Short History*; and T. L. Jarman, *Socialism in Britain*. From them further bibliographical information can be easily obtained.

The interwar Austrian labor movement has found its definitive if somewhat overwhelming account in Charles A. Gulick, *Austria from Habsburg to Hitler*. A less scholarly but much shorter and more readable introduction is Elizabeth Barker's *Austria, 1918–1972*.

The Rise of Stalinist Communism, 1919–1939   **7**

INTRODUCTION

To follow the evolution of the communist parties of Russia and the West after the end of the "Red Years" following World War I is to enter into a murky and at times exasperatingly confused situation. It transcends the purposes of a book like this one to narrate and analyze in detail the convoluted forms that Comintern policy assumed outside Russia, and only in general outline can we present the relatively less contorted story of the growth of Stalinism inside Russia.

Insofar as it is possible to find a coherent pattern in the evolution of communism in the interwar years, the following periods can be distinguished: the opening stage, one of revolutionary optimism (roughly the Red Years of 1919–21, though not clearly terminated until 1923), with civil war in Russia and repeated uprisings in the West; an ensuing period of revolutionary pessimism (approximately 1921–28, but especially 1924–28) when capitalism in the West seemed to regain its stability, Soviet Russia limped along with a semi-socialist, semi-capitalist economy, and western communist parties were "purified," while trying to build up their cadres through tactical cooperation with non-communist workers' organizations; the "Third Period," a time of renewed revolutionary offensive (1928–34), when Russia embarked on a program of collectivizing its agriculture and of rapid industrialization through five-year plans, and western communists launched into a militant rejection of cooperation with non-communists; and the "Popular Front" period (1934–39), when the struggle against fascism was paramount, and new and surprising forms of cooperation between communists and non-communist anti-fascists were worked out.

In each of these periods the internal political and economic struggles of the Soviet Union conditioned the policies of the Comintern far more than did the internal needs of the individual non-Russian parties. As a result, some awesomely contradictory situations were to develop at times within western communist parties, situations in which factional and ostensibly ideological issues within each party were couched in terms that bore little coherent relationship to the objective situation in the individual country in question. Thus communist leaders often spoke about conditions in their own country in an odd, arcane language that actually made sense only in reference to conflicts inside Russia and the foreign policy needs of the Soviet Union. Similarly, many doctrinal issues that western communists had assumed, after much initial confusion, were settled once and for all at the Second Congress of the Comintern in 1920 became twisted out of all recognizable shape. Such matters as cooperation with social-democratic parties and trade unions, participation in bourgeois cabinets, colonialism, and patriotism—concerning which the Second Congress and Lenin's writings of the time seemed to speak without equivocation—were re-interpreted in ways that contradicted what had been previously accepted. Indeed, what it finally meant to be a "communist" in terms of a body of integrated doctrine became exceedingly clouded by the late 1920s— the earlier uncertainties concerning the meaning of "Marxism" were minor in comparison. The only unambiguous definition came to be "someone who unquestioningly accepts directives from Moscow and who puts the good of the Soviet Union above all other considerations." Yet, even the most dedicated communist revolutionaries at times found this definition hard to accept, and even after the purges of the early and middle 1920s communist leaders in the West sometimes balked when confronted with new and contradictory marching orders. In the end the bolsheviks—and ultimately Stalin—had their way, but not without appalling costs to non-Russian communist movements.

THE STRUGGLE FOR POWER IN RUSSIA

The origins of Stalinist communism must be sought in the postrevolutionary dilemmas of Soviet Russia. More particularly, Stalinist communism orginated out of the bolsheviks' response to a contradictory situation: that proletarian revolutionaries now held power in a fundamentally peasant or bourgeois nation, without a realistic prospect of immediate aid from the proletariat of the West. Put in other terms, the origins of Stalinism must be sought in Lenin's legacy, both in the initial doctrinal justifications he provided for socialist revolution, and in the party he created.

In January 1924, after a series of crippling strokes that had made an invalid of him over the preceding two years, Lenin was laid to rest. His illness and death left a great vacuum. He bequeathed a party that was uniquely stamped with his personality, one that through the years he had fashioned to suit his particular talents. Under his leadership it had proved itself an effective weapon in retaining power since 1917, but there was good reason to doubt that any other individual could continue to run the party as he had. Of particular importance among Lenin's many talents was his success in winning the respect, fidelity, and obedience of the leading cadres of the party—composed of ambitious, contentious, and often jealous men. In the many hotly contested controversies that had shaken the Bolshevik Party Lenin had been consistently able to cast a deciding vote and then to consolidate his factional victory without humiliating or alienating those over whom he had triumphed.

At the same time Lenin enjoyed a broad popularity among Russia's masses, even among those without particular enthusiasm for the cause of communism. He possessed a popular touch that endeared him to the apolitical and which helped him to assume a position in the minds of masses very similar to that of the Little Father, that is, of the benevolent tsar, who cared for his people and understood their sufferings.

When the character and qualifications of the leading contenders for leadership of the party—Trotsky, Zinoviev, Kamenev, Bukharin, and Stalin—were considered, it became clear that none of them could duplicate Lenin's role of respected leader (*Vozhd'*, a term with charismatic overtones in Russian) of both party and country. Thus it seemed inevitable that a new kind of leader and a new kind of party would emerge; or, as was more often assumed at the time, that "collective leadership" would take over after Lenin's passing.

The bolsheviks in 1924 based their support primarily in a few large cities, where they could fall back on at least relative popularity. In the vast lands surrounding those cities, however, among the peasants who worked the land and who constituted the overwhelming majority of Russia's population, suspicion and even open hostility to the bolsheviks very often prevailed. These peasants had to be brought under closer bolshevik control, either through some kind of enticement or through force. Moreover, the bolshevik regime was weak not only internally but internationally; Russia was a backward country surrounded by more powerful and hostile neighbors. All of these factors spoke for some dynamically new kind of policy and leadership in the ensuing years.

In 1922–23, as hope that Lenin would ever fully recover faded, a loose coalition began to form against the one aspirant to power that all others feared: Trotsky. Their apprehensions were based on a number of factors. Trotsky's name was most usually linked with Lenin's as leader of the 1917 revolution. Indeed, Trotsky was viewed in many circles as the principal hero of 1917. His brilliance as a theoretician and his courage as a revolutionary were widely admired. In particular his performance as head of the Revolutionary Military Committee in 1917 and then as organizer of the Red Army won him far greater status both inside Russia and out than any other bolshevik except Lenin. And his continuing leadership of the military gave him direct access to a decisive source of power in any final showdown.

In a sense, however, Trotsky's links with the military were a source of weakness. A pre-occupation of all leading bolsheviks, who had in mind the model of the revolution of 1789–99, was a Thermidorean-Bonapartist reaction in Russia, now that the revolution's main leftward thrust seemed to have exhausted itself. Trotsky's military accomplishments, his overbearing vanity, his cavalier disregard for democratic and humanitarian niceties, and his ill-concealed contempt for most other leading bolsheviks, made him seem a likely candidate for the Man on Horseback in Russia.

The three leaders who most feared Trotsky's rise were, not surprisingly, men whom Trotsky held in particularly low esteem: Zinoviev, Kamenev, and Stalin, soon to be known as the "Triumvirate." Although Stalin was generally seen as the junior partner of this coalition, he had already by 1922 amassed considerable power in his hands, at least potentially. Indeed his low profile was important in this initial stage, for he grew in strength quietly and largely unnoticed, until he was so well entrenched that he was almost impossible to dislodge. Many leading bolsheviks considered Stalin a dull and unimaginative bureaucrat, a junior member who busied himself with the paperwork and the administrative drudgery that others avoided. This was certainly Trotsky's view of him at this time, although the ever-prescient Lenin, even from his sickbed, coupled Stalin with Trotsky as "the two most outstanding leaders in the present Central Committee" (Tucker, *Stalin*, p. 270). Stalin had not been part of the brilliant coterie of émigré intellectuals, was not widely known as a theorist of any importance (with the one exception of a work on the nationalities question), and had not played a role of first importance in the revolution or the civil war.

By the early 1920s Stalin held a number of important posts, both in the government and in the party. He was the Commissar of Nationalities in the Council of People's Commissars, which gave him contact with and a substantial degree of control over about 50 percent of the population of Soviet Russia, generally the less articulate, less industrially advanced, non-Russian population. Stalin's second and more important post in the government was head of the so-called *Rabkrin* (an acronym from the Russian words for Workers' and Peasants' Inspectorate). This body was charged with inspecting and overseeing all government agencies in order to ferret out corruption, inefficiency, and excessive bureaucratization. While devoting his attentions to these goals Stalin was also usually able to make replacements throughout the government with men loyal to him. Rabkrin in addition exercised a general supervision over the secret police, although at this stage in the struggle for power Stalin was discreet in using his access to police powers.

Aside from these governmental posts Stalin held two important party posts: He was a member of the Politburo and served as General Secretary. The ten-man Politburo by the early 1920s had become the most important policy-making executive body of the party, since the Central Committee had grown too large to work efficiently on day-to-day tasks. Stalin's position as General Secretary was his most important, since he was given wide discretionary power, which he used skillfully and vigorously. Stalin's later popular strength at party congresses and meetings of the Central Committee was to an important degree related to the influence that men appointed by him as party secretary were able to exercise in the local elections to higher bodies.

One of the few to perceive the potential power in the many offices held by Stalin and one of the first to become alarmed at a possible misuse of power in the party was Lenin himself. But his delicate health prevented him from taking effective action. Lenin encouraged Trotsky on several occasions to take up the offensive against Stalin, but Trotsky repeatedly held back. In December 1922, Lenin wrote the set of notes that later became known as his "Testament," in which he openly worried about Stalin's accumulation of power. Then, in a postscript dated January 1923, he strongly attacked Stalin and recommended that he be removed as General Secretary.

Soon thereafter Lenin suffered another paralyzing stroke, and his Testament was not discussed at the forthcoming party congress. (He had intended, in his own words, to present a "bombshell" to the congress.) Indeed, his notes remained locked in his office until after his death in the following January. However, after the funeral Krupskaya, Lenin's wife, saw to it that they were put into the hands of the Central Committee for presentation at the upcoming congress in May 1924.

In the discussions of the Central Committee prior to the congress, Zinoviev and Kamenev successfully argued against Stalin's removal as General Secretary, and the Central Committee voted not to discuss the Testament at the full congress (although it was discussed at various caucuses before) or to publish it for national consideration. Still, some 1,200 delegates to the congress learned of its contents and undoubtedly talked about it among themselves. Ironically, Trotsky was pressured by the Politburo to announce that any talk about a testament by Lenin was a "malicious fabrication," after one of his followers in the West had published the Testament without his authorization or knowledge.

Thus, Stalin escaped public censure and retained his posts, in spite of Lenin's deathbed wishes. In later years many observers, particularly supporters of Trotsky, would look back ruefully at this lost opportunity. But it is important to note that Trotsky's disinclination to use the Testament at this time must have been due at least in part to the criticisms it contained of *him* (and indeed of all other leading bolsheviks). Although Lenin had encouraged Trotsky to lead the attack on Stalin, the Testament also noted Trotsky's "excessive self-confidence" and his "disposition to be too much attracted to the administrative aspect of affairs" (Tucker, *Stalin*, p. 270). It sounded almost as if Lenin were leveling the accusation of bureaucratism at Trotsky more than at Stalin.

Fear of Stalin was not yet widespread because at this crucial juncture in the struggle for power he did not make blatant use of the repressive devices potentially within his power; instead, he was able to rely on the firm support of other leading bolsheviks, especially Zinoviev and Kamenev, while Trotsky repeatedly refused to make an issue of Lenin's last words.

Quite aside from the issue of the Testament, many explanations of Trotsky's puzzling reticence at this time and on several later occasions have been offered: his own recurring ill health (which meant that he was often in the south recuperating while important matters were being decided in Moscow), his confidence in his own strength within the party's rank and file (at the Party Congress in 1923 the applause which greeted him far exceeded that of any other party leader), his distaste for disrupting the party with an open struggle at a time when bolshevik rule in Russia was still precarious. Yet such consistently retiring attitudes during such a crucial period on the part of a man so decisive and courageous at other crucial times and places remain a profound puzzle.

Trotsky's reticence also seems peculiar because in historical retrospect we can see how Stalin ultimately triumphed. But at this time Stalin appeared to most observers a paragon of modesty and self-abnegation. While Zinoviev, Kamenev, or Bukharin attacked Trotsky with ferocious hostility, Stalin's statements were usually characterized by moderation and an apparent effort to strike a conciliatory stance. Trotsky far more than Stalin gave the impression of ambition and arrogance, of a man who tenaciously insisted upon the correctness of his positions and who rarely if ever recognized his own error.

The attack that Trotsky finally launched in 1924 against the Triumvirate did little to forward his cause, and indeed provided further ammunition for his detractors. In January 1924 his pamphlet *The New Course* assailed the growing bureaucratization of the party. Coupled with this attack was an appeal to the youth of Russia to keep the older generation, tempted as it was to acquiesce in bureaucracy and passivity, on the revolutionary path. *The New Course* was only the prelude to the much more pointed and explicit attacks Trotsky made in the autumn of 1924. Under the title "The Lessons of October," which was a lengthy introduction to a collection of his writings and speeches in 1917, he held up for public scrutiny the blots on the revolutionary records of Zinoviev and Kamenev. More generally, he argued that a long-standing "right-wing tendency" in the Bolshevik Party, a tendency Lenin had continually fought, had not only opposed the takeover in 1917 but thereafter had adopted a "fatalistic, temporizing, social-democratic, menshevik attitude" (Trotsky, *Essential*, p. 153).

Typically, one of the most effective responses to Trotsky's attacks was a speech given by Stalin in November 1924, entitled "Trotskyism or Leninism?" In it Stalin forcefully defended the party against the charge of bureaucratism. In the process he tried to show, with doubtful regard for historical accuracy, how even in the seizure of power and during the civil war the party "guided comrade Trotsky's every step." Particularly damaging was Stalin's detailed presentation of Trotsky's prerevolutionary conflicts with Lenin. In light of the burgeoning cult of Lenin since his death, some of Trotsky's earlier polemics were indeed stunning. For example, Trotsky had described Lenin as a "professional exploiter of every kind of backwardness in the Russian working-class movement" and had said that the "whole edifice of Leninism at present is built upon lying and falsification." Even after Trotsky had joined the party, Lenin once termed his behavior "bureaucratic, unsoviet, unsocialist, incorrect, and politically harmful." (Lenin was even less able than Trotsky to let a single adjective suffice.) (Tucker, *Stalin*, pp. 349–54).

By late 1924 it became obvious to Trotsky that he was losing the so-called "Literary Discussion," the war of words concerning who was the most "Leninist." He prepared a long rebuttal of Stalin's speech but then let it go unpublished. In early 1925 he resigned his military posts, ostensibly to demonstrate his lack of Bonapartist aspirations. In so doing, he destroyed the one solid base of power he possessed. Zinoviev and Kamenev there-upon pressed for his immediate explusion from the party, but Stalin opposed such demands, saying that Trotsky was too capable a leader for the party to lose. Again, Stalin came across as a reasonable, conciliatory person, admirably free of vindictiveness.

Once Trotsky had been successfully blocked from leadership of the party, internal differences began to dissolve the unity of Triumvirate. Stalin gradually moved to a position close to Bukharin and the right wing of the party, while Zinoviev and Kamenev began to grope about for new allies, themselves moving left in the process.

Trotsky now appeared as their only hope against Stalin, and slowly an unsteady "United Opposition," all too obviously patched together, began to form against Stalin and the party's right wing. But Stalin experienced little difficulty in stripping Kamenev and Zinoviev of their positions of authority within the party (and in Zinoviev's case, as President of the Comintern); by the end of 1925 they too had been eliminated as main contenders for party leadership.

A final dramatic confrontation between Stalin and Trotsky occurred at the October 1927 meeting of the Central Committee. This meeting had been called specifically to discuss the issue of the expulsion of Trotsky and Zinoviev from the Central Committee. Carefully maintaining his long-cultivated stance of a humble follower of Lenin, Stalin once again dredged up Trotsky's attacks on Lenin. In shocked tones he observed, "What language, comrades! . . . This is Trotsky writing, writing of Lenin. Is it any wonder that this Trotsky, who so unceremoniously slights the great Lenin, should now hurl abuse at one of Lenin's disciples, comrade Stalin?" (Tucker, *Stalin*, p. 365).

Stalin adroitly dealt with the issue of Lenin's Testament, which Trotsky had finally decided to use. Stalin unhesitatingly read to the Central Committee the full text of Lenin's postscript (which asked for Stalin's removal), something that even Trotsky had not done. But hav-

ing thus read to the assembled party leaders the most damaging passages about him in the Testament, Stalin was able to turn the "rudeness" which Lenin had complained about into a kind of virtue and to
argue convincingly that the party left him no choice but to remain in
his post. "Yes, I am rude, comrades, toward those who rudely and
treacherously wreck and split the party. I have never concealed this and
do not do so now." He then noted that he had asked the Central Committee in 1924, after the Thirteenth Congress, to release him from the
duties of General Secretary. But in the ensuing discussion virtually all
of the leaders of the party had insisted that he remain. Indeed, in the
final vote even Trotsky voted for him to remain as General Secretary.
"What then could I do? Flee the post? That is not my character. . . . that
would be desertion." A year later he again submitted a request that he
be released and again it was refused. (Tucker, *Stalin*, p. 366).

Stalin then went on to make it seem that Trotsky and others in the
United Opposition had been responsible for the suppression of the Testament since Lenin's death. Had not Lenin said even more damaging
things about them? Hadn't Trotsky vociferously denied the existence of
a testament, calling reports of one "malicious nonsense"? And why were
Trotsky, Zinoviev, and Kamenev so frightened to see the document published? Because in it Lenin accused them of fundamental inadequacies
as bolsheviks and as revolutionaries, as *politically* unreliable, while he
had found fault in Stalin only for his rudeness, not for his political positions.

The United Opposition stood further condemned in the eyes of the
Central Committee because the very existence of such a formally organized faction within the party had been outlawed by the resolutions of
the Tenth Party Congress in 1921. After 1921, organized factionalists
had been either demoted or expelled from the party. Trotsky, Zinoviev,
and Kamenev thus were guilty of violating principles they themselves
had promulgated and actively enforced. Stalin had little difficulty in
getting the United Opposition condemned, and then in having its members expelled from the party.

For Trotsky expulsion from the party meant leaving Moscow to
begin his "long night of exile," which would end only when one of Stalin's agents murdered him with a pickax in 1940. Zinoviev and others
were later re-admitted, having abundantly recognized their errors. A
foreign communist, writing a few years later to a former follower of
Trotsky who was also in exile, rendered a painfully appropriate judgment of Trotsky: "I have studied him since the beginning of the century,

and I have always seen in him a lonely meteor, in love with his own character and incapable of carrying behind him anything or anybody" (Wohl, p. 272).

Stalin's victory was still not complete. Another important figure remained to challenge him in the party: Nikolai Bukharin. But in order properly to comprehend this final stage in the power struggle, and to reach a broader understanding of the growth of Stalinist communism, it is necessary to turn back to the theoretical controversies within the party and to the growth of communist movements outside of Russia.

THE EMERGENCE OF STALINIST COMMUNISM IN THE WEST

At first glance Stalin's victory in Russia is easier to fathom than his eventual rise to mastery of western communist parties. Personally he was not the type to appeal to most western revolutionaries. In contrast to nearly all other leading bolsheviks he was not fluent in western tongues, had formed no personal friendships with westerners, knew relatively little about conditions in western Europe, and generally gave the impression of being slow in thought and provincial in culture. Stalin was apparently not even present at the first three congresses of the Communist International—an absence which is quite remarkable in that the usual Russian delegation to one of the Comintern congresses consisted of around a hundred voting and nonvoting representatives, including virtually every important bolshevik. And even after Stalin became better known in the West, the theory that was linked to his name, "Socialism in One Country," seemed to emphasize the lack of importance of western communists. Finally, Stalin did not have the same powers of appointment and supervision within western communist parties that he did within Russia. Nor could he get away with the blatant falsifications outside Russia that he eventually came to rely upon inside Russia, since in the West the press was free. It was also for the most part anti-communist and relished exposing the lies printed in Russia under Stalin's control.

And yet by the late 1920s Stalin's domination over western communists was remarkable; the eulogies heaped upon him in the 1930s by western communists would have made Lenin blush. Stalin's success, although extraordinarily complex in detail, can be easily understood from a broader perspective: The Comintern and the parties within it had already been "Stalinized"—that is, made into obedient, uncritical, uncomplaining executors of directives from Russia—by Lenin, while he was still alive, and even more so by Trotsky, Zinoviev, and Bukharin. It was they who arranged for the expulsion of western dissidents, who covered up embarassing truths, who saw to it that western communists learned to recognize that the ultimate good of communism was equivalent to the interests of the Soviet Union. All that Stalin had to do was to take over the Comintern apparatus fashioned by them, a move that was quite easily accomplished once he had gained complete control over party and state in Russia. This point should be kept in mind when trying to decide to what extent Stalinism was a natural growth from Leninism, for within the Comintern much, though certainly not all, of what later was called Stalinism was indeed initiated by Lenin and his closest associates.

A further element that went into creating the aura of uncritical adulation which eventually surrounded Stalin was his leadership of Soviet Russia into its "second revolution" of collectivization of agriculture and rapid industrialization after 1928. Western revolutionaries thus tended to see him as the personification of the revolution-on-the-march, and many felt a deep need to put aside critical carping rally to the defense of the Soviet Union, as it launched into one of the most audacious and risky adventures in modern times.

The story of the Comintern and its member parties from 1921 to 1928, especially as it relates to matters of theory, is almost ludicrously impenetrable. During this period the so-called United Front tactic, outside of Russia, was fashioned to go hand in hand with the NEP inside Russia. As theory the United Front was more intelligible than it became in practice: It was a tactic of united action with other parties of the socialist left, ostensibly suited for a period of capitalist recovery, and it represented a concomitant effort on the part of communists to nurse their wounds from previous unsuccessful revolutionary struggles and to build up their organizations for the inevitable revolutionary catacylsm. In these ways the United Front complemented in the West the sense of recovery being felt through NEP in Russia.

It was assumed that communists in this period would not plan for any immediate seizures of power. Rather, they would offer to cooperate with non-communist workers' organizations and form a "united front" with them, in the name of day-to-day benefits for the workers, who yearned for unity of organization. Such efforts on the part of communists would gain visibility for them, and would expose the democratic socialists for what they were, defenders of the bourgeois order. Capitalism, although it had made a temporary recovery, was in fundamental crisis, the argument continued, and thus capitalists could not permit meaningful advances in the condition of the working class; they would refuse demands for betterment of wages or other working conditions. Gradually the workers would perceive that the only answer was revolution, while the democratic socialists would be put in the position of watering down their demands or even abandoning them in the name of saving the existing system. This line of reasoning had a special appeal in Germany—where indeed the idea of the United Front was born— since the country's economy was extremely precarious.

The United Front was not usually interpreted to mean that communists could join in cabinets with non-communists, although there was considerable ambiguity about when and if a United Front "from above" or "from below" should be resorted to. "From above" implied some kind of open cooperation between communist and non-communist leaders, while "from below" meant merely seeking out common action with rank-and-file non-communist workers. "From above" was normally described as a right-wing tendency, "from below" as left wing.

Even more ambiguous was the question of whether the United Front was a tactic that could be adapted to the sudden appearance of a revolutionary situation. This became an issue in Germany in 1923, as will be described below. Such fundamental ambiguities as these sapped the concept of meaning, but there is reason to believe that the leaders of the Comintern were content to let it remain murky, so that it could be applied "flexibly"—that is, in a way that suited the particular needs of the moment and defeated the efforts of western communists to interpret it independent of Moscow's imprimatur.

The concept of the United Front, either from above or below, did not sit well with many recent western converts to the cause of world communist revolution. For some, such as Amadeo Bordiga, who led the Italian Communist Party, it was unsuitable because it was a non-revolutionary tactic, and they believed revolution was still imminent in their countries. For others, such as L.-O. Frossard in France, who did not believe in the proximity of revolution, the cooperation envisaged by United Front was both unrealistic and inappropriate, following as it did upon the vituperations between democratic socialists and admirers of Lenin when the SFIO split.

Thus from the time of the founding of communist parties in the West a contradiction existed between what Russian leaders believed was an appropriate policy—obviously influenced by the Russians' own needs for cooperation between communists and non-communists within Russia and by their hopes to reduce international hostility to the Soviet Union—and what western communists perceived was necessary for the growth of their movements. Even in Germany, where the United Front policy more or less meshed with the actual opportunities open to German communists, its application was fraught with irony. The notion of offering to cooperate with non-communists for short-run goals had been first put forth by Paul Levi, in late 1920 and early 1921 (after the unification of the left USPD and KPD), as a means of uniting German workers in their resentments over reparations. At that time, the Left of the KPD, which admired the bolsheviks more than Levi did, attacked Levi for "opportunism" and "revolutionary passivity." In early 1921 he was expelled for "indiscipline" (particularly because of his public criticism of the Comintern's role in the disastrous Märzaktion). Soon afterward, however, his opponents were obliged by the Comintern to take up the same policies that had been Levi's undoing.

In spite of individual expulsions, in 1921 and early 1922 lack of discipline on the part of Comintern member parties went surprisingly much unpunished, especially when it had to do with the issue of the United Front. To some observers in this first year it seemed that the Moscow International, for all its intransigent language, allowed its member parties almost as much leeway as the prewar International had done. A symptom of this lack of effective centralized control was the degree to which factionalism in many western parties, such as the German, French, and Italian, consumed the energies of party leaders to the neglect of the vital task of building up party cadres. And in most parties, opposition to the United Front was complemented by sheer confusion concerning what the United Front was supposed to entail. In the spring of 1922 the Comintern agent in France summed up the situation in a confidential letter to Moscow: "An extraordinary confusion exists on all questions," and above all on the United Front (Bahne, p. 177). These conditions virtually begged for the intervention of the Comintern leadership.

One of Moscow's most significant efforts to intervene in the affairs of a western communist party occurred in Germany, and here the issues of the meaning of the United Front, factionalism in the KPD, and the emerging struggle for power in Russia became inextricably intertwined. In October 1921 a social-democratic government was constituted in the provincial (*Land*) government of Thuringia. The new government relied not upon a coalition with bourgeois parties, as did the SPD on the federal level. Instead, it won the support, though not the actual participation, of the communists, who held the balance of parliamentary power there. The communists' action appeared consistent with the concept of the United Front from above as well as the notion "workers' governments" or "workers' and peasants' governments" which was more fully articulated at the Comintern's fourth congress in 1922. It was also one of the few instances that the social democrats consented to some kind of cooperative effort with the communists.

The line followed by the KPD leadership at this time was thus a "right-wing" one. It was promoted by Heinrich Brandler, who had taken over after Levi's demise. In spite of some bitter criticism from within the party, especially on the left, Brandler maintained relatively firm control and looked to further opportunities for cooperation with social-democratic and trade-union leaders. Brandler was generally supported by Karl Radek, a leading bolshevik, who had been given special responsibility by the Comintern to over see German affairs.

In early 1923 the French occupied the Ruhr in retaliation for what they believed was Germany's bad faith effort to pay reparations. Germany was thrown into turmoil. Inflation wiped out the savings of small property owners and reduced many relatively secure Germans to the status of paupers. Workers tended to lose confidence in their trade unions, which themselves lost their savings, and thus feelings of extreme insecurity spread through the ranks of both the petty bourgeoisie and the working class. Guerrilla warfare, conducted largely by right-wing extremists, erupted in the occupied areas.

In such a time leaders both within the KPD and in Moscow began to question whether the non-revolutionary perspective of the United Front was still appropriate, and before long communist leaders started to apply the United Front concept in some surprising directions. One of these was the "Schlageter Line" (so called after a Freikorps officer who had been killed by the French and who was then made into a national hero), which entailed communist efforts to exploit German nationalism. This new strategy outraged some members of the more internationalist KPD Left, but others took it up with gusto, even resorting in some instances to old themes of anti-Semitic anti-capitalism long abandoned by Marxists. Radek rationalized that the Schlageter Line was an appropriate application of the United Front concept, which would rally the petty-bourgeoisie to the banners of the revolutionary working class, while at the same time splitting the ranks of the fiercely anti-communist extreme Right.

The new line was not much of a success. The nationalist Right was not split, nor were many members of the petty bourgeoisie attracted to communism. On the other hand many social-democratic workers, whose sympathies were in theory most important to the United Front idea, were put off by the chauvinistic excesses that the Schlageter Line encouraged. Still, the Comintern leadership professed to see ever greater revolutionary potential in the worsening situation in Germany, and soon Moscow began to pressure the KPD leadership to prepare for an actual seizure of power. Brandler and those around him, after much initial resistance, became caught up in the enthusiasm of the Russians.

The plan to seize power that the German communists finally settled on differed strikingly from the bolshevik model, in spite of all that had been said since 1917 about the universal relevance of the Russian experience. Leading bolsheviks did make some pathetic efforts to draw parallels between the situation in Germany in 1923 and that in Russia six years earlier (Trotsky even argued that the takeover should be planned for November 7), but in most fundamental ways the array of forces was quite different, as was the projected timing. The plan called for communist ministers not only to support but to enter the social-democratic governments in Thuringia and Saxony. This was to be, in other words, an extreme example of the "right-wing" United Front from above. Then, however, under the cover of these friendly provincial governments, arms were to be stockpiled to equip the "Proletarian Hundreds," which were being organized throughout the country in preparation for violent revolution.

In retrospect this projected revolution appears wildly unrealistic. It assumed that the army and police would play a neutral role, based on the paltry reasoning that members of the working-class within those forces would not rally to the protection of the bourgeois state. Even more implausible was the argument that right-wing nationalists would refuse to assist the Weimar Republic, which they detested, in a confrontation with the communists.

The KPD was saved from a bloody fiasco by the decisive actions of Gustav Stresemann, who had just become chancellor on the basis of a broad Weimar coalition. In October, shortly before the communist plan was to be put into action, he moved against both the extreme Left and extreme Right, crushing Hitler's Beer Hall Putsch and outlawing the Nazi and Communists parties. Stresemann acted without actually knowing about the specific plans of the communists, but his actions sufficiently disrupted the KPD's timing that Brandler finally called the whole thing off.

Stresemann was able to put Germany back on its feet, both politically and economically. The KPD was spared the humiliation that had been its lot after the Märzaktion in 1921, since its plan to seize power was never made public, but still this was a very great failure, for which heads would roll. Members of the KPD left wing blamed Brandler and his faction for following the tactic of United Front from above in this revolutionary situation. And since Radek was allied with Trotsky in the power struggle, Trotsky's opponents used events in Germany as another means of discrediting him and his revolutionary theories. A typical imbroglio of charges and countercharges emerged. Trotsky, who normally considered himself on the left of the Bolshevik Party, defended the KPD right wing (although not in all aspects), while Zinoviev, who was linked to Stalin and the party's Right (at least according to Trotsky's description of the party's factions at this time), supported the KPD's Left in its attacks on Brandler.

At the Fifth Congress of the Comintern in 1924, Brandler, Radek, and, by implication, Trotsky were condemned as having applied the strategy of United Front in an erroneously "rightist" fashion. Thereafter, the Comintern made a swing a few degrees to the left in its policies. This was officially designated as a "new course." It meant that now the United Front from below rather than from above was stressed, although the possibility of future cooperation between communist and non-communist leaders was not categorically ruled out.

The year 1924 marked a turn in Comintern policy also in the sense that its executive committee stepped up its effort to discipline its member parties under the slogan of "bolshevization." This meant introducing an organization of party cells on the Russian model, controlled strictly by party headquarters. Bolshevization also meant the effort to give a more proletarian—which in effect meant a more pliant—character to the leadership of western communist parties, by bringing genuine workers up from the lower ranks to replace the former leaders, who were frequently of bourgeois origin, more intellectual, and more fractious.

The shock waves of bolshevization were felt particularly in France, where lack of discipline had been a special problem, as had factionalism, and where leadership by bourgeois intellectuals had been the rule. Frossard aspired to preserve in the New French Communist Party something of the broad and tolerant spirit of Jaurès, but such aspirations were undermined by the uncompromising hostility between the Left and Right of the party. Frossard and Marcel Cachin, the leading figures in the party, had been centrists in the SFIO, and the revolutionary Left made no secret of its contempt for them. Comintern leaders, in particular Zinoviev, had finally consented, after extended negotiations in the summer of 1920, to Cachin's and Frossard's leadership of the as yet to be created communist party. They reasoned that Cachin and Frossard seemed pliant and willing to recognize their past failings—and also that the revolutionary Left in France was too weak and splintered to form the nucleus of a significant party. But although Zinoviev's decision allowed the pro-Comintern faction to win a majority in the split of the SFIO, it also meant that divisions within the French party were ominously wide. Further major splits were narrowly averted in the party's first years, with the Left gradually asserting itself. By 1923 Frossard recognized the impossibility of reaching his goals and left the party.

Trotsky devoted special attention to matters in France, where he enjoyed a strong following in the new Communist Party and where he had formed many friendships during the war, when he spent several years in France. These friendships were mostly among anarchosyndicalists who later allied to the cause of communism and who constituted the Left of the new Communist Party. As late as February 1924, after the bolsheviks' Thirteenth Party Conference had censured Trotsky, one of his French admirers, Boris Souvarine, a contender for leadership of the French party, was able to get a resolution through the PCF's central committee that in effect upheld Trotsky. But by the end of 1924, Souvarine and the rest of Trotsky's French followers had been expelled, due to the diligent efforts of the Comintern's president, Zinoviev.

The subsequent leaders of the French, German, and other western communist parties lasted only as long as Zinoviev remained a power in the Comintern. By 1927, with Zinoviev's final humiliation and the defeat in Russia of the United Opposition (an effort which was often matched in the West by final, desperate attempts to rally all those who had been earlier expelled), a new breed of communist leaders came into power and remained there generally for the next generation. These were men who had first come into prominence with the campaign for bolshevization. They were "sons of the proletariat," men like Maurice Thorez in France and Ernst Thälmann in Germany, far less intellectual than former leaders but also more disciplined. And they clearly recognized what the leadership role of the Bolshevik Party in the world communist movement really meant.

STALINISM TRIUMPHANT

In the initial stages of the struggle for power the very term "Stalinism" would have been inconsonant with Stalin's pose of humble disciple of Lenin. Yet by the mid-1920s Stalin's aspirations to doctrinal as well as bureaucratic leadership of the Bolshevik Party had becom unmistakable. Throughout the mid-1920s he still associated himself in theoretical matters with Bukharin's right wing of the party, although at the same time he maintained a degree of separation from some of Bukharin's formulations. Stalin's name became associated with the theory of "socialism in one country," but this theory was patently based on Bukharin's writings, something which Stalin did not at this time particularly seek to disguise.

By the late 1920s Stalin had provided an answer to the question What kind of person could possible replace Lenin as the leader of the party? The other half of Lenin's legacy had not yet been solved—that is, How could the dilemma of the revolution itself be dealt with? This issue came down to the question How and at what rate could Soviet Russia industrialize and modernize? It is misleading to see the issue, as is sometimes done, as a confrontation between two factions, one arguing that Russia could not industrialize without revolution in the West, the other insisting that "socialism in one country" was possible without aid from the West. Both sides believed that some degree of socialism was possible in one country—at least they agreed on the need to *begin* building socialism—and both recognized the importance of some kind of aid from the West. Indeed, both sides freely recognized that without revolution in the West the ultimate triumph of socialism in Russia was inconceivable. Their differences centered not so much on the question of revolution in the West as on the problems of the tempo of industrialization in Russia and the manner in which the surplus capital necessary for industrial development could be obtained.

Even on the matter of surplus capital there existed a kind of consensus, for both sides recognized that as long as capital was not available from the advanced economies of western Europe, a primary source would have to be Russia's own agricultural sector, which employed something like 80 percent of Russia's productive population. Soviet Russia had no colonies to exploit, no wealthy class to tax or expropriate, nor could she count on a favorable balance of trade. She remained economically isolated and backward—her industries devastated by the revolution—and it took no great economic acumen to understand that in some sense her agrarian production would have to finance her industrial growth.

How could surplus capital be obtained from the agricultural sector? Generally, there were two choices: either cooperation or coercion. On the one hand, it could be obtained through free trade on the market, with normal rates of profit for the socialized industrial sector derived from the exchange of industrial products for agricultural products. On the other, it could be gotten through some variety of expropriation, such as direct taxation, highly unfavorable rates of exchange imposed by the state, or outright requisition at gun point. Coercion had been an important device used during the period of War Communism, between 1918 and 1921. But it had functioned adequately—if the term "adequately" can be used—only in the contexts of civil war and the intervention of foreign powers; it was thereafter abandoned because it became patently unworkable. The New Economic Policy (NEP), which had introduced free trade in the countryside, was a pragmatic response to the failure of coercion.

The question that faced the party after 1921 was, how long could NEP last—or even, if it could last, *should* it? The right wing of the party, led by Bukharin, argued that NEP, or some modified version of it, was the most efficient and realistic path for Soviet Russia to take, even though it had been resorted to initially not as a long-range approach to economic development but simply as an emergency response to save the economy from immediate collapse. The party's left wing, whose more distinguished economist was Evgenii Preobrazhensky—although Trotsky was its best-known spokesman—argued that the policy of NEP was too slow, too lacking in dynamism, too dependent upon the good wishes of a naturally anti-socialist class (that is, the rural small land-owner) to succeed over the long run.

Within these two positions subtle variations appeared in the 1920s, with new factional alliances being made that were often surprising when compared to the alliances of the years of revolution. Bukharin's own defense of NEP might at first appear strange, in that he had previously been a leading figure of the party's left wing. But there was a certain consistency in Bukharin's move from the Left to the Right of the party. As a leftist, until 1920 he had repeatedly stressed the importance of party democracy and had feared the evolution of the bolshevik regime into a new kind of exploitive bureaucracy. His fears became heightened in early 1921, for the Kronstadt uprising and the widespread unrest in the countryside made him acutely aware of the party's isolation and vulnerability. Thus he became concerned above all with reconciling the non-party masses to the new regime. As he saw it, the only alternatives to such a reconciliation were increasingly despotic and bureaucratic measures. One of his strongest objections to the program of the Left of the party was that it emphasized coercion rather than persuasion in dealing with the great mass of rural Russians. The Left called for a "plundering" of the countryside in the name of Marxist class warfare. Bukharin emphasized instead the need for a firm and lasting *smychka* (nexus, alliance) of city and country, proletarian and peasant.

Bukharin's policies, then, represented a step away from the heroic, revolution-against-all-odds image of the bolsheviks from 1917 to 1921. But, as he himself often emphasized, he was not a reformist or revisionist in the western sense, because he still advocated violent revolution to seize power from the capitalists; it was only after the revolutionary victory that he believed caution and conciliation were necessary, particularly given Russia's special problems.

Just as Bukharin feared a "bureaucratic degeneration" of the regime, so the left wing feared that NEP would lead to a "petty-bourgeois degeneration." Bukharin's belief in the smychka was precisely what disturbed the party's Leftists. They stressed that Bukharin's policies would encourage rural capitalism: Under NEP small landholders, especially the kulaks (the richest stratum of the peasantry), were to be encouraged to expand their holdings (or, in Bukharin's words, to "enrich themselves"—a phrase that smacked of Guizot's advice to those desiring the vote in the 1840s—and which the Left seized upon). The kulaks were to be encouraged in order that they accumulate the profits or surplus cash necessary to buy consumer goods produced in the state-controlled urban-industrial sector. The profit from these goods in turn could be invested in further industrial development. The Left asserted that Bukharin's policy meant the regime would indirectly encourage the exploitation of the poor in the countryside, in order for the rural capitalists to accumulate wealth—a startling contradiction for a party that had made a revolution in the name of the oppressed.

Ironically, encouragement of the kulak class had been the policy of the prewar tsarist minister, Stolypin, who had believed that creation of a sturdy and self-sufficient peasantry, on the French model, would end Russia's endemic rural unrest and make the peasants a bulwark of conservatism in Russia. The Left, looking to the prewar example, asserted that Bukharin's policies unavoidably encouraged the expansion and increased power of an inherently conservative class that would always yearn for the destruction of bolshevik rule.

The Left wanted more direct and dramatic measures; it could not accept the slow workings of the market and cooperation between city and countryside. As opposed to the "trickle of profits" (a phrase again first used by Bukharin and held up to ridicule by his opponents) that would accrue to the urban-industrial sector under NEP, the Left looked to some sort of massive and rapid infusion of capital investment in industry, particularly in heavy industry, coordinated according to a long-range economic plan. Preobrazhensky, refashioning the term "primitive capitalist accumulation" used by Marx, looked to "primitive socialist accumulation"—that is, an accumulation that in some sense would resemble the initial stages of the move into rapid industrial development in the West, but under the auspicies of a socialist government.

But still, the unvarnished reality was that labor had to be exploited, or in some sense put under pressure, in order to extract capital for investment. And Preobrazhensky did not shrink from this reality. Indeed, his frequent use of such terms as "exploit" and "expropriate" was seized upon by his opponents and was a source of embarrassment for his supporters. Trotsky also once suggested a "militarization" of the industrial sector, in order that productivity rise through longer hours, stricter discipline, and lower pay. He bemoaned the "democratic prejudices" in the party that stood in the way of such policies.

A key consideration in the Left's program was how the peasantry, as distinguished from the urban working class, was to be "plundered" or "squeezed." Could the peasants possibly be plundered without the kind of confrontation that would lead again to an economic collapse like that of 1920–21, or even to civil war? Preobrazhensky did not look to overt violence to extract a surplus from the peasants; rather he believed it would be possible to expand the use of monopolistically influenced industrial prices (which he termed "nonequivalent exchange"), that would assure the kind of profits required for investment in heavy industry. Bukharin retorted that the peasants simply would not accommodate themselves to such prices; they would refuse to trade or even to make the added effort to grow crops behond their immediate needs, since exchanges on the market would be so unfavorable.

These debates took on a special meaning in the winter of 1924–25, when serious peasant unrest coupled with unexpectedly meager harvest forced the government to expand the NEP policy of economic concessions to the peasantry. That is, more favorable grain prices were introduced, agricultural taxes were reduced, and other restrictions on free trade and the hiring of wage labor were loosened. The Left protested bitterly against this "kulak deviation," but to the Right, which had the decisive say in the government at this time, it seemed the only realistic alternative.

The struggle for power became inextricably linked to the debates on industrialization. Bukharin joined enthusiastically in the Triumvirate's attacks on Trotsky, and although he was the most fair-minded of Trotsky's opponents, as well as the most intellectually sophisticated, he too at times attacked with ferocity and without regard for historical accuracy. These attacks would come back to haunt him a few years later.

Once Trotsky had been eliminated as a serious contender for power, and as Zinoviev and Kamenev then began to move leftward in fear of Stalin, they too attacked the "peasantism" of Bukharin and Stalin. In the following four years (1924–28) Bukharin and Stalin remained doctrinally and factionally close, working together to defeat the United Opposition in 1927. Indeed, Bukharin more than Stalin became the theoretical defender of NEP and of the notion of conciliating the peasants.

In these years NEP could claim some impressive accomplishments. The harvest of 1925, 1926, and 1927 were good, and industrial recovery was spectacular. Prewar levels of productivity in most sectors of the economy were being reached. However, at the same time, the "Nepmen," the aggressive urban small capitalists who had emerged under NEP, were attaining an influence and visibility that deeply offended the party's idealists. Similarly, in the countryside social stratification was proceeding rapidly, much as it had during the generation before the war, which meant that the kulak, the aggressive rural "capitalist"-exploiter, was prospering. Bukharin was troubled by these aspects of the NEP, although he and his faction tended to play them down, suggesting that the kulak under the soviet regime was different in nature from his unsavory predecessor under the tsar, and that kulaks anyway made up only 3 or 4 percent of the rural population. The Left of course believed that the kulaks were exactly the same now as before and that they made up a much higher proportion of the rural population, perhaps as much as 20 percent.

Similarly, Bukharin thought it feasible to hope for a "socialization" of the middle and lower peasants (that is, those who were not kulaks and did not profit significantly from the labor of others). They could be encouraged, he believed, to be more receptive to the ideas of collectivism. He argued that government-sponsored cooperatives in marketing, buying, and credit would help convince the peasants of the superiority of socialist methods. The Left remained wary of such ideas. Cooperatives had existed before in Russia, and indeed they existed now in the West, but they were usually associated with non-socialist, petty-bourgeois mentalities or with Russian populism, not with Marxism. The party's leftists tended to believe that socialization through institutions that oversaw the circulation of money and goods rather than through the place of production reflected a non-Marxist perspective.

They thus called for large, collectively run farms, which would emphasize working together, and which could take advantage of economies of
scale and advanced technologies.

By the spring of 1926 or 1927 Bukharin had begun to give serious
consideration to a number of the Left's positions, even while remaining
attached to the premises of the NEP. For instance, he came to agree that
it now was necessary to move away from the heavy reliance in market
incentives that had prevailed since 1924 and to initiate a greater degree
of state intervention, in the direct of long-range economic planning. He
even accepted the Left's prediction that once Soviet Russia had rebuilt
its prewar industrial plant and had reached prewar levels of productivity, a new stage of economic development would be reached, one which
would be much more difficult to deal with. He spoke more favorably of
investment in heavy industry, openly recognized that "we are proceeding far too slowly," and granted the Left's point that a slow rate of industrial development would not safeguard Russia from the growing
threat of military intervention from the West.

All of Bukharin's rethinking of NEP was suddenly and alarmingly
echoed in developments in the countryside in November and December
of 1927. Grain procurements were only half of what they had been for
those months the year before. The problem was not a failure of production. Rather, farmers with surplus grain to sell decided to withhold
their crops, because the market price was low and the consumer goods
which they would normally buy with the profits from the sale of their
grain were in short supply. Their profit from previous years was sufficient that they did not feel pressed to sell their products immediately,
and by withholding they could presumably sell later under more favorable conditions. In addition to these considerations, a war scare in the
summer of 1927 caused many to hoard food.

The party leadership had not foreseen this eventuality. Many were
stunned and inclined to panic. To raise grain prices would have disrupted established plans for industrial investment, and there were simply not enough consumer goods in stock to flood the market in hope of
enticing the peasants to sell their hoarded grain at existing prices.
Faced with this impasse, the party leaders in January 1928 turned to
what they termed "extraordinary measures." Leading party figures
toured the provinces, putting into operation what was clearly a break
with the noncoercive policies of NEP: "Self-taxation," obligatory loans,
even requisitions were forced upon the peasants. Many were arrested
and sentenced under a law that prohibited the concealment of grain.

In retrospect it can be seen that these measures in January 1928 set in motion a fatal chain reaction, making it impossible to return to NEP. The amount of grain collected was indeed remarkable, far exceeding any corresponding period. But to collect grain in this fashion destroyed the symchka, the delicate nexus between city and country, between party and peasantry, that had been so carefully nurtured since the early 1920s. The implications were grave, for although in the short run the party could force the peasants to give up hoarded grain, it could not effectively force them to plant enough seed and work industriously enough to provide for future crop surpluses. Once peasants knew that they were subject to requisitions, they could stage something like the work slowdowns of the industrial sector. But an agricultural slowdown could lead to starvation in the cities.

Here was a showdown, a testing of power, and a confirmation of the assertions of the party's Left that the regime could not confidently build socialism if it had to rely on the cooperation of a naturally anti-socialist class. This anti-socialist class was now showing what it could do to stymie bolshevik plans. Thus the confrontation of January 1928 set the stage for the massive "second revolution" of collectivization and five year plans that followed, which was the eventual answer of Stalin and his followers to the rural show of power.

Significantly, although Bukharin resisted the conclusion that NEP was bankrupt, he himself approved the fatal first step, the "extraordinary measures" of January 1928. Moreover, his rethinking of NEP in 1926–27 provided Stalin with the ammunition with which to destroy NEP. That is, many of the ideas that Bukharin had cautiously formulated at this time in response to left-wing criticism were taken up by Stalin and gradually given an exaggerated form, eventually such an extreme form that even many leftists felt Stalin was going too far. But many did not at first recognize what he was doing, since he was using Bukharin's language.

A key question to ask in evaluating the events of the following years is whether Stalin, in directing efforts to collect grain through "extraordinary measures," unnecessarily provoked the countryside. Did he close down the options of the rest of the party, and thus intentionally make a restoration of the smychka impossible? Many historians have accepted Bukharin's belief that a return to incentives rather than a move toward coercion was possible. They point especially to the brutally provocative activities of Stalin and his henchmen later in 1928, even after the party's Politburo had officially denounced the "excesses" of January. Yet a convincing argument could be made that the point of no return had been passed in January 1928, and thereafter, if the bolshevik regime were to survive, a clean break with NEP was necessary. Stalin no doubt accelerated and exaggerated the confrontation, due to his own apparent conviction that the smychka was already irreversibly destroyed, but nevertheless the evidence suggests that a confrontation was unavoidable.

Such a clean break pointed in the direction of a bloody civil war, but neither Stalin nor other party leaders could at first bring themselves to take that path. Instead, they parried and delayed, offering price increases of 10 to 15 percent to encourage peasants to plant more seed, but then once again resorting to "extraordinary measures" in the spring of 1928. However, this time coercion did not work, and only about 8 million tons were delivered (as compared to 10 million the year before), which was almost a starvation figure for the cities. And it was widely recognized that future collections were likely to be even worse.

Trouble was also brewing between Bukharin and Stalin. Bukharin stubbornly continued to argue that the crisis could be surmounted by raising grain prices and abandoning certain industrial projects, while Stalin spoke more and more ominously of the need to wipe out the regime's enemies, and to tackle its economic difficulties directly. By the spring of 1928 the partnership was publicly broken. Stalin now openly proclaimed the need for an "offensive against the kulak," the creation of collective farms in the countryside, and a rapid, planned development of heavy industry. Bukharin, aghast at this "betrayal," denounced Stalin's plans as "neo-Trotskyism," and termed Stalin an "unprincipled intriguer." Stalin in turn denounced Bukharin as a "right deviationist" and a detested liberal "conciliator."

Stalin's victory over Bukharin was not easily accomplished. In spite of the organizational power that Stalin had built up by 1928, Bukharin retained important positions of power in the party, especially in its press. He was still personally very popular, and his theoretical positions continued to find support. Indeed, Stalin at first proceeded with caution both in the formulation of his departure from NEP and in his destruction of the Bukharinist wing of the party. But by early 1929 he felt confident enough of his power to begin to abandon this initial caution, revising his industrial goals ever upward. Similarly, by late 1929, his campaign to collectivize had taken on much bolder and ambitious outlines than he had declared to be necessary or desirable at the outset.

Stalin wished to depict this "revolution from above" as something that had caught the enthusiasm of the peasant masses themselves (except of course the kulaks, who were to be "liquidated as a class"). In an effort to give some substance to this empty language and to stimulate class warfare in the countryside, he made promises to the poor peasants that 25 percent of the grain collected would be handed over to them in the form of long-term credits. But such efforts completely failed to sway the peasants from their universal opposition to collectivization in the countryside.

In a purely abstract economic sense, the notion of a collective farm, or *kolkhoz*, was sound. By grouping many small landholders into large, combined units, the kolkhoz could overcome the natural inefficiencies of small individual farms. Economics of scale could be introduced; large-scale machinery, modern fertilizers, pesticides, and many advanced techniques could be effectively utilized. In a more practical political sense (and it is this aspect that most observers believe was decisive in Stalin's own mind), the tightly knit organization of the kolkhoz made supervision and control of agricultural labor more feasible. Under the watchful eye of the commissar, peasants could not hoard grain, and they could be subjected to something like factory discipline. Collective farms were to become, in a phrase frequently used at the time, "grain factories."

But whatever the abstract economic rationale, the reality was far different. Russia was simply not ready, economically or psychologically, for such widespread collectivization. Her industries could not produce sufficient quantities of farm machinery and chemicals to supply large-scale agricultural production. In select areas, collectivization may have been practical, and indeed a few of the kolkhozi in the Ukraine functioned relatively well in the early stages of collectivization. But for Russia as a whole the scale of the collectivization eventually launched by Stalin was economically unsound in the extreme, for the simple reason that there was no correspondence between the rate of production of farm implements and the rate that new collective farms were established. Similarly, most Russian peasants had no knowledge of modern machinery and advanced agricultural techniques; as people who lived by tradition and custom, they resisted using them. Stories circulated, perhaps apocryphal, of peasants hitching up teams of horses to pull around tractors that had run out of gas.

But to discuss collectivization with this economic-technological focus is to avoid the central reality: Russian peasants, from kulak to migrant laborer, came to see collectivization as an insane scheme by city-dwelling revolutionaries, as a declaration of war. And they fought back desperately. Their resistance meant pitched battles in some cases, but more often it took on the form of destruction, spoliation, and sabotage. Peasants slaughtered their animals, indulging in an orgy of meat eating before the commissars arrived. Or they burned their crops and destroyed their tools. The destruction of livestock was especially widespread and had serious long-range implications, for in a backward economy farm animals supply not only meat but fertilizer and the power to pull plows and transport goods. This loss, combined with the grave losses inherent in the dislocations brought on by the attempt to remake rural society, resulted in a precipitous decline to agricultural productivity and rural famine in the early 1930s. The loss in livestock was in fact not made good until well after World War II.

But the greatest loss was to the peasant population itself. Estimates of the number of peasants who died due to the rigors of the years of collectivization range up to 20 million, although a more reliable figure is probably around half of that. For those who survived, the standard of living, in terms of consumption of foodstuffs and the use of other vital materials, dropped perilously low, while the hours they worked and the tempo of their labor often reached the limits of human endurance. Only in this way could the state gather the capital necessary for planned growth in heavy industry, since production in the countryside had so plummeted. (In 1933 the grain harvest was 5 million tons less than in 1928, but state procurements doubled. These figures give some idea of the astonishing drop in rural consumption.)

In the cities too, life for workers under the Five Year Plan became bleaker and harsher, with longer hours, fewer holidays, lower pay. What occurred in Russia in the next decade was comparable to the "primitive capitalist accumulation," in Marxist terms, that western countries like England and Germany in the previous century had experienced, but it occurred under the auspices of the state rather than individual capitalists, and in far more exaggerated form than Preobrazhensky had ever envisaged. Yet whatever else may be said about these terrible years— and to note that they were years of death and destruction on an almost unparalleled scale is, for many observers, the most important observation—one cannot deny that Russia built up a modern industrial plant in a remarkably short time, entering the ranks of the world's major industrial powers within a generation. (Whether she might have reached a comparable stage within a similar period of time under a more moderate or even a capitalist regime is a tantalizing reflection.) Similarly, it cannot be denied that the once relatively autonomous and potentially rebellious peasantry, which constituted the overwhelming majority of the population, had been brought under effective party control.

Following upon the shocks of collectivization and the reorganization of industry between 1928 and 1934, even greater sufferings were visited upon the Russian people by the mass purges of the late 1930s, the totalitarian warfare of the early 1940s, and then another wave of purges. Each time, millions upon millions died. Rarely has a people endured as much the Russians did between 1914 and Stalin's death in 1953.

While historians have differing opinions about the extent to which Stalin's actions in Russia between 1928 and 1934 were justified by the country's needs and the dilemma in which the party found itself, they are virtually unanimous in condemning his actions between 1936 and 1939. The "blood purges" (so called because Stalin's disposal of his party opponents previously had been bureaucratic rather than violent) of those years have been seen as pure nightmare, a time when Stalin's paranoia and lust for power pushed him to imprison, terrorize, and exe-cute to an unprecedented extent. In these years he put to death a ma-jority of leading bolsheviks, including virtually all those who had been with Lenin in exile before the revolution, and up to 90 percent of the higher echelons of the army. Seven to 8 million ordinary citizens were arrested, of whom something like 3 million either were executed or died from brutal mistreatment.

The blood purges resulted in a renovation of Russia's ruling strata, and fundamentally changed the composition of the party, state, and armed forces. Indeed, the purges can be considered another revolution, as far-reaching as those of 1917–21 and 1928–34. The secret police, once under the reasonably effective control of state and party, now turned, under Stalin's direction, against the leading figures of the party and state. Trotsky's prophecy in his debates with Lenin, that Russia would turn into the dictatorship of a single man, had come true, perhaps more than he himself would have ever believed possible. Russia in the late 1930s ceased to be a dictatorship or party or state, central committee or commissars; all institutions took on an unreal quality. They became mere artifices through which Stalin was able to exercise an autocracy more powerful, absolute, and terrifying than any other in the history of humanity.

The background of the blood purges is obscure, in part because of the extraordinary secretiveness of Russian political life by this time. In offering explanations of these horrifying years, we often have to rely on conjecture and reasonable supposition where solid evidence is missing. The most convincing analysis of the purges emphasizes that, as the first Five Year Plan approached its end in the early 1930s, moderates among those that Stalin had brought up through the ranks began to establish independent positions of power within the party. On a number of occasions these moderates felt strong enough to resist Stalin's directives, although on most issues they gave him solid support.

Prominent among the leaders of the moderates was Sergei Kirov, a young protégé of Stalin's, who had earlier taken over Zinoviev's position as head of the Leningrad party organization. He was an energetic, handsome figure, who enjoyed a broad popularity in the party. It is unlikely that Kirov and the moderates actually sought to replace Stalin, but they did seem intent on restoring "Leninist" party rule, that is, rule based on majority decisions and open discussion among the party's leading cadres. They also appeared to be convinced that the harsh extremes of industrialization and collectivization of the preceding years were no longer necessary. Thus they sought a relaxation and liberalization, restoring former party dissidents to positions of influence, improving living conditions of town and country, and safeguarding the rights of soviet citizens. This moderate faction was behind the less ambitious second Five Year Plan that was being drawn up. Similarly, the moderates gave support to the new soviet constitution, which was written largely under the direction of Bukharin. It established such protections of individual liberties as universal suffrage and secret balloting, and it explicitly listed the civil rights of soviet citizens.

At the Seventeenth Party Congress in January-February 1934, the so-called Congress of Victors (because of the agricultural and industrial "victories" of the previous years), the moderates heaped praises on Stalin's leadership, as was expected. However, Kirov was also given an ovation which, according to some observers, equaled that given to Stalin. Bukharin, who was also allowed to address the congress, was warmly applauded as well.

On December 1, 1934, Kirov was assassinated. Although Stalin led in the official mourning, it has been suggested that he plotted the murder through his secret police, and then used the incident as a pretext for mass arrests of those who resisted his exercise of absolute power. Stalin blamed the assassination on a secret "Zinovievite center of opposition." Zinoviev, Kamenev, and many other leading party figures were charged with indirect complicity in the crime, and were arrested, tried, and sent to prison.

A milestone had been reached in the history of the party. Previously, the worst that Stalin's opponents had suffered was to be stripped of their party posts, expelled from the party, and, in a few instances like that of Trotsky, driven into exile. Now an ever-intensifying political terror began in Russia. It was punctuated by show trials, which at times were based on highly implausible accusations (for example, that Bukharin had plotted to assassinate Lenin). Most of the accused finally confessed, and their trials were followed in most cases by immediate executions. The most famous of these was the Moscow show trial in March 1938. Bukharin, the main defendant (although other leading bolsheviks were being tried with him), presented an enigmatic picture. His language was at times strangely contorted, verbose, and contradictory; he made confessions of generalized guilt but denied most of the specific acts with which he was charged (such as the above-mentioned plot to kill Lenin). His most recent biographer, Stephen F. Cohen, has called Bukharin's performance an attempt to subtly defend his record and to mock the accusations against him by speaking in a kind of Aesopian language.

Following Bukharin's public confession, he too was quickly put to death. Now Stalin was the only remaining bolshevik of those leaders who had worked closely with Lenin. By the Eighteenth Party Congress, in March 1939, Stalin's power stood absolutely uncontested. The delegates to the congress were cowed and submissive; unanimous, enthusiastic support was given to all of the reports by Stalin and his new lieutenants. This was the first congress in five years, despite a party statute stipulating yearly meetings. Of the approximately two thousand delegates that had attended the previous congress, the Congress of Victors in 1934, well over 1,100 had since been arrested for counter-revolutionary crimes and most had been executed.

Stalin was now the uncontested Vozhd' of Russia. He had stamped out all internal threats to his rule. But now an external threat was brewing, one that would come closer to bringing him down—and indeed to ending bolshevik rule in Russia—than any before faced.

GUIDE TO FURTHER READING

Much of the writing on Stalinism has been understandably emotional and polemical, although some of the most telling condemnations have been calmly and factually presented. Particularly noteworthy in this literature are the biographies of leading communists of the interwar years, Stalin included, that offer the advantage of having been written by men of sharply contrasting political persuasions and thus of fundamentally different historical perspectives. Isaac Deutscher, whose remarkable three-volume biography of Trotsky has already been discussed, has also written one of the most valuable and penetrating of the biographies of Stalin: *Stalin, A Political Biography*. Not only is this a fine work of literature, it comes the closest to a sophisticated defense of Stalinism that one can find, written as it was by a kind of Marxist-Leninist, a defender of the Soviet experience, and a former leader of the Polish Communist Party. Stephen Cohen's *Bukharin and the Bolshevik Revolution* is a masterful defense of Bukharin's life and policies, profoundly hostile to Stalin, collectivization, and five year plans. Robert C. Tucker has begun a projected three-volume biography of Stalin, the first of which is *Stalin as Revolutionary: A Study in History and Personality*. This is an ambitious work, which attempts to use the tools of psychohistory—a particularly precarious enterprise in Stalin's case. Tucker's book is cautious and intelligent throughout, however, something that cannot be said of many other works of this genre. In other respects Tucker's work maintains the highest standards of scholarship and is blessed with a clear and forthright style. It is especially effective in making Stalin's rise to power understandable, and I have relied heavily on it in the text. Adam Ulam's *Stalin* is generally in a class with the above works; it is highly readable, penetrating, and based on exhaustive scholarship. It is also—like Ulam's other writing—deeply hostile to communism and often unnecessarily flippant. Warren Lerner's *Karl Radek, The Last Internationalist* provides fascinating insights into how a left bolshevik, who was at first in Trotsky's camp, became converted to a blatant and cynical form of Stalinism.

One feels obliged to mention Alexander Solzhenitsyn's massive *Gulag Archipelago*, not as a work of scholarly history in any rigorous sense, but as a history-making and overwhelming (if sometimes nearly unreadable) condemnation of Stalin's and Lenin's rule. Another study from out of Russia, reflecting a more scholarly and less reactionary perspective, is that by Roy Medvedev, *Let History Judge: The Origins and Consequences of Stalinism*.

Herman Weber has set a high standard for the study of the Stalinization of western communist parties in his *Die Wandlung des deutschen Kommunismus*, although only the more advanced student will be equipped to approach this masterful and many-faceted work. Nothing fully comparable exists for the other major western parties. Paolo Spriano's *Storia del partito communista italiano*, the first volume of which was discussed in the bibliographical notes to Chapter 5, is also highly recommended, especially since it is one of the very few works by a communist party member and militant to approach high scholarly standards. Ronald Tiersky's *The Communist Movement in France, 1920–1972* is not a history as such but rather an attempt to articulate certain theories about French communism, relying partly on historical narrative and analysis to do so. It provides an excellent introduction to the PCF, both during and after its Stalinist period.

A general view of the earlier years of Stalinism, consisting of documents and valuable introductory sections, is Helmut Gruber's *Soviet Russia Masters the Comintern*, which also contains ample bibliographical sections. Fernando Claudin's *The Communist Movement, From the Comintern to the Cominform* gives the views—unfortunately crabbed and long-winded—of a former insider. The promised second volume of Milorad Drachkovitch and Branko Lazitch's *Lenin and the Comintern* should cover the years of Stalinization, from the standpoint of two militant anti-communists (both of these works have already been discussed in the bibliographical notes to Chapter 5).

Also recommended are Theodore H. von Laue, *Why Lenin? Why Stalin?*, an incisive, brilliant essay, and Robert Conquest, *The Great Terror: Stalin's Purge of the 1930s*.

The Fascist Threat, 1923-1939   8

Allusion has already been frequently made in the preceding chapters to the growth of fascism and its impact upon European socialist movements. Fascism represented the greatest challenge ever to the hopes of eventual victory for socialist ideals. Indeed, many thoughtful observers in the 1930s and early 1940s concluded, whether in sadness or eager anticipation, that fascist movements would eventually wipe out socialist and communist movements in every country of Europe. And the police and armies of the fascist states came very near accomplishing just that, only to be reversed at the last hour and overwhelmingly defeated. A tremendous regrowth of socialism and communism ensued thereafter throughout the world. But socialist and communist movements had to pay a terrible price to defeat the fascists, and they remain deeply marked by the experience.

The phenomenon of fascism is nearly impossible to pin down. Its ideology lacks the coherence of socialist ideology. It is less coherent even than anarchism. Yet, in some ways fascism arose the same way as socialism—as a revolt against bourgeois-liberal civilization and a yearning for pre-modern communities and verities. Fascism, like socialism, appealed to the public's widespread anxiety concerning the rapid advent of an unfamiliar, threatening modernism. It was for such reasons that Hitler's movement was called national socialism. But whereas the socialists accepted the Dual Revolution and held Enlightened values, favoring humanism and rationalism, the fascists were fundamentally and unequivocally antimodern. They were certainly willing to use some of the tools developed by modern technology, but they rejected Enlightened values and embraced—in an often diffuse, crude fashion—such notions as unreason, will, race, nation, aggression, destructiveness.

As fascist movements took root in the early 1920s, modern bourgeois-liberal society was of course in deep crisis, reeling from the impact of the most destructive war in history, with its ensuing uprisings
and civil wars, famines and epidemics, disruption of trade and wild
inflation. With the coming of the Great Depression, the number of Europeans who retained some hope for liberal-parliamentary institutions
and an open society greatly diminished. Europeans by the millions
were moved by other forces: Hitler's shrill, hate-filled denunciations of
communists, socialists, and Jews; the powerful, colorful, and brutally
simple propaganda techniques of the fascists; the call to action, the
coarse certainties, the taste for blood.

Socialists and communists also benefitted from the distress of liberal-bourgeois civilization, but not to the same degree. Beyond the myriad of tactical and strategic errors committed by socialist and communist activists, a more fundamental, troubling reality—that the appeal
of fascism exceeded that of socialism—has remained to plague the socialist vision.

THE VICTORY OF FASCISM IN ITALY AND GERMANY

In the preceding two chapters little was said about socialism and communism in Italy, because democratic socialism and Stalinist communism were stillborn there. They survived through the late 1920s and
1930s as pitiful émigré movements with only tenuous clandestine organizations inside Italy. In light of the tremendous power of the working-class offensive in Italy in the years immediately after the war—*il
biennio rosso* ("the red two years") in Italian—this early defeat may
seem paradoxical. However, the very aggressiveness and apparent
strength of Italy's socialist and communist movements contributed to
their early demise.

It will be recalled that in the years immediately preceding the
outbreak of the war the PSI, almost alone among western socialist parties, moved to the left, and when war broke out the Italian socialists,
again almost alone, tried to carry out the resolutions of the Socialist
International. Benito Mussolini had led the PSI in these revolutionary
enthusiasms, but by late 1914 and early 1915, to the horror of the other
leaders of the party, he began to speak in terms that resembled those of
the Allied patriotic socialists. He was denounced as a traitor to the ideals of international socialism and expelled from the party.

In the light of Mussolini's background, his betrayal of socialism is
not difficult to understand. He had never been much engaged by Marx-

ist theory; his revolutionary enthusiasm owed more to the instincts and teachings of the anarchists, syndicalists, and anti-positivists. Some of his socialist critics came to believe that he had taken up the banner of revolutionary socialism not through inner conviction but only because the most entrenched and powerful leaders of the PSI were on its right wing. By assuming a position on the left, Mussolini could hope for a more rapid advance of his career. There is little question that he was a man of colossal vanity whose ambitions were little fettered by doctrinal or moral considerations.

Mussolini was attracted to action, to the dramatic, the violent and the glorious. Therefore the party's militant position in 1912–14 suited him, and he gave effective leadership to it. But he could not stomach the policy of *nè aderire nè sabotare* ("neither aid nor sabotage") which the party finally adopted in response to the war. It was too negative, too passive, too lacking in vitality. War for the Italian fatherland, for exalted nationalistic principles was a far more attractive alternative.

After his expulsion from the party Mussolini volunteered for the front, where he was gravely wounded. During his convalescence, he started a new, prowar newspaper, *Il Popolo d'Italia* (The People of Italy), which was partly financed by funds from the French Foreign Office which were in all likelihood delivered by Marcel Cachin (who at this time was an ardently patriotic socialist, intent on winning Italy's participation on France's side although he would later would become a French Communist Party leader). In spite of his break with the PSI, Mussolini remained for some time an avowed socialist. He still hoped to woo the working class away from the PSI, and he looked to an eventual proletarian victory over the bourgeoisie. In other words, one might have easily characterized him at the time as being little different from the patriotic socialists of France, Belgium, or England, who were willing to defend their country but had not abandoned all of the precepts of prewar socialism.

Still, there were significant differences between Mussolini and most other patriotic socialists. His nationalism was not linked with reformism or liberalism, as was too often so often the case with other right-wing socialists. In fact, he despised such tendencies. In this respect he had more in common with Lenin than with the social patriots. They both shared a contempt for "softs," spoke in intransigent, acerbic tones, yet were capable of the greatest flexibility in the pursuit of power. In 1917 Mussolini openly admired the bolsheviks' success, although not long afterward he began to see the advantages of an anti-bolshevik stance in Italy.

By the end of the war Mussolini was moving was moving toward a clear break with socialism. He helped to organize the so-called *fasci di combattimento* (later known as the Black Shirts), composed largely of right-wing university students and ex-soldiers and dedicated to the struggle against revolutionary socialism. Superficially, Mussolini's association with the Black Shirts resembled the alliance of SPD and Freikorps in Germany, but in the latter case the alliance between the two was opportunistic and fleeting; as soon as the crisis had passed, the SPD oversaw the dissolution of the Freikorps and their replacement by regular police and army. In Italy the fasci di combattimento were not so quickly dissolved.

Throughout the years immediately after the war the Black Shirts engaged in street brawls with socialists and communists, attacked party offices, destroyed PSI and PCI printing presses, administered doses of castor oil to prominent socialists and communists, and generally waged a campaign of vandalism and terror against the "bolsheviks," as they were collectively labeled. Even in areas where the socialists enjoyed great popular support, as in the cities of Bologna and Genoa, a relatively small number of fascist toughs proved themselves able to exercise a de facto governmental authority, intimidating the legally elected socialist and trade-union officials.

Their successes inevitably attracted the attention of those who stood to lose the most from a socialist revolution in Italy, particularly the large property owners and the industrialists, but also members of the rural and urban petty bourgeoisie, who feared that the socialists would rob them of the modicum of security that their plots of land or shops afforded. The property-owning classes felt such anxieties in nearly every country of Europe but more intensely at this time in Italy because of the exalted revolutionary rhetoric of nearly all working-class leaders, the great waves of labor unrest, and most of all because the Italian state seemed little concerned to protect property and privilege. Whereas in France and Germany the state intervened forcefully to put down the revolutionary movement, in Italy the government under Giolitti pursued a policy of apparent neutrality, based on the reasoning that since there was no real revolutionary danger the socialists would, if given enough rope, hang themselves. This same attitude meant that the state did not decisively intervene in the struggles between the fascists and the socialists.

Such a strategy had worked for Giolitti in 1904 when he faced the threat of a revolutionary general strike: The strike fizzled after a few days, without significant governmental intervention, and its revolutionary syndicalist leaders were exposed as braggarts with no comprehension of the realities of power. Giolitti hoped to repeat this successful and remarkably bloodless strategy in 1920, and indeed it did "work" once again, in that when given the chance of turning the factory occupations of September 1920 in a revolutionary seizure of power, the leaders of the PSI balked. They were painfully aware of their lack of preparation for violent revolution and of the many factors that weighed against successful social revolution in Italy. Nevertheless they were at the same time unable to wean themselves from the psychic need to make constant predictions of an imminent outbreak of revolution.

This contradiction between rhetoric and action became finally too much for the Left of the party. Discouragement and indignation spread through the rank and file, and by late 1920 it seemed that labor's offensive in Italy had spent itself. In January 1921 the PSI split into socialist and communist factions, and the story of socialism and communism in Italy in the following years was one of bitter recrimination, decline, and dissolution.

However, it was not immediately obvious to all participants that the revolutionary wave had crested, and it certainly was not obvious to those classes that stood to lose from proletarian revolution. Giolitti's second miraculous cure had an unintended but serious side effect: It convinced the possessing classes, whether small property owners or large, that they had been abandoned by the liberal-democratic state and that only the fascists stood between them and anarchistic communism. From that point on, many turned to Mussolini as a savior.

Mussolini's successes and the disorientation of the Italian working class did not discourage the new communist leader, Amadeo Bordiga. On the contrary, he believed that proletarian revolution was rapidly approaching and that at last a vanguard communist party of professional revolutionaries, freed of the influence of reformists and pseudo-revolutionaries, had been created to give proper leadership to the masses. For a while in 1921 the Comintern supported Bordiga in his revolutionary enthusiasms, but as the wave of unrest receded elsewhere, and as the United Front tactic was introduced, the Italian leader and Moscow came to bitter disagreements.

Bordiga was finally removed from power in early 1923, to be replaced by Antonio Gramsci, who would later be recognized as one of the leading Marxist theoreticians of the twentieth century. The leaders of the Comintern were attracted to him at this juncture, however, because of his greater receptivity to bolshevik leadership and to the idea of the United Front. Perhaps, one wonders, if someone with Gramsci's flexibility and realism had been at the head of the PCI from the beginning, working for a broad unity of the proletariat, Mussolini's chances of coming to power would have been diminished. As it was, Gramsci took over the party too late; Mussolini had already staged his March on Rome in October 1922 and in December he had been given dictatorial powers for one year. But working-class unity was not the only important consideration. Even if the PCI and PSI had worked together, indeed if the PSI had not split, the socialists' following would have been still less than one-third of the population, and this largely concentrated in the urban centers of the north. It is thus difficult to believe that effective anti-fascist action would have been possible without some kind of alliance with the non-socialist Left. Indeed one might argue that if the socialists had remained united, and especially if they had appeared really capable of making a revolution, then the forces that rallied to Mussolini might have done so even more rapidly and decisively. As Marx himself once wrote: "The [growth of the] party of revolution rallies the party of reaction."

Thus divisiveness and factionalism in the working-class parties do not appear to have been decisive in the victory of fascism in Italy. No doubt these divisions made Mussolini's job easier, but the more serious difficulty lay in putting together an alliance of parties that was willing to fight to preserve the liberties guaranteed by the liberal-democratic state. In concrete terms this alliance might have entailed a coalition of socialists, Giolittean liberals, and the new Catholic party, the so-called *Partito Popolare*—a coalition that would have been the rough equivalent of the Weimar coalition in Germany.

But such a coalition proved much harder to put together in Italy than in Germany. Even after the break with the communists, Serrati, the leader of the PSI, resisted any cooperation with non-socialist parties in parliament, and many of his followers were even more intransigent. The reformist Turati would have been willing, but his following was too small, and when his faction did finally leave the PSI in the autumn of 1922 it was too late to be of much use. Similarly, the right wing of the Popolari wanted nothing to do with atheistic socialists, and the pope seemed to encourage those Popolari who rebuffed any efforts to build an anti-fascist coalition which included the socialists.

Further aiding the cause of the fascists at this point was the attitude of a number of leading military figures in Italy. Disgusted with parliamentary government, they lent both covert and overt aid to the fascists. Such was also the case in Germany, but at decisive points in the early history of the Weimar Republic, the regular army came to the government's support. Such support was often withheld in Italy.

While the weakness of liberal democracy in Italy contributed more to Mussolini's rise than the divisions in the working class, it would be a mistake to see the victory of fascism in Italy primarily in terms of the weakness of liberal democracy. Mussolini put together a movement of unique power, dynamism, and attractiveness to Italy's masses. Quite aside from his appeal as defender of the propertied and protector of the status quo, his florid nationalism appealed to large numbers of Italians who felt humiliated by Italy's record in the war, by her treatment at the hands of France, England, and the United States at the Paris Peace Conference, and indeed by a entrenched attitude of northern European condescension toward Italians. The lower middle class, whether in its new white-collar form or in the older shopkeeping and small landholding forms, responded with particular enthusiasm to the phenomenon of late nineteenth-century nationalism and glorification of the state. Mussolini was able to translate those emotions in Italy into a powerful political force based on genuine popular enthusiasm.

Once given dictatorial powers, Mussolini restored order with remarkable effectiveness. Strikes ceased, street fighting subsided, and throughout Italy a new calm, a new discipline, and a new efficiency seemed to prevail. The elections of 1924, while hardly a model of democratic procedure and propriety, saw the fascists' "National List" win a heavy majority (63 percent) of the popular vote. As Mussolini's popularity and power grew, he moved more forcefully against his opponents. By the late 1920s nearly all socialist and communist leaders were either in jail, in exile, or dead. His regime was never so brutal or so thoroughly "totalitarian" as Hitler's (or Stalin's) would later be; Gramsci was able to do much of his original work in a fascist prison, a most unlikely accomplishment in a nazi concentration camp. But fascism did largely suppress the socialist and communist movements in Italy for a generation.

In retrospect it is striking how little the revolutionary socialists and communists sensed the growing fascist danger and how unprepared they were to fight the fascists, not only in Italy but in most other European countries. The revolutionary socialists had a long-standing distrust of any broad coalition of the Left that included both socialists and bourgeois democrats, fatally undermining anti-fascist unity. As early as the Millerand Affair in France, revolutionaries had seen such coalitions turn out badly; the SPD's Weimar coalition was but the last and worst example, and it served to reinforce them in their intransigence. They firmly believed that bourgeois democracy could not be saved, or was not worth saving.

The KPD's initial reaction to the Kapp Putsch of March 1920 is an instructive example of this attitude. The German communists declared that revolutionary workers should remain indifferent to the efforts of reactionary officers to bring down the Weimar Republic. Therefore, the KPD refused at first to join in the general strike called by the social democrats and other republican forces, although once it became apparent that the strike was being supported by the vast majority of German workers, the KPD reversed itself and urged its followers to join in. The first instinct of the German communists, then, was to reject any notion of a broad coalition of the Left, no matter under what guise it presented itself.

A more instructive example, because its outcome was more immediately decisive, can be found in the reaction of the Bulgarian Communist Party (BKP) to a putsch in 1923 by right-wing forces, supported by the police and officer caste, against the peasant-supported democratic regime of Alexander Stambuliski. The Bulgarian communist leaders, who had behind them a relatively powerful movement, not only declared neutrality in what they termed a struggle between rival factions of the bourgeoisie but even applauded when Stambuliski's followers were prosecuted. But here their miscalculation quickly became apparent, for once the new regime had disposed of Stambuliski, it proved itself far less tolerant of the communist movement than Stambuliski had been. The belated efforts of the BKP, now urged on by Moscow, to apply the United Front tactic in cooperation with Stambuliski's shattered forces failed, and the powerful and promising communist movement in Bulgaria was brutally and thoroughly repressed. A few years later, a broadly similar sequence in Poland would bring to power Marshal Pilsudski, who then crushed the communists and set up a semi-fascist dictatorship.

In most instances this disastrous underestimation of the power of reactionaries, particularly of fascist or semi-fascist reactionaries, was characteristic of the left-wing, ultra-revolutionary tendency within the communist and socialist movements. Thus, throughout most of the 1920s, when the Russian-dominated Comintern was backing the relatively right-wing strategy of United Front, left-wing communists like Bordiga and the leaders of the BKP who refused tactical cooperation with the democratic Left against the fascist-reactionary Right did so usually in opposition to directives from Moscow. Between 1928 and 1934, when the Comintern shifted to a left-wing, "class against class" policy, however, those western communists who looked to a united working-class against the rising reactionary and fascist danger were instead rebuffed by the Russians and instructed to maintain a pure, unallied position.

Thus, when the fascist danger was assuming its most ominous form in the German nazi movement, directives from Moscow rejected the notion of a "united front from above" and opposed cooperating with other anti-fascist organizations. Indeed, orders from Moscow went to the extreme of directing western communists to combat the democratic socialists as the "real enemy," while the fascists were to be treated as a subsidiary and transitory danger. Thus social-democratic leaders were described as "social fascists," and the social reforms and constitutional protections of bourgeois democracy were passed off as mere illusions designed to dull the revolutionary class consciousness of workers. The official line held that "objectively" the fascists and the "social fascists" were the same, in that both were futilely attempting to prop up the dying bourgeois order, but the latter were the more devious and dangerous.

It might seem that after the disastrous experiences with fascist reaction in Italy and Eastern Europe, there would have been reason enough for the Comintern to give even greater emphasis to the United Front idea. How then can one explain the turnabout in 1928 to the "Class-Against-Class" policy? The easiest answer is that the Comintern's directive to reject all alliances in countries outside of Russia reflected internal developments in Russia (that is, the promotion of class warfare in the drive against the kulaks), just as the United Front policy corresponded to the NEP and the bolsheviks' need for a period of class cooperation in Russia. But, although there is no doubt internal Russian developments were decisive, there is more to the story, for outside of Russia the United Front had also seen a string of defeats, most notably in 1923 in Germany, in 1926 in Great Britain (with the general strike), and in China in 1926, when the communists' Kuomintang ally, Chiang Kai-shek, moved against them with ruthless effectiveness. Moreover, by 1928 in Germany (still the key western country in Comintern calculations) the fortunes of the SPD seemed to be reviving; the idea of the United Front was simply not working as a way of infiltrating the social democrats and winning their followers over to communism. Indeed, the opposite danger was present, as the SPD revival of 1928 seemed to suggest; that is, there was now the danger that the social democrats might raid the ranks of the communists.

The Class-Against-Class policy seemed to many German communists to be an effective propaganda device, once the SPD had been cornered into "tolerating" Brüning and supporting Hindenburg as the "lesser evil." Many workers felt that the communists' assertion that the social democrats were "social fascists" was plausible, and they agreed with the description of social democrats as the *Todfeind* or archenemy, the betrayers of socialism and the working class. Significantly, the KPD's Reichstag vote grew from 3.3 million in 1928 to almost 6 million in late 1932, while the vote of the SPD slipped from 9.1 million to 7.3 million.

As the communists' campaign of vilification further deepened the gulf between social democratic and communist workers, any eventual united action against Hitler's burgeoning forces became more and more unlikely. Even after the nazis' electoral support soared from 800,000 in 1928 to 6.5 million in 1932, the communist line did not much waver. KPD leaders described the sudden nazi growth as the beginning of the end, the high fever before the death of capitalism. They quoted Marx's remark that the growth of the party of the part of the revolution stimulated the growth of the party of reaction—but made little of the fact that the party of reaction was growing much more rapidly than the party of revolution. The attitude of the communists, which was epitomized by the slogan "Nach Hitler Uns!" ("After Hitler, Us!"), allowed them to cooperate opportunistically with the nazis in demonstrations against the Weimar republic and to employ nationalistic themes, such as accusing the SPD of treason to Germany for accepting the Versailles Treaty and reparations. In a way, it was a revival of 1923 Schlageter Line. This same tendency for communists to join ranks with the fascists against bourgeois democracy was duplicated elsewhere, most notably in France, as will be described in the following section.

As blind as Comintern policy seems in retrospect to have been, Hitler's victory cannot be attributed simply to communist blindness and the resulting divisions within the German working class. The points made regarding Mussolini hold even more for Hitler: Though the divisions in the working class made his work easier, even if the German working class had been united, it is highly doubtful that, without the help of Germany's bourgeois parties, it would have been strong enough to prevent an eventual nazi takeover. A fact of decisive importance is that popular support for liberal-bourgeois parties withered away in the late 1920s and early 1930s, and rallied with startling force to the nazi movement, which proved itself even more dynamic and ruthless than the Italian fascist movement.

The failure of the Weimar Republic was a failure for the social democrats. But it was not theirs alone, or even primarily. They had made every effort to cooperate with anti-nazi parties, and had made repeated compromises in order to maintain their links with their Weimar coalition partners or to prevent nazi access to power. As described in Chapter 5, social-democratic options narrowed to an impossible degree in the last years of the Republic. The leaders of the SPD grappled in vain with what may well have been insoluble dilemmas. They retained, nevertheless, much of their popular support, far more than their coalition partners, the Democrats and People's Party.

The Depression, which hit Germany with particular force, was the last straw for those who had never enthusiastically accepted the Republic. Those members of the lower middle class who had felt aggrieved about the new power and status of organized labor during the war and thereafter, who had seen their savings disappear in the inflation of 1923, and who had enjoyed only a short period of relative stability from 1924 to 1928 now abandoned liberalism, whether economic, political, or cultural. For these disillusioned and resentful masses Hitler's movement offered irresistible attractions. Whatever one's opinion of National Socialism, it is difficult to deny its dynamism, the genius of its leaders in the new techniques of mass propaganda, its skill in organizing the previously unorganized and focusing the rage and frustrations of millions of German citizens.

There was still another similarity to developments in Italy a decade before. Hitler's ability to recruit great numbers of ardent followers inevitably attracted the attention of the large capitalists in Germany, who were concerned about the growth of revolutionary sentiment in the population and no longer confident that the republican form of government could protect capitalism. Similarly, many Junker military leaders, while harboring ill-concealed contempt for Hitler and his plebeian lieutenants, nevertheless believed that he could be used to protect the traditional interests of the Junker class. Both of these powerful groups were ultimately wrong in their belief that they could manipulate the nazis, but at a crucial time their support significantly contributed to Hitler's victory.

Whatever the power and attraction of nazism, the ease with which it was able, once it had gained power, to destroy organized labor— whether social democratic, communist, or Christian—was surprising. The surprise must be all the greater when one remembers that organized workers in these three camps never joined the nazis in great numbers; nazism remained primarily a petty bourgeois movement. Even the communists, from whom one might have expected at least a symbolic show of resistance, given the party's ideology and its record in 1919, 1921, and 1923, put up little resistance in 1933. Several factors account for this surprising docility.

To begin with, the *Machtergreifung*, or "seizure of power," was a less decisive and dramatic affair than the term implies. The nazis took over after an extended period of crisis and long after parliamentary democracy had ceased to function in Germany. Hitler was only the last in a series of dictatorial, anti-labor chancellors. Even so, he took office with the understanding that he would respect the constitution. Already Brüning, who was ruling by decree, had introduced measures antipathetic to the interests of labor, and under von Papen's subsequent chancellorship a thorough and illegal purge of the social-democratic government of Prussia had occurred. Moreover, nazi terror had been widespread before January 1933, when Hitler formally assumed power, so that many workers perceived little immediate difference in terms of their own personal security before and after the Machtergreifung. Indeed, those workers who were influenced by the official communist line, which insisted that all non-communist parties were "fascist," believed that Hitler's government was not qualitatively different from the 1928 Weimar coalition's or Brüning's, or von Papen's. Moreover, the "Nach Hitler Uns!" mentality—the assertion, as one communist leader put it, that "the nazis will shoot their bolt sooner than any previous government"—tended to encourage an attitude of wait-and-see, of assuming that the nazis would demonstrate their ineptness and inability to rule. Thus, for workers of whatever anti-nazi persuasion, it was difficult to plan and stage an act of resistance; the situation was too full of equivocation. There was no clear-cut turning point.

Most of the leaders of the SPD and Free Trade Unions, moreover, were not the sort of men who could think in terms of a heroic, violent uprising, even if a less confused situation had presented itself. Indeed, such a situation may be said to have occurred in July 1932, when von Papen had taken over the legally constituted social-democratic government in Prussia. There, in the face of blatant provocation, the leaders of the SPD issued no call to resist. They neither called for a general strike nor summoned the party's paramilitary organizations. The party leadership argued that in light of the mass unemployment at the time a general strike had little chance of success and feared that aggressive action might lead to bloody and fruitless civil war. They hoped that von Papen's illegal actions could be undone through proper channels, and these hopes would have been dashed if violent resistance broke out. Whatever the merits of this reasoning, social-democratic inaction in

Prussia was widely interpreted as cowardice—the communists took particular propagandistic advantage of it—and it led to further undermining of the combativeness of the social-democratic rank and file. The failure to respond to von Papen's coup, when linked to the policies of toleration and lesser evil, contributed to the kind of demoralization that led many workers and their leaders to hope, and to keep on hoping even after the nazis were in power, that with a little more compromise they could preserve their organizations from total nazi domination.

In moving against organized labor, the nazis showed considerable tactical skill. They preserved as long as possible the illusion that some degree of legality and constitutional rule would be preserved. At the same time they played upon the divisions among German anti-fascists, making it easier to destroy them one by one.

As soon as Hitler had been appointed chancellor, the communists proposed to the social democrats and Free Trade Unions that a general strike be called. The offer was refused, as a similar offer had been in July 1932 at the time of von Papen's actions, because the social democrats did not believe in the sincerity of the communists (who in this case were not acting in consistency with their Class-Against-Class policy) and because they were certain a strike would be bloodily suppressed. The communists did not persist in calling for a general strike on their own.

This was perhaps the communists' and social democrats' last chance for a creditable showing. Negotiations had in fact been going on half-heartedly between representatives of the two since the autumn of 1932, but they came to nothing. On February 27, 1933, the Reichstag building burned to the ground, and the nazis, describing the fire as the communists' first step in a planned uprising, moved ruthlessly and effectively against the KPD, arresting its leaders and taking over the party offices and newspapers. Three weeks before the nazi takeover Ernst Thälmann, the leader of the KPD, had boasted that his party was so effectively organized and so strongly supported by the masses that it was inconceivable that government repression, such as that of 1923, could ever be repeated. Few modern political leaders have been so utterly and disastrously wrong.

Although the nazis accused the social democrats of complicity in the Reichstag fire, the full force of repression was withheld from the SPD for a time. Social-democratic leaders made various attempts to placate their new rulers. The most extreme example of these was the support offered by the Free Trade Unions (traditionally social-democratic in orientation) for the nazi transformation of May 1 into a "National Labor Day"—which was to replace the traditional international celebration. Union leaders went so far as to proclaim that "the victory of national socialism . . . is our victory as well, because today the socialist task is put to the whole nation." But such efforts were pathetically ineffective. On May 2 all trade-union buildings were occupied by nazi detachments, and prominent trade-union leaders were arrested. Not long afterward all trade unions were dissolved. By the end of June similar measures had been carried out against the SPD.

Within a few months the nazis had gone further in terms of totalitarian domination than the Italian fascists had in many years. Socialism and communism in Germany had gone down in overwhelming defeat—a development of particular significance, because the SPD and KPD were the leading democratic socialist and communist parties of western Europe. This defeat could not help but impress itself upon the leaders of the Soviet Union. It was becoming ever more difficult to assert that nazism simply represented the death rattle of capitalism. A new stage in the struggle against fascism had been reached.

THE POPULAR FRONT

From early 1933 until mid-1936, from East to West, vast changes occurred in Europe. New alliances were forged, not only on the diplomatic level, but on the political and social levels at well. The nazis, having established firm domestic control, were soon to launch a campaign for German domination of Europe. Soviet Russia emerged from five years of isolation and desperate struggle, proclaiming a victory for collectivization of agriculture and rapid industrialization. At the same time, the Soviets, alarmed by the new military threat from Nazi Germany, began to seek out new contacts and alliances. In France demonstrations against the Republic seemed to threaten a fascist takeover, and in Austria Dollfuss brutally repressed the labor movement. These many developments encouraged the formation of an unprecedentedly broad alliance of the Left, known as the Popular Front.

Events in France provide the most convenient focus to describe the genesis of the Popular Front, in part because these events seem to have acted as a catalyst in changing Comintern policy, and also because in France the Popular Front was more important than anywhere else in Europe. After 1933 France was the most important remaining continental democracy, and if fascists had come into power there, little hope could have remained for the labor movement, communist or socialist, or indeed for European liberal democracy.

As alluded to in Chapter 6, another *cartel des gauches*, or Left coalition (excluding the communists), was put together in 1932, but its Radical-led cabinets proved shaky and short-lived, often because of the repeated withdrawal of support by the SFIO. Dissatisfaction with the unstable and scandal-ridden Republic reached a climax in February 1934, with the so-called Stavisky Affair. Stavisky, a Jewish financier, had embezzled millions of francs with the aid of friends in parliament, most of whom were associated with the Radical Party. Even the Radical premier, Camille Chautemps, was believed to have tried to cover up Stavisky's machinations.

On February 6, a coalition of right-wing and fascist anti-republican organizations launched protest demonstration at the Place de la Concorde. The communists also appeared, in their own separate protest (another example of unofficial, opportunistic communist-fascist anti-republican collaboration). At one point, when the right-wing demonstrators broke through the police lines formed on the bridge separating the Place de la Concorde from the Chamber of Deputies, they appeared to be intent upon a coup d'état. The police were finally forced to use their guns, killing seventeen and injuring over two thousand.

Although subsequent research has failed to turn up convincing evidence of a conspiracy to take power on February 6, 1934, many observers on the left, in France and in other countries, believed that French fascists had tried to bring down the republic and had only narrowly missed. Following Hitler's victory in early 1933, leftists in France had had ample opportunity to learn what fascism meant in Germany, and the events of February 6 pushed them to the conclusion that something had to be done immediately to fend off the fascist danger in France.

In the following weeks a number of more or less spontaneous antifascist demonstrations were organized. Communists and socialists cooperated in them, even when the socialists took the initiative (a situation which in the past had usually meant that the communists would refuse to participate, since it smacked too much of "United Front from above"). The powerful push from below, from the rank-and-file membership of both parties for anti-fascist unity forced the long-hostile communist and socialist leadership to work together.

A similar but less powerful push from below had been felt in Germany in 1932 and early 1933, not only among the communist and social-democratic rank and file but more notably among middle-level communist functionaries. But a wait-and-see mentality, the belief that the nazis would not be able to rule and that a proletarian revolution would follow soon after, continued to prevail in the top echelons of the KPD and Comintern. Still, it is worth recalling that in July 1932 with von Papen's takeover of Prussia and then with Hitler's assumption of the chancellorship, the KPD had proposed United Front general strikes to the SPD. Whether these initiatives can be considered responses to pressure from below and tentative steps in the direction of new policies, or simply a familiar propaganda technique, remains unclear.

A further impetus in the direction of unity for the French Left was the chain of events in Austria. As will be recalled from Chapter 6, Dollfuss had assumed a near dictatorship in early 1933 by preventing parliament from meeting. An important factor in restraining him from more determined action against the social democrats was his promise to the Radical-led government in France, made in order to obtain French loans, that he would respect basic constitutional rights in Austria. When the Stavisky Affair led to the fall of the Radical government, and a conservative coalition temporarily assumed power, Dollfuss believed himself freed from his pledge and apparently concluded that French democracy was itself moribund. Approximately a week after the Stavisky riots, Dollfuss's police tried to capture hidden social-democratic weapons. Street fighting subsequently broke out and party headquarters issued a call for a general strike. However, largely because of poor planning and general discouragement, the strike fell apart, as did the preparations for military resistance. Even if the plans for the strike and uprising had been better coordinated, it is doubtful that the workers would have been able to successfully oppose the organized power of the Austrian state. In Vienna the army brought up crack units equipped with heavy artillery and blasted the working-class districts, completely overpowering workers' detachments.

In the face of such hopeless odds, many Austrian workers still fought with desperate courage, preserving for themselves and their institutions a kind of honor and self-respect. On the morrow of Dollfuss's bloody victory, Bauer, in recognizing defeat, could still proclaim that Austrian social democrats, unlike their counterparts in Italy and Germany, had stood up in the name of socialism and had helped to rebuild the morale of socialists in the rest of Europe, humiliated as they were by Hitler's easy victory.

In France workers were determined to do more than go down in heroic defeat. February 1934 marked what the French subsequently termed a "grand tournant," a great turning point. Even Radicals decided to join in the new-found socialist-communist unity. By July 14, 1935 (Bastille Day), the three parties came together in a huge anti-fascist rally, which looked forward to unity in the elections scheduled for the following spring.

Already as early as the end of 1932, French communist leaders appear to have been playing with the notion of a shift in tactics. Conceivably they discussed these ideas with the leaders of the KPD, who, as mentioned above, may themselves have at least thought about a move away from Class-Against-Class. But in no case would the Russian leaders of the Comintern have permitted their followers in France and Germany to proceed on their own in formulating such an about-face in policy.

By the end of 1934 it was difficult for communists to continue the rhetoric about the nazis "shooting their bolt"; moreover, communists could see that if the nazis could link hands in some military-diplomatic sense with the fervently anti-bolshevik fascists and authoritarians in Italy, Austria, Eastern Europe, and, finally, in France (assuming that fascists took power there), there seemed little hope that the Soviet Union could survive. Hitler's conclusion of an agreement with the anti-communist Polish leader Pilsudski in January 1934, in part palpably designed as a German-Polish anti-Russian alliance, gave the Soviets further cause for alarm. In short, there was much to be said in favor of Russia breaking out of its diplomatic isolation and seeking allies in western Europe.

Events inside Russia were also opening up the possibility of new initiatives. The worst throes of collectivization had passed, and the first Five Year Plan was nearing its end in 1933. The notion of heroic class conflict, the working class against all others, now appeared objectively less appropriate. Indeed, world revolution remained a distant prospect, and if Russia was going to have to brace itself for a major military confrontation with its neighbors, then it would be to the interests of the Soviet leaders to bind up the wounds of Soviet society, to de-emphasize class conflict, and to speak in nationalistic terms. As will be recalled, by the time of the Seventeenth Party Congress in 1934, the so-called Congress of Victors, moderates in the Bolshevik Party was asserting themselves in the name of a general relaxation and liberalization.

Stalin opposed such loosening of control, and he eventually purged all of the moderates, but nevertheless the moderate perspective on the international and Comintern level prevailed until 1939. The extent to which Stalin himself at this time sincerely embraced the notions of unity with the democratic Left against fascism and a Russian diplomatic alliance with western democracies is difficult to measure. Some historians believe—and there is much evidence to support this belief—

that Stalin always hoped and planned to reaffirm or even expand the 1922 Rapallo alliance with Germany. But a German-Russian alliance did not serve Hitler's interests in the early 1930s, and thus whatever Stalin's preferences, he was obliged to listen to those who advised otherwise. Certainly he had to recognize the failure of the Class-Against-Class policies and the mounting danger to the Soviet state posed by Nazi Germany. Thus he went along with the new policies, until different opportunities offered themselves.

In September 1934 the Soviet Union joined the League of Nations, and in May 1935 it signed a treaty of mutual assistance with France. The Comintern, after its Seventh Congress in 1935, where the new Popular Front policies were proclaimed, now encouraged cooperation with democratic socialists, praised the remaining liberal democracies in western Europe, and encouraged working-class patriotism in those countries where the fascists were not in power. Across the board those aspects of communist ideology that had most alienated non-communists were drastically de-emphasized. When a western reporter asked Stalin about the communists' commitment to violent world revolution, Stalin replied that the whole idea had been a "tragi-comical misunderstanding."

The decisiveness with which the Comintern and its member parties finally moved away from the Class-Against-Class tactic dazzled and confused many observers, although the new tactic undeniably struck a responsive chord in the working class of France and other western democracies. Central to the Popular Front idea was to establish the broadest possible anti-fascist coalition. This meant not only a new unity of the working class, but even more an effort by the communists to conciliate and rally the petty bourgeoisie, the class that had proved the most susceptible to the appeals of fascism in other countries. The Popular Front was more than a revival of Radek's ill-fated Schlageter Line of 1923; now there was little suggestion that revolution was a prospect. Moreover, the underlying conception of the Schlageter Line (that is, a nationalistic attack on republicanism) had always been less appropriate in France, since the French lower middle class was more favorably inclined toward republican parliamentary democracy than were members of that class in Germany. Indeed, the Third Republic had become to an important degree a petty-bourgeois republic, run by the Radical Party. Thus communist efforts to conciliate the Radicals and their petty-bourgeois following entailed not attacks on republican government but rather praise for republicanism, and attempts to associate communism with the jacobin tradition.

Many leaders of the Radical and socialist parties remained suspicious of the communists in their new-found reasonableness, and on the left of the SFIO there were murmurs that the communists were betraying the principles of revolutionary socialism. But on the whole the communists succeeded. The elections of the spring of 1936, which netted the parties of the Popular Front 370 seats out of 618, represented a particular victory for the PCF; the communists polled twice as many votes as in 1932 and won 72 seats in parliament, as compared to a mere 12 in 1932, when they had refused to have anything to do with electoral coalitions. The SFIO won 149 seats, as compared to 129 in 1932, thus making its delegation the largest in parliament, even though the party's percentage of the total vote slipped slightly, from 21 percent to 20 percent. (These puzzling differences between percentage of total vote and number of parliamentary seats were made possible because of the deals made between coalition partners; that is, the leading party in the first round of voting benefited from the withdrawal in the second round of the other coalition parties who urged their voters to support the leading party.) The Radicals' seats dropped from 157 in 1932 to 109 in 1936, and from 19 percent to 14 percent of the total vote, largely due to defections of conservative Radical voters from the Popular Front. Thus the Radical Party was the relative loser and ceased being France's largest party. Overall the Popular Front won 59 percent of the vote, as compared to 49 percent for the unallied parties in 1932. But more than a shift to the left, these percentages represented a shift away from the middle, which ominously recalled trends in the last years of the Weimar Republic. France's political community, always fragile, was now entering a period of even deeper divisions. This was not a good sign for the long-range success of the Popular Front.

As soon as the election results were known, Blum announced that he was willing to head a new Popular Front government. He had carefully prepared his party to accept this eventuality, when earlier he had articulated his distinctions between "participation," "conquest," and "exercise." Now he was ready to "exercise" power, without attacking basic bourgeois institutions, in the name of ridding France of the fascist menace. As leader of the largest party in France, his earlier stipulations were satisfied. That is, the SFIO could be the dominant coalition party, its Radical allies assuming a secondary position (the communists, while supporting the coalition, refused cabinet posts).

Almost immediately Blum ran into difficulties in guiding his government along the carefully defined lines of an exercise of power. Between the May 3 ballot and Blum's actual assumption of office on June

4, workers launched a tremendous chain of strikes and sit-downs. Not since the general strike of 1920 had anything like this been seen in France, and the leaders of the three parties as well as the leaders of the trade unions were taken by surprise. It seemed that workers were spontaneously assuming control of France's economy. By the first week of June over 2 million workers were taking part in strikes and factory occupations. French industry came to a standstill.

Revolutionaries in France, particularly those on the extreme Left of the SFIO, were exhilarated, exclaiming "anything is possible!" But social change in the direction of workers' control or socialization of industry was not on the agenda of the leaders of the Popular Front. The communist as much Blum—to say nothing of the Radicals—were convinced that unless these mass outbursts were curbed, the Popular Front would disintegrate before it had a chance to deal with the fascists in France. This latter goal was what 59 percent of the voters had supported; a far less significant percentage favored social revolution.

The genesis of the strikes and exactly what their participants hoped to accomplish have remained unclear—very likely because no precise plans or goals ever existed at the time. Rather than a planned revolution, the sit-down strikes might be better termed a celebration, calling to mind the "festival of the oppressed" in the Paris Commune. This is not to suggest that the situation did not have revolutionary potential or that the spirit of the strikers might not have changed into something more aggressively anti-capitalist. A number of factory owners were certainly near panic. In this setting representatives of management met with Blum in his office at the Hôtel Matignon, where the famous "Matignon Agreements" were worked out. Although sullen and resentful, the employers sensed that it was necessary to make concessions in order to cool down the situation in the factories.

What Blum demanded of the employers was a program of the most thoroughgoing economic reforms in the history of modern industrial France. The only challenge to private property and the market economy was in the nationalization of the armaments industries and in the imposition of greater governmental control over the privately owned Bank of France. The Matignon Agreements also established collective bargaining rights and awarded salary increases averaging 12 percent to workers. Subsequent legislation assured a forty-hour week, two-week vacations with pay, and a program of public works to reduce unemployment. The program of the Popular Front, while appearing drastic in the context of French history, did not differ fundamentally from FDR's New Deal—something that Blum openly recognized.

The Matignon Agreements did not, however, stop the strikes. The euphoria of the electoral victory lingered on, and many strikers seemed to doubt that management would implement the agreements in good faith—a thoroughly justified suspicion. At this point it was the communists who most effectively urged workers to be satisfied with the gains already achieved. By the end of June the strikers finally relented.

Thus the first accomplishments of the Popular Front in France were in the area of labor relations, although the unifying force behind the Front and its most urgent concern was the defense of democracy against fascism. This primary goal was satisfied by legislation that dissolved the various fascist organizations that had participated in the riots of February 1934. (They soon reappeared as political parties, however, which made them harder to attack under the constitution.) At any rate, the Popular Front had flexed its muscles, not only with this anti-fascist legislation but also with its impressive majority vote and the June strikes.

In dealing with the international situation Blum was from the outset less successful. In March, just before the Popular Front had assumed power, Hitler had taken his biggest and most successful gamble, remilitarizing the Rhineland. This daring move, made in opposition to advice from Germany's military leaders and in flagrant violation of Germany's treaty obligations, allowed Hitler to transform the military situation in Europe, to the immeasurable advantage of Germany. With the Rhineland fortified and secure from any invasion from France, a whole range of new options for eastward expansion opened up to Germany. France's military agreements with various eastern Europe states lost much of their credibility, since the French army could no longer rapidly reach Germany's industrial heartland in the event of war on Germany's eastern borders.

The caretaker government in France in March, which was only holding power until the spring elections, had not felt up to a confrontation with Germany on this issue, and once Blum took over it was judged too late to do anything effective. At any rate, even the powerful Popular Front coalition was not ready to face the prospect of war with Germany. So German military forces remained in the Rhineland. But soon another international crisis faced Blum, which he could not similarly disregard.

In July Generalissimo Francisco Franco raised the banners of revolt against Spain's own Popular Front, which had been formed in the early part of 1936. Within a short time, the situation in Spain threatened to develop into something like the Balkan crisis of 1914, embroiling all of Europe. From the standpoint of the fundamental goal of the Popular Front, it seemed obvious that Blum's government should offer whatever aid was necessary to defeat Franco. Yet, as Mussolini and Hitler began to aid the Spanish dictator, a general European war between the forces of democracy and fascism became a distinct possibility.

The cause of French intervention on the side of the Spanish Republic was not a popular one in France, especially outside of the parties of the Left. Even among those parties, support for the republican Loyalists was divided and often lukewarm. Conservatives were disturbed by the social revolution that was developing under the auspices of the Spanish Popular Front. Catholics were appalled—and indeed so were most Frenchmen of humane sentiments—by the anarchist atrocities against the Church (such as the dynamiting of ancient cathedrals and the rape of nuns). Fear of another general European war was especially strong among the socialists and Radicals, who were inclined to think that no threat, not even the victory of fascism, could justify dragging France into another round of the endless slaughter of trench warfare.

Blum himself, while not quite the weak and indecisive intellectual that hostile observers believed him to be, was nevertheless deeply torn between his own revulsion against war and the obvious need for a tough-minded solidarity of the Left in Europe as a whole. His foreign policy options had drastically narrowed since Hitler's remilitarization of the Rhineland; now, more than ever, France depended upon British support in the foreign policy area. In a way France's dependence upon Britain was convenient for Blum and his government since they could shift responsibility for their own inability to make decisions onto the shoulders of the British Conservative government, and that government had no taste whatsoever for fighting on the side of the Spanish Popular Front, or for giving it aid.

The British favored a policy of non-intervention in Spain, and this was the policy that Blum finally agreed to. He proposed that all powers stay out of Spain and let the Spanish solve their own problems. The resulting Non-Intervention Pact was signed by the major concerned parties—Germany, Italy, France, Russia, and England. France and England respected the pact, but Germany and Italy flouted it, as then did the Soviet Union. The nazis even stepped up their aid in weapons and military advisers, using the occasion of the Spanish Civil War to provide experience for German officers and to test new weapons.

The French government was unwilling to copy the fascists' blatant cynicism regarding signed treaties. But this unwillingness was not the most fundamental difficulty. What emerged with growing clarity in the first year of the Popular Front was that France's population was too deeply divided to permit her leaders to take effective action. Even if France had been better prepared militarily, even if the remilitarization of the Rhineland had not occurred, there is good reason to conclude that the country's internal divisions doomed it to what the French termed *attentisme*, a postponement of decisions because they threatened civil war within France itself.

Blum found decision making nearly impossible even in the economic area, where the Matignon Agreements had at first seemed to set a bracing precedent. The business and financial community was so hostile to him that it was ready to go to any length to undermine his position. Even if Blum had enjoyed greater confidence among bankers and businessmen, he would still have had great difficulty in dealing with the legacy of previous depression cabinets that had little notion of what was to be done about the economy and had tried to work with inadequate powers of taxation, thus incurring a growing governmental debt. The hostility to Blum of the monied class, who hoarded their gold and sent money abroad, merely compounded Blum's predicament by draining France of the financial reserves necessary to implement his economic programs. Even Blum's working-class supporters increased his economic troubles because with the forty-hour week (which was accompanied by a great deal more goldbricking than before), with the salary increases, and with the paid vacations, labor was less productive and profit margins sagged. Lower profit margins meant less potential income, in the form of taxes, for the government. By October 1, 1936, Blum was forced to break one of his election promises by devaluing the franc (generally viewed as a conservative economic measure), and in February 1937 he in a sense acknowledged defeat by declaring a "pause" in the implementation of the Popular Front program. The pause was a recognition that many of the clauses of the Matignon Agreements had not been fully implemented from the beginning, and that in any case France could not afford them, given the economic conditions and political climate of the time.

By early 1937 the excitement and élan of June 1936 had almost completely dissipated, not only because of the economic disappointments but because of the deep divisions brought to light by the Civil War in Spain. Blum's government lingered on until June 1937, but it was never able again to regain its June 1936 confidence and vigor. A Radical-led government, still basing itself on the Popular Front majority, took power for most of the following year, contenting itself with what was in effect an unofficial continuation of Blum's pause. Further attempts by Blum to restore and even broaden his government of June 1936 in the name of national security because of the rising aggressivity of France's neighbors came ultimately to nothing, because the Right in France wanted nothing to do with him. Many were ready to chant "Better Hitler than Blum!"

THE COLLAPSE OF INTERNATIONALISM: THE SPANISH CIVIL WAR AND THE NAZI-SOVIET PACT

The defeat of the armies of the Spanish Republic in early 1939 and the subsequent signing of the Nazi-Soviet Pact in August of that year marked a cruel end to the already battered international solidarity of the Popular Front era. Indeed, these two events put into question many of the most fundamental beliefs and commitments of socialists and communists. These years of fascist triumph after triumph represent the most gloomy, confusing, and seemingly hopeless period that internationalists and social revolutionaries had ever had to face.

The course of the Spanish Civil War and the decisive years immediately preceding it were dizzying in their complexity. Any civil conflict is inherently chaotic, but repeated uprisings, pronunciamentos, strikes, cabinet crises, and bitter factionalism seem especially to characterize the Spanish situation. The profusion of socialist factions alone—CNT, FAI, UGT, PSUC, POUM, to name some of the more important—easily taxes the patience of the uninitiated. Moreover, the passionately opposed interpretations of the events of those years make an intelligible and balanced account particularly difficult to give in a few pages.

From the standpoint of the history of socialism it is vital to note that certain areas of Spain were experiencing a social revolution of major dimensions, in many ways comparable to Russia's experience from 1917 to 1920. George Orwell, in his *Homage to Catalonia*, captured the mood of late 1936 in Barcelona:

Practically every building of any size had been seized by the workers and was draped with red flags or the red and black flags of the Anarchists; every wall was scrawled with the hammer and sickle. . . . Every shop and café had an inscription saying that it had been collectivized; even the bootblacks had been collectivized and their boxes painted red and black. Waiters and shop-walkers looked you in the face and treated you as an equal. . . . There were no private motor cars, they had all been commandeered, and all the trams and taxis . . . were painted red and black. . . . Loudspeakers were bellowing revolutionary songs all day and far into the night. . . . Practically everyone wore rough working-class clothes or blue coveralls or some variant of the militia uniform. [Pp. 4–5]

The official Spanish Popular Front government, like the Russian Provisional Government in 1917, was embarrassed by social upheaval on this scale and did what it could to dampen the spontaneous actions of the masses. Political authority was distintegrating, and Spain's propertied classes and previous ruling elites—most of whom eventually supported Franco—were all-too-often corrupt and inefficient. The country was economically backward, with a few areas of relatively advanced industrial development (Barcelona was one of them, and like Petrograd was a center of revolutionary activity), but otherwise peasant agriculture prevailed. National minorities were agitating for autonomy or independence. Among those at all attracted to revolutionary notions, a kind of indigenous anarchism exercised the greatest appeal. Although compared to the bolsheviks in 1917 the Spanish communists were weak, even here the parallels are suggestive. The bolsheviks, beginning as a party with a small following and little influence in February 1917, came to gain control over most key institutions of power by the early autumn; similarly, the Spanish communists came from modest beginnings to exercise a growing power over the institutions of government, resorting to a ruthlessness which exceeded even that of the bolsheviks in 1917.

There was one major difference between the two situations: In 1917–20 the bolsheviks identified themselves with a spontaneous revolution; in 1936–39, the Spanish communists did everything they could to slow and even reverse social revolution, in the name of preserving the Popular Front coalition against Franco. Social revolution threatened to alienate the petty bourgeois and bourgeois elements of the Popular Front, and thus effective and anti-fascist warfare and social revolution could not go on at the same time—or at least so the communists believed.

Coupled with this belief was the communist assertion that only with greater discipline and centralization could the war be effectively waged. And it was largely in the guise of this effort to wage war effectively that the communists won support and increasing institutional power. Since Soviet Russia was the only country willing to supply the Republican forces with the materials of war, the communists gained considerable leverage over how the war was to be waged.

Spanish communists were strengthened also by the influx of foreign communists, usually as members of the so-called International Brigades. The Brigades were composed of left-wing activists who volunteered to fight against fascism in Spain. Prominent among them were communists and socialists whose countries had been taken over by fascists. They were known to fight with a particularly desperate valor, perhaps tinged with a desire to make a final creditable showing, after humiliation in their own countries, but also no doubt because for them there was no turning back, no homeland to which they might return. The famous Thälmann and Garibaldi batallions, composed of German and Italian émigrés, distinguished themselves in several key battles, and of the original volunteers appallingly few survived. But young idealists from France (representing the largest contingent), Great Britain, the United States, and some fifty other countries sacrificed their lives in great numbers.

Inextricably mixed into the larger anti-fascist struggle were the sordid and brutal struggles between communists and non-Stalinist Marxists of the POUM (the Party of Marxist Unification, often termed "Trotskyist," but in fact having no formal connections with Trotsky). The non-Stalinists were treated in Spain much as were dissident communists in Russia at about the same time. They were subject to arrests in the night, denial of due process, and summary executions and accused of wildly improbable acts of collaboration with the fascist enemy.

This disturbing contrast between the communists' selfless heroism and the most abased treachery suggests a larger one in the Spanish revolution itself. Orwell, like many foreign volunteers, came away from Spain with memories of a warm and touchingly generous Spanish common people, but he could not ignore that these same Spaniards seemed to lapse easily into gullibility, suspiciousness, mendacity, and a stunning cruelty—attitudes which again suggest interesting parallels with Russia. After six months in Spain, during which he suffered a grave wound at the front, he confessed to "an overwhelming desire to get away from it all; away from the horrible atmosphere of political suspicion and hatred, from streets thronged with armed men, from air-raids, trenches, machine-guns, screaming trams, milkless tea, oil cookery, and shortage of cigarettes—from almost everything that I had learned to associate with Spain" (p. 200). Since he had been connected with the POUM, he very nearly did not make it out of Spain.

The communist efforts to discipline the Loyalist forces, bolstered by Soviet aid, could not overcome the superiority of Franco's armies, aided as they were by German and Italian intervention and by the strong support of the Spanish officer caste. Franco slowly tightened his grip, achieving final victory in early 1939. In the inevitable recriminations that followed this defeat, spokesmen for the anarchists and POUM insisted that communist influence, rather than increasing the effectiveness of the Republic's armies, contributed to their defeat. These spokesmen argued that, aside from the obvious point that Stalinist repressions removed from the front thousands of men who were by almost any standard selfless soldiers in the battle against fascism, the Spanish common people lost interest in the war when they realized that victory would entail the preservation of private property and the bourgeois class system. Such spokesmen—and many observers since, from the scholarly to the (often) shrilly partisan—have professed to believe that convinced revolutionaries represented such an overwhelming majority of the Spanish masses that the anti-Franco forces could have never been defeated so long as they believed that social revolution would accompany military victory. The initial blundering and military ineptness, this school argues, were passing and relatively insignificant matters, which were much exaggerated by the communists for their own devious purposes.

Such claims are of course inherently difficult to prove or disprove, but in considering them a larger question looms: What *were* communist purposes in Spain? Were they simply to defeat fascism, or did more complex and sinister motives finally become decisive? (For example, to draw the war out for as long as possible, in hopes of drawing in France and Great Britain and assuring that general war break out in the West.) The signing of the Nazi-Soviet Pact in August 1939, establishing a military alliance between Germany and Russia, with secret provisions for the partition of Poland, convinced many that indeed sinister motives had been at work.

News of the Pact hit the western democracies like a bombshell, and subsequently its ratification has been described as one of the most stunningly cynical acts of modern times, a deal between two rapacious totalitarian dictators to divide up the lands of their neighbors. Yet, this is not the only possible or plausible explanation.

In interpreting the Pact much depends on the extent to which one believes that Stalin, even from the early 1930s, hoped and schemed for a German alliance, to revive the Russo-German entente negotiated at Rapallo in 1922. Similarly, one's interpretation of the Pact depends on how much he believes that Stalin was ever genuinely interested in cooperation with the western democracies, or collective action through the League of Nations, or western diplomatic alliances, or the Popular Front strategy.

Obviously, Stalin went along with a western, anti-German orientation for a time, but as earlier noted it is arguable that he did so only because he saw no other immediate option, and because other members of the Soviet hierarchy (who would not be totally out of Stalin's way until 1939) effectively intervened in favor of such an orientation. It has even been suggested that the Soviet dictator discouraged the KPD in early 1933 from resisting Hitler and that he in effect made a "gift" of the KPD to Hitler in order to avoid a bloody nazi-communist showdown and an unnecessary poisoning of Russo-German relations. Akin to this line of reasoning is the assertion that even after the initiation of the Popular Front strategy by the Comintern in 1935, Stalin continued to hope and plan for a Russo-German détente. Thus his covert intention was to stay on Hitler's good side while at the same time trying to engage Germany and the western democracies in another war like that of 1914–18—so that after years of exhausting warfare in the West, Russia would be in a position to pick up the pieces. Even in Spain, the argument goes, Stalin's hopes centered around drawing France and England into a general war in the west.

If one subscribes to some variety of this reasoning, then the Nazi-Soviet Pact was merely the predictable, culminating act of duplicity by a cunning and unscrupulous Russian dictator, a man whose anti-fascism had nothing to do with the humane traditions from which communism had sprung. Therefore western statesmen were naive to hope for any sincere or lasting Soviet commitment to a unification of the Left against the fascists.

However, the argument can easily be turned around, for duplicity, bad faith, and suspicion had characterized western as well as Soviet attitudes since the time of the Revolution. Many western leaders would have been satisfied to see an exhausting conflict between Nazi Germany and Soviet Russia, and Stalin was ever alert to the possibility that western statesmen might try to divert Hitler's armies eastward. Similarly, at the same time that western leaders suspected that Stalin's intentions in Spain were to encourage the outbreak of general war in western territory, western reticence to aid the Republic strengthened the hand of those in Russia who doubted the firmness or reliability of anti-fascism in the West.

In a related but more subtle way, doubts in Russia about the viability of a pro-western strategy were no doubt fed by the profound instability of the Popular Front coalition in Spain, whose members very often seemed to hate one another more than they did Franco. Russian communists might also have begun to wonder, with some justification, whether France was an ally worth having in the event of a new world war, since the Popular Front had uncovered profound social divisions in France, which hamstrung France's leaders. And of what value was the Franco-Soviet Treaty of 1935 after the French allowed the Germans to remilitarize the Rhineland?

The ensuing policy of appeasement of Hitler—which, took many forms, the most dramatic of which were allowing the *Anschluss* with Austria and signing the Munich Agreements—could only feed Russian suspicions that western statesmen were subtly encouraging Hitler eastward, especially since the Russians, who were certainly interested parties, were not even invited to participate in the Munich negotiations.

Even if we see appeasement in the West in the least cynical (and probably most accurate) light—that is, assume that western statesmen wanted desperately to avoid war and were willing to go to almost any length toward that goal—the Russians still had real cause for anxiety, since this kind of western pacifism, if it did not intentionally push Hitler eastward, nevertheless left the way to the east open for Germany. Of course the Russians and their western communist supporters were not inclined to accept the least cynical interpretation; they saw malicious intent. After Munich the French communists publically accused western policy makers of trying to turn Germany on Russia. And as western diplomats in 1939 apparently continued to drag their feet in negotiating a new anti-German treaty with Russia to oppose Hitler's new demands, this time having to do with former German territories in Poland, communist suspicions became ever more heightened.

Much ink has been spilled in arguing which of the major powers must take the most responsibility for the failure to achieve an anti-German Anglo-Franco-Russian alliance after Munich. The assumption is that had this treaty been signed, Hitler could have been stopped earlier and with a less gruesome price in blood. Those who accept the idea that Stalin from the beginning was looking for a chance to make a deal with Hitler see Soviet diplomatic negotiations with France and England in 1939 as mere window dressing, or as a tactical maneuver to stimulate a response from Germany. Those who defend the Soviet Union point to the unseemly slowness of western negotiators and the apparent unwillingness of the western powers to put pressure on Poland and its Baltic neighbors to allow the Red Army to move troops into their territory. Of course these countries, having only recently freed themselves from the Russian yoke—and now being militantly anti-communist to boot—were not enthusiastic about the stationing of Russian troops on their lands, since they felt that this would be only the first step in a new subservience to Russia. And there is little doubt that their fears were well grounded. Yet defense against Germany was hardly feasible unless Russian troops were moved to the German border, and indeed unless some unity of command were instituted between the Red Army and the armies of these countries.

Here we come to the crux of the matter, and it is related to a point much repeated in this and the previous section: Hitler's opponents in 1939 were still too deeply divided to oppose him effectively. Conceivably France, England, and Russia could have swallowed their mutual suspicions for the moment in order to block Hitler, but for Poland and Russia to have cooperated was far less conceivable. Indeed, in the final analysis most Poles, like most other eastern Europeans, feared and hated Nazi Germany less than Soviet Russia. Even in France and England much of the political Right believed Hitler to be preferable to Stalin.

Such being the case, *both* Russia and the West must have sensed the impossibility of their forming an effective alliance against Germany at this time. Certainly the Soviets, who were hardly above restoring to *Realpolitik*—and this is true for the moderates as much as Stalin—must have perceived the virtual impossibility of making this new anti-German coalition work.

Thus one can say that there was good reason for both the West and Russia to negotiate in bad faith, each hoping that Hitler would turn on the other. Moreover, looking at the advantages to Russia of a treaty with Germany, it is easy to see how minds less perverse than Stalin's could have been powerfully attracted to such a treaty. There was, at any rate, nothing in the communist value system that made communists feel deep and lasting commitment to bourgeois democracy, particularly if they thought that bourgeois democrats were trying to turn Nazi Germany on Russia. Even if Russian communists had believed that bourgeois democracy was in every way preferable to fascism, it did not follow that turning Hitler on the West was an inacceptable policy, for a war between fascism and democracy would not have necessarily meant the victory of one or the other but conceivably the exhaustion of both, leading to the ultimate triumph of communism. And the Nazi-Soviet treaty, by turning Hitler westward, was only reversing what it seemed the western powers had been trying to do since at least early 1936. (One is tempted to remark that, had some western diplomat been able so dramatically to turn the tables on communist Russia, he would have been hailed as a hard-headed patriot and diplomatic genius.) Similarly, the Nazi-Soviet Pact allowed Russia to gain Polish territory, move the

Red Army westward, and to enjoy a breathing space in order to prepare for the nazi attack that would come in the event Germany was able to win in the West.

Of course one could blame Soviet policy for unleashing World War II by giving Hitler a "green light" to attack westward, once the Polish territories had been brought under domination (something that was done with lightning speed). This argument carries most force if one believes that Hitler could have been prevented from going to war, a doubtful proposition, and one that Stalin most likely did not believe. One might also argue that without the Nazi-Soviet Pact the war could have been fought under more favorable conditions for Russia and the West, a somewhat more convincing argument, but one that involves too many imponderables to be decisive. From Stalin's standpoint and from the standpoint of the interests of the Soviet Union the most attractive path was to encourage war to break out in the West, with the hope that it remain there as long as possible. That this second goal was dashed, that is, that France collapsed like a house of cards in the face of Nazi Germany, was obviously the cause of much disappointment in Russia. But the Russians must have been asking themselves how would it have been to have formed a binding alliance in the first place with such a militarily disappointing power.

As one can easily imagine, the Nazi-Soviet Pact however much it served Russian national interests was a disaster for western communists, especially the one remaining large party in the West, the French. In terms of international communist doctrine, the pact meant a return to something like the Class-Against-Class tactic, but an even more extreme form of it, for now communists were expected to assert not only that western democracy and fascism were essentially the same but further to affirm that friendly relations between communists and fascists were both possible and desirable. Under the Popular Front the PCF had prospered in an unparalleled fashion: By late 1936 its membership had grown to an amazing 280,000, approximately ten times its lowest figure of the early 1930s. By 1939 it peaked at 350,000, but the 1936 figure meant that for the first time since 1924 the Communist Party was larger than the SFIO (which by the end of 1936 had about 250,000 members, about twice what it had before the Popular Front was instituted). At the same time the communists moved toward control of the reunited labor movement in France. The Nazi-Soviet Pact resulted in a sharp reversal of this trend—in fact Communist Party membership plummeted—and before long the French government began a policy of repression, finally outlawing the PCF, while the party's Popular Front allies heaped vilification upon it.

Evidence indicates that news of the Pact took the French communist leaders by surprise (they were on vacation, and had to return hurriedly to Paris). Their first reactions were not entirely coherent or consistent. Although they defended the pact as the natural culmination of the Munich Agreements and the overall western policy of appeasement, they still asserted that their party would rally to the defense of France. This patriotic attitude lasted for about a month. It became untenable once the Soviet Union had actually cooperated with Nazi Germany in the partition of Poland. Now the French communists were obliged to defend Nazi-Soviet cooperation, and thus view Germany as in some sense a friendly power. The PCF became *le parti étranger*, the "foreign party," one that had overtly chosen the interests of the Soviet fatherland over those of France. When war broke out between France and Germany, the PCF denounced it as nothing more than a conflict of rival imperialisms, unworthy of the support of French workers, who should pressure their government to sue for peace along the lines of the Nazi-Soviet Pact (that is, to recognize the partition of Poland, which had been the immediate cause for the outbreak of World War II). With France's defeat, the leaders of the PCF went so far as to approach the German occupiers with the proposal that the communist newspaper, *L'Humanité*, be published legally. Their assumption was that allowing publication would be to the advantage of the nazis because the communists would advocate cooperation with them. Shortly before this, Molotov, the Soviet Foreign Minister, had conveyed the warmest congratulations of his country to the Germany foreign minister on the brilliant victory of Germany's armed forces over France.

After failing to bring the British to their knees through massive bombardment and air warfare, Hitler cast aside the Pact and turned on the Soviet Union in June 1941. And at first it seemed that the Germans would accomplish an easy victory: They plunged deep into Soviet territory, encountering an ill-prepared and apparently surprised Red Army. Yet, aided by particularly harsh Russian winters, Russia's armies began to show what the five year plans had accomplished toward building up the country for industrial warfare. In January of 1943, at the great battle of Stalingrad, the nazis met a decisive defeat, and thereafter they were mostly on the defensive.

The nazi attack on Russia once again reversed the relationship of communists, inside and outside of Russia, to western democrats. Great

Britain and Russia quickly formed an alliance, and in countries like France that were under the nazi heel, communists now took an active— and often leading—part in the Resistance. Once again it was possible for communists to associate their cause with the cause of nationalism. Coalitions of anti-fascists, now usually broader from those of the Popular Front, grew up in most countries, and in nearly every instance communists were even more active in them than they had been during the Popular Front era.

Inside Russia the communist leadership did everything in its power to rally the non-communist masses, many of whom, especially in the border areas such as the Ukraine, at first welcomed the nazis as liberators. Thus, pronouncements from the Kremlin strictly toned down any mention of class conflict or international social revolution. In Russia the Second World War became known as the "Great Patriotic War." The communists successfully identified their cause with that of Mother Russia in the centuries-old German-Russian confrontation, often evoking the language of the tsars and the Orthodox religion. In line with all of this, and in a move particularly designed to re-assure Russia's western allies, the Comintern was dissolved in 1943.

A new stage of development in the history of communism had now arrived, one dominated by anti-German nationalism far more than by class conflict and the vision of proletarian revolution. And from the dissolution of the Comintern in 1943 until around 1949, the cause of communism was to see its period of greatest expansion, not only in Europe but also—indeed most spectacularly—in Asia. Russia's victory at Stalingrad and the subsequent march of the Red Army into central Europe in a sense vindicated the many sacrifices and compromises of communists in the past generation and greatly enhanced the appeal of communism for a new generation in both eastern and western Europe.

GUIDE TO FURTHER READING

While the general subject of fascism has of course an extensive literature, the reaction of socialists and communists to it has been the subject of relatively few monographs. Many of the books mentioned in the bibliographical essays for chapters 5 through 7 contain useful chapters on the challenge of fascism, particularly those by Sturmthal, Landauer, Hunt, Gulick, Cammett, Cohen, Halperin, Colton, and Ziebura, to name the more obvious. Although Spriano's second volume of his history of the Italian Communist Party (entitled *Gli anni della clandestinità*) sees matters, as earlier noted, from the vantage point of a card-carrying party member, it is still full of interesting material. Karl D. Bracher's study of the collapse of the Weimar Republic, *Die Auflösung der Weimarer Re-*

publik. Eine Studie zum Problem des Machtverfalls in der Demokratie, has much valuable information on both the KPD and SPD and their attitudes to nazism. Detlev Peukert's *Die KPD im Widerstand: Verfolgung und Untergrundarbeit an Rhein und Ruhr 1933 bis 1945* is an example of an effort to write history "from below," on a subject that has so far seen very little of it. Peukert's is a sympathetic but not uncritical study. While probably too laboriously detailed for most students, it has some valuable chapters and an extensive bibliography.

On the Popular Front, aside from the above-mentioned works by Colton and Ziebura (which deal with Léon Blum), the following scholarly monographs can be recommended: Nathaniel Greene, *Crisis and Decline: The French Socialist Party in the Popular Front Era*; and David Brower, *The New Jacobins: The French Communist Party and the Popular Front*. An older account, still valuable, is Henry W. Ehrmann's *French Labor from Popular Front to Liberation*.

George Orwell's *Homage to Catalonia* remains the most vivid first-hand account of the Spanish Civil War. Stanley G. Payne's *The Spanish Revolution* concentrates on the Left and the social revolution in Spain. Murray Bookchin's *The Spanish Anarchists: The Heroic Years, 1868–1936* provides a needed sympathetic treatment of the anarchists. The best general account of the war and revolution is by Pierre Broué and Émile Témime, *The Revolution and the Civil War in Spain*. More controversial but also full of fascinating detail is Burnett Bolloten's *The Spanish Revolution: The Left and Its Struggle for Power during the Civil War*.

Not yet published at the time this book went to press, Helmut Gruber's *International Communism in the Shadow of Fascism* should, if it is on a par with his previous two volumes, be of considerable value.

Socialism and Communism since World War II 9

INTRODUCTION

The thirty-five years following World War II witnessed profound transformations in the conditions affecting European socialism. Soviet Russia emerged as a major power, no longer so isolated and vulnerable but soon faced with a powerful competitor, in the People's Republic of China, for leadership of world communism. Russia's altered situation had major implications for communists and socialists throughout the world. The history of socialism after the war came to coincide more than ever with the more general history of the period, since regimes identifying themselves as socialist ruled over something like two billion people, and included not only the world's second industrial and military power but also its most populous nation.

Whatever its new-found prestige, the communist system in the Soviet Union did not provide a particularly alluring model, at least in many of its details, and as Stalinist control loosened in the late 1950s a multiplicity of variant communist states and parties began to appear, not only in Europe but throughout the world. An even wider variety of perspectives and practices emerged among socialists of a non-communist persuasion, which ranged from new formulations of anarchism to reformist socialism that accepted private property in the means of production, market incentives, and a meritocratic hierarchical society based on material incentives.

This wide and often confusing diversity of socialisms was much influenced by the perplexing problems that emerged once the ruins of war had been rebuilt. In the 1970s the unparalleled persistence of both inflation and economic stagnation, dubbed "stagflation," seemed to defy all previously effective remedies. But even more fundamentally, industrial expansion itself began to present problems that could scarcely have been imagined by the optimistic socialist theoreticians of the nineteenth century. In particular it became difficult to avoid the conclusion that there were definite limits, mostly ecological and demographic, to growth. The paradox facing socialists in the last quarter of the twentieth century was succinctly stated by Robert Heilbroner, in his essay "The Human Prospect" (*New York Review of Books*, July 24, 1974, p. 21): " . . . Even more disturbing than the possibility of a serious deterioration in the quality of life if growth comes to an end is the awareness of a possibly disastrous decline in the conditions of existence if growth does not come to an end."

THE EVOLUTION OF EUROPEAN COMMUNISM, 1945–1982

It was primarily Soviet Russia, not the United States, that wiped out fascism in Europe. As Winston Churchill graphically put it, "the Red Army tore the guts out of the nazi war machine." This was a startling achievement, especially after the series of humiliating defeats suffered by Russia's military forces in the opening campaigns of the war. And for this achievement Russia paid a ghastly price: approximately 20 million dead (more than the dead of all other warring countries combined) and almost complete destruction of some of her richest and most developed territory.

The Red Army's march into eastern and central Europe on the heels of the routed nazi forces, and the subsequent stationing of Russian troops in most of the conquered areas, meant that Soviet Russia could supervise developments in those very territories where prior to the war hatred of Russia and of communism had been particularly intense. But such supervision presented problems to the Russians, for in spite of their stance as anti-fascist liberators, they could not long tolerate any form of truly representative or popular government, for the simple reason that in most cases the population of the recently liberated countries remained both anti-Russian and anti-communist—far more than the areas of American conquest remained anti-American or anti-capitalist. Given the price that Russians had paid for their victory, they were naturally not well disposed to suggestions that they allow enemies to return to control of the countries bordering on Russia. Indeed, even if their victory had not been so costly, they would have likely sought to retain as much power as possible over bordering territories. The Americans were scarcely less determined that, in the areas where they had the power to supervise political developments, control not fall into the hands of those hostile to American interests.

In a few countries, most notably Czechoslovakia, pro-Russian feelings were strong, even among bourgeois democrats, and there conceivably Russian national interest might have been reconciled with popular government. But to do so would have required a delicate balance, difficult to imagine, at least where Russians believed their national security was at stake. Growing tension between the United States and the Soviet Union developed into the so-called Cold War. By early 1948 nearly all of eastern and central Europe had been brought under communist control, and, again in Churchill's words, an "Iron Curtain" had been erected between the countries under Russian domination and those looking to American leadership.

The Cold War had a profound influence on the development of European socialism, from its democratic socialist to its revolutionary communist varieties. The hotly debated arguments concerning the origins of the Cold War both reflected and shaped ideological positions in the immediate postwar years. Conservative scholars and politicians have argued that Soviet Russia, from its inception an expansionist, totalitarian power—similar to Nazi Germany in inner dynamics and motivations—took over eastern and central Europe as part of an overall plan to conquer the world for communism. The Russians would have expanded into western Europe, this argument continues, had not the United Stated intervened. Politicians and scholars of the Left, on the other hand, have usually insisted on the primarily defensive intent of Russia's actions in eastern and central Europe. They have emphasized that in spite of her great victories, Russia had been devastated by the war and was thus extremely weak in comparison to the United States. These left-wing observers have further emphasized that in the immediate postwar period, Russia's deep-seated sense of vulnerability was rekindled by what appeared to its leaders to be unsympathetic and increasingly aggressive attitudes and actions on the part of the United States. Above all the United States's possession of atomic weapons and demonstrated willingness to use them deeply alarmed the Russians. The insistence by American leaders that popularly elected, western-style democratic regimes be established on Russia's western borders convinced the Kremlin that American policy makers hoped to undo Russia's victories and to extend American political power and economic influence in all of the recently conquered territories, in both western and eastern Europe.

This is obviously not the place to examine in depth the history of the Cold War. Suffice it to note that Russian motives, even before the bolshevik takeover, have rarely been clear. Without access to Soviet archives, a scholarly treatment of Soviet designs after the war is difficult, if not impossible. Efforts to explain Soviet actions—or indeed the actions of Nazi Germany—in terms of some abstract model of totalitarianism have attracted a growing and persuasive body of scholarly dissent. At any rate, Russian expansionism as such need not have been impelled by the dynamics of totalitarianism or even the messianism of Marxist ideology. Simple desire for national aggrandizement—or perhaps a complex mix of that desire and Marxist idealism—is quite sufficient to explain Russian actions.

The archival sources pertaining to the formulation of American policy have been much more accessible. In part the decisions of American policy makers seem to have been made in response to an overriding concern to consolidate their country's control of world markets in order to find outlets for its rapidly expanding productivity, which had been so stimulated by the war, and to avoid a recurrence of the economic chaos of the 1930s. These and related American objectives repeatedly ran afoul of what Soviet policy makers considered their country's national interest.

Quite aside from these issues of fundamental national interest, the path of conciliation and cooperation with Stalin, a dictator of proven duplicity and ruthlessness, was one of great difficulty in practical terms. Such was above all the case in a country like the United States, whose population was unaccustomed to offical positions of Realpolitik. Millions of American voters of eastern European background considered Stalin to be an oppressor and murderer of their former countrymen—and hardly without justification. They were not much impressed with arguments that the preservation of world peace required flexibility in dealing with Stalin; their votes joined with those of millions of other Americans who considered Russian communism to be an evil beyond measure. Thus those American politicians who espoused a hard line in relation to Russia found the most ardent popular support.

In more general terms, harmony between these two giant powers would have required most superhuman diplomatic and political adroitness. The very fact that now only two major powers existed, instead of the former multiplicity of roughly equal powers, threw Russia and the United States into an unprecedentedly intense relationship of opposition and competition. Even if a country with a long history of friendship with the United States had emerged after the war to challenge American leadership in the world, hostility would likely have developed.

Friendly relations and effective communication were all the more difficult between the United States and the Soviet Union because of their profoundly different historical experience, geopolitical situations, economic systems, and general cultures.

Inside Russia and the East Bloc countries (that is, those that fell under Russian domination between 1945 and 1948) the implications of the Cold War were particularly unfortunate and seemed to be linked more to Stalin's paranoiac personality than to concern for Russian national security. It appeared that the nightmarish years of 1936–39 were about to repeat themselves. This time, instead of Trotskyism, it was Titoism that supposedly presented a death threat to communist survival and thus had to be exterminated root and branch.

Titoism implied something broader than fidelity to Tito; it represented a communism that was not directly under Russian control. Ironically, Tito, the leader of the communist regime in Yugoslavia, had had the reputation prior to the war of being a dogmatic Stalinist. But his experience as leader of the victorious Partisans in his country's war against the nazis and in its civil war apparently tempered him. He emerged as the most broadly popular communist leader since Lenin. Even before the Cold War Tito had begun to show an independent streak, more significantly in making social revolution part of the wartime program of his Partisans, whereas the official line from Moscow was to play down the issue of revolution and to wage war in cooperation with all anti-fascists, whatever their political and social background.

The Partisan victory in Yugoslavia was achieved without significant help from the Red Army, which, although it passed through the north of the country, did not remain there after the war. Thus Yugoslav communists enjoyed an unusual independence and self-reliance. Indeed they made so bold as to complain about the conduct of the Soviet troops that passed through Yugoslavia. (Russian soldiers had, among other offenses, raped Yugoslav women.) And the Yugoslavs further protested when they learned that Soviet secret police agents, without making any effort to notify their Yugoslav counterparts, were at work in Yugoslavia.

Stalin was piqued by these complaints, and, as other areas of friction began to emerge, he resolved to be rid of these "troublesome idealists," as he called them. Certainly in any other eastern European country the communist leadership could not have long survived his disfavor. But Tito's great personal prestige inside Yugoslavia made it impossible for Stalin's agents to dislodge him through maneuvers within the Yugoslav party. All other expedients, such as economic blockade and military pressure, also failed. Stalin was forced to recognize that short of actual military invasion he was stymied. But military invasion would have been full of danger for Russia: The Yugoslav Partisans were battle-hardened and quite ready to fight, while Yugoslavia's long coastline meant that aid from the West could be effectively brought to bear (as was not the case in nearly all other communist countries).

Having failed in Yugoslavia, Stalin went to absurd lengths elsewhere. The murderous paranoia that seems to have motivated him in the 1930s now revived. It is quite likely that "Titoism," in the form of a desire by eastern Europe communist leaders for greater independence in dealing with local problems, was indeed making headway. From 1949 through 1952 show trials and mass arrests spread through the East Bloc countries. Anyone who had been active in the communist movement before 1939 or had spent time in the West—particularly as a member of the International Brigades in the Spanish Civil War—was now likely to be arrested, just as in the late 1930s nearly all of those who had been members of the party during the revolution were purged.

Stalin's death in 1953 ended, or at least significantly relaxed, these trends. His successors strove gradually to dismantle his machinery of terroristic despotism. Key measures were the removal of Lavrenti Beria, the feared head of the secret police (who was suddenly arrested and charged with having been a spy for the past thirty years!), and the subsequent reorganization of Russia's security apparatus so that it could be more adequately supervised. A large number of amnesties and rehabilitations were granted, and the forced labor camps run by the secret police were curtailed and put under normal state control.

While these measures seemed to promise a new respect for the rule of law in Russia, the new leaders of the Communist Party had only limited reforms in mind. They also seem to have differed sharply on which reforms were necessary. Few if any contemplated loosening the party's grip on all important aspects of Russian life, the judiciary included, and indeed many among them wished to move only slightly from established Stalinist practices.

Of Stalin's lieutenants who vied for power in the years immediately following his death, N. S. Khrushchev was among the more strongly inclined to a decisive break with former policies. At the Twentieth Party Congress in February 1956, Khrushchev delivered a six-hour, emotion-filled speech, entitled "On the Cult of Personality and Its Consequences." The speech related the details of Stalin's rise to absolute power with an accuracy and frankness unknown to the party for over a generation. In vivid language Khrushchev described how Stalin had used the secret police for tortures and brainwashing techniques to force confessions to crimes that were never committed; how dedicated communists innocent of any crime were arrested and sent to prison camps; how Stalin's extreme suspiciousness threw Russia into a maelstrom of denunciations, purges, and show trials.

Khrushchev's exposé of Stalin's rule nevertheless respected certain boundaries. For example, he did not condemn the collectivization of agriculture or the five year plans, or even the methods used to implement them. Similarly, he made no effort to rehabilitate such major bolshevik dissidents as Trotsky, Zinoviev, or Bukharin. He did not jettison the basic notion of world revolution, although he did break with Stalinist theory by asserting that war with the imperialist powers was no longer inevitable and that different countries had a right to seek out different roads to socialism—which implied a truce with Tito and a gentler domination of other communist lands in eastern Europe.

These new positions required much boldness from Khrushchev, and significantly his speech was delivered to a secret session of the congress. Not even a summary of its contents was made available to the Russian population at large. Those who believed that his efforts constituted a dangerously radical experiment saw their fears confirmed when unrest linked to demands for greater independence got out of control in the East Bloc countries. In Hungary shifts in leadership and party policy led by October 1956 to a violent uprising, spearheaded by workers and students, with strong popular support. The program of the leaders of the uprising went beyond a demand for greater independence in the building of communism; they wanted free elections and democratic institutions on western patterns. No Soviet leader could accept this, and Khrushchev used considerable brutality in putting down the uprising.

The events in 1956 in Hungary, as well as in Poland (discussed below), represented the most serious internal challenge that the bolsheviks had faced since the Kronstadt rebellion of 1921, and in the spring of 1957 those in the party who held Khrushchev responsible tried to depose him. He had numerous opponents within the party on a range of other issues, but the implications of his denunciation of Stalin were perhaps the most wide-ranging: He was putting into question the whole notion of the "leading role"—or, more bluntly, the infallibility—of the Bolshevik Party, which had been so carefully cultivated over the past three or four decades. Although he himself did not voice such conclusions, Khrushchev was implying that the party in its leading role was not only fallible but had been tragically wrong; communists in the rest

of the world should naturally scrutinize the party's pronouncements far more critically in the future.

Khrushchev's opponents failed to bring him down, and in future years the notion of the leading role of the party did indeed suffer further decline. This was due, however, not merely to Khrushchev's denunciation of Stalinism. Communist China had risen as a competitor to the Soviet Union in ideological matters, and the initial tensions between the two communist giants turned into seething hostility. The Chinese reviled the Russians as "Revisionists," "Economists," "imperialists," and even "fascists" (to say nothing of the unofficial Chinese description of Khrushchev as a "bald-headed idiot").

Khrushchev's fall from power in 1964, under a hail of criticism from his former protégés—but without bloodshed—inevitably furthered the process of exposing Russia's leaders as prone to error. Russian leaders after Khrushchev, led by Leonid Brezhnev, have shown themselves to be sober and conservative men. They have disdainfully avoided the kind of colorful if vulgar histrionics to which Khrushchev was prone. Compared to such figures as Lenin, Trotsky, or Bukharin, they come across as gray bureaucrats—cautious, limited, aging, and uninspiring. Above all they seem distrustful of radical change or passionate dissent.

Their policies in eastern Europe have been consistent with the themes of bureaucratic caution, fear of radical change, and vigilant concern for Russian national interest. Yet the forces unleashed by Stalin's death and Khrushchev's denunciation of Stalinism have not been contained: The countries of the East Bloc have continued to edge toward various forms of national communism. Indeed, it is easy to overlook that the violent repressions in Hungary in the autumn of 1956 were preceded by major efforts to conciliate nationalist communists, efforts that Khrushchev's successors could scarcely hope to reverse in any full sense. Khrushchev seems to have hoped that his denunciations of Stalin in February of that year might mollify simmering unrest in the East Bloc, might shift the blame for earlier injustices entirely onto the shoulders of Stalin. His speech was followed up by a number of gestures, including a conciliatory meeting with Tito in June, to signify Russian toleration of different roads to communism.

Very shortly after Khrushchev's meeting with Tito, working-class riots broke out in Poznan, Poland. These led to major concessions and promises of reform by the leaders of the Polish Communist Party, itself still in the throes of internal upheaval. Wladislaw Gomulka, earlier a victim of Stalinist purges but now returned as party leader, played a key role in persuading Khrushchev that Poland's proposed reforms (which included abandoning collectivized agriculture) offered no threat to Russian national interest and that the Polish party remained faithful to the Soviet Union. It was only after this—and no doubt partly because of Gomulka's success—that events got out of hand in Hungary.

The Hungarian tragedy certainly put a damper on reformist enthusiasms elsewhere, but most of the new leaders who had come in to replace the discredited Stalinists remained in place, although in many instances their rule soon became nearly as oppressive as that of their predecessors. Such was the case even with Gomulka. It was also true of the new Czechoslovakian party leader, Antonin Novotny, who was popular when he took over in 1957, but was increasingly challenged by reformers in the 1960s because of his stiff and centralized rule.

In the spring of 1968 Novotny, in a complex party shuffle, was replaced by Alexander Dubček, who was associated with the reformers. Although Dubček's credentials as a sincere communist, deeply loyal to the Soviet Union, could not be seriously questioned, he oversaw a series of liberalizing reforms that strikingly broke away from previously existing communist party practice. He called it "communism with a human face" (an ambiguous phrase, in that it implied that communism had not previously had a human face). It meant a more open and tolerant communist rule, one that retained socialization of the means of production. It would be a kind of soviet system, but far less centralized and authoritarian, and capable of generating real support from the great majority of the population. This was close to the ideal of earlier revolutionaries like Rosa Luxemburg, but it was an ideal that heretofore had remained distant from reality, even in Tito's Yugoslavia.

As might be imagined, after the seemingly endless disappointments associated with socialism and communism since 1917, this "Prague Spring" was greeted with enormous enthusiasm, not only in Czechoslovakia but on the left throughout western Europe, indeed throughout the world. But at the same time Dubček's reforms disquieted the Russians and the other leaders of the East Bloc, especially in the directly neighboring lands. They could not afford such openness nor could they hope for such popularity. They feared that demands for similar reforms might spread into their own countries. After a series of warnings and hurried conferences in the summer of 1968, Dubček seemed to have placated his worried communist neighbors. Then suddenly in August Warsaw Pact troops crashed into the country to depose him forcibly. The Czechoslovak populace resisted peacefully and at times in ingenious ways, but all in vain. Dubček's reforms were brought to an abrupt end.

Those who had admired Dubček were bitterly disappointed. Even communists in the West denounced the invasion. But no effective countermeasures were taken—just as the Russians had calculated. Still, liberalization in East Bloc countries slowly continued. Paradoxically, the country that made the most steady and permanent progress in that direction was Hungary. Janos Kádár, unpopular and even ridiculed by the man on the street in the first few years after his takeover in 1956, gradually proved himself a most capable leader. By the mid to late 1970s Hungary enjoyed a surprisingly open intellectual climate. Probably more important, its economy, gradually and carefully relieved of many of the restraints of centralized management typical elsewhere in the East Bloc, showed genuine strength. Most remarkable of all, Kádár was able to oversee these changes while avoiding major friction with the Russians.

Thus, judged by the developments in the 1960s and 1970s, the rhetoric about different paths to communism, while in many respects bogus, did have some content. Gomulka's reforms gave land to the peasants and allowed the Catholic Church wide leeway. Rumania charted an independent foreign policy, which was grudgingly tolerated by the Russians, partly because communist rule inside Rumania was easily as repressive as in Russia. And of course Yugoslavia continued in its longstanding independent course.

In all East Bloc countries material well-being increased markedly in the 1960s and 1970s. East Germany became one of the world's major economic powers, and its citizens, like those of Hungary, enjoyed a greater range of consumer goods and in general more material comfort than did the citizens of the Soviet Union, although there too notable gains were made.

In the summer of 1980, the Russians faced a new challenge to their authority in the East Bloc. By 1970 Gomulka had, like Novotny, lost his initial popularity through an inept and increasingly repressive rule, and he was brought down in that year. Again, as in 1956, working-class strikes were instrumental in challenging party policy. Gomulka's successor, Edmund Gierek, initially reversed some of the harsher and uglier aspects of his predecessor's rule (Gomulka had, for example, embarked on an anti-Semitic campaign against Poland's few remaining Jews). However, by the end of the decade Gierek and his entourage proved even more unsavory. His ambitious economic projects, depending to an important degree upon borrowing from the West, were ill-conceived and inefficiently operated. As problems emerged, his rule became ever more repressive. It also revealed itself to be astonishingly corrupt. In 1976 Gierek used brutal force in dealing with dock workers in Gdansk, but in 1980, facing strikers in the same city—and the spread of their opposition to other areas—his hold over the country failed almost completely.

This time reform efforts sprang up entirely outside of the party. An organization calling itself "Solidarity," beginning formally as a trade union, rapidly rallied a major part of the Polish working class to its banners. In strike after strike, Solidarity demonstrated its power to an increasingly impotent and panicked party apparatus. As months passed, Solidarity expanded its appeal to the general population. Even the lower and middle ranks of the party itself were infiltrated by Solidarity members, who urged a reform of the party in a more liberal direction. Lech Walesa, at the head of Solidarity, became not only a national hero but a figure who captured the admiration of the world.

Warnings sounding much like those in 1956 and 1968 began to thunder out of Moscow, but Russia's leaders were beset by many problems of their own. Violent repression by Russian forces in Poland promised to be immeasurably bloodier than in Czechoslovakia in 1968 or even Hungary in 1956. Thus the Russians played a waiting game for over a year—far longer than in 1968 or 1956—apparently hoping that the Polish Communist Party could once again gain control over the situation, or that Solidarity would destroy itself. (This latter hope was certainly not implausible, since by late 1981 factionalism within Solidarity was developing into a major problem, and in a more general way Solidarity's heady series of successes had awakened unbounded and often contradictory expectations.)

But this time the party leadership seemed unable to generate even the temporary popular enthusiasm and parallel claim to political legitimacy that had at first accompanied Gomulka's and Gierek's rule. In December 1981, in a surprisingly well-orchestrated move, General Wojciech Jaruzelski arrested Solidarity's leaders and declared martial law, declaring these measures necessary to avert a "national disaster." But although Jaruzelski was thus able to stifle Solidarity's ever-growing pretensions, his military rule was only a stop-gap measure; it did not represent a coherent program of change or needed reform. Moreover, the need for military rule in Poland was intensely embarrassing for the party, which indeed appeared bankrupt. Until this time communist parties had always insisted upon their "leading role" and had kept a tight rein on the military. Did events in Poland set a disturbing precedent for other communist regimes in times of crisis? And could the Polish Communist Party pull itself together enough to take over once again? Whatever the answers to these questions, events in Poland further underlined the point that monolithic communism was a thing of the distant and irretrievable past in Eastern Europe.

Similar remarks apply *a fortiori* to western communist parties. In the post–World War II period they hold our special interest because two of them, the French (PCF) and the Italian (PCI), have grown to impressive dimensions without the intervention of the Red Army or the machinations of the Russian secret police. This is not to ignore that Russia's victory in World War II exercised a powerful influence on people in western Europe; clearly it established Russia and her communist system as the voice of the future in the eyes of many westerners. But indigenous factors, only indirectly related to Russia's victories, played a more important role. In most western countries communists became identified as the backbone of the anti-fascist Resistance, and through the Resistance they were able, even more than had been the case during the Popular Front era, to associate their cause with that of patriotism. At the same time, western communist parties sought to broaden their appeal, particularly to the rural masses, by gradually diluting much of the barricades revolutionism that had characterized the young communist movement and by emphasizing their distance from Russian methods of rule. By the late 1960s there was good reason to question whether western communists were revolutionaries in any rigorous sense, and by the early 1980s most of them had broken decisively with the earlier notion that the Russian Communist Party was the natural leader of or the model for other communist parties.

In most western European countries communists entered into coalition governments at the end of the war. This was again consistent with wartime policy. Similar coalitions were established in those countries that were overrun by the Red Army. In both eastern and western Europe those coalitions were formed in a significantly different context from the anti-fascist coalitions of the Popular Front, for now the prewar ruling elites, particularly the large industrialists, were discredited in most countries for having cooperated with the nazis. Similarly, the postwar coalitions were generally broader than those of the Popular Front, and included even anti-fascist conservatives, as was the case in France with the cabinets under De Gaulle.

With the final defeat of Hitler's armies the mood on the left was euphoric. It is natural to assume that many communists at that time harbored hopes for the long-awaited world revolution, since the old order had been even more thoroughly discredited than after World War I. Yet the available evidence by no means clearly indicates that the communists, especially in western Europe, were at this time plotting a takeover. Indeed, much evidence points in the opposite direction. Many historians have insisted that Stalin, painfully aware of Russia's weakness and vulnerability at the end of the war, initially avoided conflict with the United States. He thus saw to it that communist parties throughout Europe maintained their wartime policy of anti-fascist class cooperation. Although Tito refused to follow Russian directives in these matters, nearly all other European communist leaders went along.

The paradoxical result was that in most western countries the communists, whatever their actual intentions, played a significant role in restoring the much-discredited capitalist system. It is tempting to compare the actions of the PCF and PCI in the year or two following World War II to those of the SFD following World War I, for in both cases these parties assumed the position of preserver of the capitalist old order in crisis, of reformer rather than destroyer of capitalism. The comparison with the SPD is even more appropriate in that the German party following World War I was deterred from a more radical path because its leaders wished to cooperate with the western democracies and understood that the leaders of France, Great Britain, and the United States would not have tolerated social revolution in Germany. At the end of World War II western communists similarly understood that the good will of the Anglo-American military authorities was vital to the reconstruction of their countries and that those authorities had the power to repress any efforts at a communist takeover.

Thus it may be that the communists who participated in the immediate postwar regimes of France and Italy did so as reliable or good-faith partners, both because of directives from Moscow and because there was every indication that efforts to incite revolution would fail. Yet even beyond these factors western communists were aware of the popular appeal of their appearing "responsible." The PCF wished to fully associate itself with the goal of restoring France to its prewar position of a major power. And, because of the special relationship that the French communists had established with France's industrial workers—including control of the largest trade unions—the Communist Party was in a key position to influence industrial productivity, which was itself essential to France's return to prestige and influence after the humiliations of the past decade. The PCF became the "party of production," within the context of the free-market economy and the private ownership of the means of production. (Although a number of major industries were nationalized in France—the nationalizations being made politically easier in those cases where former owners had cooperated with the nazis—the economy remained basically capitalist.) Being "the party of production" meant urging the working class on to greater discipline, harder work, longer hours. Talk of revolution or of other disruptive activities immediately following the war was branded as "sectarianism" by Maurice Thorez and Jacques Duclos, the leaders of the PCF.

In Italy in the spring of 1945 the largely communist-led Resistance made a strong showing in the north, taking control of factories in Milan and Turin, and meting out a summary, bloody justice to tens of thousands of fascists. In Italy's northern provinces the communists could probably have taken full power, but instead communist and other Resistance leaders cooperated with Allied efforts to disarm and control the insurgent masses. The Italian communists, like their French counterparts, entered a coalition cabinet with non-communists, and forcefully presented themselves and their party as leaders of the Italian people, regardless of class, religion, or previous political affiliation. Here also as in France important reforms in economic and institutional life were introduced, but capitalist structure remained. The communists of both France and Italy paradoxically provided their countries' demoralized industrial and financial leaders with a necessary breathing spell, a chance to re-establish themselves—under, of course, an all-important American supervision.

The Cold War put an end to this short but significant stage of communist cooperation. In the spring of 1947 the communists in France and Italy were deprived of their cabinet posts. Simultaneously, non-communists in the Russian-controlled countries were either removed or absorbed into communist parties, as a first step in the total communization of eastern Europe. Thereafter western communists reverted to a disruptive and subversive stance.

Early 1948 was critical. Czechoslovakia, a country that had long identified itself with western democratic traditions and that was no longer occupied by Soviet troops, went over to communist rule. The move was strongly supported by the working masses and only feebly resisted by the non-communists. Communist Czechoslovakia thus began by resembling Yugoslavia, in that its new leaders enjoyed relatively strong popular support. It appeared for a time that Italy as well might join the ranks of these relatively popular communist regimes: The first postwar elections of June 1946, registered about 40 percent for the PCI and the closely allied PSI, and the elections of 1948 seemed to promise further advances for the allied communists and socialists. But American influence, both overt and covert, which was linked to the stabilization of Italy's economy of the preceding three years, was sufficient to prop up the anti-communist forces. Still, the PCI remained strong, consistently polling between a quarter and one-third of the popular vote. Many westerners, perhaps not the most prescient but certainly among the most vocal, believed that a communist takeover continued to be a threat, not only in Italy but in France and in other western European countries.

In retrospect these fears appear exaggerated. Indeed, historical perspective suggests that the years of most extreme Cold War tensions (1947–53) represented an aberration. The overall trend, gradual but unmistakable in the generation following Stalin's death, was for communists throughout Europe, including Russia, to become less revolutionary and more pragmatic, and to seek integration into or cooperation with the capitalist regimes of western Europe.

After Stalin's death we have seen that Kremlin leadership of world communism became distinctly less categorical and overpowering. One of its clearest directives was to de-Stalinize, to move toward greater liberality in relations between communist parties. Another was to abandon the "cult of personality" that had grown up around individual communist leaders within each non-Russian communist party. This was a directive that many western communist parties, particularly the French (who were enduringly the most Stalinistic of the major ones), resisted. Under Stalin a similar reticence by the PCF to follow the line from Moscow would have been nearly inconceivable, but the new rulers in Russia could hardly resort to Stalinist devices in order to induce other communists to de-Stalinize!

The initial stages of de-Stalinization caused much disarray among western communists. They found it necessary to think for themselves about fundamental issues—an activity most of them had little or no practice in—and to apply new and unfamiliar standards in making their decisions. In Stalin's day the interest of the Soviet Union, as defined by Soviet leaders, provided a simple key for all non-Russian communists, and even directives as unpalatable as those given the French communists after the Nazi-Soviet Pact were diligently digested. But after Stalin's death, western communists were provided with less explicit, and often contradictory, directives. An example of the awkwardness of this new relationship can be seen in the 1965 presidential elections in France. The PCF supported the candidate of the left coalition,

François Mitterand, in opposition to De Gaulle. But the Russians were much pleased by De Gaulle's foreign policy, in particular his critical attitude to the United States and his departure from NATO. As election day approached, the leaders of the PCF were astonished and indignant to read a TASS communiqué from Russia urging France's workers to vote for De Gaulle.

Divergences like these multiplied in the 1960s and 1970s. One of the most important of them had to do with Dubček's efforts to liberalize communist rule in Czechoslovakia. As noted, a communist system based on an unprecedented openness and respect for individual rights had an enormous appeal among western communists, who saw in Dubček's regime a most attractive model of how communism might function in a country with a long democratic tradition. The suppression of this heady experiment cut into the potential popular appeal of western communist parties and provoked a deep crisis in communist relations, one that was only slowly and imperfectly patched up. Similarly, the issues raised by Solidarity evoked much sympathy among western communists, and when it was suppressed western communists protested loudly. Such was especially the case with the Italian Communist Party, whose leaders by the early 1980s routinely criticized Russia's leaders in terms that thirty years before had been heard only from intransigent anti-communists. Russia's leaders replied in kind—although the ferocity of the polemics between the Russians and Italians was not so great as that between the Russians and Chinese, when their split first became public.

The rise of Communist China had major and often paradoxical effects on Russia's relations with other communist parties. The Sino-Soviet conflict encouraged détente between Russia and the West, which in turn indirectly stimulated liberalization and differentiation within other communist parties: With tension building on her vast eastern borders, Russia naturally sought to reduce tension on her western borders, both within the East Bloc and in relation to the NATO powers; her toleration of different paths to communism must of course be seen partly in this light, and similarly her efforts to expand friendly contacts with the West were accompanied by more cordial relations between communists and non-communists in most western countries.

Sino-Soviet hostility also opened up the possibility of more cordial relations between China and the United States. China, like the Soviet Union, was concerned to avoid isolation in any further conflict with her former ally. Significantly, it was President Richard M. Nixon, the former Cold Warrior and the darling of the fiercely anti-communist

China Lobby, who took the crucial steps toward the recognition of mainland China. All of this did not abolish anti-communism in the West, but it certainly reduced its Manichean fervor.

Another factor in the 1960s and 1970s that tended to move communists and anti-communists away from the emotional bipolar confrontations of the Cold War was economic interest. The often desperate needs of Russia, eastern Europe, and China for the industrial and agricultural goods produced in the West, linked to westerners' interest in new markets and new investment opportunities, regularly chipped away at the barriers to trade established immediately after the war. Much of the previously referred to economic expansion in communist countries was palpably linked to contacts with the West, and of course the opening up of economic channels unavoidably resulted in the opening up of other kinds of contacts, intellectual, political, social.

By the late 1970s, however, many of the more optimistic expectations growing out of the previous decade of détente were proving unjustified; by the turn of the decade tension between Soviet Russia and the United States began to resemble that of the 1950s. Among the imponderables of the shifting situation were the long-range intentions of the Soviet Union: What did she hope to achieve by moving into Afghanistan? Were her ruling circles deeply afraid of "encirclement" by the United States, Western Europe, China, and Japan? Was she determined, whatever the cost, to win her "place in the sun" in world affairs? (The parallels with Wilhelmine Germany, that other "trouble maker," are obvious and were much commented upon by political observers at the turn of the decade.) Similarly imponderable and no less potentially dangerous were American intentions. Would Soviet "expansionism" provoke a sustained growth in American belligerence and militarism, in belief that American military power should be brought to bear everywhere in the world that a growth in Russian influence was perceived?

In a number of ways, however, the situation of 1981 was not that of 1951. Tensions between the United States and Soviet Russia in 1981 did not generate significant tensions between communists and non-communists in Europe. Indeed, Europeans seemed increasingly inclined to go their own way, and to preserve the fruits of détente. Western European communists were of course quite different in 1981 as compared to 1951. Notions of violent class conflict, of revolutions on the barricades attracted only limited fringe groups or sects, of vaguely anarchist provenance. The communist voter and militant in the West appeared to be no longer attracted to such concepts as proletarian dictatorship, world revolution, or even socialization of the means of production in any rapid or radical fashion. In the 1970s communist parties in western Europe became generally a force for cautious change; they began to cultivate a new respect for the methods of bourgeois democracy and technocratic industrialism. It is doubtful that western European communist parties can even meaningfully be termed Marxist-Leninist anymore.

The Italian Communist Party offers the most advanced example of this new face of communism, as has already been suggested above. Innovativeness might be expected of a party that had long been known as the least Stalinist in western Europe and had, from its beginnings, attracted leaders of unusual imagination, flexibility, and intellectual ability. These were men like Antonio Gramsci and Palmiro Togliatti, the latter of whom led the party in the postwar generation, and Enrico Berlinguer, the leader of the party in the 1970s, who became one of the most respected politicians in Italy.

Italian communists have been elected to office in most of the major cities of Italy; they have earned the reputation of being efficient and relatively uncorrupt administrators, whereas the Christian democrats, their main opponents, who have controlled the national government since the war, have set lamentable standards in those regards. In terms of the dedication and discipline of its followers, to say nothing of its power in the trade-union movement, the Italian Communist Party has long established its superiority to the ruling Christian democrats.

The steady growth in electoral support for the communists in Italy reached a peak in 1975 when the party came within a few percentage points of the Christian democrats. But even though the Christian democrats proved themselves no more capable of effective and honest government than they had ever been, communist support leveled off. Christian democrats continued to balk at Berlinguer's proposals for a "historic compromise" (a grand coalition of communists and Christian democrats), although in practice the situation developed to the point that on many levels rule without the tacit support and cooperation of the communists became impossible. As in Poland, briefly, during the heyday of Solidarity, the situation in Italy seemed to offer the potential of a new model of relationships between communists and non-communists. However, events in France in 1981 (described in the next section) offered a different, though also path-breaking model, one that might well have an important influence in Italy in the 1980s.

The Italian communists were considered the pre-eminent "Eurocommunists," a term that gained wide currency from the mid to late 1970s. The Eurocommunists included also the French communists and the newly legalized communists in Spain. Whether the term Eurocommunism has much long-range significance is open to question. It was obviously coined to underline the disparities in communist theory and practice between those countries without a significant liberal-democratic tradition and those where such a tradition has been important. But among the three Eurocommunist parties important differences remain, and indeed may become more important in the 1980s. The leader of the Spanish party, Santiago Carrillo, in spite of being a most vociferous critic of the Soviet Union, has a long and unsavory Stalinist past, and his single-minded efforts to achieve a degree of respectability in Spain (a country, it should be noted, that while in the West hardly has a deep-rooted liberal-democratic tradition) have so far not met with great popular success. The PCF and PCI have a much longer experience of legal action, have set down deep roots in the institutions of their respective countries, and enjoy from one-quarter to one-third of the popular vote. Still, their relationship has been marked by acrimonious exchanges, reflecting different perspectives and experiences. French communist leaders are often working-class in origin and retain a taste for some of the dogmatism and heavy-handed methods of the 1950s. Leading Italian communists are more often of middle and upper-middle class background, inclined to a more sophisticated and intellectual approach. The quip "Scratch an Italian communist and you find a liberal; scratch a French communist and you find a Stalinist" undoubtedly retains some truth. Whether these three parties can find enough in common to be able to work productively together, to merit, in other words, the retention of the term Eurocommunism, remains to be seen.

THE DEMOCRATIC SOCIALISTS FOLLOWING WORLD WAR II

At no time in their history did the democratic socialists achieve anything like the monolithic organization or unity of purpose that characterized the communist parties under Stalin. In the interwar period, we have seen, the democratic socialists proceeded in substantially separate directions, in spite of the existence of a reconstructed Socialist International. After 1945 the extent of their separate development was even greater. An important number of them, such as the British Labour Party, the Swedish Social Democratic Party, and the SPD assumed dominant electoral positions and gained considerable experience in ruling their countries. Others, such as the SFIO and PSI, had relatively limited governing experience. When they did govern, it was in coalition with other parties, usually larger than they. Most moved distinctly away from their earlier positions of doctrinaire socialism. They had tended to blame capitalism, the private ownership of the means of production, and the existence of social classes for all, or at least most, of the difficulties that developed in human relations. They now came to view the achievement of the good society as far more elusive and ambiguous than socialists in the earlier part of the century had viewed it.

For a number of years immediately following World War II an important unifying force for most democratic socialists was anti-communism. More precisely, they were concerned to dissociate themselves from Stalinist practices in Russia and the East Bloc. In nearly all European countries democratic socialists after the war projected an image of openness, moral earnestness, and pragmatism. They were predominantly middle-aged and not usually known for boldness or originality. To the eyes of impatient young people and to other critics on the far left, especially in the 1960s, they appeared little different from liberal reformers. And, indeed, in terms of actual practice it has become difficult for anyone to distinguish democratic socialism from liberal reformism, or what has in earlier chapters been termed democratic radicalism.

The history of the SFIO in the three and a half decades following World War II offers a good example of the range of experience and the far-reaching changes experienced by democratic socialists. During the time of the Fourth Republic (from the end of the war until 1959) the SFIO regularly participated in power. Blum's prewar strictures against "participation" as distinguished from "exercise" were no longer considered relevant; the party joined cabinet coalitions whether or not it dominated them. Yet the SFIO retained its doctrinaire, more or less Marxist program. The steady growth that the party had enjoyed in the interwar years ceased. After becoming, for a short time at least, the largest party of the Left in France at the time of the Popular Front, the SFIO began a steady decline in membership and voting strength, and by the 1960s it was unmistakably stagnating.

Declining support characterized all of the major parties of the Left in France (Radical, Socialist, and Communist) although the Communist Party declined more slowly, gradually establishing its position as the most imposing force on the left from the late 1940s through the 1970s. During these same years France was transformed by a dramatic reversal of her pre-1939 economic and demographic stagnation. A paradoxial situation developed, in that dynamic changes in the direction of urbanization, industrialization, and modernization—changes hitherto associated in Europe with the growth of socialist parties—seemed to favor parties of moderate and even conservative temper.

By the mid-1960s the SFIO seemed to have reached a blind alley. It still got its greatest electoral support for the most part from areas that had voted socialist for nearly a century, and they were not generally the areas of greatest economic change or dynamism; they tended to be rural or dominated by older industrial enterprises. The residents of those areas were inclined to be fearful of change and opposed to many aspects of modern industrial life. To vote for the SFIO often meant to express a preference for the practices and institutions of the past.

Such tendencies were not new: Modern European socialism had its origins in the early nineteenth century as a movement that favored certain anti-individualist values of pre-industrial society and that expressed at best mixed praise for industrialization. But increasingly thereafter socialists, and particularly Marxist socialists, regarded industrialization and the class it most characteristically produced, the factory proletariat, as absolute prerequisites for a socialist society. And the tendency grew to regard anything that forwarded industrial growth as progressive, while anything that impeded it was considered regressive or reactionary in tendency. Thus following World War II when socialists or other members of the Left spoke up for the preservation of traditional values and aesthetic sensitivities (as for example in opposing urban renewal projects or the building of skyscrapers in Paris), they seemed to be returning to some of the earliest concerns of modern socialism.

French socialists were not the only leftists, it should be emphasized, who were perplexed by the dilemma posed in most industrial societies by attempts to increase productivity of labor through technology on the one hand and to improve the overall quality of life on the other. Industrial societies as diverse as Japan and the United States have seen sharp clashes between those advocating rapid economic growth and those opposing such growth in the name of ecological and aesthetic considerations. But in France perhaps more than in most other industrial countries the democratic socialists of the 1960s came more and more to fit the mold of unimaginative, superannuated functionaries. Their defense of what Blum had earlier called "la vieille maison" ("the old house"—the traditional party organization and doctrine) became transparently a rationalization for unwillingness to respond flexibly to change. The aged Blum, in his return to political life immediately following the war, himself argued in favor of a less dogmatic socialism. He wanted socialism to move away from issues of class conflict and materialistic determinism, but he was outvoted by those who insisted on re-affirming the party's traditional doctrines.

Another but related kind of contradiction was the SFIO's growing separation from the industrial proletariat, especially that involved in heavy industry, a separation that had begun in the 1920s. In the period immediately following World War II the SFIO came to represent quite heterogeneous social and geographical forces in France. It became a "catch-all party," but of a peculiar sort: in the north it attracted workers in the textile industries; in the south and southwest, small farmers, especially around the theme of anti-communism; in the cities it became above all the party of postal workers, educators, and other lower civil servants. But everywhere the SFIO tended to attract to its banners— though of course not exclusively—what might be termed the less progressive social strata of French society, such as textile workers whose plants were being closed and small farmers who were unable to compete with large-scale, highly capitalized agricultural production. This failure to remain true to its progressive origins further contributed to the paradoxical situation that, in spite of a very significant increase in in the relative numbers of young people in France, the SFIO did not benefit from that increase in the 1950s and 1960s to the extent that it had before World War II.

The gradual decline in support for the Left, especially among young people, helps to explain why the French socialists so long remained out of power after the mid-1950s. Their membership declined from 350,000 at the end of the war to less than 100,000 by 1960, and in approximately the same period the SFIO's vote dropped from 23 percent to about 12 percent of the total. After a short period of cooperation with De Gaulle at the beginning of the Fifth Republic, the SFIO broke away, suffering a series of minor schisms and divisive controversies.

The unhappy experiences of these years, culminating in a complete rout in the presidential elections of 1968, impelled the party to dissolve itself, abandoning the name SFIO—a move symbolic of the effort to shake off a stultifying past—and emerging as simply the "Socialist Party." The new party retained a commitment to collectivism but articulated more flexible, up-to-date, and ultimately non-Marxist positions on such matters as the market economy and class conflict.

Since relations between communists and socialists had warmed with détente, and since a broad coalition of the Left seemed the only hope against the Gaullists, negotiations were initiated with the communists which resulted in the so-called Common Program in 1972.

These various moves soon began to bear fruit. The Socialist Party broadened its appeal considerably, and by 1978 it had regained its position as the party with the largest electoral following on the left, a development greeted with little enthusiasm by the communists. They had assumed, in consenting to the Common Program, that they would be the strong partner in any popular front government of future years. The socialists' rapid advance thus tended to unnerve the communists and to cause them to back away from the Common Program. The old communist tactic of "absorbing" democratic socialist allies—so notorious in Eastern Europe after the war—seemed to be backfiring. François Mitterand, at the head of the Socialist Party, spoke openly of his goal to lure away some 3 million of the PCF's 5 million voters.

The spring elections of 1981 proved a spectacular success for the socialists. Mitterand not only won the presidential elections, placing the powerful office of President of the Republic in the hands of a socialist for seven years, but in the ensuing elections the Socialist Party won an absolute majority in the Chamber of Deputies. The PCF's vote fell to its lowest level since the mid-1930s.

Nevertheless, Mitterand offered the communists a chance to participate in the new government—but on his terms: The PCF was asked to accept a number of conditions, including a condemnation of Russia's move into Afghanistan, that the party's leaders had firmly rejected before the elections. Fearing that they would be further cast into political oblivion, they meekly accepted all of these. The terms of Mitterand's offer made quite clear the new power relationships between the two parties. In a less immediately obvious sense he gained by bringing in communists, since as coalition partners they could not so easily play the role of spoilers or so readily make political capital out of future socialist embarrassments.

The new government was widely termed a "popular front"—words with strong emotional overtones—but in fact it differed substantially from Blum's government in 1936, if for no other reason than the tragic experience of the first popular front served as a model of what was to be avoided. But there were many other reasons. The international situation was far more favorable; Mitterand was unlikely to be obliged to squander his energies and popular support dealing with intractable international crises, as Blum had been. The economic situation, while certainly troubled compared to the 1960s and early 1970s, could not be compared in its gravity to the situation in 1936. Mitterand and his appointed premier had considerably more political power than did Blum, both because of the constitutional power of the president and because of the socialist majority in the assembly. Even within his own party Mitterand was in a far better situation than Blum had been, for the overwhelming majority of socialist voters in 1981 were moderate in temper, like Mitterand himself. The more extreme or ideological faction of the party accounted for a small percentage, perhaps 10 percent, of its popular support. Even Mitterand's political and economic opponents were not so deeply hostile as Blum's had been. Leading capitalists and financiers in 1981 were hardly happy, but they were more inclined to resignation than insurrection.

Thus, while Blum's failure was evident within six months, Mitterand's experiences in the same length of time were largely successful. Legislation to nationalize key industries as well as a number of institutions of finance and credit advanced regularly. Administrative decentralization, curtailing the great power of the prefects, was instituted, and a number of social welfare measures were introduced, including an increase in the minimum wage, higher retirement rates, and the creation of new government jobs.

These welfare measures tended to bring France more into line with the standards of other countries that had been ruled by democratic socialists since the war. France's new government was hardly rushing the country into some form of profoundly collectivized society; the private sector and market incentives still retained a decisive voice.

These successes also left a larger question unanswered: Could a socialist government remedy France's more fundamental economic problems? Since stagflation was by the late 1970s apparently endemic to all western industrial economies—and since remedies of a completely opposite nature were being applied in the United States and Great Britain—France's socialist government was widely studied as a possible countermodel, a more humane approach. Many observers believed that Mitterand's victory was more due to the personal unpopularity of former president Giscard d'Estaing and to the divisions of the conservative camp than to genuine enthusiasm for Mitterand and his promises. There was also much speculation that the socialist victory of spring 1981 represented an assertion of France's less dynamic forces, of those more interested in equality than productivity. An apprehension lingered that the new government might even make the economic situation worse.

The experience of the German social democrats differed significantly from that of the French socialists. To begin with, the SPD remained out of power for approximately the first two decades following the war, becoming the out-party in a system that more resembled the American two-party system than the multiparty systems of France and

Italy. Thus in Germany social democracy remained out of power on the national level for nearly forty years, ever since the ill-fated cabinet of Hermann Müller in 1930. (The social democrats in East Germany, or the DDR [*Deutsche Demokratische Republik*], were forcibly absorbed into a new party, the Socialist Unity Party, which was controlled by the communists.) Thus, Germany's remarkable postwar economic recovery—the so-called *Wirtschaftswunder*—as well as her re-entry as a respected member into European political and diplomatic life were accomplished under the Christian democrats.

The SPD had therefore to contend with highly successful opponents. They enjoyed the confidence of the United States, could plausibly claim great merit for the free-market system, and could charge that the social democrats would bring isolation and economic ruin to Germany. At the same time communism exercised little attraction for West Germans, unlike the French and the Italians, and the Communist Party in the Federal Republic was soon outlawed. Thus the leaders of the SPD felt scarcely any competition on their left and a great deal of it on their right. In short, powerful forces were pushing the already relatively moderate German social democrats in a reformist direction. These forces did not operate so strongly in France.

By 1949, when the Federal Republic was established, the SPD numbered approximately 800,000 members, as compared to about one million during the Weimar years. Its recovery must be considered all the more impressive when one remembers that many of the SPD's former strongholds were now under East German communist control. The SPD's renewed strength translated itself into victories at the state and local levels, but not nationally until 1969.

Willy Brandt, the first social-democratic chancellor of the Federal Republic, was in his earlier years something of an outsider, cut more in the mold of Rosa Luxemburg than of Friedrich Ebert. By the time Brandt became chancellor both he and his party had responded to the new forces working upon them. At its congress in Bad Godesberg in 1959 the SPD adopted a new program that put aside its earlier theories of economic determinism and its narrow identification with the working class. The Bad Godesberg program articulated a pluralist commitment to humanism, classical philosophy, and Christian ethics. Thus the long-standing aspiration of various social-democratic leaders to convert the SPD into a *Volkspartei*, a party of the people in general rather than of the working class alone, was at last formally achieved, although of course in the Weimar years the party had already traveled far in that direction. The SPD became a catch-all party, but with a wider and more progressive following than the SFIO. It moved away from notions of nationalization and extensive central planning, and now accepted market incentives and private ownership of the means of production. The party's new slogan was "as much competition as possible, as much planning as necessary."

The change in party program did not result in any immediate or marked increases in SPD memberships or votes. After disappointing results in several national elections, Brandt led his party into a grand coalition with the Christian democrats in December 1966. This experience of coalition was on the whole beneficial to the party. It allowed party leaders to gain respectability, visibility, and political experience on the national level. It also permitted Brandt, as Minister of Foreign Affairs, to initiate important changes in the Federal Republic's policy. Further developed when Brandt became chancellor in 1969, his so-called *Ostpolitik* (eastern policy) meant exploring new cooperative and nonconfrontational relationships with the Soviet Union, the East Bloc, and the DDR. In 1970 he negotiated a non-aggression pact with the Russians, followed shortly by pacts with the DDR recognizing the boundaries established at the end of the war, and then by agreements over the status of Berlin.

By reducing many of the points of tension or controversy between the West and the communist powers and thus helping to erase some of the bitter heritage of the Cold War, Brandt's initiatives facilitated subsequent moves toward détente between the United States and Russia, although, as discussed above, many other factors were moving the two countries in that direction. Brandt was awarded the Nobel Peace Prize in 1971, and he came to enjoy a bourgeoning popularity inside Germany, not only because his foreign policy accomplishments seemed to promise greater security and independence for the Federal Republic but also because his party's reforms of German economic and social life were made without disrupting the country's continued remarkable industrial growth and general prosperity. Under his leadership the SPD at last replaced the Christian Democratic Union as Germany's largest party (though it still did not quite constitute a majority; it was necessary to rely upon the small Free Democratic Party for a parliamentary majority). This growth was in part due to a penetration into the ranks of the middle class and Catholic voters.

Brandt's career went into a rapid and tragic eclipse in 1974, when it was discovered that one of his close aides was a spy for East Germany. He was succeeded by Helmut Schmidt, a vigorous and articulate man, known especially for his acerbic wit, prodigious memory, and efficient administrative style. By the late 1970s he had gained a wide respect—if not love—in large sections of the German population, including some that previously had had little good to say about social democrats. Indeed, the decade between 1969 and 1979, under Brandt and Schmidt, can be described as one of the more successful periods in the rather disappointing history of democratic socialist rule, although the successes had more to do with foreign policy and the efficient administration of welfare capitalism than with the formerly cherished ideals of economic reorganization and social solidarity. Important legislation designed to increase worker participation in management (so-called codetermination, discussed in the next section) was passed during Schmidt's chancellorship, but it was all too obvious that he was not interested in moving the German economy in the direction of fundamental socialization, that indeed he was comfortable with Germany's controlled market economy.

The British Labour Party following World War II offers a significantly different example of democratic socialist activity. Rather than being in exile or fighting in the Resistance, Labour leaders had participated in a coalition cabinet since the beginning of the war, and during the war they were responsible for exercising the extensive governmental control of British life made necessary by the stringencies of desperate, totalitarian conflict. Thus already by the early 1940s Labourites were able to oversee the introduction of a kind of socialism in Great Britain—in the name of seeing to it that everyone did his fair share in the war effort and that the lower classes were properly rewarded for their vital contributions. The record of Labour ministers as efficient and intelligent administrators earned them new respect, and in the elections following the war British voters returned 393 Labourites to parliament, as opposed to 213 Conservatives. In consequence, the government of Winston Churchill was replaced by a Labour government under Clement Attlee.

Labour's victory was not widely regarded as a mandate for the rapid socialization of the means of production in Britain (indeed, despite its lopsided numbers of parliamentary delegates, Labour had narrowly missed winning an absolute majority of British voters). But it unquestionably expressed a desire for wide-ranging reform and even more a fear that Conservative rule might somehow bring back the troubled 1930s. In the postwar elections Labour presented to the voters a minutely worked-out program of social welfare and nationalization, including such measures as socialized medicine, a takeover of the Bank of England, and the nationalization of many of the country's key industries. And this program was gradually put into effect in the following ten years. Owners of nationalized industries were compensated, and new state-owned industries were administered by public corporations, directed by state officials but still involving industrialists who remained in the private sector.

This wave of nationalizations and social welfare legislation gave the government greater power to assure that industrial production was directed in the public interest. Yet workers did not sense that their daily routine was being fundamentally altered or that English society had been transformed. After the pressures of war had ended, the sense of common purpose and willingness to sacrifice vanished, and the deep-rooted character of English society tended to reassert itself. Class origin continued to play a pervasive role in the careers of English people, perhaps to an even greater degree than in other western countries. Upward mobility continued to be an elusive goal. Similarly, in spite of the efforts by the Labour government to redistribute the wealth through such devices as income and inheritance taxes, the distribution of wealth in Great Britain remained in basic outline similar to that of other western, industrial societies. After more than a generation had passed under these egalitarian measures, a 1974 survey showed that 20 percent of British citizens still held 86 percent of the nation's wealth. Redistribution of personal income, as distinguished from already acquired wealth, seemed almost as difficult to accomplish, for despite the array of taxation and general social welfare measures in Great Britain, the pattern of income distribution remained surprisingly similar to that of western countries where fewer such measures had been enacted.

After the initial flurry of postwar reforms under Labour Party auspices, the Conservative Party ruled for thirteen years. In the 1960s and 1970s the two parties alternated in power with fair regularity. But these alternations saw no new reforming zeal or massive efforts to undo what had been done by the preceding government. The Conservatives did not attempt to dismantle the welfare state, since it was clear that a majority of British citizens wanted it. Leaders of the Conservative Party did maintain that they could make the welfare state operate more efficiently, and they did make some efforts at limited denationalization, but few if any of them spoke of returning to the prewar economy.

Such was at least true until 1979, when the Conservative government under Margaret Thatcher attempted to re-emphasize market incentives and private enterprise, to get Great Britain's stagnant economy moving again. But several years of Thatcher's "bitter medicine" brought few of the promised cures: The country's unemployment rate soared to levels not reached since the Great Depression, while inflation remained high.

The economic policies instituted by the Labour Party since the war, linked to the general role of organized labor in Great Britain, were widely held responsible for the worsening rates of economic growth since the war. Such a view was undoubtedly simplistic; some deeper malaise was affecting the country's productivity (Great Britain had by the mid-1970s fallen from the ranks of the leading industrial economies, surpassed even by East Germany in gross national product). But Labour's palpable inability to improve the situation had helped to prepare the English for Thatcher's radical remedies and had similarly made a return of Labour government less palatable.

At any rate, the Labour Party was in no position to benefit from Thatcher's flailings: The party was deeply troubled by factionalism, with one group clamoring for more radical and more unequivocally socialist measures and another believing that such measures would be both impractical and unpopular. As the 1980s began, a new Social Democratic Party had broken off from Labour and was making rapid progress, while the Labour Party moved leftward, wracked even more by factionalism.

All things considered, the parties with the most enviable record among democratic socialists in the postwar years have been the Scandinavian socialists, although by the late 1970s many of them had been voted from office, after nearly uninterrupted rule since the Depression. It will be recalled that the social democrats in Sweden led their country through the Depression years with considerable success. They also kept Sweden out of the war; the country actually benefited economically from its neutral position. In the generation following the war Sweden began to establish itself as one of the wealthiest nations in the world. By 1974 it had overtaken the United States in per capita income ($6,720 compared to $6,200). Swedes also benefited from a more equitable distribution of income, far better social services, little or no poverty, and generally less social strife than the residents of other industrialized countries. By the late 1970s and early 1980s, however, Sweden too was encountering new social and economic difficulties, although they were still minor compared to those of Great Britain.

Social democratic rule did not make of Sweden a socialist society, but it could be described as one of the best-run welfare states in the world, without the range of nationalizations that had occurred in England, France, and Italy. And of course, as we have already seen in Chapter 6, Sweden has many advantages over other European countries which have made the work of social democrats considerably easier.

But whatever Sweden's successes, its society remains remote from the socialist vision as first conceived in the nineteenth century. Private ownership, the market economy, and self-seeking individualism prevail. Moreover, the Swedish masses, having freed themselves to a considerable degree from material deprivation and want, and having gained unprecedented leisure, do not make use of their money and free hours to become the kind of liberated, cultivated, and creative citizens of the socialist dream. The average Swedish worker has shown little interest in "high culture" and altruistic social responsibility. In general he uses his leisure in ways that disappoint intellectual socialists, even if Swedish workers have a better record in this regard than the workers of other industrial nations (most notably the United States).

THE FUTURE OF EUROPEAN SOCIALISM

Do the final decades of the twentieth century promise any novel or dramatic changes in European socialism? What can socialists and communists realistically hope for? What do they really want? Are the various socialist visions, originally conceived in the first half of the nineteenth century, still relevant to the consciousness of Europeans and others in the final years of the twentieth? Can we still believe that the socialization of the means of production, material abundance, and social democracy will transform the human situation and create a condition of harmony, liberation, and general happiness never before known?

The changes in European society by the 1970s might have simultaneously overjoyed and appalled socialists of the nineteenth century. Serious social and economic problems undeniably remain, but many of the most flagrant abuses associated with early industrialization, which had been so important in awakening socialist awareness, have been reasonably well brought under control (such as child labor, long working hours, dangerous working conditions, festering slums). The suffrage has been extended to all adults, access to schooling has been opened up, controls have been instituted to mitigate the ravages of the free market, and so on. Still, while these are reforms that socialists fought for, they have to be considered democratic-radical rather than strictly socialist. And even from the purely democratic standpoint, it has to be recognized that although the quantity of wealth in western societies has increased immeasurably, its distribution has not fundamentally changed.

Power continues to be exercised by narrow elites, whatever the formalities of democratic participation and control. Whereas in the communist states the means of production is no longer, for the most part, in private hands, income distribution is anything but egalitarian, and political power, with its many social and economic perquisites, lies in the hands of an even smaller and far more authoritarian elite than in the West.

More subtly, the life of the masses in Europe and industrialized America has taken on qualities, most notably in cultural matters, that would have deeply troubled socialist theoreticians—although harbingers of the present situation were abundant during the lifetimes of Marx and Proudhon. Destructive competition, isolation, and a spectrum of hatreds—racial, religious, nationalist, ideological—continue to be major problems in modern industrial societies. These are by no means adequately explained as deriving from capitalism and class society. Many if not most working people, no matter which system they live under, remain locked into a pattern of dull, repetitive, and unrewarding labor, subject to alienating hierarchies and disciplines. Their leisure hours are all too often spent in mindless, degraded recreation. The socialist vision of human solidarity and psychic liberation appear still ineffably distant.

It is tempting to conclude that such a vision of the human condition has always been a pipe dream and that now more than ever it is necessary to abandon it and to stick to the unavoidably arduous and ambiguous task of working within high complex, technologically sophisticated societies. Without necessarily embracing such dour views, any clear-sighted observer who examines the forces at play in the final decades of the twentieth century must speak with guarded optimism at best, and more likely with outright pessimism.

In the past, socialist optimism about the future was founded on a belief that the increased productivity of labor, through industrial or technological advance, was the key to the solution of all problems of social relations. Growth—in material production, in technological understanding, in sheer numbers of human beings—was looked upon with satisfaction. In the same way, most socialists based their optimism about the future on the instincts of the common people (whom they variously called the masses, the workers, the proletariat). By the 1970s, if not before, these foundations of socialist optimism appear shaky, particularly in regard to the question of the growth of industry and population. The one threatens irreparable pollution of the environment and the other mass starvation. And the more we have discovered about popular opinion the less certain the foundation of humane values seems in the voice of the majority of the people. Indeed, it is not uncommon for intellectuals of both the Left and the Right to question if the interests of the working population—especially as articulated by organized labor—are compatible with the interests of society at large.

The very notion of progress and the working class's role in it have come to be questioned by thinkers of socialistic inclinations more than has been the case since the early advent of industrialism. A few have expressed doubts that industrial society itself is desirable, especially since its "advances" have brought humanity to the brink of atomic annihilation and ecological armageddon. Numerous theorists of Marxist provenance since World War II have written to the effect that the wage earner in advanced societies can no longer be considered the agent of progressive or rational change. The ruling elites of advanced societies have been able to organize their countries' economies so that the worker is provided with material comforts and satisfactions of immediate desires to the extent that he no longer, by the nature of his very existence, yearns for a fundamentally different kind of economic system. On the contrary, he and his leaders in organized labor have begun to feel a new conformity of interests with the owners of industry, particularly against those active in the efforts to protect the environment from industrial pollution, urban sprawl, and unplanned growth generally.

Herbert Marcuse, no doubt the best known of these theorists, has argued that the proletariat in Marx's sense no longer exists; if social revolution is ever to occur its cause will have to be taken up by newly important groups—such as racial minorities, young people, and déclassé intellectuals—who in various ways stand outside the enticements of modern consumer society. Another well known writer and thinker, Norman Birnbaum, has similarly argued that the industrial working class, in its economic, social, and political goals—and especially in its cultural tastes—cannot be considered a force for the further progress or elevation of humanity. Birnbaum too looks to young people and intellectuals, who are relatively free of binding and blinding obligations to the established order, or whose work allows them a degree of critical distance, to lead the way to a radically transformed society.

Such theories took on particular interest and renewed plausibility in the *annus mirabilis* of 1968, whose exhilarating spring seemed to open up whole new vistas for the advance of socialism. Several references have already been made to the "Prague Spring" of Alexander Dubček's liberal communist regime and the manifold implications it had for international communism. Concurrent and in some ways more surprising and exhilarating was the student-worker uprising in France, usually referred to as the "Events" of May and June.

The Events began as a series of student demonstrations and strikes, reflecting the deep resentments over the French government's long neglect of education, a problem compounded by the unprecedented number of young people who aspired to higher education. In the midst of unparalleled economic prosperity and general affluence students faced outrageous classroom crowding, inadequate facilities, and impossible study conditions generally. Unrest among the students set off a general strike of some 9 to 10 million workers—exceeding in numbers and scope even the legendary strikes of 1920 and 1936. Nearly all observers were astonished and bewildered—none more than the largest party of social revolution in France, the PCF.

Both the workers' and students' strikes grew partly out of "normal" kinds of grievances, having to do with wages, working conditions, and educational inadequacies. But the nature and extent of the strikes reflected something larger and far less tangible, springing from a rejection of the hierarchies and disciplines of the modern industrial state. A number of student leaders, such as Danny Cohn-Bendit, advanced vaguely anarchist positions, but in general, while the rhetoric of revolt was colorful and refreshing, its programmatic content was both confusing and confused.

A remarkable and often hilarious struggle of slogans and graffiti was waged, which in certain ways spoke more effectively of the situation than volumes of commentary. To the students' "Tout pouvoir à l'imagination!" (All power to the imagination!) De Gaulle responded with "Réforme, oui, chie-en-lit, non!" (Reform, yes, pooping in your bed, no). To the young students and perhaps to many workers it seemed that a new era was beginning. To De Gaulle and those that thought like him the Events represented scarcely more than the antics of pampered and undisciplined adolescents, or of workers blindly ignorant of social and economic reality.

For a short time it appeared that revolutionary change was indeed in the offing, or at the least that De Gaulle and the Fifth Republic were finished. But he and the leaders of his party showed themselves capable of flexible and subtle response, while his menagerie of opponents committed blunder after blunder.

One of the regime's most effective allies in diverting the revolt into non-revolutionary, electoral directions was the PCF. Communist leaders scrambled frantically to establish control over the striking rank and file, to bring the Events under established and familiar patterns of control. Cohn-Bendit referred to the French communists as "Stalinist creeps," while they in turn warned their followers against this "German anarchist." But it was ever more apparent that the French communist leaders, like their Soviet counterparts, thought primarily in bureaucratic terms and most of all distrusted any spontaneity that threatened abrupt or radical change.

This indirect aid to De Gaulle and the existing system did not turn to the advantage of the communists. As earlier alluded to, the special elections called by De Gaulle in June 1968 were a disaster for the PCF, the SFIO, and the other parties of the Left. The Gaullists greatly strengthened their position, with their coalition winning 358 out of 485 seats. De Gaulle played on the country's fear of the unknown and of what a communist-dominated Left coalition might develop into—and of course the memory of the Popular Front, some thirty-two years before, was not a pleasant one for most Frenchmen. At the same time, De Gaulle offered a program of reform, ostensibly responding to many of the demands made in May and June. He offered greater popular "participation" in government, but what this came down to was a weak rehash of traditional conservative corporatist ideas, in some ways resembling those espoused by the Vichy regime, although in 1968 of course the unchallenged existence of free institutions made the context quite different. These ideas were indeed anti-individualist and anti-liberal to some degree, stressing the need for "working together." However, they offered little or nothing to transform existing power relationships and general authoritarian modes of operation. Even the extensive and long-overdue reforms in education soon led to widespread confusion, administrative chaos, and overall discouragement.

The Soviet invasion of Czechoslovakia in August delivered a kind of coup de grâce to the exhilaration and high hopes of the spring in France. The invasion also revived suspicions concerning how much communists could be trusted to observe democratic procedure. The wave of popular revulsion that followed the invasion of course helps to explain why the leaders of the PCF hastened to condemn it, although before long they were backing away from the stridency of their initial outbursts.

In the late summer of 1968 it was easy to be a pessimist about the future of humane and democratic socialism in Europe—and in particular about the prospect of a dramatic departure from established bureaucratic modes of control. The rulers of France offered yet another example of the tenacity, flexibility, and durability of "capitalist" institutions, while the Russians in their turn made it unmistakably clear how powerful the obstacles were to any fundamental transformation of authoritarian communist rule. Visionaries of a revolutionary bent lapsed into a mood of despondency similar to that following the failure of the revolutions of 1848, and indeed some of them by the 1970s began to put forth positions that echoed the conservative anti-communism of the 1950s.

One should not conclude that in the discouragement of 1968 hope perished for the introduction of new institutions of popular participation in and control of Europe's economy and society. Hopes and projects of various sorts revived, as the "Eurocommunism" issue of the late 1970s suggests. Also, the more pragmatic, less political projects persisted, as for example the notion of "workers' control" as well as the related concern to humanize working conditions in factories. The notion of workers' control of industry dates back into the nineteenth century, but its better known and more significant practical antecedents can be traced to the workers' factory councils, or soviets, in Russia in 1905 and 1917, and to other workers' councils that grew up in Germany, Austria, Czechoslovakia, Hungary, and Italy at the end of World War I. All these various attempts had, in balance, disappointing histories. Within a few years the Russian soviets became little more than a façade for communist party dictatorship, while in other countries workers' councils either faded away, or, as in the Weimar Republic, had their functions so reduced that they were robbed of a meaningful—to say nothing of revolutionary—role.

A significant and lasting revival of these earlier efforts at workers' control of production occurred in Yugoslavia following World War II. "Workers' self-management," as the Yugoslavs called it, operated in a more democratic manner than the highly concentrated and authoritarian economic systems of the other communist states, although definite limitations were imposed upon it by the state and party. The difference between Yugoslav practice in this area and the practice of the Stalinized parties of eastern Europe constituted yet another area of friction between Tito and Stalin. After Stalin's death, various forms of workers' self-management, roughly following the Yugoslav model, did gradually spread to other eastern European states.

The operation of workers' self-management in Yugoslavia defies simple description. Suffice it to note that at least formally the voice of the workers in a given plant sets the guidelines for industrial management. Broadly stated, projects for workers' control in western Europe have had the same goals. At the end of World War II high hopes in this direction were entertained by socialists' and workers' representatives of various sorts. But once again, as following World War I, genuine control slipped out of the hands of workers and back into those of managerial elites under the direction of the factory owners. A partial exception to this trend prevailed in Germany and Austria, where "co-determination" (*Mitbestimmung*) by workers in key industries was widely viewed as a necessary democratic corrective to the notoriously undemocratic proclivities of certain segments of German industry during the Weimar and nazi years. When the German coal and steel industries were being reorganized by the occupying powers in early 1947, equal workers' representation was established in the supervisory boards of four iron and steel undertakings. Most German industrialists accepted these measures, indeed encouraged them, largely because they saw co-determination as their only alternative to outright socialization. However, by the early 1950s, once the owners of German heavy industry were firmly back in power they backed away from their initial flirtation with Mitbestimmung, not only as a limited measure for the coal and steel industries but especially as a program for all of German industry, as most of the German Left had intended. German trade unions fought tenaciously to retain co-determination, and in early 1951 its survival in the coal and steel industries was finally protected by law. Subsequent legislation extended workers' representation, and by the time of the social-democratic governments of Brandt and Schmidt, extensive co-determination programs were instituted, though their legality was soon challenged by the leaders of German industry.

In spite of the many initial disappointments in the immediate postwar period, democratic socialists in most countries still looked to some variety of co-determination, in the general sense of extending workers' control into managerial functions, although both the communists and the American AFL-CIO adamantly rejected the idea of workers' control. The exact way that workers would involve themselves in industrial management is not easily summarized, and it varies from country to country, but it is important to understand that while co-determination cannot be considered socialization of the means of production, it does attempt to redefine the prerogatives of ownership, in that workers can claim rights that were formerly associated with private ownership, such as having a voice in financial policies, personnel matters, long-range planning, plant renovation, and so on.

It is possible to consider co-determination to have developed organically out of collective bargaining, and as such it has implications for nearly all western economies. From the hard-won recognition, dating from the 1930s in most countries, that trade unions could represent workers in negotiating matters having to do with wages and working conditions, the further demand is being made that workers' representatives have a voice in managerial decisions. This is not a revolutionary escalation in workers' demands, but it does differ qualitatively from traditional collective bargaining.

Some observers believe that to permit workers to move into the arena of managerial decisions will result in more socially responsible industrial policies. It will further help transform the work place, so these observers argue, into a less authoritarian and more humane environment, where workers can be rescued from the subjection, drudgery, and monotony of their operations. For others the very idea that workers might be able to make intelligent managerial decisions is laughable; their education, background, and perspective are considered to be too limited. Workers' influence will lead, these observers contend, to declining productivity and general inefficiency—and even to less socially responsible policies. It would be too easy to conclude that the truth lies somewhere between these two extremes. Undoubtedly, national peculiarities will play a decisive role, and whereas workers' control may in one country lead to needed reforms, it may in another be a disaster.

In the area of making the work place less monotonous and generally more satisfying, a number of industrial concerns, most notably in Sweden, have experimented with production-line reorganizations that provide the individual workers with a greater sense of creativity, independence, and responsibility by allowing them to follow through in the production of commodities, in order that they might better identify with the end product. For example, they work in a production team to put together an entire automobile instead of each monotonously adding one part of it. But such ideas have generally come from management. Often they are a response to declining productivity because of low worker morale, rather than a direct response to pressure from workers' organizations or from the workers themselves.

Where such initiatives, designed to mitigate the harshness and alienation of modern industrial production, will lead is difficult to say. Much debate surrounds them, and results so far have been equivocal, particularly in terms of their long-term viability, since initial enthusiasms can easily encourage premature optimism. A related and even more fundamental question, one that has bothered socialists since Fourier, is how to reward and motivate workers to fulfill tasks that are essential to society but unpleasant, no matter how one reorganizes them. Obvious examples can be found in work involving dangerous, noxious, or disgusting materials—garbage collecting, to cite the classic example. In a society where inequality of fortunes exists and where people are encouraged to seek wealth in whatever quantities they can accumulate it, it is normally easy to find people to do unpleasant work, either because of their poverty, their avarice, or some combination of the two. But without the disciplines provided by want or the desire for extraordinary gain, it might prove extremely difficult to find workers willing to do a wide variety of labor vital to the well-being of society. Similarly, different degrees of skill, preparation, and diligence are easily rewarded in a society of inequality, but under a system of social equality it is likely that many would lose interest in working hard or in devoting themselves to the often arduous study necessary to perform complex and socially vital tasks.

Expressed in other terms, social inequality, while it can be considered a root cause of many social ills, such as robbery, prostitution, or drug abuse, can at the same time be considered socially useful. Moreover, it would take a rather dogmatic and simple-minded socialist to believe that the above-mentioned social maladies can be explained solely in terms of social inequality under capitalism. Even if capitalism and social inequality were to end, many of them would likely persist. Similarly, only the most sanguine and visionary of socialists can ignore the serious threats that would be posed to social cohesion and a secure life if the harsh edge of economic necessity were removed from the lives of ordinary citizens. Talk of how these threats could be avoided through a radically transformed value system remains vague and invites disbelief. Certainly in the communist states little that would even suggest such a transformation has occurred, in spite of the abolition of private ownership of the means of production. If anything, the opposite has happened and continues to be the case: The planned economies of the communist states have increasingly resorted to incentives for individual material gain and have established considerable degrees of social inequality, for the obvious reason that these appear necessary in the context of an advanced technological society. Some observers have seen in the history of these communist states a reversal of the Marxian historical progression. Instead of the historically inevitable march to socialism, they seem to be marching back toward competition and authoritarian social hierarchies.

Where does this leave a person, whether he calls himself a socialist or not, who yearns for enhanced cooperation, altruism, and social harmony, and who is troubled by the many ugly by-products of competitive social inequality and the self-serving ideologies that facilely equate misfortune with moral turpitude? It would be deeply satisfying if, at the end of this history of European socialism, confident answers could be provided. While it is all too obvious that they cannot, it would be cowardly to avoid offering at least some tentative conclusions.

The old visions of unlimited material abundance were always shallow. By the 1980s they are clearly outdated and must be abandoned. The romantic-liberal hopes for the unending betterment of the human condition—or indeed its transcendence into a different realm— through industrial production and technological innovation must be abandoned as well. The phrase "era of limits" became a cliché in the 1970s, but it is a cliché that nevertheless reflects a profound if unpleasant reality. Furthermore, the last two hundred years of socialist experience in Europe do not give us much cause to believe in the panacea of dramatic social revolution. The failures of violent social revolution are legion: 1793, 1834, 1848, 1871, 1905, 1914, 1919–20, 1923, 1936–38. And its "successes" in Russia in 1917, in eastern Europe, and in Asia following World War II, while arguably entailing great advances in material security for the broad masses in those areas, do not offer appealing models for the peoples of advanced industrial societies.

Pragmatic or reformist socialism does not lend itself to such humiliating and bloody defeats—this is a conclusion that even western European communists have apparently given careful consideration. But gradualistic socialism also lacks much of the mystique, the emotional appeal to idealism and self-sacrifice, of revolutionary socialism. Still, considering the terrifying crimes that have been committed in the name of social idealism in the twentieth century—in every century for that matter, but especially in the twentieth—one can feel justified in viewing the mystique of social revolution with hesitation (which is not the same as rejecting it out-of-hand, in whatever context). At any rate, strong evidence—which even someone with socialist sympathies must soberly recognize—indicates that some form of market discipline and social hierarchy will continue to exist long into the future in all advanced industrial economies. A society of equals is most unlikely—indeed, powerful evidence again suggests that such a society is neither possible in industrial nations nor desired by the overwhelming majority of the people in such nations.

Yet, we do not necessarily have to abandon the socialist vision to accept a degree of inequality as both useful and unavoidable, as a glance back at Fourier's theories might remind us. Nor does the use of market incentives rule out harmony and cooperation in economic and social matters. The world would be a pitiful place if all visions of a more harmonious human condition and a more perfect humanity were abandoned. Knowledge of the history of socialism is a heavy burden for those who persist in cherishing such visions. But, at the same time that we work to assure dignity, comfort, and emancipation for all people through intelligent planning and control of the anti-social tendencies of the market economy, we must also recognize that the pursuit of individual gain in the context of liberal economic institutions has proved to be a potent force for the growing productivity of labor and for social vitality in general. This paradox is hardly a new one, and it hardly promises to be resolved in the foreseeable future.

GUIDE TO FURTHER READING

There is no dearth of articles, monographs, and larger studies dealing with the nature and evolution of socialism and, especially, communism since World War II. Many of the studies written by western scholars in the 1950s and early 1960s were distorted by militant anti-communism, while in the late 1960s and the early 1970s the pendulum swung in the other direction, especially in works written by Americans. By the mid to late 1970s a degree of scholarly balance seemed to be emerging.

The concluding chapters of Leonard Schapiro's previously cited book, *The Communist Party of the Soviet Union*, provide a solid introduction to post–World War II Russia. As a partial antidote to Schapiro's hostility to Soviet communism, one might look at Herbert Marcuse's *Soviet Marxism: A Critical Analysis*, although its scope and focus are quite different. To gain some sense of post-Khrushchevian Russia, Zbigniew Brzezinski's *Dilemmas of Change in Soviet Politics* can be recommended.

Gabriel Kolko's *The Politics of War: Allied Diplomacy and the World Crisis of 1943–1945* offers insights, particularly interesting from the standpoint of the history of socialism, but to be accepted with great caution, into the developments within each major European country at the end of the Second World War. A less polemically left-wing account, putting the Cold War into broad historical perspective, is Louis Halle's *The Cold War as History*.

On the East Bloc countries, Zbigniew Brzezinski's *The Soviet Bloc: Unity and Conflict* remains a most impressive and thorough study. Concentrating more on recent developments is François Fetjö's *A History of the People's Democracies: Eastern Europe since Stalin*. An older, excellent study is Hugh Seton-Watson's *The East European Revolution*.

The French communists are the subject of two fine studies: Ronald Tiersky, *The Communist Movement in France, 1920–1972*, and Annie Kriegel, *The French Communists*. A useful comparative study is by Donald L. M. Blackmer and Sidney Tarrow, *Communism in Italy and France*. A most valuable collection of essays is *Eurocommunism: The Italian Case*, Austin Ranney and Giovanni Sartori, eds.

A light and highly readable introduction to the democratic socialists in the twentieth century, including the post–World War II period and discussing most of the major parties at crucial periods, can be found in Nathaniel Greene, *European Socialism since World War I*, a collection of articles from the *New York Times*. A stimulating study, with considerable space devoted to the SFIO, is Frank L. Wilson, *The French Democratic Left, 1963–1968: Toward a Modern Party System*. An intelligent introduction to the history of the SPD in this period is by David Childs, *From Schumacher to Brandt: The Story of German Socialism, 1945–1965*. Once again mention can be made of Samuel Beer's *British Politics in the Collectivist Age*, which stands out as both stimulating and comprehensive. Very little in English exists concerning Swedish social democracy, but a helpful general study is Donald M. Hancock's *Sweden, The Politics of Post-industrial Change*. See also Andrew Martin's *The Politics of Economic Policy in Social Democratic Sweden*.

An overview of the general issue of workers' control, covering nearly every country in Europe, can be found in Charles Levinson, ed., *Industry's Democratic Revolution*, although the contributors to this collection of essays are mostly labor leaders, and the quality of the writing is not always up to the best scholarly standards.

Robert Heilbroner's *Between Capitalism and Socialism* offers an excellent and beautifully written series of articles dealing largely with matters relevant to the future of socialism. Erich Fromm has edited an ambitious anthology, including papers from both East and West: *Socialist Humanism, An International Symposium*. Perhaps the most influential works in this area are Herbert Marcuse's *Eros and Civilization* and *One-Dimensional Man*. Two further works that have particularly stimulated discussion are Norman Birnbaum's *Crisis of Industrial Society* and C. A. R. Crosland's *Future of Socialism*.

Bibliography

EXPLANATORY NOTE

This alphabetical listing should provide easy access to titles that might be difficult to retrieve in the Guides to Further Reading. Fuller bibliographical information is provided here, as are a number of titles that seemed inappropriate or unnecessary to discuss in the Guides. A large number of these works exist in several editions, sometimes originally in foreign languages; no attempt has been made here to provide a bibliographical history of them. The places and dates provided are those judged to be the most accessible; when the original date of publication is much earlier it is so noted. An asterisk marks the availability of a paperback edition.

Agulhon, Maurice. *La République au village: Les populations du Var de la revolution à la Second République.* Paris, 1970.

———. *Les Quarante-huitards.* Paris, 1976.

*Althusser, Louis. *For Marx.* New York, 1969.

Anderson, Evelyn. *Hammer or Anvil.* London, 1945.

Angress, Werner. *Stillborn Revolution.* Princeton, N.J. 1963.

*Ashton, T. S. *The Industrial Revolution, 1760–1830.* Oxford, 1948, many reprinted editions.

Avrich, Paul. *The Russian Anarchists.* Princeton, N.J., 1967.

Bahne, Siegfried. *Les Archives de Jules Humbert-Droz.* Dodrecht, Holland, 1970.

Barker, Elizabeth. *Austria, 1918–1972.* New York, 1973.

Beecher, Jonathan, & Bienvenu, Richard. *The Utopian Vision of Charles Fourier.* Boston, 1971.

Beer, Max. *A History of British Socialism.* New York, 1953, 2 vols.

*Beer, Samuel H. *British Politics in the Collectivist Age.* New York, 1969.

Bell, Daniel. "In Search of a Marxist Humanism: The Debate on Alienation," *Soviet Survey* 32 (April-June 1960).

*Berki, R. N. *Socialism.* New York, 1975.

*Berlin, Isaiah, *Karl Marx, His Life and Environment*. New York, 1959.

Bernstein, Samuel. *Auguste Blanqui and the Art of Insurrection*. London, 1971.

———. *The Beginnings of Marxian Socialism in France*. New York, 1965.

Bezucha, Robert J. *The Lyons Uprising of 1834: Social and Political Conflict in the Early July Monarchy*. Cambridge, Mass., 1974.

Billington, James H. *Fire in the Minds of Men: Origins of the Revolutionary Faith*. Boston, 1980.

*Birnbaum, Norman. *Crisis of Industrial Society*. New York, 1964.

Blackmer, Donald, & Tarrow, Sidney. *Communism in Italy and France*. Princeton, N.J., 1975.

Blackmer, Donald. *Unity in Diversity: Italian Communism and the International Communist Movement*. Princeton, N.J., 1975.

Blumenberg, Werner. *Karl Marx*. London, 1972.

*Bober, M. M. *Karl Marx's Interpretation of History*. New York, 1965. First published, 1927.

*Bolloten, Burnett. *The Spanish Revolution: The Left and Its Struggle for Power during the Civil War*. Chapel Hill, N.C., 1979.

*Bookchin, Murray. *The Spanish Anarchists: The Heroic Years, 1868–1936*. New York, 1976.

*Bottomore, Tom, ed. *Karl Marx*. Englewood Cliffs, N.J., 1973.

Bourgin, Georges. *La Guerre de 1870–1871 et la Commune*. Paris, 1971.

Bracher, Karl Dietrich. *Die Auflösung der Weimarer Republik: Eine Studie zum Problem des Machtverfalls in der Demokratie*. Stuttgart, 1955.

Brand, Carl F. *The British Labour Party: A Short History*. Stanford, 1964.

Braunthal, Julius. *History of the Internationals*. New York, 1967, 2 vols. Vol. 1, 1864–1914; Vol. 2, 1914–43.

*Brinton, Crane. *A Decade of Revolution*. New York, 1963.

Broué, Pierre, & Temime, Émile. *The Revolution and the Civil War in Spain*. Cambridge, Mass., 1970.

Brower, Daniel R. *The New Jacobins: The French Communist Party and the Popular Front*. Ithaca, N.Y., 1968.

Brown, Bernard. *Eurosocialism, Eurocommunism*. New York, 1978.

Brzezinski, Zbigniew K. *Dilemmas of Change in Soviet Politics*. New York, 1969.

*———. *The Soviet Bloc: Unity and Conflict*. Cambridge, Mass., 1960.

*Buber, Martin. *Paths in Utopia*. London, 1949.

Calvez, Jacques-Yves. *La Pensée de Karl Marx*. Paris, 1956.

*Cammett, John M. *Antonio Gramsci and the Origins of Italian Communism*. Stanford, 1967.

*Carr, E. H. *The Bolshevik Revolution, 1917–1923*. Baltimore, Md., 1966. 3 vols. First published, 1950.

Carsten, F. L. *Revolution in Central Europe, 1918–19*. Berkeley, 1972.

*Chamberlin, William H. *The Russian Revolution, 1917–1921*. New York, 1965, 2 vols. First published, 1935.

Charléty, Sébastien. *Histoire du saint-simonisme, 1824–1864*. Paris, 1964.

Chevalier, L. *Classes laborieuses et classes dangereuses à Paris en 1848*. Paris, 1958.

Childs, David. *From Schumacher to Brandt: The Story of German Socialism, 1945–1965*. Oxford, 1966.

Claudin, Fernando. *The Communist Movement, From the Comintern to the Cominform*. New York, 1975.

*Cohen, Stephen. *Bukharin and the Bolshevik Revolution*. New York, 1973.

*Cohn, Norman. *In Pursuit of the Millennium*. New York, 1959.

Cole, G. D. H. *The History of Socialist Thought*. New York, 1953–60. 5 vols.

*Colton, Joel. *Léon Blum: Humanist in Politics*. New York, 1960.

Conquest, Robert. *The Great Terror: Stalin's Purge of the 1930s*. New York, 1969.

Conze, W., & Groh, D. *Die Arbeiterbewegung in der nationaler Bewegung*. Stuttgart, 1966.

Cornu, Auguste. *Karl Marx et Friedrich Engels*. Paris, 1955–70. 3 vols.

Crew, David F. *Town in the Ruhr: A Social History of Bochum, 1860–1914*. New York, 1979.

Crosland, C. A. R. *The Future of Socialism*. London, 1964.

*Daniels, Robert V. *Red October*. New York, 1967.

Degras, Jane, ed. *The Communist International, 1919–1921*. New York, 1965.

Deppe, Frank. *Verschwörung, Aufstand, und Revolution: Blanqui und das Problem der sozialen Revolution*. Frankfurt am Main, 1970.

*Derfler, Leslie. *Socialism since Marx*. New York, 1973.

Derry, John W. *The Radical Tradition, Tom Paine to Lloyd George*. London & New York, 1967.

*Deutscher, Isaac. *The Prophet Armed: Trotsky, 1879–1921*. Oxford, 1954.

*———. *The Prophet Unarmed: Trotsky, 1921–1929*. Oxford, 1959.

*———. *The Prophet Outcast: Trotsky, 1929–1940*. Oxford, 1963.

*———. *Stalin: A Political Biography*. New York, 1967.

Dobb, Maurice. *Studies in the Development of Capitalism*. New York, 1963.

Dodge, Peter. *Beyond Marxism: The Faith and Works of Hendrik De Man*. The Hague, 1966.

Dolléans, Édouard. *Histoire du mouvement ouvrier*. Paris, 1939, 1946, 1953. 3 vols.

Dommanget, M. *Les Idées politiques et sociales d'Auguste Blanqui*. Paris, 1957.

Drachkovitch, Milorad, & Lazitch, Branko. *The Comintern: Historical Highlights*. Stanford, 1966.

———. *Lenin and the Comintern*. Stanford, 1972.

Drachkovitch, Milorad, ed. *The Revolutionary Internationals, 1864–1943.* Stanford, 1966.

Droz, Jacques. *Histoire générale du socialisme.* Vol. 1: Origins to 1875. Paris, 1972. Vol. 2: 1875–1918. Paris, 1974.

*Duveau, Georges. *1848.* New York, 1968.

*Edwards, Stewart, *The Paris Commune, 1871.* London, 1971.

*————, ed. *The Communards of Paris, 1871.* Ithaca, N.Y. 1973.

Ehrmann, Henry W. *French Labor from Popular Front to Liberation.* New York, 1947.

Eisenstein, Elizabeth L. *The First Professional Revolutionist: Filippo Michele Buonarroti, 1761–1837.* Cambridge, Mass., 1959.

Engels, Friedrich. *The Condition of the Working Class in England in 1844.* Oxford, 1958.

Esch, Patricia van der. *La Deuxième Internationale.* Paris, 1957.

Feldman, Gerald. *Army, Industry, and Labor in Germany, 1914–1918.* Princeton, N.J. 1968.

Fetjö, François. *A History of the People's Democracies: Eastern Europe since Stalin.* New York, 1971.

*Fischer, Louis, *Life of Lenin.* New York, 1964.

*Fried, Albert, & Sanders, Ronald. *Socialist Thought.* New York, 1964.

*Fromm, Erich. *Marx's Concept of Man.* New York, 1961.

*————. *Socialist Humanism, An International Symposium.* New York, 1956.

Gay, Peter. *The Dilemma of Democratic Socialism: Eduard Bernstein's Challenge to Marx.* New York, 1952.

*————. *The Enlightenment.* New York, 1966 & 1969. 2 vols.

Goldberg, Harvey. *Life of Jaurès.* Madison, Wis., 1962.

*Gray, Alexander. *The Socialist Tradition.* New York, 1968. First published, 1946.

Greene, Nathaniel. *Crisis and Decline: The French Socialist Party in the Popular Front Era.* Ithaca, N.Y. 1969.

*————. *European Socialism since World War I.* Chicago, 1971.

*Gruber, Helmut. *International Communism in the Era of Lenin.* New York, 1972.

*————. *Soviet Russia Masters the Comintern.* New York, 1974.

*Guérin, Daniel. *Anarchism.* New York, 1971.

Gulick, Charles A. *Austria from Habsburg to Hitler.* Berkeley, 1948.

*Haimson, Leopold. *The Russian Marxists and the Origins of Bolshevism.* Cambridge, Mass., 1955.

Halévy, Elie. *Era of Tyrannies: Essays on Socialism and War.* London, 1967.

————. *Histoire du socialisme européen.* Paris, 1948.

*Halle, Louis, *The Cold War as History.* New York, 1971.

*Halperin, S. William. *Germany Tried Democracy.* New York, 1965. First published, 1946.

Hamerow, Theodore S. *Restoration, Revolution, Reaction: Economics and Politics in Germany, 1815–1871*. Princeton, 1958.

Hamilton, Richard F. *Affluence and the French Worker in the Fourth Republic*. Princeton, 1967.

Hammen, Oscar. *The Red Forty-Eighters: Karl Marx and Friedrich Engels*. New York, 1969.

*Hammond, J. L., & Hammond, Barbara. *The Town Labourer*. New York, 1968.

Hancock, Donald M. *Sweden: The Politics of Post-industrial Change*. Hillsdale, Ill., 1972.

Harding, Neil. *Lenin's Political Thought*. Vol. 1: *Theory and Practice in the Democratic Revolution*. London, 1977. Vol. 2: *Theory and Practice in the Socialist Revolution*. New York, 1981.

*Harrington, Michael. *Socialism*. New York, 1972.

Harrison, J. F. C. *The Quest for the New Moral World: Robert Owen and the Owenites in Britain and America*. New York, 1969.

*Heilbroner, Robert. *Between Capitalism and Socialism*. New York, 1970.

*———. *The Worldly Philosophers*. New York, 1961.

Hicks, John, & Tucker, Robert. *Revolution and Reaction: The Paris Commune of 1871*. Cambridge, Mass., 1971.

*Hill, Christopher. *The Century of Revolution*. Edinburgh, 1961.

———. *Society and Puritanism in Pre-revolutionary England*. New York, 1964.

*Hobsbawn, E. J. *The Age of Capital, 1848–1875*. London, 1976.

*———. *The Age of Revolution, 1789–1848*. London, 1962.

*———. *Labouring Men*. New York, 1964.

*Hook, Sidney. *From Hegel to Marx*. Ann Arbor, 1962. First published, 1950.

*Howe, Irving, ed. *The Essential Works of Socialism*. New York, 1971.

Hulse, James W. *The Forming of the Communist International*. Stanford, 1964.

*Hunt, Richard N. *German Social Democracy, 1918–1933*. New Haven, 1964.

———. *The Political Ideas of Marx and Engels*. Vol. 1: *Marxism and Totalitarian Democracy, 1818–1850*. Pittsburgh, 1974.

Jarman, T. L. *Socialism in Britain*. New York, 1972.

Jaurès, Jean, ed. *Histoire socialiste, 1789–1900*. Paris, 1901–08. 13 vols.

*Jellinek, Frank. *The Paris Commune of 1871*. New York, 1937. First published, 1937.

Johnson, Christopher. "Communism and the Working Class before Marx: The Icarian Experience," *American Historical Review* 76, no. 3 (1971): 642–89.

———. *Utopian Communism in France: Cabet and the Icarians, 1839–1851*. Ithaca, N.Y. 1974.

*Joll, James. *The Anarchists*. New York, 1964.

————. *The Second International, 1889–1914*. New York, 1955.

Jones, David. *Chartism and the Chartists*. New York, 1975.

Judt, Tony. *Socialism in Provence, 1871–1914: A Study in the Origins of the Modern French Left*. Cambridge, Eng. 1979.

Keep, John L. H. *The Russian Revolution, A Study in Mass Mobilization*. London, 1976.

Kelley, Robert. *The Transatlantic Persuasion*. New York, 1968.

*Kilroy-Silk, Robert. *Socialism since Marx*. New York, 1972.

*Kolakowski, Leszek. *Main Currents of Marxism*. Vol. 1: *The Founders*, vol. 2: *The Golden Age*, vol. 3: *The Breakdown*. Oxford, 1978.

Kolb, Eberhard. *Die Arbeiterräte in der deutschen Innenpolitik, 1918–1919*. Düsseldorf, 1962.

Kolko, Gabriel. *The Politics of War: Allied Diplomacy and the World Crisis of 1943–1945*. London, 1969.

König, Helmut. *Lenin und der italienische Sozialismus, 1915–1921*. Tübingen, 1967.

Kriegel, Annie. *Aux origines du communisme français*. Paris, 1964. 2 vols.

————. *The French Communists*. Chicago, 1972.

————. *Le Pain et les roses: Jalons pour une histoire des socialismes*. Paris, 1968.

*Krimerman, Leonard I., & Perry, Lewis. *Patterns of Anarchy*. New York, 1966.

*Kropotkin, Peter. *The Great French Revolution*. London, 1909.

*Laidler, Harry W. *History of Socialism*. New York, 1968.

Landauer, Carl. *European Socialism*. Berkeley, 1959.

*Landes, David. *The Unbound Prometheus: Technological Change and Industrial Development in Western Europe from 1750 to the Present*. London, 1969.

*Langer, William L. *Political and Social Upheaval, 1832–1852*. New York, 1969.

*Lasky, Melvin. *Utopia and Revolution*. Chicago, 1976.

*Lefebvre, Georges. *The Coming of the French Revolution*. New York, 1947.

*————. *The French Revolution*. New York, 1965. 2 vols.

Lequin, Ives. *Les Ouvriers de la région lyonnaise, 1848–1914*. Lyons, 1977. 2 vols.

Lerner, Warren. *Karl Radek, The Last Internationalist*. Stanford, 1970.

Leroy, Maxime. *Histoire des idées sociales en France*. Paris, 1946–54. 3 vols.

Levinson, Charles, ed. *Industry's Democratic Revolution*. London, 1974.

*Lichtheim, George. *Marxism, An Historical and Critical Study*. New York, 1961.

*————. *The Origins of Socialism*. New York, 1969.

*————. *A Short History of Socialism*. New York, 1970.

Lidtke, Vernon. *The Outlawed Party: Social Democracy in Germany, 1878–1890*. Princeton, 1966.

Ligou, Daniel. *Histoire du socialisme en France, 1871–1961*. Paris, 1962.

Lindemann, Albert S. *The "Red Years": European Socialism versus Bolshevism, 1919–1921*. Berkeley, 1974.

Loubère, Leo A. "The Intellectual Origins of Jacobin Socialism," *International Journal of Social History* 4 (1959): 415–31.

——. *Louis Blanc: His Life and His Contribution to the Rise of French Jacobin Socialism*. New York, 1961.

*Lougee, Robert W. *Midcentury Revolution, 1848: Society and Revolution in France and Germany*. Lexington, Mass., 1972.

Louis, Paul. *Histoire du socialisme en France*.

McKay, Donald. *The National Workshops*. Cambridge, Mass., 1933.

*MacKenzie, Norman. *Socialism, a Short History*. New York, 1966.

*McLellan, David. *Karl Marx, His Life and Thought*. New York, 1973.

——. *Marx before Marxism*. London & New York, 1970.

——. *The Young Hegelians and Karl Marx*. London, 1969.

Maione, Giuseppe. *Il biennio rosso*. Bologna, 1975.

Maitron, J. *Histoire du mouvement anarchiste en France, 1880–1914*. Paris, 1955.

*Malia, Martin. *Alexander Herzen and the Birth of Russian Socialism*. Cambridge, Mass., 1961.

*Mandel, Ernest. *Marxist Economic Theory*. New York, 1968. 2 vols.

Manuel, Frank. *The New World of Henri Saint-Simon*. Cambridge, Mass., 1956.

——. *The Prophets of Paris*. New York, 1965.

Marcus, John T. *French Socialism in the Crisis Years, 1933–1936*. New York, 1958.

*Marcuse, Herbert. *Eros and Civilization*. Boston, 1955.

*——. *One-Dimensional Man*. Boston, 1964.

*——. *Soviet Marxism: A Critical Analysis*. New York, 1961.

Martin, Andrew. *The Politics of Economic Policy in Social Democratic Sweden*. New York, 1980.

Mason, Edward S. *The Paris Commune*. New York, 1967. First published, 1930.

*Medvedev, Roy. *Let History Judge: The Origins and Consequences of Stalinism*. New York, 1971.

*Mehring, Franz. *Karl Marx: The Story of His Life*. Ann Arbor, 1962. First German ed., 1918.

*Meyer, Alfred G. *Leninism*. New York, 1957.

*——. *Marxism, The Unity of Theory and Practice*. Ann Arbor, 1963.

Miller, Martin. *Kropotkin*. Chicago, 1976.

*Mitchell, Harvey, & Stearns, Peter. *Workers and Protest: The European*

Labor Movement, the Working Class, and the Origins of Social Democracy, 1890–1914. Itasca, Ill., 1971.

*Moore, Barrington, Jr. *Injustice, The Social Basis of Obedience and Revolt.* New York, 1978.

*———. *The Social Origins of Dictatorship and Democracy.* Boston, 1966.

Moore, Stanley. *Three Tactics: The Background of Marx.* New York, 1966.

Moss, Bernard H. *The Origins of the French Labor Movement: The Socialism of Skilled Workers.* Berkeley, 1978.

Munro, D. H. *Godwin's Moral Philosophy.* Oxford, 1953.

*Nettl, J. P. *Rosa Luxemburg.* Abridged paper ed., Oxford, 1969.

*———. *The Soviet Achievement.* New York, 1967.

*Nicolaievsky, Boris, & Maenchen-Helfen, Otto. *Karl Marx, Man and Fighter.* London, 1973. First German ed., 1933.

Noland, Aaron. *The Founding of the French Socialist Party, 1893–1905.* Cambridge, Mass., 1957.

Noyes, P. *Organization and Revolution, Working Class Associations in the Revolutions of 1848–9.* Princeton, 1966.

*Ollmann, Bertell. *Alienation: Marx's Concept of Man in Capitalist Society.* Cambridge, Eng. 1972.

*Orwell, George. *Homage to Catalonia.* Boston, 1966.

*Page, Stanley. *Lenin and World Revolution.* New York, 1959.

*Palmer, R. R. *The Age of Democratic Revolution.* Princeton, 1959 & 1964. 2 vols.

*———. *Twelve Who Ruled.* New York, 1965. First published, 1941.

*Payne, Stanley G. *The Spanish Revolution.* New York, 1970.

Peukert, Detlev. *Die KPD im Widerstand: Verfolgung und Untergrundarbeit an Rhein und Ruhr 1933 bis 1945.* Wuppertal, 1980.

Pierson, Stanley. *Marxism and the Origins of British Socialism.* Ithaca, N.Y., 1973.

*Plamenatz, John. *German Marxism and Russian Communism.* New York, 1965. First published, 1954.

———. *The Revolutionary Movement in France, 1815–1871.* New York, 1952.

*Popper, Karl, *The Open Society and Its Enemies.* New York, 1962. 2 vols. First published, 1945.

*Poster, Mark, ed. *Harmonian Man: Selected Writings of Charles Fourier.* New York, 1971.

Price, Roger. *Revolution and Reaction: 1848 and the Second French Republic.* London, 1976.

———. *The Second French Republic, A Social History.* Ithaca, N.Y., 1972.

*Rader, Melvin. *Marx's Interpretation of History.* Oxford, 1979.

*Rabinowitch, Alexander. *The Bolsheviks Come to Power.* New York, 1976.

———. *Prelude to Revolution: The Petrograd Bolsheviks and the July 1917 Uprising.* Bloomington, 1968.

Ranney, Austin, & Sartori, Giovanni. *Eurocommunism: The Italian Case.* Washington, D.C., 1978.

Riasanovsky, Nicholas V. *The Teachings of Charles Fourier.* Berkeley, 1969.

Ridley, F. F. *Revolutionary Syndicalism in France.* Cambridge, Eng. 1970.

Ritter, Gerhard. *Die Arbeiterbewegung im wilhelmischen Reich, 1890–1900.* Berlin, 1959.

*Robertson, Priscilla. *The Revolutions of 1848.* New York, 1960.

Rose, R. B. *The Enragés: Socialists of the Revolution?* Sydney, 1965.

*Roszak, Theodore. *The Making of a Counter-Culture.* New York, 1969.

Roth, Günther. *The Social Democrats in Imperial Germany.* Totawa, N.J., 1963.

Rousseau, Jean-Jacques. *The Social Contract and Discourses.* New York, 1950.

*Rudé, George. *The Crowd in History, 1730–1848.* New York, 1964.

Ryder, A. J. *The German Revolution of 1918.* Cambridge, Eng. 1967.

*Schapiro, Leonard. *The Communist Party of the Soviet Union.* New York, 1960.

———, & Reddaway, Peter. *Lenin: The Man, The Theorist, The Leader.* London, 1967.

Scheidemann, Philipp. *The Making of a New Germany.* New York, 1920. 2 vols.

*Schorske, Carl E. *German Social Democracy, 1905–1917.* Cambridge, Mass., 1955.

Schulkind, E. *The Paris Commune of 1871: The View from the Left.* London, 1972.

*Schumpeter, Joseph A. *Capitalism, Socialism and Democracy.* New York, 1962. First published, 1942.

*Schwarzchild, Leopold. *Karl Marx: The Red Prussian.* New York, 1948.

Scott, J. A. *The Defense of Gracchus Babeuf.* Amherst, Mass., 1967.

Scott, Joan Wallach. *The Glassworkers of Carmaux: French Craftsmen and Political Action in a Nineteenth Century City.* Cambridge, Mass., 1974.

*Serge, Victor. *Memoirs of a Revolutionary.* Oxford, 1963.

Seton-Watson, Hugh. *The East European Revolution.* New York, 1956.

*Soboul, Albert. *The Sans-Culottes.* New York, 1972.

———, ed. *Babeuf et les problèmes du babouvisme.* Paris, 1963.

*Solzhenitsyn, Alexander. *The Gulag Archipelago.* New York, 1974–78. 3 vols.

Spitzer, A. B. *The Revolutionary Theories of Auguste Blanqui.* New York, 1957.

Spriano, Paolo. *Storia del partito communista italiano.* Vol. 1: *Da Bordiga a Gramsci.* Turin, 1967. Vol. 2: *Gli anni della clandestinità.* Turin, 1969.

Stadelmann, Rudolf. *Social and Political History of the German 1848 Revolution.* Athens, O., 1975.

Stafford, David. *From Anarchism to Reformism.* Toronto, 1971.

*Stearns, Peter. *European Society in Upheaval.* New York, 1967.

———. *Revolutionary Syndicalism and French Labor.* New Brunswick, N.J., 1971.

Steenson, Gary. *Karl Kautsky, 1854–1938.* Pittsburgh, 1978.

———. *Not One Man! Not One Penny! Germany Social Democracy, 1863–1914.* Pittsburgh, 1981.

Sturmthal, Adolf. *The Tragedy of European Labor.* New York, 1943.

Sweezy, Paul. *The Theory of Capitalist Development.* New York, 1942.

*Talmon, J. L. *The Origins of Totalitarian Democracy.* New York, 1960.

Tenfelde, Klaus. *Sozialgeschichte der Bergarbeiterschaft an der Ruhr im neunzehnten Jahrhundert.* Bad Godesberg, 1977.

Thompson, David. *The Babeuf Plot.* London, 1947.

*Thompson, E. P. *The Making of the English Working Class.* New York, 1966.

Tiersky, Ronald. *The Communist Movement in France, 1920–1972.* New York, 1975.

*Tocqueville, Alexis de. *The Recollections of Alexis de Tocqueville.* London, 1948.

Trempé, Rolande. *Les Mineurs de Carmaux, 1948–1914.* Paris, 1971. 2 vols.

*Trotsky, Leon. *The Essential Trotsky.* New York, 1963.

*———. *The History of the Russian Revolution.* New York, 1959. 2 vols. First published, 1932.

Tsuzuki, C. *H. M. Hyndman and British Socialism.* Oxford, 1961.

*Tucker, Robert. *Philosophy and Myth in Karl Marx.* Cambridge, Eng. 1961.

*———. *Stalin as Revolutionary: A Study in History and Personality.* New York, 1973.

*———, ed. *The Marx-Engels Reader.* New York, 1972.

*Ulam, Adam. *The Bolsheviks.* New York, 1965.

*———. *The Unfinished Revolution.* New York, 1960.

*———. *Stalin.* New York, 1974.

van der Esch, Patricia. *See* Esch.

*Venturi, Franco. *The Roots of Revolution.* New York, 1966.

Vidalenc, J. *Louis Blanc.* Paris, 1948.

*Von Laue, Theodore. *Why Lenin? Why Stalin?* New York, 1964.

Wachenheim, Hedwig. *Die Deutsche Arbeiterbewegung, 1844 bis 1914.* Cologne, 1967.

Wearmouth, Robert F. *Some Working-Class Movements of the Nineteenth Century.* London, 1948.

Weber, Hermann. *Der deutsche Kommunismus, Dokumente.* Cologne, 1963.

———. *Die Wandlung des deutschen Kommunismus.* Frankfurt am Main, 1969.

Wehler, Hans Ulrich. *Moderne deutsche Sozialgeschichte*. Cologne, 1966.

Williard, Claude. *Les Guesdistes*. Paris, 1965.

*Williams, Roger. *The French Revolution of 1870–1871*. New York, 1967.

*Wilson, Edmund. *To the Finland Station*. New York, 1953. First published, 1940.

Wilson, Frank. *The French Democratic Left, 1963–1968: Toward a Modern Party System*. Stanford, 1971.

Wittke, Carl. *The Utopian Communist, A Biography of Wilhelm Weitling*. Baton Rouge, La., 1950.

Wohl, Robert. *French Communism in the Making, 1914–1924*. Stanford, 1966.

*Wolfe, Bertram. *Marxism: One Hundred Years in the Life of a Doctrine*. New York, 1965.

*———. *Three Who Made a Revolution*. New York, 1964. First published, 1948.

Wolfe, Willard. *From Radicalism to Socialism: Men and Ideas in the Formation of Fabian Socialist Doctrines, 1881–1889*. New Haven, 1975.

Wolin, Sheldon. *Politics and Vision*. Boston, 1960.

*Woodcock, George. *Anarchism: A History of Libertarian Ideas and Movements*. New York, 1962.

*Zeitlin, I. M. *Marxism: A Re-examination*. New York, 1967.

Ziebura, Gilbert. *Léon Blum, Theorie und Praxis einer sozialistischen Politik*. Berlin, 1957 & 1965. 2 vols.

Index